T0330597

Confronting Land and Property Problems for Peace

This collection clarifies the background of land and property problems in conflict-affected settings, and explores appropriate policy measures for peacebuilding. While land and property problems exist in any society, they can be particularly exacerbated in conflict-affected settings – characterised by unstable security, weak governance and loss of proper documentation, as well as the return of refugees and Internally Displaced Persons. Unless these problems are properly addressed, they can destabilise fragile political order and hinder economic recovery. Although tackling land and property problems is an important challenge for peacebuilding, it has been relatively neglected in recent debates about liberal peacebuilding as a result of the strong focus on state-level institution building, such as security sector reforms and transitional justice. Using rich original data from eight conflict-affected countries, this book examines the topic from the viewpoint of the state-society relationship.

In contrast to previous literature, this volume analyses land and property problems in conflict-afflicted areas from a long-term perspective of statebuilding and economic development, rather than concentrating only on the immediate aftermath of the conflict. The long-term perspective enables not only an understanding of the root causes of the property problems in conflict-affected countries, but also elaboration of effective policy measures for peace. Contributors are area specialists and the eight case study countries have been carefully selected for comparative study. The collection applies a common framework to a diverse group of countries – South Sudan, Uganda, Rwanda, Burundi, Cambodia, Timor-Leste, Colombia and Bosnia and Herzegovina.

Shinichi Takeuchi is a visiting fellow at the JICA Research Institute and Director of the African Studies Group at the IDE–JETRO (Institute of Developing Economies – Japan External Trade Organization). He has a PhD from the University of Tokyo. Having specialised in the political economy of Central African countries, his current interest lies in the processes of statebuilding and peacebuilding in the area with particular focus on land problems.

Routledge Explorations in Development Studies

This Development Studies series features innovative and original research at the regional and global scale.

It promotes interdisciplinary scholarly works drawing on a wide spectrum of subject areas, in particular politics, health, economics, rural and urban studies, sociology, environment, anthropology, and conflict studies.

Topics of particular interest are globalization; emerging powers; children and youth; cities; education; media and communication; technology development; and climate change.

In terms of theory and method, rather than basing itself on any orthodoxy, the series draws broadly on the tool kit of the social sciences in general, emphasizing comparison, the analysis of the structure and processes, and the application of qualitative and quantitative methods.

Confronting Land and Property Problems for Peace

Edited by
Shinichi Takeuchi

Routledge
Taylor & Francis Group

LONDON AND NEW YORK

First published 2014
by Routledge
2 Park Square, Milton Park, Abingdon, Oxon, OX14 4RN

and by Routledge
711 Third Avenue, New York, NY 10017

Routledge is an imprint of the Taylor & Francis Group, an informa business

British Library Cataloguing in Publication Data
A catalogue record for this book is available from the British Library

Library of Congress Cataloging-in-Publication Data
Confronting land and property problems for peace / edited by Shinichi
Takeuchi.
pages cm. – (Routledge explorations in development studies)
Includes bibliographical references and index.
1. Peace-building–Case studies. 2. Land tenure–Political aspects–Case
studies. 3. Land tenure–Economic aspects–Case studies. 4. Right of
property–Political aspects–Case studies. 5. Right of property–Economic
aspects–Case studies. I. Takeuchi, Shin'ichi, 1962– , author, editor of
compilation.

JZ5538.C668 2014
333.3'1–dc23
2013043293

ISBN13: 978-0-415-85585-3 (hbk)
ISBN13: 978-0-203-73423-0 (ebk)

Typeset in Times New Roman
by Cenveo Publisher Services

Contents

Figures and tables

Figures

Tables

Contributors

Christopher Burke has been based in Uganda, working on conflict and development issues for over 12 years. He has a strong interest in land governance and has worked with a broad range of institutions, including UNDP, USAID, Institut Géographique National-France International (IGN-FI) and Oxfam. He is an advisor to the Secretariat of the Joint Acholi Sub-Region Leaders' Forum and the chairperson of the Northern Uganda Land Platform.

Sergio Coronado Delgado is a researcher at the Centre for Research and Popular Education – CINEP – and is also a professor in the School of Environmental and Rural Studies at Pontificia Universidad Javeriana in Bogotá. He is a lawyer with Masters degrees in Constitutional Law and Rural Development. His work and research are related to human rights, land policy, territorial conflicts and the territorial rights of indigenous people, afro-descendant communities and peasants. Currently, he is working on a research and advocacy project focused on the impact of mining on the rights, territories and livelihoods of rural communities.

Antero Benedito da Silva is a founder and currently Director of the Institute for Peace Conflict and Social Studies based at the Faculty of Social Science, Universidade Nacional Timor Lorosa'e. He has a PhD in Education for Peace, with Justice, and his areas of interest are peace and conflict studies. He is interested in promoting a new education paradigm that would favour education for transformation and peace in his newly independent country. He is also active in national and regional social movements.

Kiyoko Furusawa is a professor in the Department of Economics at Tokyo Woman's Christian University. She has been involved in human rights activities on Timor-Leste since 1985. She was a UN certified observer during the popular consultation in 1999. Her research field is economic development with gender perspectives. Her focus is on the development of social capital relating to irrigation management, and she has given papers on West Java/Indonesia, Saga/Japan, Lao PDR and Timor-Leste. With reference to Timor-Leste she has conducted participatory research in several districts, collaborating with farmers' groups and the Ministry of Agriculture and Fishery since 2008.

Noriko Hataya is a professor in the Department of Hispanic Studies, Faculty of Foreign Studies at Sophia University in Tokyo. She is a self-trained sociologist and holds a PhD in human geography from University College London. Having focused her research interest on urban poverty and self-help housing in Colombia since 1985, she is now concerned with peasant movements and resistance to sustain livelihoods under the threat of displacement.

Mari Katayanagi is a senior research fellow at the JICA Research Institute, Tokyo. She served the Office of the High Representative in Bosnia and Herzegovina as a political advisor. Her earlier positions include senior advisor and First Secretary of the Embassy of Japan in Bosnia and Herzegovina, and special advisor for JICA. She received an LLM in international human rights law from Essex University and a PhD in law from Warwick University. Her research interests are peacebuilding, conflict prevention and international law, particularly international human rights law. She is the author of *Human Rights Functions of United Nations Peacekeeping Operations* (Kluwer Law International, 2002).

Jean Marara is currently a researcher at Institut Catholique de Kabgayi (ICK) in Rwanda. He worked as a researcher at the Institut de Recherche Scientifique et Technologique at Butare, Rwanda, from 1994 to 2011. His main research interest is the transformation of the rural economy in Rwanda after the genocide in 1994. He has published a number of articles and reports on this issue. At the ICK, he is a member of research teams on 'Socioeconomic impact of population displacements on the development of local communities in Rwanda' and 'Socio-economic impact of the development of marshland and the land consolidation in Rwanda'.

Ryutaro Murotani is a research fellow at the JICA Research Institute, Tokyo. Having worked in the field of development and peacebuilding for the Japanese government and JICA in various post-conflict situations including those in Bosnia and Herzegovina, Aceh (Indonesia) and Iraq, he now conducts research on peacebuilding, development aid in fragile situations and human security. He holds a Masters in Public Policy (MPP) from the Harvard Kennedy School.

Sylvestre Ndayirukiye is currently a professor at the Université du Burundi. He is in charge of the doctorate course *Sciences Humaines et Sociales: Société, Pouvoir, Espace et Environnement*. During 2006–7, he worked as a researcher at the Institut de Recherche Scientifique et Technologique at Butare, Rwanda. He has a doctorate from the Université Nice Sophia Antipolis (France) in Geography and Planning. He has a particular interest in the spatial reconfiguration of rural and urban Burundi and countries in the African Great Lakes region, following the crises since the end of the twentieth century.

Flor Edilma Osorio Pérez is a professor in the Department of Rural and Regional Development, Faculty of Environmental and Rural Studies of Pontificia Universidad Javeriana in Bogotá. She is a social worker, and has an MA in Rural Development from Pontificia Universidad Javeriana and a doctorate in Latin American Studies from Université Toulouse le Mirail (France). Currently, she coordinates the research group on 'Conflict, region and rural societies'. Her central research interests are the processes of deprivation and domination, as well as those of resistance and reconstruction of livelihood, of forcibly displaced people in Colombia.

Fumihiko Saito is a professor in the Faculty of Intercultural Communication, Ryukoku University, Japan. He is the author of *Decentralization and Development Partnerships: Lessons from Uganda* (Springer-Verlag, 2003) and the editor of *Foundations for Local Governance: Decentralization in Comparative Perspective* (Physica-Verlag, 2008). He has also published books in Japanese covering international development studies and participatory development. Until recently, he was co-leading a comparative research project examining the complex interfaces between local governance reforms and sustainable development with selected countries in both developed and developing worlds.

Nadarajah Shanmugaratnam is Professor Emeritus in Development Studies at the Department of International Environment and Development Studies (Noragric), Norwegian University of Life Sciences, Aas. He was previously Head of Research and Director of Studies in the Department. He is a political economist with a background in agricultural economics and agronomy. His academic interests include conflict, development and peacebuilding. He has published widely and edited the book *Between War and Peace in Sudan and Sri Lanka* (James Currey, 2008).

Shinichi Takeuchi is a visiting fellow at the JICA Research Institute and Director of the African Studies Group at the IDE–JETRO (Institute of Developing Economies – Japan External Trade Organization). He has a PhD from the University of Tokyo. Having specialised in the political economy of Central African countries, his current interest lies in the processes of statebuilding and peacebuilding in the area, with particular focus on land problems.

Nicolás Vargas Ramírez graduated as an ecologist from Pontificia Universidad Javeriana in Bogotá. He works as a researcher at the *Observatorio de Territorios Étnicos y Campesinos* (OTEC) at the School of Environmental and Rural Studies at Pontificia Universidad Javeriana. His work is focused on the construction of geographical information systems with rural communities in Colombia. His areas of interest are human geography and political ecology.

Foreword

Peace and development are mutually reinforcing and dependent on each other. This is an old cliché, but clarifying how these issues are related and how they can be put into a virtuous cycle remains a huge challenge. In recent peacebuilding literature, there has been a growing awareness of the importance of helping local people to regain their peaceful lives and improve their livelihood. Unless local people can see 'peace dividends' through improved health services, education, income-generation opportunities and basic infrastructure, their societies will not achieve long-term sustainable peace.

One key issue in this peace and development conundrum is land and property, which form the basis for people's lives in many ways: as a place to live, for cultivation and even for worship. Sometimes working as public goods, land and property can also create situations in which people contact and deal with their government directly. In fact, the land and property issue provides a policy space in which public institutions and local people's efforts to improve their daily lives meet.

In the past several years, land and property problems have been receiving more international attention. Despite this heightened awareness, however, our knowledge of the nature of these problems and potential policy measures to address them is still limited, particularly in relation to statebuilding and peacebuilding. Clearly, more efforts are required for the accumulation of information and experience, and the exchange of knowledge and ideas leading to appropriate policy responses.

Intended as a contribution to this endeavour, this volume publishes the outcomes of a research project of the Japan International Cooperation Agency Research Institute (JICA-RI). Since its foundation in 2008, the institute has aimed to fill the knowledge gap in emerging issues in international development, and, with 'Peace and Development' as one of its top-priority research domains, it has conducted policy-oriented research substantiated by academically solid methodologies and analyses. It would be a great pleasure to us if this volume turns out to be useful both for researchers and practitioners.

Hiroshi Kato
Director, JICA Research Institute
Vice-President, Japan International Cooperation Agency

Preface and acknowledgements

This volume is the result of a research project funded by the Japan International Cooperation Agency Research Institute (JICA-RI), which was established in 2008 to conduct policy-oriented research on the challenges currently faced by developing countries. The research project was launched in 2011 under the title 'Land and property problems in post-conflict statebuilding and economic development'. The views expressed in this book are those of the authors and do not represent the official position of either the JICA-RI or JICA.

As an organiser of the project, I wanted to address the following three issues. The first was to think about peace from the perspective of ordinary people. There is a voluminous literature in peace studies on such 'big issues' as peace negotiations, peacekeeping operations, DDR (disarmament, demobilisation, reintegration) and SSR (security sector reforms). There is no doubt that these studies are significant and should be better promulgated. However, my interest is rather in people's everyday security, which I consider to be decisive in establishing a durable peace. Second, I wanted to examine peace on the basis of area studies. The assessment of peace policies is not easy, because their meanings and effects are always contextual. What contributes to peace in the short term may be harmful in the long run. Having studied Central African countries for more than two decades, I strongly believe that the comprehensive approach of area studies is needed to understand the context, and that area specialists could make a much greater contribution to peace studies. That is why the project members mainly comprised area specialists. The third objective was to communicate our ideas to an audience across the world. I have so far published research papers mostly in Japanese. Other participants in the project have also published mainly in their own languages, including Japanese, French and Spanish. The circulation of their views and ideas has therefore been limited to one country or region. By presenting our findings in English, I wished to establish constructive conversations with researchers and practitioners across different regions and enrich discussions at the global level.

To this end, we have made efforts so that the results of the project would stimulate discussion over the topic. The participants gathered in Tokyo three times during the course of the project. Each time, we had intensive discussions about our case studies, their comparative features and their policy implications. At the final meeting, drafts of the chapters were presented and reviewed by all participants. Daniel Fitzpatrick kindly joined us and provided exceptionally important insights regarding our drafts. I believe these vigorous debates contributed to sharing the analysis framework among the authors and improved the quality of the papers. Our readers must now judge whether our attempts were successful or not. We would welcome any comments and criticism.

*

As with my other works, this publication owes a great deal to a number of colleagues. First of all, I would extend my deep gratitude to Keiichi Tsunekawa, who was Director of JICA-RI and suggested to me the importance of land issues in peace studies. It was his advice that made me conceive this research project. The financial, practical and moral support of JICA has been substantial in the realisation of the project. I gratefully thank Akio Hosono and Hiroshi Kato, the former and current Directors, respectively, of JICA-RI. JICA staff provided many helpful suggestions on the basis of their practical experience; the comments of Koji Makino and Naoshi Sato were particularly helpful. A number of insightful comments and suggestions from Daniel Fitzpatrick were indispensible for the elaboration of each chapter. Liz Alden Wily and Gregory Myers also kindly read some drafts and provided valuable comments.

At the preliminary stage of this project, just after the Great East Japan Earthquake in March 2011, Mari Katayanagi and I visited Essex University. Our meeting with John Packer and Sally Holt was very useful in initiating this research project on land and conflict. In February 2012, on the occasion of my visit to Leiden University, Marco Lankhorst kindly organised a small but warm meeting. During the last stage, in July 2013, the authors of the concluding chapter visited Washington DC, and had a number of opportunities to receive constructive comments from experts on land issues. We are particularly indebted to Carl Bruch and Gregory Myers, who helped us to organise meetings. Conversations at institutions including the World Bank, Rights and Resources Initiative, Engility, USAID and the Environmental Law Institute were extremely valuable. We would like to express our sincere gratitude to Klaus Deininger, Thea Hilhorst, Yongmei Zhou, Roisin de Burca, Andy White, Alexandre Corriveau-Bourque, Thomas P. Baltazar, Philip J. Decosse, Cynthia Brady, Peter Giampaoli and Rick Gaynor.

In comparison to the generous hospitality and useful suggestions that these people have offered to me, the result might be quite insufficient. However, my fervent hope is that this volume will promote lively debate among academics and practitioners. It is only through such debate, I believe, that effective policy and practice can be designed.

Shinichi Takeuchi
September 2013

Abbreviations

ADB	Asian Development Bank
ADR	alternative dispute resolution
AfDB	African Development Bank
ASEAN	Association of Southeast Asian Nations
AUC	African Union Commission
CFS	Committee on World Food Security
CHS	Commission on Human Security
CPA	Comprehensive Peace Agreement
DFID	Department for International Development (UK)
DRC	Democratic Republic of the Congo
ECA	Economic Commission for Africa
ECHR	European Convention for the Protection of Human Rights and Fundamental Freedoms
ECtHR	European Court of Human Rights
FAO	Food and Agriculture Organization of the United Nations
GFAP	General Framework Agreement for Peace
HLP rights	housing, land, and property rights
HRW	Human Rights Watch
ICG	International Crisis Group
IDMC	Internal Displacement Monitoring Centre
IDPs	internally displaced persons
IFIs	international financial institutions
INGO	international nongovernmental organisation
IOM	International Organization for Migration
JICA	Japan International Cooperation Agency
JICA-RI	JICA (Japan International Cooperation Agency) Research Institute
MDG	Millennium Development Goals
NGO	nongovernmental organisation
OCHA	UN Office for the Coordination of Humanitarian Affairs
ODA	Official Development Assistance
OECD	Organisation for Economic Co-operation and Development
OSCE	Organization for Security and Co-operation in Europe

PPP	public–private partnerships
PTSD	post-traumatic stress disorder
SSR	security sector reform
TOI	The Oakland Institute
UBN	unsatisfied basic needs
UDHR	Universal Declaration of Human Rights
UN	United Nations
UNDP	United Nations Development Programme
UNHCR	United Nations High Commissioner for Refugees
USAID	United States Agency for International Development
WTO	World Trade Organization

1 Introduction

Land and property problems in peacebuilding

Shinichi Takeuchi

Land and its associated real estate often cause serious disputes in war-torn societies. In Burundi, Hutu refugees returning to their home villages after a 30-year absence saw that their family lands had been occupied by migrants from other regions. In post-war Bosnia and Herzegovina, property rights became a major source of social conflict, as these had often been appropriated by the time the original rights-holders returned. While problems with land and real estate exist in any society, they tend to be markedly exacerbated in conflict-affected situations, characterised by unstable security, weak governance and loss of proper documentation, as well as the presence of large numbers of refugees and internally displaced persons (IDPs). Such problems with the basic requirements for living, if not properly addressed, may destabilise the fragile political order and hinder the return to peace. Tackling these problems should therefore be regarded as an important challenge in consolidating peace. This book refers to these issues as 'land and property problems', and explores the realities on the ground in order to suggest the appropriate measures that can be taken to ensure peace.

This book has three main objectives. First, it attempts to analyse the nature of land and property problems in conflict-affected countries through an in-depth examination of eight case studies (Bosnia and Herzegovina, Burundi, Cambodia, Colombia, Rwanda, South Sudan, Timor-Leste and Uganda). While there is a considerable range of variation in the nature of the problems, each chapter, written by an area specialist, clarifies their characteristics in terms of causes, actors and patterns. Second, the book tries to elucidate the policy measures that have been implemented in order to tackle land and property problems. In many conflict-affected countries, land and property problems are not a new challenge, and a number of measures have already been implemented not only by governments but also by the international community and civil society. Some of these have been effective and some have not. In the following chapters, typical responses will be presented and analysed. Third, based on analyses of the nature of land and property problems and the policy measures used to address them, we will examine the lessons learned and desirable measures for consolidating peace.

In this introduction, I begin by clarifying the perspective of this book and its importance as well as uniqueness. In the next section, I will offer a definition of land and property problems in order to elucidate the target of our analyses. Following this, the necessity of analysing land and property problems in the context of peacebuilding will be explored. Here, the close relationship between land and property, statebuilding and peacebuilding is highlighted. Then I provide some background information to the case studies. First, the main reasons for land and property problems in conflict-affected settings are illuminated, and the necessity of analysing both factors directly connected to armed conflict and those not directly connected will be stressed. Second, major policy interventions to alleviate these problems are examined. Finally, a brief summary of each chapter will be presented.

Land and property problems in peacebuilding

The notion of the 'land and property problem' has a wide scope. Conceptually, property refers to the 'relationship between and among persons with regard to things' (Moore 1998: 33). In the real world, this means any physical or intangible entity that is owned by an individual or a group, such as a community or state. The owner has a bundle of rights, which are generally protected by political authorities – typically the state – so that he or she can derive benefit or income from the entity. Land is one such property. From the perspective of this book, land is particularly important. Land is indispensable to people's survival, whether in urban or rural settings. It is not only the most basic means of making a livelihood, but also a critical resource in politics, as well as a social basis for identity formation. Land is of cardinal importance in developing countries, where a huge number of people depend directly on land for their everyday life in agriculture and cattle raising; and it is mostly in such developing countries that serious armed conflicts have broken out and efforts towards peacebuilding have been made. Our use of the term 'land and property' should not be understood as a simple juxtaposition. Rather, it is intended to emphasise the importance of land.[1] Our focus on *land* and property is based on the conviction that everyday security for ordinary people is crucial for the establishment of durable peace.

In the context of violent conflicts, the most visible 'land and property problem' may be sharp disagreements over competing rights to property, such as those between returnees and secondary occupants. Some of these visible conflicts may be brought before conflict resolution mechanisms, including courts. However, behind the visible, recordable and often violent conflicts over land and property, a huge number of tensions exist between persons and/or groups. These tensions may not be palpable, since they are not necessarily brought before the courts and may only be expressed through verbal complaints or impatient grumblings. Yet this kind of discontent may be mobilised by some trigger and result in eruptions of violence. We call the visible and recordable tension 'conflict', while the term 'dispute' will be used for discontent that may not be clearly expressed, though the distinction between the two is often blurred.

Land and property problems are not necessarily confined to inter-human or inter-group tensions. Insecurity of property rights may also be caused and aggravated by the lack of capacity and/or willingness of the state. Recognition and protection on the part of political authorities are indispensable for the effective exercise of property rights. When the value of property rights is critically high, as with land and housing, the political authority protecting these rights needs to have the status and power to assume its responsibilities. In today's world, it is typically the sovereign state that endorses and protects land and property rights, but other customary authorities, including local communities and extended families, also often play an important role. However, such endorsement and protection are severely undermined in the case of state dysfunction, which has often been observed in developing countries and is exacerbated by armed conflict. In addition, there can be excessive disparity in property ownership. It is well known that great inequality in land holding in Latin American countries has constituted a major cause of armed conflicts. In short, the scope of analysis needs to be sufficiently broad to understand the whole picture of land and property problems that threaten peace.

Activities for consolidating peace are called 'peacebuilding'. This is a relatively new concept that has developed since the 1990s (UN 1992). Peacebuilding is not simply the absence of war. We understand the concept as 'activities undertaken on the far side of conflict to reassemble the foundations of peace and provide the tools for building on those foundations something that is more than just the absence of war' (UN 2000: para. 13). From this perspective, peacebuilding should be regarded as a long-term process that accompanies substantial social transformation, largely overlapping with long-term social changes towards positive peace, which refers not only to the absence of physical violence but also of structural violence (Galtung 1969). Although positive peace per se is a difficult objective to achieve, efforts to curb structural violence are indispensable in preventing the recurrence of war.

Dealing with land and property problems is one of the crucial elements in peacebuilding. The main reasons for this are threefold. First, land and property problems have a significant influence on the lives of huge numbers of people. Considering the enormous impact that these problems have, they should be given high priority among the policy measures taken for peacebuilding. Second, the causal relationship between an armed conflict and property problems is two-way and interactive. While an armed conflict can lead to significant land and property problems, it has often been observed that land and property problems have been behind large-scale violence, even if they are not direct causal factors (Homer-Dixon 1999).[2] Ignoring the problems, therefore, can endanger the fragile peace of war-torn societies. Third, dealing with such problems is important as it contributes to social change for durable peace. Such policy measures as ensuring property rights, enhancing gender equality in land ownership and improving land governance are essential not only for alleviating land and property problems, but also for improving social welfare in general and inducing positive social change. We consider such changes to be crucial for the consolidation of peace in conflict-affected societies.

Problems over land and property are relatively new topics in peacebuilding debates. Although the importance of this issue was recognised in several peace negotiations in the 1990s,[3] related debates have been considerably promoted in the 2000s, as indicated by the establishment of the Pinheiro Principles (UN 2005), which focus on the property rights of displaced people, as well as numerous academic publications (Unruh 2003; Leckie ed. 2008; Pantuliano ed. 2009; Leckie and Huggins 2011; Unruh and Williams eds 2013). Through these efforts from practitioners and academics, the topic has attracted increasingly serious attention. With the aim of making a contribution to the debate, this book particularly stresses the importance of adopting a long-term perspective in the analysis of land and property issues in peacebuilding. The authors attempt to illuminate the structural causes of the problems and assess policy measures in the case study countries by paying close attention to the development of state–society relations. In other words, we try to understand the problems and evaluate policy measures in the context of statebuilding, which is now considered to be the core element of peacebuilding. This approach, we believe, enables light to be shed on the root causes of land and property problems in conflict-affected situations, and suggests appropriate measures for their alleviation.

Let me make a minor caveat with regard to terminology. Though the term 'peacebuilding' is frequently used in this book, the focus of our studies is not limited to post-conflict countries in the strict sense. The reason is twofold. First, it is not only very difficult to provide a rigorous definition of 'post-conflict', but it is often futile as the shift from war to peace tends to proceed gradually and moves back and forth. In addition, peacebuilding includes attempts made before the complete cessation of armed conflict for the purpose of its mitigation.[4] This is why we believe that significant implications for peacebuilding can be drawn from the case study on Colombia, where civil war has continued for five decades.

Peacebuilding, statebuilding and land and property problems

Peacebuilding and statebuilding

For a long time, problems over land and property have attracted great interest in many academic fields, including philosophy, economics, political science, law and development. However, it is only recently that the topic has become the subject of ardent debates within peacebuilding. Since the publication of the 'Agenda for Peace' (UN 1992), most of the activities carried out under the name of peacebuilding have aimed at alleviating the direct legacies of war and/or improving various levels of governance. The former includes the disarmament of warring parties, destruction of weapons and assistance for refugee return, while activities such as monitoring elections, encouraging efforts to protect human rights and strengthening democracy fall into the latter (UN 1992: para. 55). Although the UN document put forward the idea that an agricultural development project linking warring parties could be a good example of post-conflict peacebuilding,[5] there are not many examples of this kind in past peacebuilding activities. During the early 1990s, peacebuilding activities were mainly carried out by UN agencies and their peacekeeping missions, and were characterised by the standard strategies of democratisation and marketisation (Paris 2004). During this period, attempts to tackle land and property problems were rarely made. Nevertheless, efforts that culminated in the adoption of the Pinheiro Principles in 2005 were initiated in the 1990s, clearly motivated by the experience of armed conflicts that had erupted during the period, particularly the conflict in Bosnia and Herzegovina.

Since the mid-1990s, with the increasing involvement of development actors, peacebuilding has seen a significant change in its activities. On the basis of their experience in long-term commitment, donors have actively promoted institution building. The mainstreaming of security sector reforms (SSR) was one of the most outstanding examples in this context (Smith 2001; OECD 2007a). Donors' focus on institution building derived from concern over the state capacity of failed states,[6] namely countries in crisis due to internal conflicts and economic stagnation.[7] Moreover, the awful shock of 9/11 attracted international attention to the issue. State dysfunction is now perceived to be a serious concern for international security. Following urgent calls to deal with failed states (Mallaby 2002; Crocker 2003; Rotberg ed. 2004; Eizenstat *et al.* 2005; Fukuyama 2005), the international community has become increasingly involved in statebuilding, which is now regarded as an integral part of peacebuilding (DFID 2005; USAID 2005; OECD 2007b). In the statebuilding project, which has an ideological basis in liberalism, democracy and the market economy are promoted, as these are supposed to enhance a constructive relationship between state and society (OECD 2007b; 2008; Whaites 2008). In other words, not only the state's capacity to provide security and social services, but also its legitimacy in the eyes of its citizens are critically required in order to establish sustainable state–society relationships and prevent the recurrence of armed conflicts (Manning and Trzeciak-Duval 2010).

However, the results of statebuilding have not been as successful as was expected. Recent projects of international statebuilding have often been condemned for failings including neglect of local ownership, bias in favour of state security to the detriment of human security, weak governance, poor human rights records, increasing economic inequalities and endangering subsistence economies (Paris and Sisk eds 2009; Newman *et al.* eds 2009; Richmond and Franks 2009). As a consequence, state fragility continues to be a serious challenge for the overwhelming majority of conflict-affected countries. The causes behind the disappointing results are various, but the fragility derives fundamentally from the difficulty in establishing constructive state–society relationships (Takeuchi *et al.* 2011). Some conflict-affected countries have faced serious difficulties in enhancing state capacity, particularly in maintaining political order in their territories. Countries such as Afghanistan and the Democratic Republic of the Congo (DRC) have not been able to establish governmental control over their territory in spite of the huge amount of resources that have been injected. Those post-conflict countries, which have succeeded in enhancing the state capacity to restore order, often face problems with state legitimacy. Although the overwhelming majority of conflict-affected countries have introduced democratic institutions since the 1990s, the quality of their governance has often been questioned. In particular, the process of political monopoly and social exclusion has been observed in many such countries (Zürcher 2011).

The latter point may be understood as a tension between peacebuilding and statebuilding (Rocha Menocal 2011). As Tilly (1992) argues, coercive power strengthens as a state develops its organisation. It is necessary to enhance the state's capacity for controlling territorial security and deterring armed conflicts. However, if the rule depends only on coercive power and lacks legitimacy in the eyes of its citizens, it is questionable whether such statebuilding could contribute to peacebuilding. As the 'Arab spring' has clearly shown, an oppressive regime that appears to be stable and successful in deterring people's discontent may suddenly collapse. Sustainable peace cannot materialise without state legitimacy, which derives not only from formal procedures but also from a wide range of other elements, including custom.[8] This perspective is deemed to be particularly important when we examine statebuilding with regard to land and property problems in conflict-affected settings.

State and property problems

A connection between the state and property is essential, as has been repeatedly emphasised in classics of political philosophy. However, there are a variety of understandings with regard to the relationship between the two. For instance, John Locke states that every human being is able to have property through his own labour, and the most important function of the state is to protect property rights.[9] Possession of property is the basis of citizenship and civil society, to which the state is required to be accountable. On this point, Thomas Hobbes makes a completely different assumption with regard to state and society in positing that a human being does not have property unless the state, namely the sovereign, recognises him or her and provides it. Property rights in land therefore originate from the arbitrary distributions of the sovereign.[10] Hobbes's argument does not assume the existence of a citizen who derives property rights from his labour. For Hobbes, the state deals not with citizens but with subjects, who cannot establish property rights without permission of the sovereign. In other words, with total control of the social order, the state has dominant power over the provision of property rights.

As one of founders of liberalism, Locke's ideas on the state–society relationship as well as property rights are basically adopted by the logic of liberal peacebuilding and statebuilding as advocated by the international community (OECD 2008). On the contrary, the sombre picture described by Hobbes seems to fit with the realities of today's conflict-affected settings. If the administrative capacity to maintain order is weak, property rights remain unstable due to the state's fragility in general. However, while property rights endorsed by a strong authoritarian state may be stable as long as the regime exists, these rights may be completely denied when the regime collapses and the next regime establishes its own property order. This is what we have observed in countries such as Burundi, Cambodia, Rwanda and Timor-Leste.

Although the ideas of the two philosophers contrast, two implications can be drawn. First, the functioning of property rights depends critically on the nature of the state, namely the state–society relationship. This has been repeatedly stressed by North (1981), who demonstrates that the state's role in ensuring property rights has been a decisive factor in the economic development of European countries.[11] Conversely, the weakness of the state exacerbates property problems by reinforcing legal pluralism (Unruh 2003).[12] The second implication is that enhancing the legitimacy of the state vis-à-vis its citizens will be crucial in ensuring property rights over the long term. A despotic state tends to have a much more difficult time surviving today than it would have had in the age of Hobbes. Once the sudden shift of political power has taken place in such a country, it will cause a drastic change in the property order. Therefore, attempts to secure property rights in peacebuilding are inseparable from efforts to establish a sustainable state–society relationship, which in turn ensures a stable property order. In this regard, enhancing state legitimacy in statebuilding will be crucial as a policy measure for tackling land and property problems.

Land and property problems in recent debates

From the middle of the 2000s, the importance of land and property in peacebuilding began to be stressed in a number of research projects, which can be roughly classified into three categories. The first group consists of research on housing, land and property (HLP) rights in post-conflict settings (Leckie ed. 2008; Pantuliano ed. 2009; Leckie and Huggins 2011). Strongly motivated by humanitarian concerns, and urged on by the adoption of the Pinheiro Principles in 2005, this research insists on the necessity of taking HLP rights into consideration in post-conflict peace operations, particularly in humanitarian actions as well as peacekeeping operations. The second category includes research focusing on land problems in relation to local communities in conflict and fragile situations (Unruh 2003; Huggins and Clover eds 2005; Shanmugaratnam ed. 2008; Anseeuw and Alden eds 2010). Based on the micro-level anatomy of livelihoods in conflict-affected settings, this research succeeded in clarifying the structural causes of land problems and the way ordinary people could survive in war-torn societies. Among recent work in this category, a book edited by Unruh and Williams (2013) deserves special attention, as it includes a number of interesting case studies and provides important policy implications. The third group consists of research on critical approaches to peacebuilding debates. Criticising liberal peacebuilding and donor-led statebuilding for neglecting the needs and logics of local communities, these academics have emphasised the importance of local ownership as well as human security in peacebuilding (Richmond and Franks 2009; Newman *et al.* eds 2009; Richmond 2009; Newman 2011). Although they do not necessarily discuss land and property problems explicitly, their logic, stressing particularly the significance of human security in peacebuilding, inevitably implies the value of tackling land and property problems.

While the contributors to this book have learned a lot from previous literature, our framework of analysis is unique. We completely agree with the view of the first group of researchers, who emphasise the significance of HLP rights, but the timeframe of our analyses is much longer. Searching for the causes of property problems in the past, often going back as far as pre-colonial times, we tried to understand the structural and historical reasons behind current land and property problems, and examined policy measures from the viewpoint of their contribution to durable peace and sustainable statebuilding. We also share a common perspective with the literature in the third group, emphasising the significance of human security in peacebuilding. While research in the third category tends to adopt a theoretical approach to peacebuilding, our main objective is to explore policy implications from in-depth case study analyses. The methodology and the perspective on research of the second group may be the closest to ours. The difference, however, lies in our stance on analysis: this book looks at land and property problems in conflict-affected settings through the framework of the state–society relationship. The authors therefore share an interest in historical and structural approaches.

Causes of land and property problems

The following case-study chapters clarify the nature and causes of land and property problems, as well as policy measures taken to tackle the problems in each country. This section and the next will therefore present an overview of these two points. With regard to the causes of the problems, two different kinds of factors can be singled out. In conflict-affected settings, factors directly caused by the armed conflict tend to be intertwined with factors not directly related to it. Analysing both of these types of factors is indispensable to understanding the mechanism of erupting land and property problems.

Factors directly caused by armed conflict

Violent armed conflicts are likely to inflict damage on land and associated real estate and paralyse the administration that governs land issues. Administrative institutions and documents relating to property titles may be intentionally destroyed. In Timor-Leste, land administration offices were attacked by pro-Indonesian militia and documents were systematically destroyed and carried off in the course of the violence that followed the referendum in favour of independence in 1999. The administration was entirely paralysed as virtually all the senior civil servants, who were either non-East Timorese or anti-independence, fled to Indonesia (Fitzpatrick 2001: 3). The intentional attacks on title documents indicate that property rights are often so strategically important that they become the targets of destruction in war.

Displacement caused by armed conflicts is a critical trigger of land and property problems. While an intense armed conflict naturally forces people to abandon their homeland, displacement has often been the purpose of the violence rather than its consequence. The 'ethnic cleansing' in the former Yugoslavia was such a case. In Colombia, a huge number of peasants[13] have been forced to leave their homeland as a result of the activities of both para-military and guerrilla groups. Displacement has been especially exacerbated by the actions of the paramilitaries seeking to control key areas for the benefit of the drug industry (Thomson 2011: 344). Government policy may also cause massive displacement. In northern Uganda, while the rebel army (the Lord's Resistance Army, LRA) was undoubtedly a source of insecurity for inhabitants from the mid-1980s, it was in 1996, when the government forced civilians into 'protected villages', that the displacement crisis began there (Rugadya 2006: 2).

Displacement can trigger serious problems related to land and property, which may be occupied by others during the absence of the original owners. In cases in which the displaced people do not have clear evidence of property rights, their return is likely to cause competition over claims for a plot of land. As land registration has not yet been carried out in the majority of developing countries, returnees tend to face disputes over land in conflict-affected settings. Obviously, competition over land claims becomes more intense as the period of displacement lengthens. Unfortunately, long-term refugees have not been the exception in the contemporary world (Crisp 2000). In Rwanda, the victory of the Tutsi-led rebels (the Rwandan Patriotic Front, RPF) in the civil war in 1994 triggered the return of a tremendous number of Tutsi refugees who had escaped their homeland around independence in 1962. Following the conclusion of a peace agreement in 2000, Burundi has seen a massive return of Hutu refugees, who had fled the country after 1972.

Returnees may have no place to settle if their birthplaces have been occupied by others during their long absence, or if they did not have land before the displacement. A tremendous number of refugees returned to Afghanistan after the Bonn Agreement in December 2001, and landless returnees were not unusual: 'more than 1.4 million returnees, or just over 60% of all returnees between March 2002 and October 2003, were landless' (Ozerdem and Sofi-zada 2006: 86). In Cambodia, property rights were systematically denied under the Pol Pot regime (1976–79). As the mass slaughters and massive displacement that took place in the 1970s and 80s led to general confusion in the country until the conclusion of the peace agreements in 1991, refugees often did not know where exactly to go when they returned to the country.[14] Many of the returnees settled in the areas near refugee camps in Thailand without effective land rights, and they have seen their social status become marginalised as time has passed (Eastmond and Öjendal 1999). Because the experiences of returnees during the armed conflict may have been quite different from and even in contrast to those of inhabitants who remained behind, relations between the two groups may be tense (Unruh 2003). In particular, in countries that have experienced ethnic conflicts, retur- nees and original inhabitants often have different ethnic affiliations, thus making their coexistence more complicated (Huggins 2009; Jansen 2011; Fransen and Kuschminder 2012).

In addition to visible effects such as physical destruction and displacement, armed conflicts often produce invisible changes to norms among people by transforming power relations.[15] Territorial control by an armed group will make existing rules and norms invalid, as we have seen in many wars and revolutions. The two entities in Bosnia and Herzegovina created by the Dayton Peace Agreement (Republika Srpska and the Federation of Bosnia and Herzegovina) have different norms in favour of their respective majority ethnic groups, rendering the property rights of minority groups in each entity extre- mely vulnerable. This is the main reason why many of them chose not to return to their place of origin even after the restitution (Von Carlowitz 2004; Williams 2006; Jansen 2011). The two entities in Bosnia and Herzegovina are clear and visible legacies of the war, but legacies that influence norms in this way are often invisible. In Rwanda, where the Tutsi-led RPF took power in 1994, Tutsi returnees have been privileged in gaining land from Hutu neighbours. Needless to say, this policy of 'land sharing' could be carried out because the RPF monopolised state power following its victory in the war. In South Sudan, after the conclusion of the Comprehensive Peace Agreement (CPA), soldiers, offi- cials and IDPs of the Dinka people – the largest ethnic group in the former rebel and current ruling party, the Sudan People's Liberation Movement – often claimed rights over the lands of other ethnic groups on the grounds that they 'have bought the land during wartime with the buckets or tins of their blood' (Leonardi 2011: 217). Here, land was demanded on the basis of two logical notions: compensation for the sacrifices of their ethnic group members during the civil war and the group's advantageous position in post-war politics. The claim could be made because the war and the CPA had transformed power relations among communities in South Sudan.

In order that a property right delivers benefits for its owner, it needs to be endorsed and protected by the political authority. The state is the most common and the most important among a variety of political authorities, though other alternatives are possible, such as a traditional community or a rebel group. An armed conflict tends to have a considerable impact on the power relations within a state. It may lead to a total power shift, as in the cases of Rwanda, South Sudan and Timor-Leste; power sharing following a peace deal, as in Bosnia and Herzegovina, and Burundi; or a power shift in a limited territory, as in the case of Colombia. A sudden shift of political authority will cause a collision between the property rights endorsed by the previous regime and those established by the new forces. In addition to such a 'diachronic' collision of property rights between new and old right holders, an armed conflict may cause 'synchronic' collisions if one or more rebels occupy part of the national territory and assert their rule as well as their own property order, as in the case of the eastern DRC (Autesserre 2010). In short, in disrupting the existing political order and state governance, an armed conflict promotes conditions of legal pluralism, 'with different sets of normative rules regarding land, property, and territory intricately bound up in the conflict itself' (Unruh 2003: 353).

Factors not directly caused by armed conflict

Legal pluralism, which is exacerbated by armed conflicts, constitutes a significant background to the land and property problems erupting in conflict-affected settings. However, legal pluralism with regard to land can be observed in many developing countries, in which customary authorities exist more or less independently from the state and play important roles in land distribution. In the same vein, conditions contributing to the undermining of land governance, such as the weak rule of law, identity politics and corruption, can be found not only in conflict-affected settings but also in many countries, particularly in developing areas, where there is no outright armed conflict. Moreover, factors directly related to armed conflict may not play a significant role in current land and property problems in conflict-affected countries. For instance, the majority of land disputes both in Rwanda and Burundi derive from intra-familial problems such as inheritance (Van Leeuwen 2010; Takeuchi and Marara 2011). In short, as the causes of land and property problems in conflict-affected settings are in part the same as those in normal settings, the former must be understood in continuity with the latter. This perspective is indispensable in seeking methods for the alleviation and resolution of such problems. In this regard, three factors independent from armed conflict deserve mention, namely the nature of the state, demand from the private sector and the vulnerability of customary land rights.

Since property rights need to be endorsed and protected by the political authority, it is a corollary that the nature of the state has a strong influence on the function of property rights. Deininger and Feder point to three governmental functions indispensable for ensuring land rights security: unambiguous definition and enforcement of property rights, provision of reliable information, and cost-effective management of land-related externalities (2009: 235). These requirements, however, are not so easily met in developing countries, particularly in conflict-affected settings, in which state capacity tends to be weak almost by definition. In addition, the problem often lies less in the limited administrative capacity per se than in the politically biased practice of land governance, which often privileges the elite or a particular group. Although applying the concept of neo-patrimonialism (Médard 1982; Chabal and Daloz 1999) to conflict-affected countries in general would be an exaggeration, it is true that arbitrary distribution of land has been regularly carried out as a means of maintaining patronage networks.[16] The situation where 'property rights are not "guaranteed," protected, or relatively insulated from political decision making by prior constitutional fiat' (Boone 2009: 196) has formed the general background of the land and property problems plaguing not only conflict-affected settings, but also developing countries in general.

Strong demand from the private sector is another important factor in land problems. Due to the recent global rise in demand for food and raw materials, caused mainly by the rapid economic growth of emergent countries such as China and India, interest in farmland has escalated, causing large-scale land acquisitions. In Latin America, commercial agriculture areas such as soybean production and livestock have developed considerably following the liberalisation of markets and trade in the 1980s. Southeast Asian countries, particularly Malaysia and Indonesia, have recently seen their palm oil production soar. In these regions, a marked increase in agricultural production has been made possible by turning a high volume of land into farms, plantations and ranches. Circumstances have also drastically changed in countries in transition from former socialist regimes, in which the dissolution of collective and state farms has produced smallholder farms on the one hand, and large-scale integrated companies on the other. Large-scale land acquisition has been especially conspicuous recently in Africa (Cotula *et al.* 2009), although reliable statistics are lacking. In relatively land-abundant African countries such as Ethiopia, Mozambique and Sudan (both North and South), as well as in Asian countries such as Cambodia, an enormous amount of land has been recently 'acquired' by domestic and foreign actors (Deininger and Byerlee 2011: chap. 2). Large-scale land acquisition and the subsequent eviction of inhabitants has been one of the central causes of the protracted Colombian armed conflict. Although extensive expulsions have not been widely observed in African countries, their potential danger is quite obvious.

The third issue to be considered is the vulnerability of customary land rights. In conflict-affected settings, land disputes tend to break out in areas where customary land tenure prevails. Either land conflicts between returnees and secondary occupants, large-scale land acquisitions, or land disputes over inheritance are likely to take place in areas under customary tenure. The most important reason for this is the ambiguity and instability of land rights. Customary lands have hitherto been virtually governed by customary authorities including local communities and extended families, but in many countries these have been categorised as state lands and therefore the state has had the formal power to distribute them. As people who use the land every day do not have formal titles, they tend to encounter enormous difficulties in claiming their rights once they have fled the place as a result of armed conflict. In addition to conflict-related problems, tenure security in customary lands has been in danger because of a complex mixture of factors affecting local land governance, including rapid population growth, weakened solidarity in local communities, increasing demand for farmland and the patrimonial nature of the state. Securing customary lands has been, therefore, one of the central issues in recent debates and practices in land governance. This point will be discussed in the next section.

Policy measures for tackling land and property problems

Analysing and assessing the policy measures taken to tackle land and property problems in conflict-affected countries is a main objective of this book. As land and property are fundamental issues for human societies, the range of related policy measures will be extremely wide, including promotion of agricultural technologies, job creation, urban planning, investments for infrastructure and so forth. Clearly, a narrow policy focus will not resolve land and property problems. While completely acknowledging this point, we confine ourselves to examining only policy measures directly relating to land and property problems, since limiting the scope of our arguments will make comparisons among the case studies more effective. As a thorough examination of the policies and their assessment will be carried out in the concluding chapter, only brief background information about three related policy fields is provided here.

The first policy field is concerned with direct assistance for the displaced. These policy measures are implemented to assist victims of forced migrations, which are the direct consequence of armed conflicts. There is a wide range of assistance of this kind, but recently the paramount importance of restitution tends to be stressed. It was particularly after the experience in post-war Bosnia and Herzegovina, where the restitution of housing was one of the most critical issues, that restitution and other assistance for the displaced began to attract significant attention from the international community. The success of the restitution process in Bosnia and Herzegovina led to the adoption of the Pinheiro Principles in 2005 at the UN Economic and Social Council (UN 2005). Although the most thorough and effective way to assure returnees' property rights is through restitution, the conditions that enabled the implementation of restitution in Bosnia and Herzegovina are not necessarily prevalent in other countries. In fact, for the majority of conflict-affected countries, systematic and organised restitution such as that carried out in Bosnia and Herzegovina would be very difficult, not only because of resource constraints, but for reasons including, in particular, ambiguity over which properties should be returned. This is why various types of policy measures have been established to assist returnees. Such policies include land sharing (Rwanda and Burundi), land allocation (Cambodia) and housing arrangement (Rwanda). To assess these measures, we need to know the conditions in the countries as well as their historical contexts. Each case study analyses these points.

The second area of policy intervention is related to conflict resolution mechanisms. Against the backdrop of an increase in land and property disputes caused by the return of large numbers of refugees, measures have been taken to strengthen the capacity of conflict resolution mechanisms. A number of countries, including Bosnia and Herzegovina, Burundi and Cambodia, have established organisations that specialise in the resolution of this kind of conflict. Reinforcing conflict resolution mechanisms is important, as it contributes to the reduction of social tension, thus promoting peace and reconciliation. However, we should note that such mechanisms cannot address the social structure that frequently causes land and property problems. In addition, in many conflict-affected countries the justice sector tends to be subordinated to the state, and judgements may follow the intentions of the state authority. In this case, strengthening a conflict resolution mechanism may only contribute to the empowerment of a means for repression. A real challenge for policy intervention in conflict resolution mechanisms is to figure out how to enhance their capacities for effective judgements and execution, while at the same time ensuring their political impartiality.

The third issue is concerned with measures for ensuring the property rights of vulnerable people. While these policy measures do not directly derive from armed conflicts, they can have a considerable effect in improving the situation by addressing the major causes of land and property problems. It is, however, important to note that the approach to strengthening the land rights of the poor has markedly changed since the end of the Cold War (Boras *et al.* 2007; Sikor and Müller 2009). In the Cold War era, land reform referred first and foremost to the redistribution of land for the benefit of the poor. The same practice of land redistribution was adopted in the two opposing capitalist and socialist camps, though the ideology buttressing the policy was in contrast. In capitalist countries such as Japan, the Philippines, South Korea and Taiwan, land was redistributed to tenants and landless farmers for the purpose of attenuating rural poverty and breaking down pre-modern social subordination. The redistribution of land with clear property rights was expected to reduce social unrest and foster conservative farmers, thus resisting the invasion of communism. Redistribution of land was systematically pursued in socialist countries as well. The purpose here, however, was to create collective farms and to abolish private property rights so as to further the establishment of socialism and communism. In addition, in countries such as Algeria and Egypt the nationalist regimes that emerged out of wars of independence or revolution, often adopting leftist ideology, undertook land redistribution through appropriation from the old elites (Borras *et al.* 2007; Lipton 2009).

However, since the 1990s, property rights reform, rather than redistribution, has been mainstreamed among approaches to land reform. The policy aims at ensuring land tenure for people living mainly in rural areas through indirect legal as well as administrative measures, rather than direct redistribution. The major reasons for this change were threefold. First, the effectiveness of customary land tenure was increasingly recognised and appreciated. Research has emphasised the relative efficiency as well as the flexibility of indigenous customary land and resource use arrangements (Feder and Noronha 1987; Ostrom 1990; Bruce and Migot-Adholla eds 1993). In contrast to the stereotyped image, indigenous land tenure systems function rationally and cost-effectively and are capable of adapting themselves to social changes, including population increases and the development of a market economy. The World Bank economists, who were once strong advocates for the establishment of private property rights, also began to recognise the efficiency of communal land tenure systems (Deininger and Binswanger 2001; Deininger 2003). Second, practices of land redistribution in the Cold War era were severely criticised. Redistribution policies under the socialist regimes were completely repudiated and reversed following the end of the Cold War. Even in capitalist countries the policy has often been blamed for such problems as inefficiency and corruption.[17] Third, the positive effects of land tenure security for economic development were widely recognised. The trend was underpinned by the theoretical development of institutional economics (North 1981; 1990) and reinforced by other influential works such as that of De Soto (2000).

A number of land tenure reforms have thus been carried out and many new land laws have been promulgated since the 1990s. Unlike the experiences in the capitalist camp in the Cold War era, when a standardised policy promoting land registration to establish private land rights was uniformly applied, approaches to ensuring land rights today vary, as the failure of such a one-size-fits-all policy has been widely recognised (Green 1987; Platteau 1996; Place and Migot-Adholla 1998). Rather, the importance of ensuring various rights over land has been stressed (Le Roy *et al.* eds 1996; Toulmin and Quan eds 2000; Benjaminsen and Lund eds 2003). As a result, a number of countries, including our case-study countries, have officially recognised customary land rights (Alden Wily 2011). While this is a significant change, it should be remembered that protecting customary rights has always been difficult in practice (Otto and Hoekema 2012). Even in the event that community land governance is officially endorsed, as in Tanzania, its effectiveness is questionable.[18] In other cases, such as Rwanda and Burundi, policies recognising customary tenure aim mainly at establishing private property rights, though whether this is an adequate approach for land governance in these countries is debatable. Effective methods for land governance must address the different conditions that a given country and its inhabitants face. We would therefore echo Otto and Hoekema's statement that 'the way forward should be based on careful assessments of the very specific local situations within a country' (2012: 21).

The attention paid to land governance has recently been on the rise, particularly following a surge in food and energy prices in the late 2000s and large-scale land acquisitions. In this context, attempts have been made actively to coordinate land policies throughout the international community and to develop policy tools for the elaboration of land governance. A number of guidelines have been proposed. While the most conspicuous result of this process is that initiated by the Food and Agriculture Organization of the United Nations (FAO 2012), similar attempts have been made by other actors. The African Union Commission, the Economic Commission for Africa and the African Development Bank, established in 2006, launched the Land Policy Initiative, which has produced important results on this issue in terms of knowledge management and policy mainstreaming (AUC–ECA–AfDB 2009; 2010; 2011). In addition, private actors have developed their own guidelines for investment, such as the Equator Principles and Santiago Principles.[19] Policy tools for the assessment and improvement of land governance have been developed either by international organisations such as the World Bank and UN-Habitat (Deininger *et al.* 2012; UN-Habitat 2012; Byamugisha 2013) or by donors (USAID 2007; 2011; 2012). Although these policy tools and guidelines focus on land governance in general, they have significant implications for measures taken to tackle the problems in conflict-affected settings because the nature of such problems is considerably affected by the quality of land governance. For this reason, a policy tool particularly focusing on 'land and conflict prevention' (Bruce and Holt 2011) is very useful. Moreover, these guidelines and policy tools afford valuable insights for alleviating possible tensions between statebuilding and peacebuilding.

Case studies

This book comprises eight case-study chapters. The location of the eight countries discussed and some basic data relating to them are indicated in Figure 1.1 and Table 1.1. Table 1.1 shows that the countries vary considerably in terms of population size, land area, population density, level of national income, international commitment in the form of Official Development Assistance (ODA) and their level of political liberty and civil rights (as estimated by Freedom House). However, the countries share a common feature: all of them have experienced serious armed conflicts. The armed conflict is still ongoing in Colombia, and peace is not well consolidated in countries such as Burundi and South Sudan. Peacebuilding is the primary policy goal in all of these countries.

The causes, progress and conclusion of the armed conflicts are again quite different among the eight case studies. Land and property problems were important backgrounds for the armed conflicts in Colombia and Rwanda, but the situation was not the same in the cases of other countries. While Rwanda's civil war ended in a one-sided victory, armed conflicts were brought to an end through international mediation, which resulted in the installation of power-sharing mechanisms in Burundi, Bosnia and Herzegovina, and Cambodia. In Bosnia and Herzegovina, South Sudan and Timor-Leste, it has been the newly independent states that have dealt with daunting tasks in the post-war period. These differences have affected the state–society relationship and the nature of land and property problems.

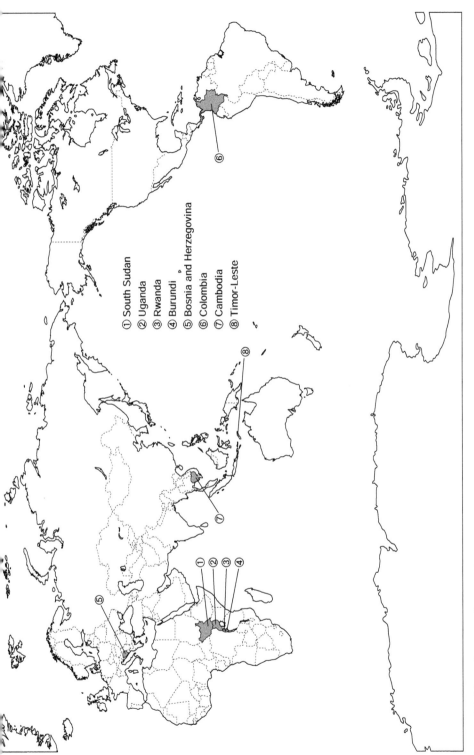

① South Sudan
② Uganda
③ Rwanda
④ Burundi
⑤ Bosnia and Herzegovina
⑥ Colombia
⑦ Cambodia
⑧ Timor-Leste

Figure 1.1 Map of case study countries

Table 1.1 Basic data on case study countries

	Population (2012)	Land Area (km²)	Population Density (persons/km²)	GDP / cap. Current US$ (2012)	Net ODA / cap. Current US$ (2011)	Freedom House Rating (2013)**	Recent armed conflicts (year)
Bosnia and Herzegovina	3,833,916	51,200	75	4,447	162	3.0	1992–95
Burundi	9,849,569	25,680	384	251	61	5.0	1993–2000
Cambodia	14,864,646	176,520	84	946	54	5.5	1978–91
Colombia	47,704,427	1,109,500	43	7,752	22	3.5	1964–ongoing
Rwanda	11,457,801	24,670	464	620	113	6.0	1990–94
South Sudan	10,837,527	619,745*	17	862	105	5.5	1983–2005***
Timor-Leste	1,210,233	14,870	81	1,068	241	3.5	1999, 2006
Uganda	36,345,860	197,100	184	547	45	4.5	1988–2006

Source: *Official website of government of the Republic of South Sudan (www.goss.org/, accessed July 2, 2013)
** Freedom House, Freedom in the world 2013 (www.freedomhouse.org/report-types/freedom-world, accessed August 30, 2013)
Others: World Development Indicators (http://data.worldbank.org/, accessed September 1, 2013)
***South Sudan has been again in de facto civil war since December 2013

By comparing countries with experiences of serious armed conflict, this book aims to gain a deep understanding of the causes of land and property problems in such settings as well as policy measures to address them. We do not claim that our selection of eight case studies covers the entire pattern of property problems in conflict-affected countries. However, we believe that in-depth analyses and comparison of the cases will enable us to identify the general characteristics of the problems, conduct balanced assessments of policy measures and attain our final objective of distilling elements that contribute to durable peace.

The case-study chapters start with South Sudan, which gained independence after a long civil war. This new country suffers from disorganised land governance. Although the 2009 Land Act has a progressive nature and has widely recognised the validity of customary land rights, huge tracts of land were seized before its enactment, and the execution of the law has always been difficult due to the weak state capacity. In addition, the power shift at the state level resulting from the war has impacted on ethnic relations regarding land, thus exacerbating antagonisms between ethnic groups. The predicament that this country is caught in derives from multi-dimensional collisions including those between customary and statutory property orders, various customary rights, and returnees and secondary occupants, as well as politically powerful and powerless groups; these issues are commonly observed in many conflict-affected countries.

Chapter 3 deals with Uganda, whose northern region was devastated by a long-term civil war that lasted until the mid-2000s. The analysis of factors in the post-conflict land disputes reveals that they are closely related not only to the civil war and societal transformation, but also to national policies and the nature of the state. Factors such as displacement, the death of elders, population increase and the erosion of traditional authorities have been closely intertwined with factors such as people's distrust of the southerner-led government and the commoditisation of land. In other words, the eruption of land disputes in northern Uganda has taken place as a consequence of the statebuilding under Museveni.

Chapter 4 examines the case of Rwanda. After the military victory of the former rebel RPF in the civil war, the regime, which is mainly based on the minority Tutsi ethnic group, has delivered remarkable results on land-related policies. In spite of severe problems including high population pressure and extreme land shortages, it has succeeded in providing the huge numbers of Tutsi returnees with land and housing, securing women's land rights and proceeding rapidly with land registration. Moreover, it has so far controlled the outbreak of returnee-related land disputes. Assessments of these consequences are not simple, because they have been the result of authoritarian and top-down policy interventions by the RPF. The authors argue that in order to sustain the positive results achieved under the RPF regime serious efforts should be made to enhance state legitimacy in the eyes of all nationals, including the majority ethnic group, the Hutu.

Chapter 5 discusses Burundi, in which a strict power-sharing mechanism between ethnic groups, mainly Tutsi and Hutu, has been introduced as a consequence of the civil war. A specialised conflict resolution mechanism, the CNTB, was established to mediate in land disputes between returnees and secondary occupants. However, as the former Hutu rebel party CNDD-FDD has dominated the government, its political influence has extended over the CNTB, thus ensuring that its policy systematically favours Hutu returnees. This change in the nature of the conflict resolution mechanism has caused the politicisation as well as the intensification of land and property conflicts.

Chapter 6 discusses the case of Bosnia and Herzegovina, which has often been cited as a laudable example in that acute property problems after the armed conflict were satisfactorily resolved, particularly as a result of the serious engagement of the international community. However, we should be cautious in deeming the Bosnian case a simple success story. In addition to the well-known fact that the restitution did not necessarily result in the return of refugees and IDPs, property problems in the country remain contentious, as the author convincingly argues with the examples of the apartments of the Yugoslav National Army, restitution of nationalised properties and the distribution of state properties, as well as agricultural land use. These difficulties illustrate uneasy statebuilding in Bosnia and Herzegovina.

Chapter 7 examines the case of Colombia, in which an enormous disparity of land holdings has been one of the central causes of the five-decade-long civil war, in turn exacerbating population displacement as well as land deprivation. Although attempts at land redistribution have repeatedly been made, they have produced only poor results because of the obstruction of the elites. Recent policy measures to clarify property rights for vulnerable people in rural areas, as well as to promote restitution, were undoubtedly positive steps. In addition to institutional reform, the authors stress, it is crucial to address the unequal politico-economic power structure, which lies at the centre of not only the land problems but also the protracted civil war.

Chapter 8 deals with Cambodia, which has recently suffered an eruption of land disputes despite relative political stability and rapid economic growth. Exploring the reasons, the author stresses the importance of the statebuilding process under the Cambodian People's Party (CPP), which took power after the fall of the Pol Pot regime in 1979. While abolishing all pre-1975 land rights, the CPP regime, which at the outset embraced a socialist ideology, provided plots of land equally for all nationals in the mid-1980s, but subsequently recognised private land rights during the transition to a market economy following the end of the Cold War. As the CPP's hold over power has been consolidated, the disparity in land holdings has increased, causing a considerable number of land disputes. Elite capture of state institutions, weak governance and rapid marketisation are major elements behind this.

Chapter 9 discusses the case of Timor-Leste. Following long and harsh domination under Portugal and Indonesia, the country gained independence only in 2002. A centuries-long history of external rule has created complex land and property problems, not only because property rights deriving from different contexts (customary, Portuguese and Indonesian) compete with each other, but also because large-scale violence has seriously damaged the regulation of property through massive displacement and the intentional destruction of property records. While various attempts have been made since independence to reconcile competing rights and establish a new property order, these efforts are still in their infancy. This young state therefore faces enormous challenges.

On the basis of these eight case studies, policy measures to address land and property problems are comprehensively examined and evaluated in the conclusion, and reflections made on their general policy implications. We will not propose a panacea. The current land and property problems in conflict-affected settings are too complex to be solved with a wave of a magic wand. What we wish to emphasise in this volume is that the general background of land and property problems needs to be clarified and understood in order to elaborate appropriate and effective policies for tackling them. Detailed case studies like those in this volume will certainly contribute to this objective.

Notes

1 We thus use the terms 'land and property problems' and 'property problems' interchangeably.
2 Although to state that the Rwandan mass killings in 1994 were caused by land problems would be an obvious exaggeration, it was true that land scarcity helped the ethnic mobilisation and ordinary people's participation in the slaughter (André and Platteau 1996; Uvin 1998). In addition, land problems have often exacerbated local-level violence, thus connecting it with a national-level armed conflict. A typical case can be found in the eastern part of the Democratic Republic of the Congo (DRC). While the area has seen land problems dating back to the colonial period, local conflicts over land have become much more complicated and aggravated during the civil war since the 1990s, thereby resulting in intractable instability and the eruption of ethnic violence (Mathieu and Willame eds 1999; Autesserre 2010).
3 For examples of peace agreements touching on issues of land and property in the 1990s, see the chapters on Rwanda, Burundi and Bosnia and Herzegovina.
4 Unlike the understanding of peacebuilding in the 'Agenda for Peace' (UN 1992), in which the concept was framed in terms of activities specifically in the 'post-conflict' phase, we agree with the 'Brahimi report' (UN 2000: para. 13), which considers that peacebuilding activities can begin before the complete cessation of hostilities.
5 As a peacebuilding project in the aftermath of international war, an idea of 'projects that bring States together to develop agriculture' was indicated in UN 1992: para. 56.
6 There is no clear difference in definition between 'failed states' and 'fragile states'. We use the two terms interchangeably.
7 On the one hand, the 1990s saw a number of serious armed conflicts particularly in Africa, Eastern Europe and the former Soviet Union. Problems involving failed states were serious concerns of the international community (Helman and Ratner 1992–93; Zartman ed. 1995). In the case of the World Bank, the 'Post-Conflict Unit' was set up in 1997 for dealing with recovery after armed conflicts. On the

other hand, contrasting economic performances between African and East Asian countries aroused keen interest in the institutions and governance (World Bank 1989; 1993). In this context, weak governance has been considered a major cause of the failure of economic development. Concern over the state as well as governance therefore derived from both political and economic reasons.

8 OECD (2010: 8) identifies four main sources of legitimacy: 1) input or process legitimacy, which is tied to agreed rules of procedure; 2) output or performance legitimacy, defined in relation to the effectiveness and quality of public goods and services; 3) shared beliefs – including a sense of political community – and beliefs shaped by religion, traditions and 'charismatic' leaders; and 4) international legitimacy.

9 In his *Two Treatises of Government*, Locke stated: '(a)s much land as a man tills, plants, improves, cultivates, and can use the product of, so much is his property. He by his labour does, as it were, inclose it from the common' (Book II, para. 32). With regard to the role of the state, he stated: '[t]he great and chief end, therefore, of men's uniting into common-wealths, and putting themselves under government, is the preservation of their property' (Book II, para. 124).

10 According to Hobbes in *Leviathan*, 'where there is no coercive power erected, that is, where there is no Commonwealth, there is no propriety [*sic*], ... but the validity of covenants begins not but with the constitution of a civil power sufficient to compel men to keep them: and then it is also that propriety begins' (chap. 15). With regard to the possession of land, he stated: '(i)n this distribution, the first law is for division of the land itself: wherein the sovereign assigneth to every man a portion, according as he, and not according as any subject, or any number of them, shall judge agreeable to equity and the common good' (chap. 24).

11 Previously, economists tended to explain the creation of property rights by the logic of cost–benefit analysis. For example, Demsetz (1967: 350) stated that 'property rights develop to internalize externalities when the gains of internalization become larger than the cost of internalization'. He considered that rising resource values led to the creation of private property rights when the benefits of private ownership outweighed the costs. However, as Fitzpatrick (2006) pointed out, in the reality of developing countries, the rise of a resource value has not necessarily established private property rights systems. In order for property rights to function, the state is expected to protect them and exclude illegitimate claimants in favour of the legitimate holders. Without such state action, the rise of a resource value will put it under open access. In fact, the state often does not play this expected role in developing countries, particularly in the case of conflict-affected countries. Demsetz's theory totally lacks consideration of the state or political aspects. Careful consideration of political factors is indispensable for the analysis of property rights.

12 Legal pluralism exists in all countries, as Moore (1973) pointed out, and it does not directly cause property problems. However, the legal pluralism that derives from state weakness will destabilise the property order as a whole, thus exacerbating property problems. With regard to legal pluralism, see also Griffiths 1986.

13 In the Colombian context, the term 'peasant' has connotations of small-scale and subsistence-level agricultural producers.

14 This means that refugees did not know where they could acquire land rights. In many post-conflict countries, this is a serious problem, particularly for young returnees who do not know their father, and women who have lost their husbands.

15 Here, we use the word 'norms' in its sociological sense – i.e. denoting the common standards or ideas which guide members' responses in all established groups. This term may describe actual rather than expected behaviour (Michell ed. 1968: 125–26).

16 For a case study in Africa, see Boone 2007. For Cambodia, see Global Witness 2007.

17 It is, however, important to notice that not all of the redistribution policies have necessarily been discarded. With regard to the excessive disparity of land holding that is observable in Latin America and southern Africa, the land redistribution policy has been naturally regarded as legitimate and necessary (Tucker *et al.* 2004; Lipton 2009).

18 More than a decade after the passage of Tanzania's land act, which formalised village-level customary land rights, only 7 per cent of villages have received a certificate of village land (Deininger and Byerlee 2011: 102). For the Tanzanian case, see also Alden Wily 2012.

19 The Equator Principles are a risk management framework developed by private financial institutions for determining, assessing and managing environmental and social risk in projects (www.equator-principles.com/index.php/about-ep/about-ep, accessed 17 August 2013). The Santiago Principles were set up in a similar vein by the International Working Group of Sovereign Wealth Funds (www.iwg-swf.org/pubs/gapplist.htm, accessed 17 August 2013).

References

Alden Wily, L., 2011, 'The law is to blame: the vulnerable status of common property rights in sub-Saharan Africa', *Development and Change*, 42(3): 733–57.

——2012, 'From state to people's law: assessing learning-by-doing as a basis of new land law', in *Fair Land Governance: How to Legalise Land Rights for Rural Development*, ed. J.M. Otto and A. Hoekema, Leiden: Leiden University Press, 85–110.

André, C. and Platteau, J.-P., 1996, 'Land tenure under unendurable stress: Rwanda caught in the Malthusian trap', *Cahiers de la Faculté des Sciences Economiques et Sociales*, 164: 1–49.

Anseeuw, W. and Alden, C. (eds), 2010, *The Struggle over Land in Africa: Conflicts, Politics and Change*, Cape Town: HSRC Press.

AUC–ECA–AfDB (African Union Commission–Economic Commission for Africa–African Development Bank), 2009, 'Declaration on land issues and challenges in Africa', available online at www.au.int/en/sites/default/files/ASSEMBLY_EN_1_3_JULY_2009_AUC_THIRTEENTH_ORDINARY_SESSION_DECISIONS_DECLARATIONS_%20MESSAGE_CONGRATULATIONS_MOTION_0.pdf (accessed 3 August 2013).

——2010, 'Framework and guidelines on land policy in Africa', available online at http://rea.au.int/en/content/framework-and-guidelines-land-policy-africa (accessed 3 August 2013).

——2011, 'Nairobi action plan on large-scale land-based investments in Africa', Addis Ababa.

Autesserre, S., 2010, *The Trouble with the Congo: Local Violence and the Failure of International Peacebuilding*, Cambridge: Cambridge University Press.

Benjaminsen, T.A. and Lund, C. (eds), 2003, *Securing Land Rights in Africa*, London: Frank Cass.

Boone, C., 2007, 'Property and constitutional order: land tenure reform and the future of the African state', *African Affairs*, 106(425): 557–86.

——2009, 'Electoral populism where property rights are weak: land politics in contemporary Sub-Saharan Africa', *Comparative Politics*, 41(2): 183–201.

Borras, S., Kay, C. and Akram-Lodhi, A.H., 2007, 'Agrarian reform and rural development: historical overview and current issues', in *Land, Poverty and Livelihoods in an Era of Globalization: Perspectives from Developing and Transition Countries*, ed. A.H. Akram-Lodhi, S. Borras and C. Kay, Abingdon: Routledge, 1–40.

Bruce, J.W. and Migot-Adholla, S.E. (eds), 1993, *Searching for Land Tenure Security in Africa*, Dubuque, IA: Kendall/Hunt Publishing Company.

Bruce, J.W. and Holt, S., 2011, 'Land and conflict prevention', Initiative on Quiet Diplomacy, University of Essex, Colchester.

Byamugisha, F.F.K., 2013, *Securing Africa's Land for Shared Prosperity: A Program to Scale Up Reforms and Investments*, Washington, DC: The World Bank.

Chabal, P. and Daloz, J.-P., 1999, *Africa Works: Disorder as Political Instrument*, Oxford: James Currey.

Cotula, L., Vermeulen, S., Leonard, R. and Keeley, J., 2009, *Land Grab or Development Opportunity? Agricultural Investment and International Land Deals in Africa*, London: IIED/FAO/IFAD.

Crisp, J., 2000, 'Africa's refugees: pattern, problems and policy challenges', *Journal of Contemporary African Studies*, 18(3): 157–78.

Crocker, C.A., 2003, 'Engaging failing states', *Foreign Affairs*, September/October: 32–44.

De Soto, H., 2000, *The Mystery of Capital: Why Capitalism Triumphs in the West and Fails Everywhere Else*, New York: Basic Books.

Deininger, K., 2003, *Land Policies for Growth and Poverty Reduction*, Washington, DC: The World Bank.

Deininger, K. and Binswanger, H., 2001, 'The evolution of the World Bank's land policy', in *Access to Land, Rural Poverty, and Public Action*, ed. A. de Janvry, G. Gordillo, E. Sadoulet and J.-P. Platteau, Oxford: Oxford University Press, 406–40.

Deininger, K. and Feder, G., 2009, 'Land registration, governance, and development: evidence and implications for policy', *The World Bank Research Observer*, 24(2): 233–66.

Deininger, K. and Byerlee, D., 2011, *Rising Global Interest in Farmland: Can it Yield Sustainable and Equitable Benefits?*, Washington, DC: The World Bank.

Deininger, K., Selod, H. and Burns, A., 2012, *The Land Governance Assessment Framework: Identifying and Monitoring Good Practice in the Land Sector*, Washington, DC: The World Bank.

Demsetz, H., 1967, 'Towards a theory of property rights', *American Economic Review*, 57(2): 347–59.

DFID (Department for International Development), 2005, 'Why we need to work more effectively in fragile states', London.

Eastmond, M. and Öjendal, J., 1999, 'Revisiting a "repatriation success": the case of Cambodia', in *The End of the Refugee Cycle? Refugee Repatriation and Reconstruction*, ed. B. Richard and K. Koser, New York: Berghahn Books, 38–55.

Eizenstat, S.E., Porter, J.E. and Weinstein, J.M., 2005, 'Rebuilding weak states', *Foreign Affairs*, January/February: 134–46.

FAO (Food and Agriculture Organization of the United Nations), 2012, *Voluntary Guidelines on the Responsible Governance of Tenure of Land, Fisheries and Forests in the Context of National Food Security*, Rome: FAO.

Feder, G. and Noronha, R., 1987, 'Land rights systems and agricultural development in Sub-Saharan Africa', *The World Bank Research Observer*, 2(2): 143–69.

Fitzpatrick, D., 2001, 'Land issues in a newly independent East Timor', Parliamentary Library Research Paper, No. 21 2000–2001, Department of the Parliamentary Library, Commonwealth of Australia, available online at www.aph.gov.au/binaries/library/pubs/rp/2000–2001/01rp21.pdf (accessed 4 September 2013).

———2006, 'Evolution and chaos in property rights systems: the third world tragedy of contested access', *The Yale Law Journal*, 115: 996–1048.

Fransen, S. and Kuschminder, K., 2012, 'Back to the land: the long-term challenges of refugee return and reintegration in Burundi', *New Issues in Refugee Research, Research Paper*, No. 242, UNHCR, available online at www.unhcr.org/5040ad9e9.html (accessed 4 September 2013).

Fukuyama, F., 2005, *State Building: Governance and World Order in the Twenty-first Century*, London: Profile Books.

Galtung, J., 1969, 'Violence, peace, and peace research', *Journal of Peace Research*, 6(3): 167–91.

Global Witness, 2007, *Cambodia's Family Trees: Illegal Logging and the Stripping of Public Assets by Cambodian Elite*, Washington, DC: Global Witness Publishing.

Green, J.K., 1987, 'Evaluating the impact of consolidation of holdings, individualization of tenure, and registration of title: lessons from Kenya', LTC Paper 129, Land Tenure Center, available online at http://pdf.usaid.gov/pdf_docs/PNABB825.pdf (accessed 4 September 2013).

Griffiths, J., 1986, 'What is legal pluralism?', *Journal of Legal Pluralism and Unofficial Law*, 24: 1–55.

Helman, G.B. and Ratner, S., 1992–93, 'Saving failed states', *Foreign Policy*, 89: 3–20.

Homer-Dixon, T., 1999, *Environment, Scarcity, and Violence*, Princeton, NJ: Princeton University Press.

Huggins, C., 2009, 'Land in return, reintegration and recovery processes: some lessons from the Great Lakes Region of Africa', in *Uncharted Territory: Land, Conflict and Humanitarian Action*, ed. S. Pantuliano, Rugby: Practical Action Publishing, 67–93.

Huggins, C. and Clover, J. (eds), 2005, *From the Ground Up: Land Rights, Conflict and Peace in Sub-Saharan Africa*, Pretoria: Institute for Security Studies.

Jansen, S., 2011, 'Refuchess: locating Bosniac repatriates after the war in Bosnia-Herzegovina', *Population, Space and Place*, 17: 140–52.

Le Roy, E., Karsenty, A. and Bertrand, A. (eds), 1996, *La Sécurisation foncière en Afrique: pour une gestion viable des ressources renouvelables*, Paris: Karthala.

Leckie, S. (ed.), 2008, *Housing, Land, and Property Rights in Post-conflict United Nations and Other Peace Operations: A Comparative Survey and Proposal for Reform*, Cambridge: Cambridge University Press.

Leckie, S. and Huggins, C., 2011, *Conflict and Housing, Land and Property Rights: A Handbook on Issues, Frameworks, and Solutions*, Cambridge: Cambridge University Press.

Leonardi, C., 2011, 'Paying "buckets of blood" for the land: moral debates over economy, war and state in Southern Sudan', *Journal of Modern African Studies*, 49(2): 215–40.

Lipton, M., 2009, *Land Reform in Developing Countries: Property Rights and Property Wrongs*, Abingdon: Routledge.

Mallaby, S., 2002, 'The reluctant imperialist: terrorism, failed states, and the case for American empire', *Foreign Affairs*, March/April: 2–7.

Manning, R. and Trzeciak-Duval, A., 2010, 'Situation of fragility and conflict: aid policies and beyond', *Conflict, Security, and Development*, 10(1): 103–31.

Mathieu, P. and Willame, J.-C. (eds), 1999, *Conflits et guerres au Kivu et dans la région des Grands Lacs: entre tensions locales et escalade régionale*, Paris: L'Harmattan.

Médard, J.-F., 1982, 'The underdeveloped state in tropical Africa: political clientelism or neo-patrimonialism', in *Private Patronage and Public Power: Political Clientelism in the Modern State*, ed. C. Clapham, London: Frances Pinter, 162–92.

Mitchell, G.D. (ed.), 1968, *A Dictionary of Sociology*, London: Routledge & Kegan Paul.

Moore, S.F., 1973, 'Law and social change: the semi-autonomous social field as an appropriate subject of study', *Law & Society Review*, 7(4): 719–46.

——1998, 'Changing African land tenure: reflections on the incapacities of the state', *European Journal of Development Research*, 10(2): 33–49.

Newman, E., 2011, 'A human security peace-building agenda', *Third World Quarterly*, 32(10): 1737–56.

Newman, E., Paris, R. and Richmond, O.P. (eds), 2009, *New Perspectives on Liberal Peacebuilding*, Tokyo: United Nations University Press.

North, D.C., 1981, *Structure and Change in Economic History*, New York: W.W. Norton.

——1990, *Institutions, Institutional Change and Economic Performance*, Cambridge: Cambridge University Press.

OECD, 2007a, *OECD DAC Handbook on Security System Reform: Supporting Security and Justice*, Paris.

——2007b, 'Principles for good international engagement in fragile states and situations', Paris.

——2008, *State Building in Situations of Fragility*, Paris.

——2010, *The State's Legitimacy in Fragile Situations: Unpacking Complexity*, Paris.

Ostrom, E., 1990, *Governing the Commons: The Evolution of Institutions for Collective Action*, Cambridge: Cambridge University Press.

Otto, J.M. and Hoekema, A., 2012, 'Legalising land rights, yes but how? An introduction', in *Fair Land Governance: How to Legalise Land Rights for Rural Development*, ed. J.M. Otto and A. Hoekema, Leiden: Leiden University Press, 7–30.

Ozerdem, A. and Sofizada, A.H., 2006, 'Sustainable reintegration to returning refugees in post-Taliban Afghanistan: land-related challenges', *Conflict, Security & Development*, 6(1): 75–100.

Pantuliano, S. (ed.), 2009, *Uncharted Territory: Land, Conflict and Humanitarian Action*, Rugby: Practical Action Publishing.

Paris, R., 2004, *At War's End: Building Peace after Civil Conflict*, Cambridge: Cambridge University Press.

Paris, R. and Sisk, T.D. (eds), 2009, *The Dilemmas of Statebuilding: Confronting the Contradictions of Postwar Peace Operations*, Abingdon: Routledge.

Place, F. and Migot-Adholla, S.E., 1998, 'The economic effects of land registration on smallholder farms in Kenya: evidence from Nyeri and Kakamega Districts', *Land Economics*, 74(3): 360–73.

Platteau, J.-P., 1996, 'The evolutionary theory of land rights as applied to sub-Saharan Africa: a critical assessment', *Development and Change*, 27(1): 29–86.

Richmond, O.P., 2009, 'Becoming liberal, unbecoming liberalism: liberal-local hybridity via the everyday as a response to the paradoxes of liberal peacebuilding', *Journal of Intervention and Statebuilding*, 3(3): 324–44.

Richmond, O.P. and Franks, J., 2009, *Liberal Peace Transitions: Between Statebuilding and Peacebuilding*, Edinburgh: Edinburgh University Press.

Rocha Menocal, A., 2011, 'State building for peace: a new paradigm for international engagement in post-conflict fragile states?', *Third World Quarterly*, 32(10): 1715–36.

Rotberg, R.I. (ed.), 2004, *When States Fail: Causes and Consequences*, Princeton, NJ: Princeton University Press.

Rugadya, M.A., 2006, 'A Review of Literature on Post-conflict Land Policy and Administration Issues, during Return and Resettlement of IDPs: International Experience and Lessons from Uganda', Northern Uganda Recovery and Development Program (RDP).

Shanmugaratnam, N. (ed.), 2008, *Between War and Peace in Sudan and Sri Lanka: Deprivation and Livelihood Revival*, Oxford: James Currey.

Sikor, T. and Müller, D., 2009, 'The limits of state-led land reform: an introduction', *World Development*, 37(8): 1307–16.

Smith, C., 2001, 'Security-sector reform: development breakthrough or institutional engineering?', *Conflict, Security & Development*, 1(1): 5–20.

Takeuchi, S. and Marara, J., 2011, 'Features of land conflicts in post civil war Rwanda', *African Study Monographs*, Supplementary Issue, 42: 119–35.

Takeuchi, S., Murotani, R. and Tsunekawa, K., 2011, 'Capacity traps and legitimacy traps: development assistance and state building in fragile situations', in *Catalyzing Development: A New Vision for Aid*, ed. H. Kharas, K. Makino and W. Jung, Washington, DC: Brookings Institution Press, 127–54.

Thomson, F., 2011, 'The agrarian question and violence in Colombia: conflict and development', *Journal of Agrarian Change*, 11(3): 321–56.

Tilly, C., 1992, *Coercion, Capital, and European States: AD 990–1992*, Malden, MA: Blackwell.

Toulmin, C. and Quan, J. (eds), 2000, *Evolving Land Rights, Policy and Tenure in Africa*, London: DFID/IIED/NRI.

Tucker, A., Ruibal, A.M., Cahill, J. and Brown, F., 2004, 'The new politics of property rights', *Critical Review*, 16(4): 377–403

UN (United Nations), 1992, 'An agenda for peace: preventive diplomacy, peacemaking and peace-keeping', UN Doc.A/47/277 – S/24111.

——2000, 'Report of the panel on United Nations peace operations', UN Doc.A/55/305-S/2000/809.

——2005, 'Economic, social and cultural rights, housing and property restitution in the context of the return of refugees and internally displaced persons, final report of the special rapporteur, Paulo Sérgio Pinheiro, principles on housing and property restitution for refugees and displaced persons', UN Doc.E/CN.4/Sub.2/2005/17.

UN-Habitat, 2012, *Handling Land: Tools for Land Governance and Secure Tenure*, Nairobi.

Unruh, J.D., 2003, 'Land tenure and legal pluralism in the peace process', *Peace & Change*, 28(3): 352–77.

Unruh, J.D. and Williams, R.C. (eds), 2013, *Land and Post-conflict Peacebuilding*, Abingdon: Earthscan.

USAID, 2005, *Fragile States Strategy*, Washington, DC.

——2007, *Land Tenure and Property Rights: Volume I Framework*, Washington, DC.

——2011, *Land Tenure and Property Rights (LTPR): Situation Assessment and Intervention Planning Tool*, Washington, DC.

——2012, *Land Tenure and Property Rights (LTPR): Impact Assessment Tool*, Washington, DC.

Uvin, P., 1998, *Aiding Violence: The Development Enterprise in Rwanda*, West Hartford, CT: Kumarian Press.

Van Leeuwen, M., 2010, 'Crisis or continuity? framing land disputes and local conflict resolution in Burundi', *Land Use Policy*, 27(3): 753–62.

Von Carlowitz, L., 2004, 'Setting property issues in complex peace operations: the CRPC in Bosnia and Herzegovina and the HPD/CC in Kosovo', *Leiden Journal of International Law*, 17(3): 599–614.

Whaites, A., 2008, 'States in development: understanding state-building', DFID working paper, London.

Williams, R.C., 2006, 'The significance of property restitution to sustainable return in Bosnia and Herzegovina', *International Migration*, 44(3): 39–61.

World Bank, 1989, *From Crisis to Sustainable Growth – Sub-Saharan Africa: A Long-term Perspective Study*, Washington, DC.

——1993, *The East Asian Miracle: Economic Growth and Public Policy*, Oxford: Oxford University Press.

Zartman, I.W. (ed.), 1995, *Collapsed States: The Disintegration and Restoration of Legitimate Authority*, Boulder, CO: Lynne Rienner Publishers.

Zürcher, C., 2011, 'Building democracy while building peace', *Journal of Democracy*, 22(1): 81–95.

2 The land question, internal conflicts and international statebuilding in South Sudan

Nadarajah Shanmugaratnam

South Sudan became an independent country on 9 July 2011, following the referendum held in January–February of that year under the Comprehensive Peace Agreement (CPA) of January 2005 between the government of Sudan and the Sudan People's Liberation Movement/Army (SPLM/A). The CPA, which was the outcome of an internationally sponsored, mediated and financed peace process, marked the end of the two-decades-old second civil war in Southern Sudan. It provided for an interim phase of six years and the establishment of an interim Government of Southern Sudan (GOSS). 'The Interim Constitution of Southern Sudan' (ICSS) promulgated in 2005 was superseded by 'The Transitional Constitution of the Republic of South Sudan, 2011' (TCSS), which came into force on the day of independence. The new Republic has a territory of 619,745 sq km, with a projected population of 9,157,745 in 2011.[1] It has a federal system of government with an elected president, and a National Legislature comprising an elected National Legislative Assembly and an upper house known as the Council of States, consisting of 20 members appointed by the president to represent the ten states of the Republic. Each state has its own elected government. There are many political parties in South Sudan.[2] The content of the ICSS, TCSS and the CPA strongly reflects the influence of hegemonic liberal international conflict resolution and statebuilding policies, although a Swiss team of constitutional experts pointed out certain shortcomings in the TCSS that needed to be addressed to ensure a more democratic functioning of the state (Auer *et al.* 2011). It is also important to note that the GOSS is highly dependent on external financial and professional aid for statebuilding, humanitarian relief and development in this era of 'the drift from internal to external statebuilding' (Tilly 1992), a 'drift' that has assumed an institutional form of international trusteeship.[3] The international paradigm of post-war statebuilding incorporates institutional prescriptions to enable economic liberalisation as well. The SPLM/A-led GOSS also embraced this neoliberal development policy. Indeed, the liberal peace and development agenda is an international directive (Duffield 2005), and the essence of this project has been succinctly stated by one of its critical defenders: 'the surest foundation for peace within and between states is market democracy, that is, a liberal democratic polity and a market economy' (Paris 1997: 56; see also Paris 2004; Paris and Sisk 2009).

The 'hegemonic image of the ideal state' rests on the Western liberal premises of 'rule of law, democratic institutions, and market-driven development' (Barnett and Zurcher 2009: 28). 'Rule of law' presupposes the state's capacity to monopolise coercion and to institutionalise and ensure the functioning of the other arms of government such as the police, judiciary and civil administration. Privatisation, deregulation and integration into the global economy are the key elements of development policy, to which is added a programme of poverty reduction. It is now well known that the implementation of this economic policy alters property relations in terms of ownership and actual control over resources and their allocation, while setting in motion processes of accumulation and social differentiation. When it comes to statebuilding and state effectiveness in the South, sovereignty has been redefined with reference to human security and in terms of contingent and not absolute (Westphalian) sovereignty (Duffield 2007). The Commission on Human Security sees human security as centred on people, not states, and links it to livelihood security as well. It addresses human security as a development issue 'increasingly linked to conflict resolution, peacebuilding and statebuilding in Africa' (CHS 2003: 5). In this view, citizens' security would seem to be a key factor in building a legitimate state.

The state, however, is no longer the main provider of social security in a neoliberal world where, ideally, each individual as an autonomous being is expected to pursue his or her economic interests in the marketplace. In aid-dependent countries that have adopted state reforms prescribed by international financial institutions (IFIs) in order to qualify for aid, the programming and delivery of key economic and welfare functions of the state have largely come under the control of multilateral agencies, bilateral donors and NGOs. This is an aspect of contingent sovereignty (Duffield 2007). Thus, the state's capacity to secure domestic legitimacy in such countries is circumscribed by external conditionalities. In fact, the marginalised, the displaced and the poor in these countries have become accustomed to look towards international agencies for relief and livelihood support. This situation is more acute in countries emerging from protracted civil wars. The danger, however, is that the conditionalities themselves may generate threats to post-war peacebuilding, with serious implications for statebuilding, as documented by Paris in his case studies (Paris 2004). Neoliberal reforms may exacerbate exclusion and unwittingly help forces opposed to peacebuilding to gain support. There are also other factors that have a direct and indirect bearing on the domestic legitimacy of the post-civil war state. These include a persistent culture of militarisation and impunity, and the conduct of the political and military elite and other members of the dominant classes, including those who took advantage of war and post-war economies to accumulate wealth. Resource capture may be monopolised or dominated by particular ethnic groups, which may create new or reinforce existing horizontal inequalities with adverse consequences for reunification and nationbuilding (Cramer 2006; 2009).

What is going on in South Sudan is not a transformation of an existing state, but the building of a new state under international trusteeship. This has unique features and challenges. It is a case of building a new state not on a 'clean slate' but in an environment of historical structures such as communally entrenched customary rights to land, and problems inherited from the past amid continuing turmoil in a multi-ethnic society. Moreover, past experiences with the Sudanese state seem to have left a deep-seated fear of the state as a disenfranchising oppressive power among the people. Though officially in a 'post-war' situation, the GOSS has been spending heavily on defence and the country remains on a war footing due to tensions between the two Sudans.[4] Thus, militarisation is a dominant feature of statebuilding in South Sudan. Indeed a full-scale inter-state war appeared imminent in April 2011, when, at the height of the military clashes in Heglig, the government of Sudan officially declared South Sudan an enemy state.

At the end of the interim phase, as the peoples of South Sudan were getting ready to make their historic choice to secede and establish an independent country, the GOSS had rather little to show in terms of achievements in such key areas as infrastructure development, attracting productive investments, resettlement, food security, provision of basic educational and health facilities, disarmament of civilians, human security and inter-communal reconciliation. The 50 per cent share of oil revenues it was entitled to under the CPA accounted for almost all the revenue of the interim GOSS.[5] Most of the oil revenue, which fluctuated widely, was used to meet current expenditures such as salaries and operating costs, including the maintenance of the SPLA. The government thus had to depend on foreign aid for relief and development. South Sudan's dependence on the UN and international NGOs for humanitarian relief, health services, resettlement and livelihood revival was almost total. The situation has got worse since January 2012, when the GOSS decided to shut down oil production in retaliation for Khartoum's illegal confiscation of US$850 million worth of oil. The government introduced a range of austerity measures while leaning more on foreign aid.

Recurrent episodes of inter-communal resource conflict, anti-GOSS militia activities, mass displacements, humanitarian emergencies and other challenges to law and order, which existed in the interim phase, continue in post-independence South Sudan. Ethnic cleavages seem to have deepened due to the rise of competitive ethno-politics dominated by the Dinka and the Nuer, the first- and second-largest groups respectively in the country. There are clear signs of resentment among the ethnic minorities against majoritarianism. This is a major challenge to building a coherent national social formation around an imagined common identity. It would seem that, in regard to statebuilding, South Sudan displays signs of what Barnett and Zurcher (2009: 27) call a 'dual crisis of security and legitimacy'. It must, however, be noted that the GOSS was an outcome of a popular struggle against an oppressive state and secession was a voluntary choice of the people. It may be too hasty to conclude that the new state lacks legitimacy, but it cannot be denied that statebuilding in South Sudan is ridden with issues and conflicts that pose a challenge to building an internally legitimate state, although the same state already enjoys international recognition and patronage. The legitimacy of the struggle and the domestic legitimacy of the new state are two different things both contextually and in terms of the political, economic and institutional challenges. Besides, the GOSS does not seem to have earned wide public consent for its development policy.

This chapter explores some aspects of this problem by focusing on the land question, which was not only a major structural factor behind the protracted war, but has also come to encompass a variety of issues – with serious implications for accountability, internal pacification and unification, and statebuilding in South Sudan.[6] Historically, the North–South conflict was fuelled by several factors, such as the underdevelopment and marginalisation of the South, Arabisation and Islamisation, and the appropriation of the region's resources by the dominant classes of the North and their allies. However, over the years the conflict intensified as the inventory of the South's natural resources expanded. This became particularly evident during the second civil war (1983–2004), as mass depopulation and deaths were caused by the Sudanese government's aerial bombardments of particular areas to expropriate land for oil development (HRW 2003). This was primitive accumulation or 'accumulation by dispossession' (Harvey 2005) of a most violent kind. Moreover, the government of Sudan, while introducing new laws to abolish customary land tenure to legalise collective dispossession, was also redrawing the boundaries of the South by incorporating oil-rich areas into northern territories, thereby violating the Addis Ababa Agreement of 1972 that had brought the first civil war to an end. It would seem that the discovery of oil deposits in the South and the Khartoum regime's moves to change provincial boundaries had reinforced secessionism in the South.

The land question thus assumed central importance in the conflict and its resolution. People from all ethnic groups in South Sudan rallied round the SPLM/A's slogan 'All land in New Sudan belongs to the community'. Even though, as was to be expected, the land question was a major issue at the negotiations, no agreement was reached as neither party was willing to relent on its position on land ownership. As the CPA states, it was agreed 'to establish a process to resolve this issue'.[7] The Republic of South Sudan is now saddled with both the inherited issues over land and a host of new ones, which are a source of internal conflict, new displacements, deprivation and instability in a country in which the vast majority of the ethnically diverse citizens are farmers, pastoralists and agro-pastoralists operating at subsistence levels and vulnerable to livelihood failures.

This study contextualises and reviews the Land Act of 2009 and proceeds to examine three sets of interrelated issues with a view to capturing some key features of the ongoing conflict-ridden land redistribution and statebuilding process in South Sudan. The issues addressed are large-scale land grabbing by potential investors, resettlement, urban migration and residential land grabbing, and land-related violent conflicts and the governance crisis in the states. Land grabbing by powerful individuals and corporate capital has been happening throughout the interim phase and beyond. Most of the large-scale acquisitions took place before the promulgation of the Land Act. Large-scale land transfers to private companies have taken place at the expense of communal lands, which account for most of the land and inland water bodies in South Sudan. This has been viewed as a part of the ongoing 'global land grab' (Deng 2011a; TOI 2011), that is, accumulation by dispossession again.

The transnational land grabbers' rush into South Sudan showed the aggressive nature of present-day financialisation. This, however, did not happen in Africa's newest country without the acquiescence and collaboration of its ruling elite. In fact, during the interim phase, leaders of the GOSS were already inviting large-scale foreign investments in agriculture and other land-based ventures. While the wisdom of this policy may be debatable, it clearly conforms to the neoliberal paradigm of growth and development. Importantly, it is also a reflection of the dominant interests within the domestic power structure. The new ruling elite consists of a mix of government politicians, high-ranking military officers and senior level bureaucrats at the centre and in the states. The close links between corporate interests and the ruling elite are relevant to an understanding of the emerging class relations and some of the land conflicts in South Sudan. Resettlement of returnees and residential land grabbing are also a source of social tensions and conflicts over land rights both in rural and urban areas. At another level, in different parts of the country conflicts over land (and water) tend to turn violent and may also metamorphose into larger-scale inter-communal clashes. The overall situation of extensive ungoverned spaces and humanitarian emergencies makes South Sudan's state liable to be labelled 'fragile'. It raises the question of whether the state has the capacity to meet the basic neoliberal conditionalities of 'good governance', such as transparency, accountability and the rule of law.

Post-war land legislation: a balancing act with inherent tensions

The Land Act: a contextualisation

At its founding in 1983, the SPLM/A adopted a radical 'socialist' ideology and aligned itself with the Soviet bloc through its links with the pro-Soviet Ethiopian government (Johnson 2003). In the early days of the post-Cold War era, the SPLM went through an ideological transformation as it adopted a pro-West and pro-liberalisation position. As already noted, the SPLM and GOSS are now explicitly committed to the development policy prescriptions of the IFIs. Indeed, the South Sudan Development Plan 2011–13 is premised on a market-led development policy. However, the issue of land rights and

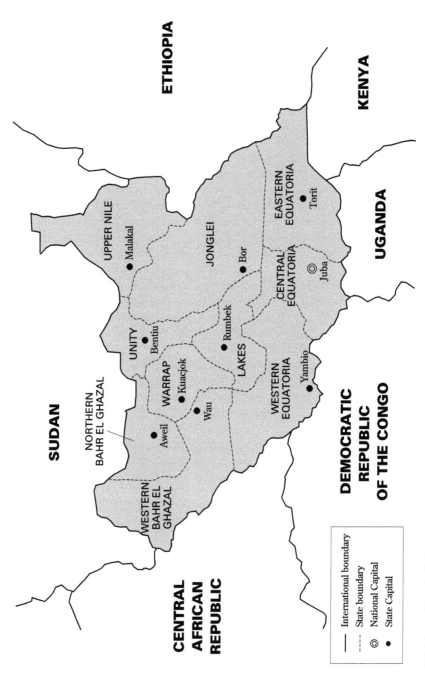

Figure 2.1 Map of South Sudan

land policy posed a challenge, as the GOSS had to address conflicting interests. In 2003 the SPLM envisioned the economy of the New Sudan in the following terms:

> The New Sudan economy shall be a mixed free market economy in which both public and private sectors shall complement each other and be encouraged, with the public sector based on social welfare, competitiveness, efficiency and provision of social overhead service. … Foreign investment in New Sudan shall be allowed and encouraged and repatriation of profits shall be guaranteed.
> (cited in Sundnes and Shanmugaratnam 2008; see also Shanmugaratnam 2008)

In this globalisation-friendly, futuristic vision of modernisation, the role of the state may be read as one of enabling the development of a 'free market economy'. A necessary condition for the translation of such a vision into reality is a land tenure system conducive to private investment and accumulation in a country in which most of the land is communal and subject to customary laws. Having won mass support for the struggle with the slogan that all land in 'New Sudan' belonged to the community (as opposed to the government of Sudan's position that all land belonged to the state), the SPLM-led interim GOSS was confronted with an apparent dilemma. It had to deliver on the promise of protecting customary rights to land, while at the same time instituting changes in the very same land tenure to create alienable or commodifiable property rights to promote economic expansion and modernisation through private investment and accumulation through integration with the global economy. The GOSS was also under pressure from the 'donor community' and corporate interests to introduce appropriate land legislation to attract large-scale investment in agriculture and other sectors such as oil. During the years of armed struggle, customary land laws and institutions prevailed in the areas controlled by the SPLM/A, which explicitly rejected the laws of the Sudanese state and created its own rather rudimentary civil administrative structures (Shanmugaratnam 2008). 'The people', notes a study of land issues in an area under SPLM/A's control in 2003, 'were by and large content with the situation: their rights to resources were being governed by the customs and rules they were familiar with, and the Movement had assured them that the same land tenure system would continue under the new regime. The SPLM/A's approach also helped to enhance its political legitimacy among the people' (Sundnes and Shanmugaratnam 2008: 72).

The Land Act 2009 appeared to offer a way out of the dilemma by declaring that 'All land in Southern Sudan is owned by the people of Southern Sudan and its usage shall be regulated by the Government' (§7: 8). Prescribing that land may be acquired through customary, freehold and leasehold tenure, the Act classifies all land in the country into three categories: public, community and private.[8] It provides statutory recognition of customary rights to land, including protection of the migratory rights of pastoralists. Under the

Act, traditional authority within a specific community may allocate customary land rights for residential, agricultural, forestry and grazing purposes. The Act also entitles returnees displaced due to the civil war from 16 May 1983 to the restitution of rights to their original lands, or to compensation if restitution cannot be effected.

However, the Act's use of the term 'people' and not 'community' for the owners of all land in Southern Sudan marks a significant departure from the SPLM's long-held position. This terminological shift would seem to be a necessary condition to enable tenure reforms and redistribution of land under the different types of property rights identified in the Land Act. It also implies a civic notion of citizenship and homeland, as opposed to the existing ethno-territorially based sense of citizenship and homeland. On the other hand, it is seen by local critics, including chiefs, civil society activists, intellectuals and politicians, as a move that would progressively weaken customary institutions and 'community values', while promoting individual interests, privatisation and inequalities.[9] They fear that it may well be a transitional step for a future amendment to the Land Act to transfer ownership of all land to the South Sudanese state.[10] Others argue that the Act's conception of the people as the owners of all land in the country is a necessary condition for envisioning and constructing an overarching identity that can unify the diverse ethnic communities to build a 'South Sudanese nation' in which every citizen is free to choose his or her place of residence. At the same time, some of them warn that it could cause more harm than good in the absence of consensually evolved policy and institutional arrangements and democratic participation. Sharing this concern, Ann Itto, Deputy Secretary General of the SPLM and a former Minister for Agriculture, said that community-based tenure was protective of community members and worked well, but it also promoted 'tribalism'. Land was 'central to nationbuilding' but the challenge of realising an inclusive vision of the South Sudanese as 'a people' had to be addressed carefully, taking into consideration such factors as ethnic diversity and women's rights. In her view, the Land Act was helpful for the commercialisation and modernisation of agriculture based on large and small holdings.[11]

Two youthful activists from the South Sudan Land Alliance were critical of the manner in which the Land Act was framed and passed as law.[12] They said that 'experts' formulated the Act without any consultation with the communities, and even the chiefs in the country were not aware of its contents until after it became law.[13] They noted that the idea that all land belonged to the people of South Sudan was not without merit from the point of view of citizenship rights and nationbuilding, but it was imperative that everyone who sought access to community land followed the customary law and the rules of obtaining land from particular communities. They believed that community tenure was flexible enough to accommodate requests for land from persons belonging to different ethnic groups. Similar views were expressed by some others, including local professionals working for INGOs. Apparently, they were suggesting a way to connect the top-down process of statebuilding with a customary-law-based approach to land distribution. Such a proposition appears far removed from current realities on the ground. Some interviewees spoke openly of minorities' apprehensions about influxes of Dinka and Nuer settlers into their territories in Equatoria. Land indeed plays a key role in South Sudan's ethno-politics.

Inherent tensions

Under the Act, the state government is responsible for the overall management and administration of land, while the ownership of subterranean resources rests with the central government. It has various provisions for expropriation of land for public purposes and for alienation of large tracts for private investment. The GOSS, state governments and any other public authority may expropriate land for public purposes through a procedure 'based on a consultative process with the communities or individuals concerned prior to conception of the plan of expropriation' (§74.1). The Act sets out a formal procedure for leasehold contracts not exceeding 99 years on communal land for commercial investment.[14] Traditional authority in consultation with the County Land Authority and the Payam Land Council may grant not more than 250 *feddans* (105 hectares).[15] A similar procedure may be followed for a lease contract exceeding 250 *feddans,* but the grant has to be approved by the concerned Ministry in consultation with the Investment Authority. On the subject of leasehold contract, 'community interest' figures prominently along with 'consultation' in the Act, which expects private investment on land acquired from a community to 'contribute economically and socially to the development of the local community' (§61.2). It may be added that the Local Government Act reinforces the provisions of the Land Act that require the government to consult local communities on decisions about community land.

The abovementioned and other provisions of the Land Act would seem to constitute a legal framework for a set of institutions to protect the customary land rights of the people, including the millions of returnees, while providing for land acquisitions for public purposes and commercially oriented private investments. However, therein lies the potential for tensions and open conflict over the conversion of communal lands into public and private lands. Indeed, there are already major problems in this regard. The Land Act is an exercise in balancing different interests which are not easy to reconcile in practice as they are competing for the same resource, which is largely under community tenure. Basically, the Act is about redistributing the country's land resources between different actors such as the communities (including individuals), foreign and domestic investors, and state and central government agencies. Redistribution of land is about restructuring or transforming power relations and such an undertaking is no cakewalk anywhere. And the realities on the ground make it even more challenging in South Sudan. Community tenure is characterised by a plurality of customary rules and practices reflecting ethnic and intra-ethnic diversity, and ethno-territorialities, as well as the diverse land use practices of pastoralists, agro-pastoralists and farmers. Mass displacements and secondary occupation of vacated homesteads and productive lands during the war in different parts of the country, land grabbing by SPLA soldiers and armed civilian groups, the large-scale flow of returnees back to their original areas, which still have substantial numbers of secondary occupants, and the growing trend of migration of young men and women to urban areas in search of livelihood opportunities have brought the customarily ethnic and clan-based community tenure system under strain. These trends contribute to local resource conflicts and tenure insecurity. This situation is further complicated by several factors such as a lack of information and awareness about the Land Act among the people, and enforcement failures. At the local and intermediate levels, there is an evident lack of knowledge and understanding about the power, authority and roles of different governmental and customary institutions. Moreover, in many areas local institutions are not fully functional and the local authorities themselves are not well informed about the Land Act and the interpretations of its provisions regarding customary rights and community land. Most people, particularly in the rural areas, remain poorly informed about the contents of the Land Act. The lack of information is even more acute among returnees.[16]

According to a post-Land Act study of tenure issues, communities were apprehensive about entrusting 'the power of land acquisition to GOSS and State governments because of the likelihood of abuse of such powers as well as the equal likelihood of marginalisation of traditional leaders' and the possible consequence of 'alienation of communities from their ancestral lands' (USAID 2010: A-5-6). There is also a fear that conversion of community land into public land may be a step towards privatisation in the future, which was a practice adopted by the government of Sudan. Such a fear is reasonably founded given the pronouncements by the president and other senior government leaders in favour of large-scale foreign investment in agriculture and other land-based activities, and the large-scale land transfers of the recent past.

Until the promulgation of the Land Act in 2009, there was uncertainty and confusion as to which laws of Sudan the interim GOSS should follow in matters concerning land. This situation was exploited by large- and small-scale land grabbers. The Land Act requires all categories of land to be demarcated and registered with the Land Registry before they are given titles. However, this has not been done for most of the community land. There have been transfers of unregistered community land to private investors. Lack of registration before transfer undermines the community's claim to the land. State governments did not seem to have a clearly defined method for delineating the boundaries of community land (Deng 2011a; 2011b). The Land Registry is extremely weak due to a lack of capacity and financial resources to cover the entire country.

GOSS did not have a formally approved land policy until February 2013, although the Southern Sudan Land Commission (SSLC) set up under the

CPA had been working on it for a long time. The SSLC finally produced a draft land policy in February 2011, which was approved by the Council of Ministers in February 2013. The approved draft policy identifies widespread tenure insecurity as the principal policy problem. 'Widespread tenure insecurity and violation of land rights', states the draft, 'impedes achievement of peace and security; forestalls individual, community and public sector efforts to increase wealth and reduce poverty; and can undermine the authority of new government institutions' (SSLC 2011: 3). The document lists several problems that contribute to this situation. These include dislocations due to civil war and natural calamities, post-war conflicts over land rights, weak land administration, lack of transparency and accountability, gender discrimination, informal settlements in cities and towns, land grabbing, conflicts between groups of pastoralists and between pastoralists and farmers, and border disputes between counties and *Payams*. It says that the right of eminent domain should be restricted to 'securing land for public use only and not for subsequent transfer or sale to private individuals' (SSLC 2011: 15).

These problems are part of the fluid and conflict-ridden realities on the ground, and I shall be addressing some of them and their implications for statebuilding and peacebuilding. However, amid all the institutional shortcomings, violations, enforcement failures and the absence of a formally approved land policy, there is a discernible logic in the processes at work when they are seen in the light of post-war economic opportunities, demographic shifts and power relations at different levels. Persons in powerful positions have been taking advantage of the weaknesses of the fledgling state, the legal ambiguity of the interim phase and the public's lack of knowledge of the contents of the Land Act to cut questionable deals with investors. Similarly, powerful individuals and armed groups have been grabbing high-value residential land with impunity.

Nevertheless, it can be argued that the Land Act provides a legal basis for operationalising the neoliberal prescription to attract foreign direct investment through long-term renewable lease contracts in legally valid and potentially transparent ways. The potential areas for such investment include the production of food and non-food agricultural commodities for export, eco-tourism based on protected areas and nature reserves, and the exploitation of high-value subterranean resources including oil and minerals. The Act, however, is not applicable retroactively without further amendment or additional legal enactment to deal with the dubious land transactions that happened during the interim phase. The GOSS has yet to reach a decision on this matter. Whatever its ambiguities may be, there is no question that the Land Act embodies a significant reform of the pre-existing tenure system to promote privatisation, accumulation and class formation in South Sudan. On the other hand, the present realities on the ground, as will become clearer in the sections that follow, expose 'the gap between the state as a formal or legal entity and its organisational or empirical capacity to govern' (Duffield 2007: 171).

The post-CPA land rush: privatisation of community and public assets and its consequences for state–society relations

Large-scale land grabbing

> I urge investors worldwide to come and invest in Southern Sudan. In terms of agriculture, it will be the bread basket of the region and the world.
>
> President Salva Kiir, October 2010 (cited in Deng 2011b: 4)

Large-scale land acquisitions (> 500 hectares each) had actually begun in post-CPA South Sudan before President Kiir's open invitation to investors worldwide and before the Land Act was passed. In a baseline survey of large-scale, land-based investment in South Sudan, Deng found that in just four years, between 2007 and 2010, a total of 2.64 million hectares were sought or acquired for agriculture, forestry and biofuel plantations alone. This figure rises to a staggering 5.74 million hectares (approximately nine per cent of South Sudan's land area) if the pre-CPA large-scale foreign investments in land-based business projects are added. Deng notes that the post-CPA foreign corporate interest in agriculture and biofuels in South Sudan is associated with the current global rush for African farmland; he raises questions about the legal validity of the deals while doubting the practical feasibility of several of them (Deng 2011a). Some international organisations have also expressed concerns about the possible adverse social consequences of these deals, while strongly criticising the non-transparent manner in which they were made behind the backs of the communities to which most of the lands belonged (TOI 2011; Oxfam 2011). Privatisation of community and public property was happening through flawed long-term lease contracts in all ten states.

The following findings of Deng's baseline survey are relevant to an understanding of the nature of the large-scale and long-term land transfers and their possible impact on state–society relations in South Sudan (Deng 2011a).

- Prior consultations with the affected communities were made in only nine out of a total of 28 transactions in the ten states. In respect of the ownership of the lands leased out, 15 projects are on community-owned land, eight on state-owned, and five on land owned by both the state and communities.
- There was no uniform procedure for managing large-scale land acquisitions, due to the legal ambiguity of the transitional phase.
- Most of the proposed foreign investments are in the three states of Central Equatoria, Western Equatoria and Unity, which are known to have large tracts of prime agricultural land. In the 'Green Belt',[17] 1.265 million hectares, or 25 per cent of the land, has been taken over by seven foreign investors for agricultural, biofuel and timber production projects. The agro-ecological zones with the most foreign investment have the least domestic investment. Projects of domestic investors are mostly smaller in

terms of land area (not more than 500 ha/project) and are found mostly in states that do not attract foreign investors.

• The displacement potential, and consequently the potential for conflict, is high in many of the projects, as they are 'located in highly populated areas where tens or even hundreds of thousands of people rely on land and natural resources for their daily livelihoods' (Deng 2011a: 28).

• There are inconsistencies between the Land Act and the Investment Promotion Act on the length of the renewable lease periods. According to the former, land may be leased for 99 years to foreign investors, while the latter prescribes 30 and 60 years of renewable contracts for agriculture and forestry projects, respectively. The baseline survey found that leases on state-owned land were on average 31 years, compared with 55 years for those on community-owned lands. Two of the large-scale land leases were for 99 years.

• While the agreed lease payments are rather low, the potential for employment generation by large-scale land investment is also low if past and current experience with large agricultural projects is any guide.

Non-transparency and corruption

The Oakland Institute reported in June 2011 that the largest land deal so far in South Sudan had been negotiated between Nile Trading & Development Inc. (NTD), a Dallas-based firm, and Mukaya Payam Cooperative in Lainya County, Central Equatoria State, in March 2008. Communal land of 600,000 hectares was leased out for 49 years for an annual rent of 75,000 Sudanese pounds (approx. US$25,000). The area transferred may be extended to 100,000,000 hectares under the lease contract. The deal 'allows NTD full rights to exploit all natural resources in the leased land' (TOI 2011: 1). In May 2008 NTD president David Neiman spelled out his firm's priorities in a letter to the governor of Central Equatoria, General Wani Konga. These included, 'without limitation, the harvesting of current tree growth' and planting and harvesting of palm oil trees and biofuel plants such as Jatropha. Further, NTD also intended to trade any carbon credits that resulted from the timber on the leased land (TOI 2011: 2). The deal between NTD and the cooperative was followed by a lease agreement between the government of Central Equatoria (Ministry of Physical Infrastructure) and the cooperative in October 2008 (TOI 2011).

However, what is most intriguing about this deal is that the Mukaya Payam Cooperative was neither legally registered nor representative of the *Payam*'s community. It was a fictitious body formed by the paramount chief of the *Payam* and two other members of his family. Unlike the other transactions, much has come to light about this deal as a result of interventions by concerned groups and individuals, including natives of Mukaya residing in Juba. With the support of these groups, the Mukaya community mounted a campaign against the lease. A delegation of community leaders from

Mukaya made representations to the president of the country and the state governor, who had authorised the lease. Both the president and the governor assured the delegation that no investment would take place without the community's consent (Deng 2012). The campaign has had some initial success in the sense that the governor and county officials admit that due process was not followed. Moreover, the extents of land to be acquired were far in excess of the land belonging to the Mukaya *Payam*. The paramount chief has also alleged that he was duped by the members of his own family, as he was made to believe that the lease period was shorter and the area leased out smaller. Apparently, he was both a perpetrator and a victim (Oxfam 2011). The final outcome of the campaign is yet to be seen. The case of NTD and Mukaya Payam Cooperative is exceptional in the sense that so far it is the only one in which the local communities have been able to receive vital information about the deal as well as support from concerned groups to stage a campaign against it. In most of the other cases, the communities had little or no information about deals that had serious consequences for their livelihoods. Clearly, the state governments concerned have exposed themselves to allegations of complicity in land leases behind the backs of the legitimate owners of the lands.

An important question about all these transactions concerns how many of them have actually become operational. As of January 2013, investment activities were going on in a few. For example, in 2009, after the promulgation of the Land Act, the Australian agribusiness company Concord Agriculture obtained 105,000 hectares of land on a 25-year lease from the government of Unity State for an agricultural project in Gwit and Pariang counties. Citadel Capital, an Egyptian equity firm, has invested in land development and the production of crops such as maize and sorghum in a part of the project area. According to Concord Agriculture, the project 'was entirely conceived and built to serve local needs' and 'will continue to serve the needs of the domestic market for the foreseeable future' (Sadek 2012: 1). However, an investigative report from the field has raised some critical issues. Although all the land leased to the company belongs to the community, the lease agreement, which includes an annual rent of US$125,000, was signed with the state government. The community was not a party to the agreement, nor is it entitled to any share of the agreed lease payment. Employment opportunities for locals were limited as most of the employees were from other countries in Africa. The CEO of Concord Agriculture also admitted that the agreement, with its tax exemptions on the import of machinery and on profits for the first 10 years, was strongly tilted in favour of the lessee. The company had not carried out the mandatory environmental and social impact assessment required by the Land Act. The CEO said that neither the government nor the agreement required it. Locals complained that the company had not honoured its promises of providing social services and agricultural training (Johnson 2012).

No major activity has begun in most of the projects. Uncertainty about the legality of the transactions and lack of basic infrastructure are among the disincentives for investment. The lessees may be waiting until these problems have been solved. They also have the option of profitably subleasing all or part of the land acquired. This has indeed happened in some cases.[18] The farming and herding communities that enjoy customary rights to the lands leased out in many areas have so far not felt or observed any real changes in the form of enclosures or land use changes by foreign or local firms. According to several sources interviewed in January 2013, these communities will definitely resist and may even resort to violent actions when such changes happen on the ground and adversely affect their housing, farming, herding, fishing, gathering and other needs. It is likely that some of the projects, such as that of NTD, will be terminated by the GOSS due to sustained opposition. However, the same cannot be said about all other questionable deals. As acutely observed by Deng, several 'influential Southern Sudanese are also deeply involved with many of these deals, and a project that does not seem viable today may nonetheless come to fruition through the political weight of its supporters' (Deng 2011a: 35).

Return, resettlement, residential land grabbing: local challenges to reconciliation and state legitimacy

Ad hocism and unrealistic assumptions

The CPA was a major inducement for millions of South Sudan's internally displaced persons (IDPs) and refugees living in neighbouring countries to return. Keen to get as many people as possible back into South Sudan in time for the census to be held by the end of the second year of the interim period, the GOSS also actively encouraged these people, particularly those who had migrated to the north and to other countries, to return to their original homes.[19] By the end of 2009 more than two million IDPs and refugees had returned to South Sudan. The trend continues. The scale of return migration and the consequent resettlement and livelihood needs posed major logistical, humanitarian and socio-economic challenges, which the interim GOSS was ill-prepared to face. The government was not unaware of its lack of capacity, but the motive behind its call to the displaced and the refugees to return was political: first the census and then the referendum. Unsurprisingly, the government became almost totally dependent on international donors and NGOs to deal with this massive and multifaceted responsibility.[20] The international actors created structures outside the emerging state to deliver humanitarian relief and material aid to returnees. The returnees (and the non-displaced) regarded the INGOs and other external agencies operating in their areas as the providers of their basic needs such as food relief, materials for temporary shelter, healthcare, and production inputs such as seeds and farm tools. Indeed, this perception has grown even stronger over the years. The reliance of aid agencies on parallel structures to deliver assistance quickly to the needy had adverse effects on the development of state structures, which were relegated to a passive secondary role. Moreover, INGOs attracted the better-qualified locals with offers of higher wages and perquisites. The result, obviously unintended but not unforeseeable, was an undermining of the development and legitimacy of the fledgling state structures. In reality, the role of the external agencies in humanitarian relief, resettlement, livelihood revival and social services has turned into a form of international trusteeship. This situation continues due to the persisting incapacity of the state.

Resettlement, livelihood revival and reintegration are official priorities, but the challenges they pose are immense. The experience so far exposes the absence of a systematic policy or a proactive approach and the dominance of ad hocism and unrealistic assumptions regarding resettlement and 'reintegration' on the part of the government (Pantuliano *et al.* 2008; Shanmugaratnam 2010; Martin and Mosel 2011; Deng 2011a; 2011b; Mennen 2012). 'The authorities in Southern Sudan', observes a study by the Internal Displacement Monitoring Centre,

> have so far focused exclusively on return to areas of origin as the only durable solution for IDPs and returning refugees. However, many IDPs would prefer to integrate in the towns they fled to, or to settle in other urban areas, to better access services and livelihoods.
>
> (IDMC 2009: 7)

The official conception of 'reintegration' suggests that the authorities had assumed that all returnees would choose to return to their original areas of residence. According to the Land Act, reintegration 'means the re-entry of formerly internally displaced persons into the social, economic, cultural and political fabric of their original community'. Surprisingly, this definition is silent about returning refugees. In an earlier study, I noted that the assumption that all returnees would go back to their original community was rather unrealistic and inflexible, and the belief that reintegration was simply 're-entry' reflected the lack of a deeper understanding of the spatial, socio-economic and political dynamics of resettlement and reintegration and their links to land rights, livelihood revival and development. The result was a lack of coherence in GOSS's approach to resettlement and reintegration (Shanmugaratnam 2010). As the UNHCR sums up, in its own past experience in other post-war situations, 'return and reintegration is not a simple reversal of displacement but a dynamic process involving individuals, households and communities that have changed as a result of their experience of being displaced' (UNHCR 2008: 5). The fieldwork and literature review carried out for the present study reinforce the foregoing assessment and the key land-policy-related issues are discussed below with reference to urban migration, residential land grabbing by powerful groups, returnee-IDP conflicts in urban and rural areas and the dilemmas of ethnicity-based customary institutions in multi-ethnic localities.

***Urban migration, residential land grabbing and governance crisis – the case
of Juba***

> Community land is being taken by outsiders without the community's
> consent ... It is OK if people are coming to Juba for employment but
> many have come here to grab plots of land to sell and make money ...
> The land grabbers include powerful politicians and generals.
>
> (Paramount chief of Juba County, 17 January 2013)

> Gazetted land in Juba city is too small compared to the rising popula-
> tion. It is so difficult to get land legally. The powerful just grab it. The
> customary rights to land have their limitations in a rapidly changing
> situation. Resettlement in Juba is about managing coexistence but there is
> no policy or mechanism for it.
>
> (A resident of Juba, 23 January 2013)

The urban population has been growing rapidly in the post-CPA period, and
the trend continues. In 1993 Juba had a population of 114,980, which according to estimates rose to 250,000 in 2005 and to 500,000 in 2010 (Martin and
Mosel 2011). Current estimates (January 2013) of the population in Juba City
Council's three *Payams* (Munuki, Kator and Juba Town) range between
700,000 and 900,000.[21] In fact, the city has already expanded beyond these
three into the rural Northern Bari and Rajaf *Payams*. The urban pull factors
for returnees and migrants include easier access to humanitarian relief and
services, and employment prospects. Juba has also been attracting land grabbers in big numbers. Indeed, urban land grabbing by the rich and powerful
appears to be a more blatant form of accumulation by dispossession. The
violence associated with it is an additional cause of human insecurity. People
are also driven by war and deprivation-related push factors to migrate to Juba
and other cities. Returnees from Khartoum and abroad who were used to
urban lifestyles preferred to move to cities such as Juba and Yei. The returnee
population was a mix of well-educated, semi-skilled and unskilled persons.
Nearly 90 per cent of the returnees who moved to Juba were not displaced
from there, and many returnees who were originally from Juba found their
plots occupied by IDPs (Pantuliano *et al.* 2008) and land grabbers. The changing urban residential geography of Juba reflects the social differentiation of its
population. There are the upper- and middle-class residential areas and the
slums where the migrant casual workers live. While post-war urban development and migration are major contributors to rising demand for land, a variety of issues has emerged over access to land and customary rights in the
evolving multi-ethnic urban settings, with implications for reconciliation,
integration and state–society relations. Juba, being the national as well as
Central Equatoria's capital, displays these issues on a bigger scale than other
urban areas in the country. The problematic relationship between the central
and the state governments on expropriation of land for public purposes is also

evident in this congested and land-conflict-ridden city. This situation contributed towards hastening GOSS's long-delayed decision to relocate the national capital to Ramciel in the neighbouring Lakes State.

The foregoing account highlights some aspects of an ongoing transformative process that throws up many challenges to the existing property regimes and structures of governance in an ethnically diverse and socially differentiated population. On one side, there is a growing demand for land for urban infrastructure development and other public utilities, social services, commercial enterprises, housing and recreation. On the other, most of the land to meet this demand has to be acquired from the local community, which holds it under customary tenure. Institutionally, it is not a free market situation, nor is it governed by functioning regulatory mechanisms. As already shown, formally the conversion of community land into public or private land involves legal and consultative procedures. The situation in Juba, however, is characterised by institutional paralysis compounded by corruption and capacity constraints on the part of the state and central governments, and local resistance to appropriation of community land, particularly for distribution to 'outsiders' – that is, migrants belonging to other ethnic groups. Powerful groups and individuals have taken advantage of governmental weaknesses and grabbed land for personal use and to profit from the burgeoning urban land lease market. A construction boom is evident in Juba, although the country is in austerity mode.

Juba's ethno-demographic landscape has been changing since it became the regional capital of Southern Sudan in 1956. Its population, however, has fluctuated because of war-induced displacements on the one hand, and influxes of IDPs on the other. Juba and the areas around it are predominantly inhabited by the minority Bari community. Most of the land in the county is under customary tenure, while areas within the municipality were gazetted as state land in earlier times. The gazetted lands were parcelled out to individuals and organisations on transferable leases. During and after the interim phase, the Bari have resisted attempts by the GOSS and the government of Central Equatoria to expropriate community land. Resentful of the large influxes of returnees belonging to other ethnic groups and the violent occupation of community land by SPLA soldiers and armed groups, Bari chiefs often invoked the SPLM's wartime slogan that the land belonged to the community. They insisted that they would consider transferring land to the government only if it agreed to conditions such as the reservation of a third of the plots for the Bari themselves and the provision of services on the plots allocated (Pantuliano *et al.* 2008). On the other hand, according to local sources, some chiefs in Juba and other parts of the state have leased land to 'outsiders' without consulting the community.

In January 2013 Juba County's paramount chief told me that he and the chiefs under him had cooperated with the state government in identifying and transferring land for public purposes and for private investment that brought benefits to the community. What he and his community were opposing was the forcible occupation of community land by powerful persons and armed groups, which always caused inter-communal clashes. The armed groups included SPLA officers and civilians from the larger Bahr el Ghazal, mostly Dinka and Nuer. He said the land grabbers were in the business of leasing out plots of the grabbed land to foreign and local investors. 'We are powerless against them', he said, and went on to recount the violence that erupted in the Kemiru village of Muniki Payam in March 2012 between Dinka and Nuer migrants and the local Bari residents. Several people, including women and children, were killed in the clash, and Bari residents were displaced by the Dinka and Nuer settlers. The Dinka have named the area they occupy *Jebel Dinka* ('Hill Dinka'). The displaced Bari are staying in Juba town. 'The Kemiru problem', he said, 'is not solved yet. The vice president delegated the matter to the deputy governor, but no result so far.'

Land acquisition, gazetting and allocation by the government involve lengthy and expensive procedures. This process has actually ground to a standstill in recent years. Military officers, politicians and other powerful persons have taken the law into their own hands and have forcibly occupied land and caused displacements in Juba. This form of land grabbing was often marked by overt violence. State officials claimed that soldiers did more than 80 per cent of the land grabbing within Juba, as they chose to move out of the barracks to be with their families (Martin and Mosel 2011). While confirming this, Central Equatoria's Minister for Agriculture and Forestry said that armed civilians were also engaged in land grabbing in Juba city and the villages around it in well-planned ways.[22] High-level officials of the state's Ministry of Physical Infrastructure (MPI), which is responsible for land allocation, admitted that the ministry was unable to prevent the illegal occupation of gazetted lands by members of the SPLA and groups of civilians from the larger Bahr el Ghazal protected by them. For instance, Class I plots in 3K South (an area known as Tong Ping or Juba na Bari, where embassies and international organisations are located), gazetted and allocated in the 1980s, had been forcibly occupied since 2006–7. The original leaseholders were displaced. The governor appointed a committee to look into the matter with a view to getting the land back. The ministry's effort to encourage the land grabbers to vacate the plots, by offering them land elsewhere in the city, did not help. The problem remained unresolved as of January 2013. An official of the MPI said that the land grabbers were after high-value land. A 1,200 sq m plot in 3K South, which fetched an annual rent of around US$10,000 (in addition to a one-off down payment) in 2005 would go for more than US $24,000 (plus down payment) in 2013. Normally, plots leased out for individual housing are 20 sq m in size. The grabbers attached forged lease titles to the sale agreements. According to the official, some 7,000 plots had been usurped within the municipality and in the Northern Bari and Rajaf *Payams*.

The direct involvement in land grabbing of SPLA personnel, other armed groups allegedly linked to them and powerful individuals is a serious affront to the country's laws and system of government. Their conduct has had a paralysing effect on the weak fledgling structures responsible for land administration. The situation in Juba is a more extreme manifestation of the GOSS's and state governments' failure to adopt a carefully planned strategy for resettlement and land distribution. It also shows that urbanisation constantly challenges the survival of ethnicity-based customary land tenure and exposes the urgency of more effective state intervention – through transparent regulatory mechanisms – to enable land acquisition and distribution to meet different needs. The scale of urban migration has exposed both the limits of customary institutions to deal with the demand for land and the failure of the state authorities responsible for acquisition and allocation of land and the rule of law. The customary law and the conventional practices of customary courts on land matters appear too ethno-centric to allow 'non-indigenous' returnees and IDPs to be legally settled on community land. It is not a case of few individuals but thousands of persons, including large numbers of women, who are invariably poor and powerless. These vulnerable groups were directly affected by the forced evictions and demolitions of informal settlements in Juba in 2008 and after (IDMC 2012). On the other hand, many locals were being driven out of their land by armed land grabbers.

Even as land grabbing and resettlement remain serious problems, the government of Central Equatoria has decided to stop gazetting and allocating land for housing in and around the city area from January 2013 and opted to offer land to private investors for real estate development. Land has already been allocated to two foreign investors for the construction of apartment blocks in Juba. The MPI sees this as a land-saving approach to urban housing, while avoiding the release of more plots of land in a situation of uncontrolled land grabbing. This will help meet the housing demand of the richer sections, but the poorer returnees and migrants will end up in Juba's slums as cheap labour for urban development. There is no guarantee that this will stop urban land grabbing, which has to do with abuse or usurpation of power.

Customary land institutions in emerging multi-ethnic settings

It has been noted that urbanisation and the changing ethnic profile of Juba are a challenge to the ethnicity- and clan-based customary land tenure and local social organisation. This, however, is not an exclusively urban phenomenon. Many rural areas have also become more multi-ethnic as a result of migration and relocation during and after the war. Conflicts between locals, returnees and IDPs also exist in these areas. As a socially embedded institution, customary tenure has its procedures for the allocation of land to an individual from another ethnic group and for temporary sharing of land resources with other groups. However, experience shows that the rules and norms of this tenure system were not meant to deal with situations of large numbers of migrants seeking land. Since everyone belongs to a particular clan within a larger ethnic or sub-ethnic group, it is not uncommon for migrant groups to reconstitute their own customary institutions in places belonging to other communities. This often leads to communal confrontations, which invariably begin over access to housing land and grazing resources and turn into identity conflicts. The outcome is not coexistence of mutually recognised customary institutions, but confrontation and institutional impasse.

This has been happening in many areas. The Madi–Dinka conflict in Nimule, Eastern Equatoria, is an example of protracted tension between returnees and IDPs with serious implications for the functioning of local customary institutions and for inter-communal relations.[23] Nimule Payam is Madi territory and the Dinka IDPs are a minority who settled in some parts of Nimule in 1994, when the locals were away in neighbouring Uganda as refugees. Conflicts over land began when the Madi returned home in large numbers after the CPA. The Dinka had constituted their own customary institution and refused to recognise the local institutions. They enjoyed a close relationship with the Dinka SPLA soldiers stationed in Nimule. Many of them were armed. They openly displayed their disregard for the local authority and customs, and claimed they had their own chiefs and customs. The conflict over land rights and governance continues in a state of institutional impasse. The asymmetry in power relations is extreme. In the larger national context, the Madi are a tiny minority compared to the Dinka, who are not only the largest ethnic group but also the most dominant in the government and the armed forces. In Madi perception, the SPLA, the judiciary and the bureaucracy were partial towards the Dinka IDPs. In terms of power, it is a case of inter-ethnic (horizontal) inequality at the local level. The Madi would like the Dinka repatriated to their native Bor under an agreement reached in January 2009, but thousands of Dinka have chosen to remain in Nimule. The question of integration looms large but it cannot be meaningfully addressed without disarming the Dinka IDPs and overcoming the institutional impasse in land governance. The Land Act does not seem to have any provision to deal with issues of this nature. This is another issue to be addressed at policy levels, as similar cases exist in other parts of the country as well (Shanmugaratnam 2010).

Resource conflicts, rebel militias and governance failure in the states

Conflicts between different groups of herders and between herders and farmers over land resources are not new in South Sudan. In pre-war times, these conflicts were largely confined to local levels and casualties were quite low even when disputes turned violent. The weapons used were mostly the traditional sticks and spears. The local conflict resolution mechanisms were also reasonably effective (USAID 2010). The war and its consequences over the years have radically altered the frequency, intensity and scale of internal conflicts in South Sudan. Competition for land resources often plays a crucial role in inter-group conflicts, but the latter invariably become linked to larger political and military factors. An enduring culture of militarisation, failure of disarmament campaigns, widespread livelihood insecurity, elite capture and ethno-political imperatives and manipulations have transformed the environment in which resource conflicts happen. Moreover, there has been a re-emergence of proxy arming in post-independence South Sudan, and rebel militia groups are well equipped with newer and more sophisticated weapons acquired through different channels, including the Sudanese army (Small Arms Survey 2012a).[24] Not all violent clashes in different states are triggered by seasonal conflicts over access to land and water or by cattle rustling, but they are more often than not connected to them in one way or another, as well as to the lack of space for meaningful political opposition and negotiation; this means 'the use of violence remains one of the few ways to negotiate for political and economic improvements' (Small Arms Survey 2012c). Tragically, unarmed women and children are the worst-affected victims of the communal clashes.

Inter-communal conflicts over land resources occur in all ten states, although their frequency and magnitude, including the scale of violence, vary widely from state to state. There are also intra-communal resource conflicts, although they are generally smaller in scale and intensity of violence compared to conflicts that assume inter-communal forms. During 2009 there were close to 400 incidents of resource conflicts that displaced hundreds of thousands of people in nine of the ten states in the country (USAID 2010). In 2009 these conflicts and other types of violence claimed some 2,500 lives and displaced more than 350,000 people (ICG 2009; OCHA 2009). The more extreme cases are the states of Jonglei, Western Equatoria, Lakes, Eastern Equatoria, Unity and Upper Nile. Resource conflicts have become intertwined with larger ethno-political issues, vested interests and clashes between rebel militias and the SPLA in Unity, Warrap, Lakes, Jonglei and Upper Nile. I discuss the case of Jonglei to illustrate the complexity of the conflicts and their implications for human security, governance and state–society relations.

The cycles of inter-communal violence involving the Lou Nuer, Dinka and Murle in Jonglei State have defied many efforts at reconciliation, disarmament and demilitarisation. Jonglei is the largest state in South Sudan in terms of both area (122,000 sq km) and population (1.3 million). It is also one of the most underdeveloped regions in an underdeveloped country. Poverty and violence have caused widespread food insecurity and dependence on humanitarian relief. Unemployment seems to be a grievance pushing the young to join armed groups and militias. Ethno-politics in the state is dominated by Dinka and Lou Nuer elites, while the Murle and three other groups are small minorities. The Lou, however, complain about Dinka domination and about being singled out for disarmament. Their leaders, including a GOSS minister, have justified the Lou being armed on the grounds that the government had failed to give them protection against other armed groups (ICG 2009). 'There is widespread belief', observes a report based on local consultations, 'that some politicians and educated people are the instigators, e.g., politicians providing their own constituents with satellite radios (*thuraya*) and guns' (SSI 2012: 11). The ethnicisation of politics and security is also linked to elite capture of resources, as in other states. It has also been reported that cattle raiding has 'evolved into a more complex business' involving cross-border trade (Rands and LeRiche 2012: 4). A recent survey on 'inter-tribal violence' in Jonglei sums up the role of class interests in these conflicts as follows:

> It is clear that local and national politicians have vested interests in the cattle stocks raided by one tribe or another. Politicians still maintain a good portion of their wealth in cattle. The youths involved in raiding are often employed by politicians to look after and expand their herds. It is uncertain to what extent politicians instigate raids to enlarge their stocks, but it is conceivable that they would support retaliatory attacks if rival tribes stole their cattle.
>
> (Small Arms Survey 2012b: 7)

Jonglei, where the second civil war originated in 1983, saw the most violent consequences of a major split in the SPLM/A in 1991, when Commander Riek Machar, belonging to the Nuer community, led a breakaway faction that allied itself with the Khartoum government. Forces aligned with Machar, which included the Nuer 'White Army', massacred more than 2,000 Dinka in Jonglei's capital, Bor. This led to a mass exodus of the Dinka from Jonglei into Equatoria, where resource conflicts and ethnic tensions exist to this day between Dinka IDPs and locals in several areas. Machar later returned to the SPLM/A and is currently the vice-president of the country. This, however, has not helped prevent the revival and escalation of communal violence in Jonglei – nor have the various disarmament and reconciliation efforts.

In the post-CPA period, the Lou Nuer in Jonglei felt politically marginalised by the Dinka, who dominated the newly established state institutions. The location of the state's capital and governmental agencies in Bor in Dinka territory was perceived by the Lou as a move to restrict their access to institutions and markets. Besides, in the dry season the Lou herders must enter Dinka or Murle territory with their cattle to find water and grazing areas (ICG 2009). The forced disarmament of the Lou Nuer by the SPLA in February 2006 was viewed by them as one-sided, since the Murle and Dinka were not disarmed at the same time. The SPLA's action was also seen as being biased towards the Dinka, who wanted the Lou disarmed before the latter began their seasonal migration to grazing areas in Dinka Duk County. The Lou refused to disarm and their White Army staged a surprise attack on the SPLA, killing many of its soldiers in 2006. The SPLA retaliated with a vengeance, and the subsequent clash left 1,200 Lou and 400 SPLA soldiers dead. The SPLA collected more than 3,000 weapons from the two Lou counties, while the Murle and the Dinka remained armed (ICG 2009; Chol 2012). Though now a loose collective of Lou youths, the White Army was able to rearm itself due to the ready availability of arms from the rebel militias in Jonglei and neighbouring Upper Nile (Small Arms Survey 2012b). Since 2006 the White Army has been involved in several incidents of violence, including clashes with the SPLA, in spite of Machar's appeals to them to withdraw and disarm. Distrust between the Lou Nuer and Dinka runs deep (Rands and LeRiche 2012). This is exploited by anti-GOSS militias, who aim to destabilise the country by supplying arms to groups such as the White Army.

The animosity between the Lou and the Murle has also worsened. There have been mutual accusations of not just killing and cattle raiding but the killing and abduction of women and children. The Murle, in particular, have stolen children from other groups. The conflict turned extremely violent in March 2009, when the Lou White Army launched a major attack on the Murle in Pibor County. This was followed by cycles of violence, which culminated in new attacks by the White Army on the Murle in December 2011–January 2012. The thousands of youths of the White Army did not heed Machar's call to halt their well-organised cattle raids and attacks on Murle settlements. Some of the active Murle leaders have a history of collaboration with the forces of the government of Sudan and of fighting the SPLA. The White Army has a similar record. This factor has serious implications for reconciliation and pacification.

The security situation in Jonglei is a more extreme manifestation of a national crisis of governance. Access to dry season grazing and water resources, protection of cattle and human security are key issues, but they cannot be understood in isolation from the larger issues of ethno-politics and the conditions of underdevelopment. The SPLA's coercive disarmament has not been productive. It seems to be aggravating the already politicised ethnic conflicts and unwittingly helping rebel militias and the flow of weapons into the troubled states, and thereby contributing to destabilisation and insecurity.

Concluding remarks

South Sudan represents a more recent example of conflict resolution and post-war statebuilding under international tutelage. As noted in the introduction, building a state in a newly independent country such as South Sudan has its unique challenges. After setting out the background, this chapter addressed this dimension with reference to the land question.

The land issues and conflicts identified and analysed in this chapter shed light on the gap between the complex realities of a newly independent multi-ethnic country emerging from protracted wars and underdevelopment and the rules and norms that underpin the international paradigm of statebuilding. Yet they are linked to global forces of accumulation by dispossession in this era of high mobility of capital. The legal ambiguities of the interim phase were exploited by corporate interests to acquire large extents of land. This could not have happened on the scale it did without the acquiescence and collaboration of powerful groups and individuals within the GOSS. Residential land grabbing by powerful politicians, military officers and armed groups has been continuing, causing displacements and social tensions. In Juba, the urban property boom appears to be a driver of this process. Considerable land redistribution has taken place through large- and small-scale land grabbing in South Sudan. Evidently, unruly events have overtaken the institutionalisation of neoliberal rules and norms of statebuilding and 'good governance'. The situation is not only a reflection of the limits of top-down international statebuilding based on a universal model without due consideration of the country's internal complexities, but also the indifference of the domestic political class to accountability and legitimacy.

The Land Act introduced significant changes in customary land tenure to enable the redistribution of land for private investment and public use in legally valid and potentially transparent ways, while granting statutory recognition to customary rights. However, the problems highlighted and analysed expose the Act's shortcomings and the lack of functioning enforcement mechanisms. Moreover, the Act is not helpful in challenging the dubious large-scale land transfers of the past, as it is not applicable retrospectively. An official land policy was conspicuous in its absence for nearly 8 years after the establishment of the interim GOSS.

The government was not adequately prepared to face the demands of resettlement and urban migration. The latter challenges ethnicity-based customary tenure in its present form, as shown by the case of Juba. Land plays a key role in South Sudan's ethno-politics, and land grabbing may be reinforcing inter-ethnic and intra-ethnic inequalities with adverse consequences for national integration and inclusive development. Ethnic minorities harbour strong apprehensions about large-scale migrations of Dinka and Nuer into their territories in Equatoria. The governance crisis, due to the escalation of resource conflicts and their links to rebel militias, as exemplified by the case of Jonglei, shows that the violent phase of statebuilding in South Sudan is not over yet. The South Sudanese state enjoys international recognition but it remains fragile in the face of internal challenges to its capacity to monopolise coercive power, enforce the rule of law, ensure human security, foster national unification and gain popular legitimacy. However, this situation has its winners and losers and the link between land grabbing, ethnic conflict and class formation deserves a deeper study. In South Sudan, peacebuilding, statebuilding, nationbuilding and development are intertwined and the land question cuts across all of them.

Notes

1 South Sudan Development Plan 2011–13.
2 The SPLM is the biggest party and the ruling party at present. The Sudan People's Liberation Movement for Democratic Change (SPLMDC) is the main opposition party. There are ten political parties including the SPLM and SPLMDC.
3 Around 98 per cent of state revenue comes from the oil sector, whose fortunes have been fluctuating. This has made GOSS even more dependent on foreign aid. The

CPA identified the international community as the principal source of funding for post-war reconstruction and development. A Joint Assessment Mission led by the World Bank and UNDP was created to assess the immediate rehabilitation and recovery needs, and to develop a framework for reconstruction and recovery up to the end of 2010 in line with the Millennium Development Goals (JAM, Sudan 2005; Shanmugaratnam 2008). In June 2011 USAID unveiled the 'USAID Transition Strategy for South Sudan 2011–13', which also involved non-USAID donors. The total funding to be mobilised for this strategy was US$17,764 million (USAID 2011). The EU allocated €260 million in development aid to South Sudan for the period 2011–13, while the UN Mission in South Sudan was engaged in supporting and overseeing the statebuilding process (Lacher 2012). Since 2006 the US has been supporting South Sudan's defence transformation programme with an estimated budget of US$150–300 million (Small Arms Survey 2012a).

4 The GOSS has been receiving military aid from the US since 2006.
5 This is evident from the annual budgets presented by the Ministry of Finance and Economic Planning.
6 The study draws on the author's previous field research, secondary sources including published research and official documents, and two weeks of fieldwork carried out in January 2013 in Juba, where interviews were conducted with a variety of stakeholders including politicians, senior government officials, university academics, civil society activists and community leaders.
7 *Comprehensive Peace Agreement*, 9 January 2005, Chapter III, 2.1 (Intergovernmental Agency for Development, 2005).
8 The TCSS reaffirms these provisions of the Land Act.
9 In an interview on 17 January 2013, Paramount Chief Dennis Garmolo of Juba County said, 'The Arabs were grabbing our land saying it belonged to the state and now powerful outsiders are grabbing our land saying it belonged to the people of South Sudan.' Similar sentiments were expressed by several persons interviewed by me in January 2013. The civil society activists interviewed were from the newly created (2012) South Sudan Land Alliance. Other interviewees included senior academics at the University of Juba and professionals involved in development programmes. In an interview on 10 January 2013, Michael Roberto Kenyi Legge, Minister for Agriculture and Forestry, Government of CES, said that the Land Act's replacement of 'community' with 'people' changed the meaning of the original position 'completely' and has encouraged land grabbing by individuals and groups. 'People' in this instance, he said, actually meant 'individuals', not the 'community'.
10 It would seem that discussions have been taking place at top policy levels on the pros and cons of such an amendment to the Land Act. This was alluded to by the chairman of the SSLC during an interview on 15 January 2013.
11 Interviewed 15 January 2013.
12 Chairperson (female) and Secretary General (male) of the Central Equatoria State Land Alliance. Interviewed in Juba on 15 January 2013.
13 It is well known in INGO and civil society circles in Juba that international consultants, USAID and the EU played a major role in the framing and finalisation of the Land Act.
14 The Investment Promotion Act limits the lease period for foreign investments in agriculture and forestry to renewable terms of 30 and 60 years, respectively.
15 Administratively, a state is divided into counties, which are divided into units known as *Payams*, which in turn are further divided into *Bomas*, the lowest administrative units which consist of villages.
16 The need to create awareness among the people about the contents of the Land Act was recognised by the GOSS and, in March 2011, a major project on awareness capacity building at local levels was launched by Norwegian Peoples

Aid. The present author is familiar with this project, which is ongoing at the time of writing.
17 South Sudan's 'Green belt' is a contiguous area running across the southern parts of Western, Central and Eastern Equatoria. It is an area with high rainfall, fertile soils and large tracts of forest (Deng 2011a).
18 For example, it was reported that the Commonwealth Development Corporation (Britain) and the Finnish Fund for Development Cooperation (Finnfund), which obtained a majority interest in forest concessions in the states of Central Equatoria and Western Equatoria in 2007, sold it to 'unnamed investors' in 2010 'without the knowledge of the government or affected populations' (TOI 2011: 2).
19 The census actually took place in 2008.
20 This section draws on Shanmugaratnam (2010).
21 Sources include local professionals and the Ministry of Agriculture and Forestry, Government of CES.
22 Interview, 10 January 2013.
23 See Shanmugaratnam (2010) for documentation and analysis of this conflict.
24 While the anti-GOSS militia groups receive arms from the Sudanese army, they have also captured weapons during clashes with the SPLA. In addition, defectors from the SPLA, who join these groups, are already armed. The estimated total strength of non-state militias is 10,150. The active militias are the South Sudan Liberation Movement/Army (SSLM/A), which is predominantly Nuer; the South Sudan Democratic Movement/Army (SSDM/A), an 'inter-tribal' movement located in Jonglei and Upper Nile states; and the Nuer White Army (Small Arms Survey 2012a).

References

Auer, A., Bisaz, C., Mendez, F. and Thurer, D., 2011, *The Transitional Constitution of the Republic of South Sudan: An Expert View from the Outside*, Aarau: Center for Research on Direct Democracy.
Barnett, M. and Zurcher, C., 2009, 'The peacebuilder's contract: how external state-building reinforces weak statehood', in *The Dilemmas of State Building, Confronting the Contradictions of Postwar Peace Operations*, ed. R. Paris and T.D. Sisk, Abingdon and New York: Routledge, 23–52.
Chol, A.L., 2012, 'Jonglei state conflict analysis: why second disarmament is not a solution', available online at www.southsudannewsagency.com/opinion/analyses/jonglei-state-conflict-analysis-why-second-disarmament-is-not-a-solution (accessed 11 November 2012).
CHS (Commission on Human Security), 2003, *Human Security Now*, New York: Commission on Human Security.
Cramer, C., 2006, *Civil War is Not a Stupid Thing: Accounting for Violence in Developing Countries*, London: Hurst.
——2009, 'Trajectories of accumulation through war and peace', in *The Dilemmas of State Building, Confronting the Contradictions of Postwar Peace Operations*, ed. R. Paris and T.D. Sisk, Abingdon and New York: Routledge, 129–48.
Deng, D., 2011a, *The New Frontier: A Baseline Survey of Large-scale, Land-based Investment in Southern Sudan*, Report 1/11 (March), Oslo: Norwegian People's Aid.
——2011b, '"Land Belongs to the Community": Demystifying the "Global Land Grab" in Southern Sudan', LDPI Working Paper 4, The Institute for Poverty, Land and Agrarian Studies, University of Western Cape, South Africa.

——2012, 'Investment-related conflict, contested rights and the power of information in South Sudan', *Haki Legal Empowerment Network*, 15 February 15, available online at www.hakinetwork.org (accessed 18 April 2012).

Duffield, M., 2005, *Global Governance and the New Wars: The Merging of Development and Security*, London: Zed Press.

——2007, *Development Security and Unending War: Governing the World of Peoples*, Cambridge and Malden, MA: Polity Press.

Harvey, D., 2005, *A Brief History of Neoliberalism*, New York: Oxford University Press.

HRW (Human Rights Watch), 2003, *Sudan, Oil and Human Rights*, Washington, DC.

ICG (International Crisis Group), 2009, 'Jonglei's tribal conflicts: countering insecurity in South Sudan', Africa Report No. 154, 23 December, available online at www.crisisgroup.org/en/regions/africa/horn-of-africa/sudan/154-jongleis-tribal-conflicts-countering-insecurity-in-south-sudan.aspx (accessed 16 April 2012).

IDMC (Internal Displacement Monitoring Centre), 2009, 'Sudan: 4.9 million IDPs across Sudan face ongoing turmoil', Norwegian Refugee Council, Geneva, 27 May, available online at www.internal-displacement.org/8025708F004BE3B1/(httpInfoFiles)/136DAB1151929646C12575C30038075A/$file/Sudan%20-%20May%202009.pdf (accessed 30 October 2010).

——2012, 'South Sudan: a profile of the internal displacement situation', Norwegian Refugee Council, Geneva, 26 June, available online at www.internal-displacement.org/8025708F004BE3B1/(httpInfoFiles)/B25C16A58C5BC4A6C1257A2900522F10/$file/South%20Sudan%20-%20June%202012.pdf (accessed 3 January 2013).

Intergovernmental Agency for Development, 2005, 'The Comprehensive Peace Agreement between the Government of the Republic of Sudan and the People's Liberation Movement/Sudan People's Liberation Army', Secretariat on Peace in the Sudan, IGAD, Nairobi, 9 January.

JAM (Joint Assessment Mission) Sudan, 2005, 'Framework for sustained peace, development and poverty eradication', *Synthesis*, 1, 18 March, available online at http://pcna.undg.org/index.php?option=com_docman& Itemid=25 (accessed 18 October 2013).

Johnson, D., 2003, *The Root Causes of Sudan's Civil Wars*, Oxford: James Currey.

Johnson, N., 2012, 'Rigging the rules: unfair land deals in South Sudan', available online at www.oaklandinstitute.org/rigging-rules-unfair-land-deals-south-sudan (accessed 27 January 2013).

Lacher, W., 2012, 'South Sudan: international statebuilding and its limits', SWP Research Paper, German Institute for International and Security Affairs, Berlin, available online at www.swp-berlin.org/en/publications/swp-research-papers/swp-research-paper-detail/article/south_sudan_state_building.html (accessed 18 October 2013).

Martin, E. and Mosel, I., 2011, *City limits: urbanisation and vulnerability in Sudan Juba case study*, London: Humanitarian Policy Group, Overseas Development Institute.

Mennen, T., 2012, 'Strengthening access to land in plural tenure systems', available online at www.hakinetwork.org (accessed 10 December 2012).

OCHA (UN Office for the Coordination of Humanitarian Affairs), 2009, 'Humanitarian action in Southern Sudan', report no. 38, 20 November, available online at http://ochaonline.un.org/sudan/SituationReports/SouthernSudanReports/tabid/3369/language/en-US/Default.aspx (accessed 16 April 2012).

Oxfam, 2011, 'Land and power: the growing scandal surrounding the new wave of investments in land', Oxfam Briefing Paper, 22 September, available online at www.oxfam.org/grow (accessed 4 January 2012).

Pantuliano, S., Buchanan-Smith, M., Murphy, P. and Morsel, I., 2008, *The Long Road Home*, report of phase II, London: Humanitarian Policy Group, Overseas Development Institute.

Paris, R., 1997, 'Peacebuilding and the limits of liberal internationalism', *International Security*, 22(2): 54–89.

——2004, *At War's End: Building Peace after Civil Conflict*, Cambridge: Cambridge University Press.

Paris, R. and Sisk, T.D. (eds), 2009, *The Dilemmas of Statebuilding: Confronting the Contradictions of Postwar Peace Operations*, Abingdon and New York: Routledge.

Rands, R.B. and LeRiche, M., 2012, 'Security responses in Jonglei state in the aftermath of inter-ethnic violence', available online at www.saferworld.org.uk/downloads/pubdocs/6726%20Saferworld%20Security%20responses%20in%20Jonglei%20State.pdf (accessed 18 October 2013).

Sadek, K., 2012, 'Concord doing good for Sudan', available online at www.the-star.co.ke/news/article-25560/concord-doing-good-sudan (accessed 27 January 2013).

Shanmugaratnam, N., 2008, 'Post-war development and the land question in Southern Sudan', in 'Proceedings of the International Symposium on Resources Under Stress', Afrasian Centre for Peace and Development, Ryukoku University, Kyoto, 23–24 February 2008.

——2010, 'Resettlement, Resource Conflicts, Livelihood Revival and Reintegration in South Sudan: A Study of the Processes and Institutional Issues at the Local Level in Magwi County', Noragric Report No. 58, Norwegian University of Life Sciences, Aas.

Shanmugaratnam, N. (ed.), 2008, *Between War and Peace in Sudan and Sri Lanka: Deprivation and Livelihood Revival*, Oxford: James Currey.

Small Arms Survey 2012a, 'Reaching for the gun: arms flows and holdings in South Sudan', Human Security Baseline Assessment, no. 19, April, available online at www.smallarmssurveysudan.org (accessed 4 August 2012).

——2012b, 'My neighbour, my enemy: inter-tribal violence in Jonglei', Human Security Baseline Assessment, no. 21, October, available online at www.smallarmssurveysudan.org (accessed 5 August 2012).

——2012c, 'Southern dissident militias', available online at http://reliefweb.int/report/south-sudan-republic/southern-dissident-militias (accessed 4 January 2013).

SSI (South Sudan Institute), 2012, 'Peace of Neighbours', Final report by Ambassador Group on Jonglei, available online at http://lirs.org/wp-content/uploads/2012/07/Peace_of_Neighbors_Report_July2012_lowres1.pdf (accessed 18 October 2013).

SSLC (Southern Sudan Land Commission), 2011, 'Draft Land Policy, Government of South Sudan', February, unpublished draft obtained from SSLC through Norwegian People's Aid Juba.

Sundnes, F. and Shanmugaratnam, N., 2008, 'Socio-economic revival & emerging issues related to land & customary institutions in Yirol, Southern Sudan', in *Between War and Peace in Sudan and Sri Lanka: Deprivation and Livelihood Revival*, ed. N. Shanmugaratnam, Oxford: James Currey, 59–76.

Tilly, C., 1992, *Coercion, Capital, and European States, AD 990–1992*, Malden, MA and Oxford: Blackwell.

TOI (The Oakland Institute), 2011, 'Understanding land investment deals in Africa: Nile Trading and Development, Inc. in South Sudan', land deal brief, June, available online at www.oaklandinstitute.org (accessed 3 May 2012).

UNHCR, 2008, 'UNHCR'S role in support of the return and reintegration of displaced populations: Policy framework and implementation strategy', available online at www.unhcr.org/47b06de42.pdf (accessed 4 November 2010).

USAID, 2010, 'Land Tenure Issues in Southern Sudan: Key Findings and Recommendations for Southern Sudan Land Policy', available online at http://usaidlandtenure.net/sudan/land-tenure-issues-in-southern-sudan-key-findings-and-recommendations (accessed 3 May 2012).

——2011, 'South Sudan Transition Strategy 2011–13', available online at http://reliefweb.int/report/south-sudan-republic/usaid-transition-strategy-south-sudan-2011%E2%80%9313-june-2011 (accessed 6 November 2012).

3 Land disputes in the Acholi sub-region in Uganda[1]

From displacement to dispossession

Fumihiko Saito and Christopher Burke

The Acholi sub-region of northern Uganda suffered war for over 20 years. Since the arrival of relative peace in 2006, approximately two million people, who for a decade had been forced to live in camps as internally displaced persons (IDPs), began to return home, hoping to restore normality to their lives (Burke and Egaru 2011). Unfortunately, the majority of them have been involved in disputes over land.[2] The reasons for these disputes and widespread land grabbing are complex. Because the soils in the north, especially in the Acholi sub-region, constituted an important national bread basket before the war, the land that lay unutilised during the prolonged conflict now presents a new frontier in the process of rebuilding peace and economic growth. These land disputes are related to political and economic changes that have taken place in Uganda under the National Resistance Movement (NRM) government (1986–present). As the political situation has become increasingly characterised by neo-patrimonialism, land in the north has become an essential resource for political patronage. In addition, as the economic policies of the NRM focus increasingly on economic growth, land has also become a valuable economic commodity.

Land disputes in the Acholi sub-region have begun to attract considerable attention, resulting in new research findings. However, while there have been insightful reports written by donors, very few academic works have appeared. Based on these new findings and our own field investigation, this chapter complements recent research with two detailed case studies of land conflicts on the ground. The first was a case in which an HIV-affected widow almost lost her land as a result of claims by her neighbour. This dispute was successfully resolved by the intervention of an NGO. The second is more complex, having two phases. The conflict unfolded between two key members of the local clan, and the attempted mediation by the local leader did not reach a successful conclusion, so that the case is still ongoing.

This chapter discusses how these cases in the north relate to broader political and economic dynamisms in Uganda. It examines the land conflicts in the Acholi sub-region within the wider historical, political and economic context (Nakayi 2012). This approach has been relatively under-emphasised until very recently, and the chapter makes a novel contribution to this

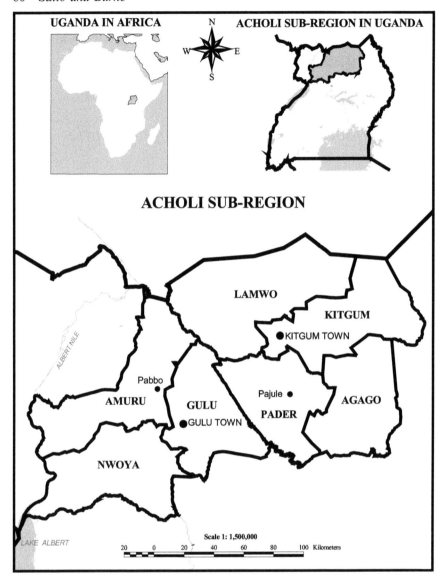

Figure 3.1 Map of Uganda and the Acholi sub-region

important intersection between disputes over land and peacebuilding. We argue that land disputes deserve serious attention from both academics and policy makers, as the socially disadvantaged continue to suffer in the transition from war to peace. As securing land rights in the Acholi sub-region relates to customary and statutory institutions, both of which continue to operate without due coordination, more orchestrated efforts are urgently

needed. Multiple remedial measures to increase the capacities of both traditional and government institutions at various levels are required. Without
coordinated efforts from multiple institutions, the suffering of the most
vulnerable is likely to continue.

Background to war, peace and land disputes

Northern Uganda is in an important transition from protracted conflict to
recovery and peacebuilding. Relative peace returned to the north when the
Cessation of Hostilities (COH) was signed in August 2006. However, it is
essential to understand the COH from a wider perspective. The seeds of the
disparity and tension within Uganda between the north and the south were
gradually sown during the colonial period. After independence in 1962,
Milton Obote and Idi Amin, both from the north, formed successive governments. After the establishment of the NRM government in 1986, led by
Yoweri K. Museveni, who originated from the south-west of Uganda, some
affiliates of the Obote and Amin administrations rebelled (Lucima 2002). This
north–south tension directly and indirectly influenced the ways in which a
series of rebellions developed in the north. Depending on the analyst, there
were five to seven phases of the insurgence in northern Uganda (Atkinson
2008; 2010; Mabikke 2011: 3). The peak period of the conflict (from 1994 to
2006), conducted by the Lord's Resistance Army (LRA) under Joseph Kony,[3]
which has attracted international media attention, constitutes only the last
phase of the enduring insurgence in northern Uganda.[4]

During this prolonged conflict, human rights violations were widespread
and the suffering among the Acholi people was deplorable. While estimates
vary, a significant proportion of the Acholi population witnessed members
of their families and neighbours being abducted, killed and mutilated
(Pham *et al.* 2005). By 2005 more than two million people, or about 86 per
cent of the local population, had been involuntarily displaced from their
homes and villages (Pham *et al.* 2007: 2). Uganda accommodated approximately 869,000 IDPs, the fifth largest number in the world at the time
(Carfield 2011: 130). Basic services provided in these camps were often
woefully inadequate (Atkinson 2010: 298). Alarmingly, 93 per cent of the
former residents did not feel safe in the camps, and the incidence of post-
traumatic stress disorder in northern Uganda is among the highest in post-
conflict populations in the world (Roberts *et al.* 2008). The LRA insurgency
was described as 'the biggest neglected humanitarian emergency in the
world' by Jan Egeland, the Under-Secretary General for Humanitarian
Affairs of the United Nations.[5]

A significant number of Acholi people do not believe that the NRM
government took sufficient measures to protect them. Instead, they tend
to consider that the government exploited the situation to marginalise the
sub-region socially, politically and economically. According to Dolan, while
about 70 per cent of the traumatic experiences of individuals were caused by

the rebels, the remaining 30 per cent were the responsibility of the government forces. Moreover, the relative share of damage to personal property was more or less 50:50 (Dolan 2009: 62). The government forces could not protect the 'protected camps', the official name given to the IDP camps. Dolan argues that under the disguise of the war the reality was 'social torture'.[6] Though this characterisation may not be fully assented to by everyone, it expresses the extent of the collective suffering that significantly affects the Acholi people's perceptions even today.

For many Acholis, the war between the government and the LRA was closely linked to underlying tensions between the NRM government and the Acholi people. While the popularity of the NRM in the Acholi sub-region has increased significantly in recent years, a certain level of animosity towards central government continues. There is deep mistrust between the Acholis and the southerners. In 2005 a public opinion survey conducted in four districts in the north revealed that the majority of the respondents (76 per cent) believed government soldiers should be held accountable for their crimes (Pham *et al.* 2005: 5). In 2010 only 30 per cent of respondents to a survey suggested that the government had done 'very well' or 'well' in uniting the north and the south of Uganda (Pham and Vinck 2010: 2, 19).[7] These surveys demonstrate a compelling picture of northerners' misgivings concerning the way in which reconciliation and rehabilitation have been pursued by the NRM government.

It is against this background that land disputes are now taking place. The north is viewed as a newly opened frontier because of its vast, unused and fertile tracts of land (Tumushabe *et al.* 2009: 2; Mabikke 2011), which are attracting the attention of those within and outside the Acholi sub-region. Land disputes are closely related to the national political and economic policy direction of Uganda as a whole. Politically, with the long-lasting hold on power by the NRM, there has been a remarkable degree of personalisation of power (Tangri and Mwenda 2010) and rampant corruption in a variety of institutions (EPRC 2010). Some land grabbers are politically well connected to the NRM regime (Atkinson 2010: 333; Nakayi 2012: 673). The Ugandan state is now typical of a neo-patrimonial state (Tripp 2010). Economically, the NRM government has shifted its relative emphasis from poverty reduction to economic growth. Thus, land is considered a valuable commodity to be traded on the market. The government is interested in promoting land markets and is also keen to attract investment for developing large-scale commercial agriculture, as stipulated by the National Development Plan, officially launched in 2010 (GoU 2010).

These changes have critical socio-cultural implications. Given also the newly found oil reserves in Uganda, land is increasingly perceived as a means for acquiring personal wealth rather than as a common asset for preserving cultural heritage. For some, especially for the elderly and traditional elites, these changes represent a worrying deterioration of the social fabric (IOM *et al.* 2010: 17).

Land tenure systems and tenure reforms in Uganda

Current land legislation in Uganda reflects a complicated history. The British colonial rule introduced a division of systems: one for the protectorate government, and another for the king, chiefs and notables in the Buganda Kingdom. Governments since independence, including the NRM, have attempted to implement land reforms with little success.[8] The land problem was one of the most controversial issues in the formulation of the current constitution (Marquardt and Sebina-Zziwa 1998: 182). Under the NRM rule, a number of significant laws have been enacted, including the 1995 Constitution and the 1998 Land Act.

During these changes, four different tenure arrangements emerged, all of which were recognised by the 1998 Land Act (Hunt 2004; Okuku 2006).[9] Freehold tenure, originally introduced by the British as a modern tenure system, signifies that land-holders – who must be citizens – enjoy full ownership of the land. Leasehold tenure is common for state-owned land held for a specific period by non-citizens and urban residents. Mailo tenure, still prevalent in central Uganda, results from the 1900 Buganda Agreement between the Kingdom of Buganda and Britain. The king, his family and clan chiefs were given one-square-mile tracts of land, hence the name *mailo*. Where the landowners were absent, these lands were inhabited by squatters, which often led to conflicts (Tripp 2010: 124). Customary tenure, the predominant tenure arrangement in Uganda, is a system whereby land tenure is regulated by clan leaders applying customary rules. Customary tenure can involve collective (communal), family and individual land ownership, depending on use. Although often misunderstood (Okuku 2006: 13–14; Adoko and Levine 2008: 107; IOM *et al.* 2010: 37), customary tenure does not necessarily mean that agricultural production is conducted collectively. Collective tenure applies to grazing and hunting grounds (Tumushabe *et al.* 2009). What is important is that these different tenure systems have experienced a transformation as a result of various factors including population increase, economic development and urbanisation. Thus, the typology does not imply that the tenure systems are fixed without any adjustment (Marquardt and Sebina-Zziwa 1998).

The 1998 Land Act was significant. While the Act stipulates that land is vested in the citizens of Uganda, its orientation is to encourage agricultural development through land markets and securing land rights in all four tenure systems. The Act also aimed to improve land administration by transferring key functions from central to local governments. Whereas the Uganda Land Commission was to oversee several key aspects of government land, including sales and management of properties, district land boards and parish land committees were to be established in order to handle local land matters. The Act also clearly stipulates that women are equally entitled to land rights, although the implementation of gender equality continues to be problematic in reality.

The 1998 Land Act was amended in 2001, 2004 and 2010. The 2001 amendment extended the time period during which magistrates' courts and the local councils were authorised to deal with land cases brought to them before the enactment of the 1998 Land Act. The 2004 amendment introduced a number of broad changes, including the redefinition of terms and adjustment of legislation concerning annual nominal ground, subdivisions, spousal and family consent, and the role of relevant statutory institutions. The 2010 amendment enhanced security of occupancy for *bona fide* occupants, in accordance with Article 237 of the Constitution.

Although the Land Act was passed and amended three times, it was only in February 2013 that the cabinet finally approved the draft National Land Policy (GoU 2013). Discussion over the land policy had been ongoing for over a decade. Although it is commonly understood that land policy is a very sensitive issue, the significant time lag between the passing of the Land Act and a newly proposed policy contributed to the weakening of land governance. Accordingly, the current land legislation suffers from a number of gaps and inconsistencies relating to succession, marriage and divorce. Among the most problematic of these issues is the fact that while the Act clearly recognised the legality of customary land tenure on communal land ownership, the customary tenure system still faces significant challenges. The implementation of the Act is poor, largely because of weaknesses in the capacity of national and local government institutions, as well as traditional authorities. Probably more important is increasing doubt regarding the political will of the current government to take the necessary measures to correct the situation. This unwillingness relates to the prevailing political situation in the country (Okuku 2006). It is also a result of a poor understanding of the customary tenure system. The socially weak and minorities, therefore, face enormous challenges in accessing statutory laws to settle land disputes and protect their rights (Young and Sing'Oei 2011: 10–11).

General description of land disputes

More than 90 per cent of the Acholi population, who once lived in the IDP camps, have returned home since 2006 (IDMC 2012). Their return has been associated with a significant rise in land disputes. The rise was previously attributed to the fact that people had been away from their homes and had forgotten the boundaries of their land, as well as to the fact that the normal functions of local government and land administration had been practically suspended during the war. But recent research suggests that the rise has more to do with opportunism and a breakdown in the social fabric, and is compounded by demographic changes. It also suggests that traditional institutions were not given sufficient recognition in customary land management.

The increasing number of land disputes has serious consequences. As land is almost the only asset that the rural Acholi population can rely on for their livelihoods, land disputes prevent proper reintegration in peacebuilding processes (Atkinson 2008: 8; IOM *et al.* 2010).[10] Furthermore, land is important for burial, connecting ancestors to the living and 'unborn children'. In these ways, land plays a crucial role in the cultural identity of the Acholis.

The magnitude of land disputes

Different research reports focussing on land issues in the Acholi sub-region over recent years provide a very rich collection of data. The estimated numbers and frequency of land disputes vary due to methodological differences. A 2008 study reported that approximately 35 per cent of households across Uganda had experienced land conflict (Rugadya *et al.* 2008: iii). Pham and Vinck found in their third series of public opinion surveys in northern Uganda that 35 per cent of the respondents had experienced land disputes since the cessation of hostilities in August 2006 (Pham and Vinck 2010: 28).[11] Another UN study suggested that approximately 12,000 land disputes were brought before the local council courts across the Acholi sub-region in one year (Burke and Egaru 2011: 9). But a more recent study conducted by Atkinson and Hopwood (2012), examining data gathered by a series of sub-country-level detailed surveys, identified only 4,300 disputes in a half-year period (Burke and Egaru 2011: 6). While the figures vary, together these findings suggest a common pattern. It is probably the case that roughly 30 to 40 per cent of the Acholi population have encountered land disputes in one way or another. Given the complexity of the history of prolonged conflict in this area, this proportion may not be regarded as high, although such a judgement depends on particular viewpoints.[12]

Another issue is that of whether the overall trend in the number of land disputes is upwards or downwards. Atkinson and Hopwood recently suggested that there are now far fewer disputes than there were six months ago (2012: 7). Yet much care is required in interpreting this assertion. Land conflict is seasonal, with a higher incidence of disputes occurring through the planting season, and grassroots surveys using questionnaires targeting semi-literate respondents are often problematic. The people our research team met during field visits reported that the number of incidents was increasing. It is therefore reasonable to conclude that land grabbing and disputes over land remain prevalent (Akin and Katono 2011).

Diverse types of disputes

Land disputes come in many forms. A significant proportion of conflicts are at the grassroots level, related to contested boundaries and competing claims of ownership among family members, some of which flare up during inheritance negotiations. Boundary disputes occur among neighbours. In the past, when land was perceived as plentiful relative to population density, Acholis were very generous and commonly gave land to newcomers. Today, people are reclaiming such land, and these claims cause disputes.

At the other extreme, high-profile disputes result from investment by large commercial companies (World Bank 2008: ii). Such investments displace large numbers of local residents and readily attract media attention. While different stakeholders have different justifications, this type of conflict tends to be politically sensitive. It is important to note that Acholis are not against investment per se, but are concerned that such investments reduce their prospects of re-establishing their livelihoods (IOM *et al.* 2010: 13).

Between these extremes there is a wide range of conflicts. Some disputes take the form of struggles between different clans. Others are between individuals and institutions such as churches and schools (as some lands were 'given' to these institutions in the past by clan elders, etc.); between communities and individuals and the Uganda Wildlife Authority, which manages national parks and game reserves;[13] and between different local governments where administrative boundaries are concerned, as some of the new districts and local governments were created recently as a result of decentralisation. Owners of the (former) IDP camps also claim that their land should be returned in view of the limited number of IDPs who remain there. There is also a dispute over the border between Uganda and South Sudan.[14]

Of these different types, which are more common than others? Because of the different methodologies adopted in recent research activities, it is not easy to compare the results (Rugadya *et al.* 2008; Pham and Vinck 2010; Akin and Katono 2011: 30; Burke and Egaru 2011: 6). However, they do suggest a consistent pattern: border disputes, family wrangles especially associated with inheritance, and competing claims about ownership are the most common types of land disputes.

Different types of disputes have different complexities of resolution. Akin and Katono, observing cases brought to NGOs for resolution, report that the magnitude of difficulty (from relatively manageable to more difficult to resolve) is as follows: family land disputes; boundary/encroachment; land grabbing; contested land sale; contested land gift; inter-clan land dispute; and contested ownership (2011: 6). Atkinson and Hopwood have recently found that complex cases are usually more protracted. About one-third of the cases lasted for more than six months and one-third lasted from two to five years (2012: 22). Their preliminary findings also suggest that about two-thirds of serious land disputes involved some form of violence, including killing, assault and destruction of property (Atkinson and Hopwood 2012: 21).

Finally, it is important to understand the gender dimension in land disputes (Immanuel 2010). The 1998 Land Act clearly stipulates that women are equally entitled to land. However, some men, intentionally or unintentionally, do not observe this gender equality. In traditional culture, not only in Uganda but in most of sub-Saharan Africa, women are not allowed to *own* land in their own names, although *access to* land is granted by customary tenure. As elaborated by Adoko and colleagues, the vulnerabilities women experience in relation to land tenure security are specific to their status as a widowed, unmarried, separated, divorced, cohabiting, or married woman. Unfortunately, concern for land rights has mainly centred on married and cohabitating women, leaving aside the more nuanced analysis of each of these different 'types' of women, each of which are uniquely susceptible to land rights abuses.

(Adoko *et al.* 2011: 3)

These challenges are most acute in fragmented families and weak clans. In such cases, it is common for brothers or other male relatives of a deceased husband to claim the land. In contrast, strong clans and coherent families tend to maintain customary practices, and women usually enjoy secure access to land, irrespective of their marital status or social situation. A recent Oxfam study suggests that 84 per cent of women across northern Uganda believe they have secure access to land (Burke and Kobusingye, forthcoming).

Dispute resolution mechanisms

In Acholi, there are two parallel systems for settling land disputes. One consists of the traditional (clan) authorities and the other is the state structure. There are positive and negative sides to having two systems. On the one hand, it is good that people have different avenues to explore. On the other hand, the current situation facilitates 'forum shopping' and creates confusion over which institution should be or is in control over what issues (Burke and Egaru 2011: 8). This situation is expected to continue for the foreseeable future, partly because both authorities have roles to play.

The traditional authorities in Acholi are clan-based. The heads of royal clans form a loose coalition led by the paramount chief known as *Ker Kwaro Acholi*, which is different from the hierarchical structure of the Buganda Kingdom. It is important to note that under the current political system in Uganda traditional leaders have no political power. They only enjoy cultural and social authority. The *Rwot Kweri*, instituted under British colonial rule, is a leader elected by the community to coordinate agricultural activities at the grassroots level. (The term means 'chief of hoes' and its plural is *Rwodi Kweri*.) As such, these leaders have a good understanding of land boundaries and are well positioned to mediate land disputes (Mabikke 2011).[15] Other traditional leaders include the *Rwot Apoka*, *Rwot Okoro*, *Rwot Aktekere*, *Rwot Lawang*, *Rwot Kaka* and *Rwot Moo*, and each has their own respective roles and responsibilities. These *Rwodi* are primarily hereditary, but are nominated by the clans. The *Rwot Apoka* focuses on social issues. The *Rwot Okoro* is concerned with traditional rituals, land use and hunting. The *Rwodi Atekere* mobilise community members at the village level. The *Rwodi Lawang* are deputies to the *Rwodi Kaka* and *Rwodi Moo*. The *Rwodi Kaka* are the clan heads. Among the clans there are 57 royal clans, and the heads of these are the *Rwodi Moo*, who loosely represent the clans in their area and are recognised, at the apex of this hierarchy, by the *Ker Kwaro Acholi* (the paramount chief and his political institution). Several donors have assisted with their functions, particularly in dispute resolution in recent years. The traditional leaders are usually considered very knowledgeable of old customs and are highly respected in local communities. If land disputes are considered too complex or difficult to resolve, cases may be referred either to statutory institutions of local government or to higher levels of the traditional authority, although the *Rwodi Moo* and *Ker Kwaro Acholi* are rarely involved in settling land disputes, except for those between clans.

Local government comprises a hierarchal system of councils and committees ranging from local council (LC) 1 at the village level to LC 5 at the district level. All levels of local government endure serious capacity deficits. The LC 1 courts are legally mandated as the first court of instance, although there is considerable confusion on this issue. Furthermore, the legality of the LC 1 and LC 2 leaders is questioned. They should have been elected in the general elections in 2006, but the elections were not upheld and the Constitutional Court ruled them unconstitutional in 2006 (Burke and Egaru 2011: 9). Nonetheless, community members have expressed a particularly high degree of trust in the LC 1 and 2 levels, which continue to receive a large number of cases for mediation. Informal collaboration between traditional and local council leaders is common. The LC officials often consult clan leaders and request their assistance in mediating disputes.

Among those who had experienced disputes, 82 per cent had approached someone to resolve them. LC 2 was most frequently contacted (42 per cent), followed by LC 1 (33 per cent), traditional leaders (20 per cent) and elders (12 per cent) (Pham and Vinck 2010: 28–29). There are various reasons why people choose particular forums for dispute resolution, including the nature of land disputes, the claimants' understanding of dispute mediation procedures, the degree of reliability and trustworthiness of the mediator, the distance to the mediator and the costs incurred by dispute resolution. A recent study shows some of the reasons why people choose either traditional or statutory forums in order to settle land disputes. It is interesting to note that familiarity, fairness and the legal mandate of the dispute resolution process matter more than distance and costs. The notion of fairness in particular gained more importance after the return of relative peace (World Bank 2008: 18).

A growing number of NGOs also provide alternative dispute resolution (ADR) and legal aid services that fill important gaps in justice service delivery. ADR mechanisms have succeeded in resolving some disputes, yet such interventions have both advantages and limitations. ADR only works as long as the contesting parties voluntarily accept the mediation, and as such it is not effective in dealing with land grabbing. Land grabbers will use any forum to pursue their predetermined goals, as is illustrated later in our case studies, and enforcement of ADR agreements is an acute problem.[16] Hence, the multiplicity of dispute resolution opportunities raises an important issue. Some deliberately choose one forum instead of others in the expectation of a favourable result. On other occasions, an individual may try, for example, the relatively less costly traditional mediation mechanism first and then pursue other avenues if the clan leaders do not show sufficient sympathy (Carfield 2011; Nakayi 2012). Ongoing research suggests that ADR is only appropriate when the contending parties participate in good faith. The criminal elements implicit in 'land grabbing' attempts, on the other hand, demand a stronger state-backed response (Akin and Katono 2011).

Reasons for land disputes

Just as the types of land disputes vary, so there are different reasons for them (Mabikke 2011; Mercy Corps 2011).

Increase of population

The area around Lake Victoria has one of the highest rural population densities in the world. The population of Uganda was forecast to grow by 3.1 per cent annually from 2010 to 2015 (UNDP 2013). The Acholi population, which stood at about 1.12 million in 2002, had increased to 1.57 million in 2011 (Burke and Egaru 2011: 3). With the population approximately doubling every 20 years, the amount of available land has effectively been halved every two decades. This change has apparently contributed to competition for scarce resources, which tends to undermine the customary land tenure system, which had originally developed during a period of relatively small population and land abundance (Young and Sing'Oei 2011: 12, 19). Even with the rapid population increase in the Acholi sub-region, the Acholi land that has remained relatively unused as a result of the prolonged conflict is seen as an attractive frontier for the southerners.

The complexity of the land tenure system

Land under freehold tenure is mostly found in the capital, Kampala. Land tenure in the rest of Uganda is mostly customary. While the National Land Policy and the majority of observers suggest that 80 per cent of land in Uganda is held under customary tenure, a recent study suggests that over 99 per cent of land in the Acholi sub-region is held under customary tenure (Atkinson and Hopwood 2012: 2; Burke and Kobusingye, forthcoming). Yet customary tenure is not a single system but a cluster of sub-systems covering different types of land usage (settlement, grazing, hunting) managed by different levels of traditional authority (clan, sub-clan, family members, etc.) and incorporating diverse reasons for transfer (inheritance, gift, purchase, etc.). 'Ownership' in the customary sense thus refers to bundles of rights, with different actors having different rights over the same piece of land. Misunderstanding this concept may lead to conflict in the form of illegal land sales, abuse of trusteeship (of orphans by uncles and of widows by caretakers), and restrictions from common easements such as boreholes and cattle paths.

Eroded authority of cultural and traditional leaders

Customarily, Acholi people have sought assistance from their elders and clan leaders when disputes involved communal land. Although the way in which the prolonged conflict affected how the traditional authority of the Acholi exercised their influence is complex, erosion of such authority became noticeable among certain segments of Acholi society, primarily because they could not protect one of the most precious assets: land (Adoko and Levine 2008: 106, 111). The passing of elders who were the custodians and guardians of land rights, combined with the changing attitudes of the youth in Acholi, has had a significant impact.[17]

In addition, the 1998 Land Act did not initially recognise the important role of the traditional institutions – for example in setting rules, marking boundaries and managing hunting and grazing land. This deficiency also eroded the authority of traditional leaders. While the 2004 amendment acknowledged the importance of protecting family and individual land rights, actual policy implementation on the ground continues to reflect the various difficulties in allowing the traditional institutions to play their roles fully.

Lack of understanding of the 1998 Land Act

Even though the Land Act was passed by the legislature, public under-standing of this important Act has been poor. This situation has been compounded by the three major amendments to the Act, each of which brought important changes. Insufficient understanding of the legislation results in different interpretations of the law. Furthermore, for those Acholis who would like to remain under customary tenure, there has been little incentive to try and understand the Land Act, as it is primarily directed towards converting customary tenure to the freehold tenure system.

Ill effects of decentralisation and the increasing number of districts

With the establishment of the NRM government in 1986, the resistance council system, originally a mechanism of communication between the NRM in the bush and the local population of south-western Uganda, was intro-duced nationwide. The new Constitution promulgated in 1995 renamed the resistance council the 'local council system'. However, historical experiences differ from region to region. In the north, the Acholis generally do not grant the NRM the same legitimacy as do the Ugandans in the south. The Acholi population initially regarded the LC system as a foreign organisation implanted on their soil by the NRM government, though with time they have accepted it. While LC leaders are now considered useful, in the case of com-plicated disputes the historical background may taint the way in which people approach the LC system.

Recently the NRM government has dramatically increased the number of districts, ostensibly to deliver services more closely to the people. There were only 39 districts before decentralisation commenced in the early 1990s. This has increased to 112 in 2013, and may continue to increase (Green 2010). Critics claim this to be election manoeuvring, since it has been mainly in the north and the east that new districts have been established, as these are the places where the NRM initially experienced difficulty in gaining political support (Dolan 2009: 64; Tripp 2010). The result is that scarce resources are spread widely across numerous new local governments, further exacerbating the serious problem of institutional weakness in local governance.

Weak implementation mechanisms in land matters by the states

Land governance suffers from capacity deficiencies, both for those who want to convert their land to freehold and for those who want to remain under customary tenure. While land administration is now entrusted to local governments, the district land boards and area land committees function poorly, especially in the north. With limited budgets, a lack of qualified personnel and a mushrooming number of new districts, many land officer positions remain vacant, resulting in extreme ineffectiveness of land governance (Burke and Egaru 2011: 13). In addition, although the Land Act recognises the customary tenure system in Uganda, the government does not appear to sufficiently understand how customary land tenure governance actually works on the ground. Thus, support from central government to local governments in this critical area of land governance management has been limited.

Increased commodification of land

Many of these factors – increased population, weakened authority vested in the clan elders, weak government structures for implementing the Land Act – have directly and indirectly fostered new attitudes among the Acholi youth and diaspora. One manifestation of this new thinking is the valuing of land as commercial property. This conception is significantly at odds with conventional understandings, in which land is valued as a cultural asset and origin of ethnic identity.[18] The situation is further exacerbated by the recent discovery of oil, highlighting the fact that foreign investment would bring more cash income (International Alert 2009).

Case studies

The previous sections have considered the historical background of different land tenure systems, the general pattern of land disputes and their magnitude, issues related to conflict resolution mechanisms, and the reasons for land conflict. This section introduces two case studies. One explores a land dispute that was successfully resolved through mediation by a locally based NGO.

The other case is more complex, with two stages and fighting between two families from the same clan. (In this section, pseudonyms have been used, as the cases involve sensitive matters.) Our purpose here is to illustrate the intricate nature of land disputes as they unfold on the ground. The cases provide interesting insights into how land disputes evolve, which are of great value for understanding the interplay of dynamics between land disputes in the Acholi sub-region and the national political and economic landscape across Uganda.

Land grabbing against a widow in Pader District (2008–12)

Mary is a 65-year-old HIV-positive widow born in Pader District. She married her husband, a farmer, in 1973 and moved to his home village in Pader District. They had nine children, although several are now dead. Mary's husband died in 2000, and she remained in the family home. She currently has nine dependents.

When the security situation became seriously deteriorated in the late 1990s, the villagers moved to an IDP camp. Around 2008, the villagers, including Mary's family, started returning home. Nelson, Mary's neighbour, who was in southern Uganda from 1998 until 2010, began to claim a two-acre portion of Mary's land upon his return. Nelson was in his late 30s and had a wife and six dependents. After returning to the village, Nelson quickly established a reputation for heavy drinking, but he has generally been perceived a 'good man'.

Nelson was the son of the LC 1 chairman in the area. When Nelson destroyed Mary's maize garden on the disputed land, Mary complained to the LC 1, but it refused to act against the interests of the chairman's son. Mary then approached the district LC 5 vice-chairman, who organised a meeting with Nelson and local community members, but no one turned up to the meeting.

Nelson based his claim on information, provided by his father, that the disputed land was his. Nelson did not doubt his father's claim. Nelson threatened Mary with violence if she returned to the garden. Mary then reported the case to the police in the town (approximately 8 km away), with the assistance of a Catholic Church Justice and Peace Commission human rights volunteer resident in the village. The police do not usually intervene in land disputes in the absence of a court order, but explained that they could respond to threats of violence. Mary wrote a statement outlining the threats that Nelson had made and noted the mobile telephone number of the police. It is important to note that the mobile telephone network throughout northern Uganda is patchy and unreliable. Mary went back to her garden and planted sorghum. After three months, when the crop was halfway to being harvested, Nelson returned and destroyed the entire crop with an ox plough. Mary contacted the police, but they never appeared. The police were understaffed, and had only one motorcycle at their disposal and no fuel allowance.

In March 2011 Mary heard on the radio about Uganda Land Alliance (ULA), an NGO based in Pader that worked to alert people to the Land Act and assist with mediation and legal support. She approached ULA and decided to try mediation. The ULA paralegals spent approximately one month preparing the mediation before inviting the parties to a meeting in the village comprising community leaders, elders and the LC 1 leader.

Nelson and his friends and neighbours explained to us later that the dispute was a regular topic of conversation in social situations, especially at a modest local kiosk that stocked alcohol. Apparently, public opinion concerning the dispute was relatively evenly divided at that point within the village. From the start, Nelson said that he was completely against the idea of mediation. He claimed to be certain about the location of his property boundaries and believed he was entirely correct, despite the fact he had been away from the area for an extended period. Nelson explained that he only listened to friends and acquaintances who supported him and gave no time to people who were against him.

In May 2011 approximately 30–40 people from the village participated in a one-day mediation facilitated by the ULA staff. Nelson agreed to participate out of respect for community opinion, as well as fear of legal action. He explained that he was sober on the day of the mediation. He was reportedly rude and obstinate throughout much of the hearing, but eventually agreed to accept Mary's claim to the land and participated in the planting of trees as boundary markers. Within one week Nelson had changed his mind and uprooted the trees to demonstrate his disgust with the situation. The ULA paralegals returned. They sternly warned Nelson that, should he persist, legal action would be pursued. They also assisted Mary in planting bananas to mark the boundary. Nelson reflected on his agreement to the outcome of the mediation and explained that his views were based on a mixture of:

1 respect for community opinion, especially that of his relatives and friends;
2 pity for Mary and her situation, in light of the fact she was a member of the same clan;
3 the fact that it was not a large piece of land and so he could do without it;
4 concern that the violence might get out of hand; and
5 fear of legal action.

Both the parties and the surrounding community consider the dispute fully resolved. Mary thinks that she became a victim because she is a woman. Nelson claims that he does not regret the fact that he accepted the community-backed resolution. For the community, this case was unusual because Nelson threatened the neighbours with violence. However, since the case has been amicably resolved, it has become very well known throughout the area and is regularly cited by community members and civil society institutions as an example of the peaceful resolution of a land conflict.

Contested ownership in Amuru District (2004–ongoing)

Fred claims that three generations of his family have lived on disputed land first settled by his grandfather. The land is located approximately 6 km from a major road between Gulu and Pabbo. In 1986 several families living along the road asked Fred to allow them to settle on his land temporarily to escape fighting between the government and the National Resistance Army.

After the restoration of peace the displaced families still remained on the land and refused to relocate. Fred reported the matter to the traditional leaders, but could not reach a solution. In 1987 Fred sued seven people in the LC 1 court. The LC 1 chairman at the time was Adam. The court ruled in Fred's favour and ordered the people to vacate the disputed land, but they refused. Subsequently, Fred took the matter to the LC 2, as well as to LC 3 courts for a further judgement and for enforcement of the earlier judgement. The accused seven continued to ignore the order until 1999, when they finally vacated the land.

This settlement curiously led to another dispute between Fred and Adam, who had chaired the LC 1 court in 1987. Adam claims that his father first settled on the disputed land in 1947, when he cleared virgin forest. Adam argues that his father had lived peacefully with Fred until his death. Adam was born on the land in question in 1952 and insists he is familiar with the boundary of the land. However, Fred and his son claim that Adam's father was given land by Fred, and that, over time, Adam's family started encroaching beyond the given area.

Whether this land is the same as that dealt with in the earlier case is controversial. Fred claims that this land is precisely the same land that Adam mediated over in 1987. But Adam claims that the land involved in the current dispute is different. Some members of the LC 2 court from the earlier judgement now support Adam. It is interesting to note that the majority of the local government leaders, including Adam, support the ruling NRM party. Fred and his sons argue that Adam has connived with political leaders to frustrate Fred's efforts to reclaim his land because one of Fred's sons (Ken) is LC 3 chairperson of the opposition party, Forum for Democratic Change (FDC), in Pabbo sub-county.

Fred's family claims that Adam accused them of colluding with the LRA (the anti-government rebels) and mobilised government soldiers to attack Fred's home in May 2001. The soldiers killed two of Fred's sons and injured his fifth-born son, Ken, who carries visible scars today. The use of this kind of violence was not uncommon during the conflict in northern Uganda. After the attack, several suspects, including Adam's children, were arrested by the police. The clan leaders intervened and asked Fred to release Adam's children from police custody and seek compensation for the deaths by customary means, as both families are prominent members of the same clan. Fred complied and Adam's sons were released. The traditional leaders performed the ritual known as *mato oput* (bitter root) to appease the spirits of those who were killed. However, when the two families were negotiating compensation, the government ordered the population back into the 'protected camps'. To date, Adam's family has not compensated Fred's family. Instead, the hatred and bitterness between the two families has steadily increased. As a result, the current land conflict is threatening to tear the clan apart. The situation has deteriorated further with the death of the clan leader, who is yet to be replaced.

In 2008 Adam took Fred to court for encroaching on his land. The LC 2 ruled in Adam's favour. As Fred was now getting old, one of his sons, Jack, took over the case. The court ruling was not acceptable to Jack, who took the matter to the LC 3 court on appeal, where he lost the case. In the meantime, the two families continued fighting and accusing each other. Malicious damage to property and threats of violence became common. The police were hesitant to respond because the case was before court. There are also credible claims that at some point the police officer in charge was not entirely transparent and was subsequently transferred to another duty station.

In April 2012 there were additional claims from both parties that they had been attacked and their properties damaged. This time the LC 2 chairperson organised a meeting to help resolve the protracted conflict, with support from other partners including the Acholi Religious Leaders Peace Initiative, a local NGO working on protection of land rights, the LC 5 vice-chairperson and traditional leaders. They met in April 2012, and the meeting resulted in the following agreement:

- both parties would cease fire and desist from violence;
- the parties would divide the land among themselves;
- trees would be planted to mark the agreed boundary; and
- mediation should be the only option used in resolving this conflict, and not court.

A date in May 2012 was set for finalising the mediation, demarcating the boundary, planting trees and signing the agreement. On this date, as people converged for the meeting, it was discovered that Adam's family was armed with *pangas* and other items. The situation was defused and no one was harmed. Another date in June 2012 was then set for the planting of demarcation trees under the supervision of the LC 3 chairperson. Unfortunately, on that day the chairperson was involved in a motor accident and was unable to attend.

As both parties waited for the chairperson to recover and organise another day, there was another claim by Fred that his family had been attacked and property stolen by Adam's family. The police arrested six members of Adam's family, who now face charges of criminal trespass, among other alleged offences. In late November 2012 a final hearing was conducted, at which the six accused denied committing any of the offences. They also claimed that the police were bribed to arrest them.

Meanwhile, Jack has lost all trust in the mediation process. He accused the LC 3 of bias. He now wants to pursue the criminal case against the six members of Adam's family, and a civil case simultaneously. He would like to reinstate his case and wants the previous proceedings to be declared null and void. This situation is compounded by arguments over the legitimacy of the

LC 2 court that first heard this case. Even if the case starts afresh, the entire proceedings will take time. It appears that unless concerted efforts by local leaders and the clan leadership are made, the case will remain unresolved. In the meantime, the relationship between the two contesting families continues to deteriorate.

Discussion of the land dispute cases

Both of the cases are factually complex and analytically interesting. The first case demonstrates how opportunists typically take advantage of the vulnerability of the socially disadvantaged (Adoko and Levine 2008). The HIV-positive widow was physically weak, and nobody protected her. She testified that if she were not a woman, the situation would probably not have been the same. Indeed, IOM and its partners report that about 30 per cent of the Acholi households are female-headed (IOM *et al.* 2010: 8). It is common for such vulnerable households to be targeted by land grabbers.

Many public institutions have proven ineffective. The fact that the LC 1 leader used his position to support his son's attempt to take over the land demonstrates nepotism among local government officials. While the police officials might have been sympathetic to the widow, they could not take effective action because of a lack of resources (fuel), a very common problem across rural Africa.

The governance void was filled by the ULA. The case reveals the importance of informal ADR mechanisms and the role played by NGOs, although the sustainability of such institutions remains a serious challenge. Analysts appreciate the role played by the ULA, especially its orientation towards strengthening the capacity of existing traditional and modern institutions (Carfield 2011; see also Aciro-Lakor 2008).

The second case in Amuru is more complex. It shows the shortcomings of both traditional and statutory dispute resolution mechanisms. The clan failed in this case, partly because the contending families are key members of the same clan. State institutions also proved inadequate. Political rivalry between the ruling NRM and opposition FDC parties has also complicated the situation. Furthermore, the police were allegedly bribed and could not maintain fairness and transparency.

As is typical of protracted disputes, the case has become increasingly complicated, compounded by hatred, animosity and manipulation. The case had almost been resolved when, unfortunately, the LC 2 chairperson was involved in an accident, which suggests that there are only subtle margins between bitterly contentious and peacefully resolved disputes.

While it is far from certain, the fact that the earlier dispute led to the subsequent dispute appears to signify opportunism. Since Adam was the LC 1 chairperson, it was advantageous for him to gain information that was not readily disclosed. It is probable that this situation affected the way he approached the second phase of the dispute.

While each case might simply reflect sheer personal greed, they provide valuable links with the overall political and economic situation in Uganda. Although the cases may not directly provide tangible evidence of the neo-patrimonial state and neoliberal economic policies in Uganda, the context in which numerous land disputes currently develop in the Acholi sub-region is indicative of neo-patrimonialism and growth-oriented economic policies. These considerations are essential for a full understanding of prevalent disputes over Acholi land.

In both cases, the disputes were brought to the LC system for mediation. Yet the local leaders failed to meet these expectations. These failures clearly demonstrate the weak institutional capacity of local government. Ironically, as a result of Uganda's ambitious decentralisation, many districts have recently been created, which has worsened the serious deficit in local capacity. The creation of new districts reflects the increasing clientelism in Ugandan politics (Saito 2010). As the LC system has now become a patronage-based political machine to maintain the NRM regime in power (Tripp 2010: 4 and chap. 5), creating more districts serves their political purpose. Indeed, the new districts were created as compensation for the loss of other patronage resources as a result of politico-economic reforms by the government (Green 2010). In short, what may be seen as distinct issues – weak institutional capacity in local government in the Acholi sub-region and increasing neo-patrimonialism in Uganda – are two sides of the same coin.

This complex interplay is further explained by the question of the legitimacy of the LC 1 and LC 2 leaders. The elections for the lower-level councils, which should have taken place in 2006, have still not been carried out. Officially it was explained that sufficient funds for these elections were not secured, though many observers suggest that the NRM was anxious that these elections would elect grassroots leaders who would not support the NRM. The current LC 1 and LC 2 leaders thus fill the institutional gap informally and temporarily. This situation reflects the political landscape in which the NRM attempts to maintain power through all sorts of means (Tripp 2010).

This political reasoning is further illustrated by the way in which the government supports customary tenure. Though officially recognised by the 1998 Land Act, the way in which the policy has been implemented suggests that government is reluctant to protect this tenure system. This reluctance partly derives from the difficulties the policy makers face in understanding the complex nature of the customary tenure system, which still tends to be misunderstood.[19] Thus, the official position and the actual situation on the ground present a stark contrast. This gap has been exacerbated by delays in articulating the National Land Policy. Although caution should be exercised in interpreting the context of this policy, such gaps are arguably characteristic of a neo-patrimonial state.[20]

Neo-patrimonialism involves duality of a legal-bureaucratic apparatus and its arbitrary use dominated by the interests of clientelism. Under neo-patrimonialism – although there are official procedures – leaders usually control public affairs personally, outside official systems. In such circum-stances, the gap between official rhetoric and reality is acute. Leaders and followers are connected through a perverted legitimacy: leaders distribute benefits according to their own interests, and followers seek to satisfy their particular demands (Chabal and Daloz 1999; Bayart 2009). Even though this is advantageous for those who are connected to the leader–follower network in the distribution and receiving of benefits in various forms, the end result is considerable inefficiency, injustice and malfunction at broader societal levels. Neo-patrimonialism evidently fosters opportunistic behaviour; the framework for judgement is not society at large, but individual viewpoints. The same logic leads to the deterioration of governance institutions.

In such a neo-patrimonial context, weak capacity and a dysfunctional state provide the ideal opportunity for the 'big man' to demonstrate that he is the only viable option to solve complex matters. By so doing, he can convince his audience that he is indispensable. As has been pointed out by scholars on African politics, disorder serves the political interests of these 'big men' (Chabal and Daloz 1999). Because land is one of the few readily available economic assets in rural Africa, it often becomes one of the key resources traded within the patron–client networks (Bayart 2009: 82–83). It is not illo-gical at all, then, that the widespread land conflicts in the Acholi sub-region, combined with the 'forum shopping' that arises from the plurality of tradi-tional and statutory dispute resolution mechanisms, present ideal opportu-nities for 'big men' to exercise patronage. Relatively unutilised, land in the Acholi sub-region has come to be highly valued as an essential resource for political patronage.

The importance of politics is further illustrated by the relative shift in eco-nomic policy by the NRM from poverty reduction to economic growth. Uganda was commended internationally for its remarkable success in imple-menting its Poverty Eradication Action Plan (PEAP). Because PEAP was considered more endogenous and participatory than similar policies in other developing countries, it was emulated as a good model for poverty reduction strategies. The PEAP was launched in 1997 and revised in 2000 and 2003–4. It undoubtedly facilitated economic reform in Uganda and contributed to reducing poverty from 56 per cent in 1991 to 25 per cent in 2010 (Kjær and Katusiimeh 2012: 7), although other factors also obviously contributed to this reduction. In 2010 a new National Development Plan (NDP) was launched. The aim of the NDP is to increase income levels so that all Ugandans can enjoy prosperity. The orientation of the NDP is towards economic moder-nisation, with an emphasis on infrastructure development (GoU 2010). However, this bulky 400-page document clearly shows that while the NDP is all-encompassing it lacks any clear strategic vision. While Uganda (like other African countries) was eager to learn from the successes of East Asian eco-nomic transformation experiences, it is increasingly clear that the NDP has not articulated key issues such as human capital formation. One of the most acute problems is that the NDP has not elaborated the crucial role of the state, especially regarding how to guide economic transformation processes, mobilise appropriate technology and redistribute anticipated benefits to the population (Hickey 2013: 201). Nor does it adequately address how inequality between the north and south is to be overcome (Hickey 2013: 202).

Furthermore, although the NDP recognises agriculture as one of the key economic sectors, it focuses on the role of large-scale farmers in order to realise economies of scale. But the document reflects a half-hearted approach by the government; as the contribution of agriculture to GDP declines, there is little articulation of which crops should be promoted strategically. The NDP also hardly discusses land reform, which is still important for rural poverty reduction in Uganda (Hickey 2013: 202; see also Lipton 2009). It is no wonder that this lack of clear policy direction perpetuates deep-seated suspicions, mistrust and fear among the Acholi people towards those in power, as they strongly believe they have remained marginalised within Uganda for the last two decades.

The major shift in development policy reflects important changes in the background political situation. In short, particular policies are promoted by particular clusters of political and economic situations (Hickey 2013). While the PEAP was enabled by a combination of key domestic stakeholders (the Ministry of Finance, Planning and Economic Development, and representatives of civil society), as well as key donors (the World Bank and the UK government, which financed a significant proportion of Uganda's budget), the NDP is now supported by different stakeholders (a new National Development Authority and the private sector) and emerging donors (particularly China). In addition, this shift is clearly influenced by newly discovered oil resources – oil having profoundly changed the political landscape as a promising source of state income to replace declining aid from conventional donors.

Therefore, although the pursuit of economic growth in itself is far from unique in Uganda, the way in which economic policies are framed is significantly affected by the political situation. Indeed, the NDP could be considered the culmination of the political attitudes of the incumbent party, pursuing economic growth without structural transformation. Pursuing real economic transformation is risky for those who would like to remain in power for as long as possible, because it takes time to realise such a transformation, and also because the transformation might entail unexpected outcomes that would upset the ruling coalition (Kjær and Katusiimeh 2012). Thus, the all-inclusive NDP in fact suits the political convenience of those who are in power. The NDP is a 'politically-attuned approach to development' (Hickey 2013: 198).

Although there is no single understanding of the relationship between economic growth and neo-patrimonialism, economic and political aspects interact in a compounded fashion. While markets are useful if properly governed by regulatory regimes, markets without such regulation tend to result in social injustice. If markets are backed by public access to information and are generated by open and competitive transactions, they can harness productive forces. However, markets subject to collusion of interests are inclined to encourage sheer greed. When neo-patrimonialism becomes a political norm, coupled with the decline of traditional authorities that no longer provide common norms and secure land governance, political connections and economic opportunism go hand in hand. Thus, the neo-patrimonial state is a useful mechanism for forging an alliance between foreign capital interests and local African establishments. Northern Uganda is no exception. Interestingly enough, the NDP often refers to public–private partnerships (PPPs) – language typical of neoliberalism. But the sort of alliance justified in the rhetoric of PPPs often exploits natural resources for personal benefits at the cost of local communities (Nelson 2010: 20 and chap. 14).[21]

The reintroduction of multi-party elections in 2001 has also occurred in the meantime. This shift signified a change of polity from a non-party democracy (in which all electoral candidates competed as individuals) to multi-party democracy. This political change was made when the ruling coalition was becoming increasingly fragmented, and the cost of maintaining it thus became more expensive than before (Kjær and Katusiimeh 2012).

All of these factors demonstrate that economic and political aspects are deeply entangled, which in turn encourages essential actors to reconfigure their positions. This complexity affects patronage networks in one way or another. The commodification of land in the Acholi sub-region has taken place in this context. This land commodification is welcomed by neo-patrimonialism because more land becomes available to be used for patronage purposes. Thus, economic rationale and political calculation, in the contemporary context of Uganda, have become inseparable. The creation of satisfactory outcomes for a small elite linked to power and wealth is taken for granted at the cost of society at large. It is important to remember 'the historical fact that the state and its many agencies in Africa have been central to land control and invariably enforced land dispossession' (Greco 2013: 460). This unfortunate story is unfolding in the Acholi sub-region in Uganda.

Conclusions

It has become clear that many unresolved land dispute cases demonstrate complex layers of factors mutually entangled with each other: the deteriorating authority of traditional leadership in Acholi; the weak capacity of local government; the increasing number of districts; rampant corruption among politicians and administrators taking advantage of institutional weakness; the subordinate social status of women; lack of protection for the socially disadvantaged; opportunism associated with greed and gender disparity; institutional confusion and non-cooperation; and interference by local and/or national politicians. Protracted cases demonstrate how these factors are inextricably linked.

These linkages are particularly important for an understanding of the broader political and economic situation in Uganda. With the same government remaining in power for more than 25 years, increasing personalisation of power, systematic clientelism using state and public resources, and widespread corruption, contemporary Uganda is a typical neo-patrimonial state (Tangri and Mwenda 2010; Tripp 2010). With increasingly growth-oriented economic policies and the accelerating commodification of land, the social fabric of Acholi society has changed significantly as well. Economic changes affect how political patronage is distributed. Against this background, resolving land disputes is a daunting task. Even given the significant limitations on the exploration of possible solutions under such circumstances, effective solutions are more likely to be achieved through a holistic vision and approach rather than with narrow and technical thinking (Nelson 2010).

Without such an approach, the vicious circle is likely to continue. As particularly illustrated by our second example, institutional weakness and opportunistic behaviour reinforce each other. There is no easy solution to this complex situation. What is needed is a coordinated strategy to address multiple issues simultaneously. Traditional authorities, NGOs (including faith-based institutions) and statutory institutions all have crucial roles to play. While traditional leaders do not enjoy political power, they are still respected in many parts of the Acholi sub-region. As such, they can enhance the legitimacy of the system in coordination with others. As seen in the case of the widow, NGOs such as the ULA provide invaluable and affordable services at the grassroots, especially in reconciliation and ADR. However, they cannot enforce arbitrated agreements. This role can only be played by the state. Collaboration among these three entities is urgently required. Each contributes an indispensable function: mediation and reconciliation by NGOs, legitimacy granted by clan leaders and enforcement by state organisations. Each needs capacity building to effectively discharge its function. Improving land-dispute resolution is an urgent matter because until the Acholis feel confident they are being treated as fairly as other communities in Uganda, all endeavours towards recovery and peacebuilding are likely to fail. Even if the return of civil war in the region is unlikely, if popular discontent continues it would not surprise us to see another armed rebellion, given the long history of conflict in this area.

Notes

1 The fieldwork for this chapter was conducted by Christopher Burke and Emmanuel Egaru during three visits between July and November 2012. Without these on-site investigations this chapter could not have materialised. The draft chapter was reviewed and commented on by, inter alia, Judy Adoko, Jeremy Akin, Daniel Fitzpatrick and Liz Alden-Wily.

2 Disputes arise due to incompatible interests and/or objectives, whereas conflicts describe a situation whereby one party perceives the situation as threatening and thereby takes action accordingly.

3 The Holy Spirit Movement (1986–87) was led by Alice Lakwena, which gave rise to the LRA of Kony; Kony is understood as 'her cousin' in the African sense (Behrend 1999).

4 The northern Uganda conflict was intertwined with diplomatic tensions between Uganda and neighbouring countries, which is another factor that made the resolution of the conflict difficult (Atkinson 2010: 283, 295).

5 This comment was widely reported in the media. See, for instance, *Guardian* (2004).

6 Dolan continues to argue that throughout the 'protected villages', widespread debilitation, dread, disorientation and dehumanisation were perpetuated on a daily basis to subordinate the population in northern Uganda (Dolan 2009: chap. 1).

7 The same survey points out that more than half (54 per cent) of the respondents thought that southerners do not understand the Acholis (Pham and Vinck 2010: 31).

8 For instance, the Amin government issued the Land Reform Decree of 1975, by which all land in Uganda was vested in the state. However, this decree was never fully implemented (Marquardt and Sebina-Zziwa 1998: 177; see also Okuku 2006: 11).

9 The Act and subsequent amendments can be found at http://ulaug.org/departments-and-programs/knowledge-management/the-land-observatory/land-laws/ (accessed 18 September 2013).

10 Although land disputes are important, such disputes are not the only type of struggle that ordinary people face on returning to their homelands after the long stay in the IDP camps. Indeed, it is important to note that most of the Acholis face many disputes at once: competition with other clans and families and struggles against state authorities, as well as against corporate investments (Young and Sing'Oei 2011).

11 This frequency appears reasonably consistent with the database of the Norwegian Refugee Council, an international NGO, which reported that 40 per cent of the IDP returnees experienced land disputes after they left the IDP camps (IOM *et al.* 2010: 9).

12 One related issue is that of whether land disputes are more concentrated in certain places than in others. The report by IOM and its partner organisations (2010: 30–31) reported that Amuru and Nwoya tended to encounter more disputes than other districts, partly due to the discovery of oil there. More recent research finds that the political, economic and social conditions behind land disputes are broadly similar throughout the Acholi sub-region, and thus land disputes can and most likely do occur anywhere. Hence, there may not be particular 'hot spots' of land disputes, as previously suggested (Burke and Egaru 2011: 5; Atkinson and Hopwood 2012).

13 The background of the dispute over the game reserves and the national parks is complex (Tumushabe *et al.* 2009: 40).

14 Tumushabe and his colleagues (2009: 61–69) classify the diverse disputes into three categories: supply-induced disputes, demand-induced disputes and disputes over structural scarcity. For more about the types of disputes, see also Mabikke (2011) and Mercy Corps (2011).

15 As they were introduced by the colonists, they are not 'traditional' leaders in the historical sense, but their broad categorisation contrasts with modern statutory institutions.

16 Mediated compromises – such as when an in-law steals two gardens from a widow, but 'compromises' by giving one back – may fail to uphold the customary land rights of the vulnerable and serve to legitimise the impunity of those seeking to grab land that is not rightfully theirs.

17 Land boundaries are commonly remembered by the clan elderly. One recent study found that about 43 per cent of respondents equate the death of recognisable chiefs and clan elders with loss of evidence and thereby dispossession of their land (IOM *et al.* 2010: 8).

18 The changing understanding sometimes results in another issue, whereby family heads who are managing family land have started to treat land as their personal property and sell it without family or clan consent.

19 While it is beyond the scope of this chapter, it is useful to consider the new issue of the certificate of customary ownership (CCO). This new CCO was launched in

March 2012 in Gulu for those who would like to have an official title to customary land. While the government's intentions are not considered malicious, land-issue NGOs have voiced their deep concerns. Some officials simply cannot understand why the new certificate undermines Acholi society as the land activists suggest. See also Okuku (2006: 14) and Hunt (2004).

20 Under such circumstances, the burden of clarifying and implementing policies rests with local governments that suffer compounded deficiencies.

21 The investment by the Madhvani Group illustrates this concern. The Madhvani Group attempted to obtain approximately 40,000 hectares of land through the district land board. However, the Acholi political leaders and residents were upset that they were not being consulted. They were informed of this land acquisition while many Acholis were still in IDP camps (Mercy Corps 2011: 12). The local people perceived this land acquisition as a reflection of economic greed on the part of non-Acholis. In March 2012 the High Court in Gulu ruled in favour of Madhvani (Nakayi 2012: 485–502). Concerned human rights activists immediately appealed to the Constitutional Court in Kampala. The case is ongoing. The Madhvani incident is not unusual.

References

Aciro-Lakor, R.H., 2008, 'Land rights information centres in Uganda', in *Legal Empowerment in Practice: Using Legal Tools to Secure Land Rights in Africa*, ed. L. Cotula and P. Mathie, London: International Institute for Environment and Development, 71–76.

Adoko, J. and Levine, S., 2008, 'Falling between two stools: how women's land rights are lost between state & customary law in Apac District, northern Uganda', in *Women's Land Rights and Privatization in Eastern Africa*, ed. B. Englert and E. Daley, Oxford: James Currey, 101–19.

Adoko, J., Akin, J. and Knight, R., 2011, 'Understanding and Strengthening Women's Land Rights under Customary Tenure in Uganda', Land and Equity Movement in Uganda (LEMU) and International Development Law Organization (IDLO), Kampala.

Akin, J. and Katono, I., 2011, *Examining the A-D-R-history of Land Dispute Mediators in Northern Uganda*, Gulu: Northern Uganda Land Platform.

Atkinson, R.R., 2008, 'Land issues in Acholi in the transition from war to peace', *The Examiner: Quarterly Publication of Human Rights Focus*, 4: 3–9, 17–25.

——2010, *The Roots of Ethnicity: Origins of the Acholi of Uganda*, 2nd edn, Kampala: Fountain Publishers.

Atkinson, R.R. and Hopwood, J., 2012, 'Land Conflict Monitoring and Mapping Tools for the Acholi Sub-region', first report prepared for Human Rights Focus, United Nations Peacebuilding Program, Gulu.

Bayart, J.-F., 2009, *The State in Africa: The Politics of the Belly*, 2nd edn, Cambridge: Polity Press.

Behrend, H., 1999, *Alice Lakwena and the Holy Spirits: War in Northern Uganda, 1986–97*, London: James Currey.

Burke, C. and Egaru, E., 2011, *Identification of Good Practice in Land Conflict Resolution in Acholi*, Gulu: UN Resident Coordinator's Office.

Burke, C. and Kobusingye, D. (forthcoming), *Securing Women's Land and Property Rights in Northern Uganda: West Nile, Acholi, Lango, Teso and Karamoja*, Kampala: Oxfam Uganda.

Carfield, M., 2011, 'Land justice in Uganda: preserving peace, promoting integration', in *Working with Customary Justice Systems: Post-conflict and Fragile States*, ed. E. Harper, Rome: International Law Development Organization, 127–43.

Chabal, P. and Daloz, J.-P., 1999, *Africa Works: Disorder as Political Instrument*, Oxford: James Currey.

Dolan, C., 2009, *Social Torture: The Case of Northern Uganda, 1986–2006*, New York: Berghahn Books.

EPRC (Economic Policy Research Centre), Makerere University 2010, *First Annual Report on Corruption Trends in Uganda: Using the Data Tracking Mechanism*, Kampala: EPRC.

GoU (Government of Uganda) 2010, 'National Development Plan: 2010/11–2014/15', National Planning Authority, Kampala.

——(2013), 'The Ugandan National Land Policy', Ministry of Lands, Housing and Urban Development, Kampala.

Greco, E., 2013, 'Struggles and resistance against land dispossession in Africa: an overview', in *Handbook of Land and Water Grabs in Africa: Foreign Direct Investment and Food and Water Security*, ed. J.T. Allan, M. Keulertz, S. Sojamo and J. Warner, London: Routledge, 456–68.

Green, E., 2010, 'Patronage, district creation, and reform in Uganda', *Studies in Comparative International Development*, 45: 83–103.

Guardian, 2004, 'Northern Uganda "world's biggest neglected crisis"', 22 October, available online at www.guardian.co.uk/world/2004/oct/22/2 (accessed 7 August 2013).

Hickey, S., 2013, 'Beyond poverty agenda? Insights from the new politics of development in Uganda', *World Development*, 43: 194–206.

Hunt, D., 2004, 'Unintended consequence of land rights: the case of the 1998 Uganda Land Act', *Development Policy Review*, 22(2): 173–91.

IDMC (Internal Displacement Monitoring Centre), 2012, 'UGANDA: need to focus on returnees and remaining IDPs in transition to development, a profile of the internal displacement situation', 24 May, IDMC, Geneva.

Immanuel, K.F., 2010, 'Challenges and opportunities for women's land rights in post-conflict northern Uganda', MICROCON Research Working Paper 26, MICROCON, Brighton.

International Alert, 2009, 'Harnessing oil for peace and development in Uganda', International Alert Uganda, Kampala.

IOM (International Organization for Migration), UNDP (United Nations Development Programme) and NRC (Norwegian Refugee Council), 2010, *Land or Else: Land-based Conflict, Vulnerability, and Disintegration in Northern Uganda*, Kampala.

Kjær, A.M. and Katusiimeh, M., 2012, 'Growing but not transforming: fragmented ruling coalitions and economic developments in Uganda', DIIS Working Paper 2012:07, Danish Institute for International Studies, Copenhagen.

Lipton, M., 2009, *Land Reform in Developing Countries: Property Rights and Property Wrongs*, London: Routledge.

Lucima, O., 2002, *Protracted Conflict, Elusive Peace: Initiatives to End the Violence in Northern Uganda*, special issue of *Accord*, London: Conciliation Resources.

Mabikke, S.B., 2011, 'Escalating land grabbing in post-conflict regions of northern Uganda: a need for strengthening good land governance in Acholi region', paper presented at the International Conference on Global Land Grabbing, University of Sussex, 6–8 April.

Marquardt, M.A. and Sebina-Zziwa, A., 1998, 'Land reform in the making', in *Developing Uganda*, ed. H.B. Hansen and M. Twaddle, London: James Currey, 176–84.

Mercy Corps, 2011, 'Land disputes in Acholiland: a conflict and market assessment', Mercy Corps, Portland.

Nakayi, R., 2012, 'The dynamics of customary land rights and transitional justice: the case of the Acholi sub-region of northern Uganda', PhD dissertation, University of Notre Dame.

Nelson, F., 2010, *Community Rights, Conservation and Contested Land: The Politics of Natural Resource Governance in Africa*, London: Earthscan.

Okuku, J.A., 2006, 'The Land Act 1998 and land tenure reform in Uganda', *Africa Development*, 31(1): 1–26.

Pham, P. and Vinck, P., 2010, 'Transition to peace: a population-based survey on attitudes about social reconstruction and justice in northern Uganda', Human Rights Center and School of Law, University of California, Berkeley.

Pham, P., Vinck, P., Wierda, M. and Stover, E., 2005, 'Forgotten voices: a population-based survey on attitudes about peace and justice in northern Uganda', International Center for Transitional Justice and the Human Rights Center, University of California, Berkeley.

Pham, P., Vinck, P., Stover, E. and Moss, A., 2007, 'When the war ends: a population-based survey on attitudes about peace, justice and social reconstruction in northern Uganda', International Center for Transitional Justice and the Human Rights Center, University of California, Berkeley.

Roberts, B., Ocaka, K.F., Browne, J., Oyok, T. and Sondorp, E., 2008, 'Factors associated with post-traumatic stress disorder and depression amongst internally displaced persons in northern Uganda', *BMC Psychiatry*, 8: 1–38.

Rugadya, M.A., Nsamba-Gayiiya, E., Mutyaba, R.L., Kamusiime, H., Asiimwe, J.B. and Namakula, V., 2008, *Final Report on the Integrated Study on Land and Family Justice*, Kampala: Ministry of Justice and Constitutional Affairs.

Rugadya, M.A., Nsamba-Gayiiya, E. and Kamusiime, H., 2008, 'Northern Uganda Land Study: Analysis of Post-conflict Land Policy and Land Administration: A Survey of IDP Return and Resettlement Issues and Lessons: Acholi and Lango Regions', a report for the World Bank, available online at www.landcoalition.org/sites/default/files/legacy/uploads1/northern_uganda_land_study_acholi_lango.pdf (accessed 18 October 2013).

Saito, F., 2010, 'Decentralization for local democracy? Lessons from recent policy "reversals" in Uganda', *Journal of the Socio-Cultural Research Institute* (Ryukoku University), 12: 115–37.

Tangri, R. and Mwenda, A.M., 2010, 'President Museveni and the politics of presidential tenure in Uganda', *Journal of Contemporary African Studies*, 28(1): 31–49.

Tripp, A.M., 2010, *Museveni's Uganda: Paradoxes of Power in a Hybrid Regime*, Boulder, CO: Lynne Rienner.

Tumushabe, G.W., Bainomugisha, A. and Mugyenyi, O., 2009, 'Land tenure, biodiversity and post-conflict transformation in Acholi sub-region: resolving the property rights dilemma', ACODE Policy Research Series No. 29, Advocates Coalition for Development and Environment, Kampala.

UNDP (United Nations Development Programme), 2013, *Human Development Report 2013*, New York: Palgrave Macmillan.

World Bank, 2008, 'Post-conflict land policy and administrative options: the case of northern Uganda', World Bank Report No. 46110-UG, Kampala.

Young, L.A. and Sing'Oei, J., 2011, *Land, Livelihoods, and Identities: Inter-community Conflicts in East Africa*, London: Minority Groups Rights International.

4 Land tenure security in post-conflict Rwanda

Shinichi Takeuchi and Jean Marara

Land has been Rwanda's pivotal issue for a long time. As the country is one of the most densely populated in Africa, fragmentation of land holdings has always been a focus of concern for the Rwandan government. Rural pauperisation due to land shortage is considered an important background element to the genocide in 1994. Although land shortage cannot be considered as the direct cause of the mass killings, it is true that the land issue was actively utilised as a means for mass mobilisation in the civil war (Prunier 1995: 248; André and Platteau 1996; HRW 1999: 299; Mamdani 2001: 231; Bigagaza *et al.* 2002; Rose 2007). The acuteness of the land problem in Rwanda was exacerbated after the war, as the military victory of the former rebels, the Rwandan Patriotic Front (RPF), induced a massive return of Tutsi[1] refugees after decades of absence. For the newly established RPF-led government, dealing with the land problem was therefore one of the most urgent imperatives.

Against this backdrop, a series of radical policy interventions have been made in post-conflict Rwanda with regard to land, resulting in drastic changes in the rules relating to land and its ownership. For example, mass Tutsi returnees were provided with land without exception; women's land rights were strengthened; villagisation made considerable progress; and land was systematically registered all over the country. In addition, in spite of the massive refugee return, the government has so far managed to control the outbreak of land-related conflicts. How should these policy measures and their consequences be assessed? This study reflects on this point by focusing on land tenure security in post-conflict Rwanda. Securing land rights is particularly important for Rwanda: contributing to the promotion of investment as well as social stability, land tenure security serves to create the basis of economic development and sustainable peace (North 1981). In fact, Rwanda emphasised the importance of land tenure security in its National Land Policy (NLP), whose overall objective was to 'establish a land tenure system that guarantees tenure security for all Rwandans and give guidance to the necessary land reforms with a view to good management and use of national land resources' (Republic of Rwanda 2004: 22). Did post-conflict Rwanda succeed in ensuring land tenure security through radical policy interventions?

To examine the policy impacts on land tenure security, we tentatively adopted the concept of Place *et al.* (1994: 19), according to which 'land tenure security can be defined to exist when an individual perceives that he or she has rights to a piece of land on a continuous basis, free from imposition or interference from outside sources, as well as ability to reap the benefits of labor and capital invested in that land, either in use or upon transfer to another holder'. Despite this definition, the concept includes ambiguities because this personal perception is not only impossible to measure, but also relative in the sense that it may vary depending on the person's social status (Lavigne Delville 1998). A simple example is that policy intervention may strengthen the land tenure security of tenant farmers and at the same time undermine that of landlords. The relative nature of land tenure security has been clearly observable in Africa, where people 'have gained access to land, labour, and capital for agricultural production both through exchange and through membership and status in various social units', and '[i]ndividuals' access depended on the political structure and dynamic of the resource-controlling group' (Berry 1989: 41–42). A policy may bring about contrasting effects for members of two different ethnic groups if the members of each group have totally different degrees of access to power. Considering that Rwandan society has never been monolithic and has been deeply affected by repeated armed conflicts, the effects of post-conflict land policies might be expected to vary from one social group to another. In addition, the divisions in Rwandan society are not solely ethnic, but involve other factors, including economic and regional differences.

Land policies in post-conflict Rwanda have attracted attention from a number of researchers (Van Hoyweghen 1999; Hilhorst and Van Leeuwen 2000; Musahara and Huggins 2005; Pottier 2006; Wyss 2006; Bruce 2009; Huggins 2009; Payne 2011; Ali *et al.* 2011). On the basis of the previous literature, this study attempts to make contributions particularly regarding the following two points. First, it clarifies the whole picture of Rwanda's post-conflict policy interventions regarding land. Since the end of the civil war, a wide range of policy interventions have been made regarding land. Although the timeframe may not yet be sufficient for ex-post evaluations, the analysis elucidates the configuration of these interventions, thus helping the analysis of their effects on land tenure security. Second, in addition to the previous literature, this chapter is also based on information collected during field research that the authors have carried out since 1999 in two cells[2] in the southern and eastern provinces (Cell B and Cell R, respectively).[3] In particular, information about local land conflicts collected in the two cells will be referred to for the examination of land tenure security.[4] In our argument, therefore, land tenure security in rural areas will be the main focus.

First of all, we attempt to elucidate the historical context of the social setting in which post-conflict policy interventions have been made. In Rwanda, political interventions in the distribution of land can be traced back to the period of the pre-colonial kingdom. The effects, as well as the meanings, of a

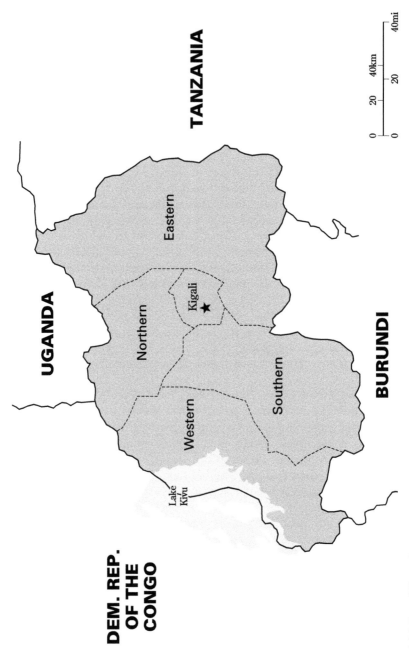

Figure 4.1 Map of Rwanda

policy intervention cannot be understood without knowledge of previous interventions. The second section illuminates post-conflict policy measures on land. While the NLP comprehensively set out post-conflict Rwandan land policy, several important measures had been taken before the adoption of the NLP. The complete picture of post-conflict interventions regarding land will be indicated in this section. The third section analyses land disputes in post-conflict Rwanda on the basis of recent studies, as well as our own field research. The last section reflects on land tenure security in post-conflict Rwanda.

Historical context

Repeated interventions on land

Interventions on land holding have a long history in Rwanda. For an understanding and an assessment of the land policies, these need to be contextualised in a long historical trajectory. In the pre-colonial kingdom of Rwanda, the land tenure system was composed of two major elements: *isambu-igikingi* and *ubukonde*.[5] Simply put, the former was a landlord system in which agriculturalists had to provide tributes and sometimes labour for their pastoral chiefs, while the latter was a system of family-owned lands, whose ownership was collectively assumed by the family members who had originally opened them up. *Igikingi* (pl. *ibikingi* – pastoral estates granted by the king) was introduced during the 1840s, against a backdrop of population increase and pressure on land (Nkurikiyimfura 1994). It enabled land exploitation by a small number of powerful pastoralists, which was detrimental to other small pastoralists and agriculturalists (Vansina 2001: 168).[6] Roughly speaking, pastoralists here could be considered as Tutsi, and agriculturalists as Hutu. As the kingdom established its dominance and expanded its control over territory, the *ubukonde* system was transformed into the *isambu-igikingi* system, in which small pastoralists and agriculturalists had to face arbitrary interventions from their chiefs. In colonial times, the vast majority of Rwanda's territory was considered to be 'customary land', in which the pre-colonial land system was in principle maintained under the authority of the king. However, the king's power was undermined relative to high-class administrators such as chiefs and sub-chiefs, who wielded power as delegates of the colonial authority, thereby promoting their intervention in the distribution of land.[7]

The traditional Tutsi-centred political system collapsed following the 'Social Revolution'[8] which broke out in November 1959 and accompanied the country's first-ever large-scale ethnic conflict. The conflict was ignited by a confrontation between supporters of the Tutsi-led UNAR party (*Union nationale rwandaise*) and those of the Hutu-led PARMEHUTU party (*Parti du mouvement de l'émancipation Hutu*), and spread quickly throughout the country. The eventual victory of the PARMEHUTU, aided by the colonial authorities, resulted in the overthrow of the existing political system, which was dominated by Tutsi elites. As a consequence, as many as 200,000 to 300,000 UNAR supporters and their families,[9] most of them Tutsi, had been expelled or had fled the country by the mid-1960s.[10] They are referred to as 'old-case' refugees.

The impact of the 'Social Revolution' on land was enormous. The refugees left behind vast ownerless tracts of land. Huge areas of this, along with the *ibikingi* that had been abolished in 1960, were confiscated and integrated into the national land, over which the local officials,[11] particularly the Burgomasters (chiefs of communes), wielded enough power to control distribution (André and Lavigne Delville 1998: 161).[12] Thus, enormous areas of land that had been owned by Tutsi families, or reserved as *ibikingi*, were summarily distributed to other peasants. We observed in Cell B several households that had acquired land from the commune authority. They were relatively poor Hutu households, often migrants, who had originally had no land in the cell and had acquired some plots by relying on personal favours from the authorities (Takeuchi and Marara 2005). Such redistribution of land was frequently carried out in areas where land scarcity was already a serious issue. The local authority provided certificates for receivers of land on the occasion of its redistribution after independence. However, the papers were deemed invalid when the RPF won the war in 1994. Those who had acquired lands from the local authorities were obliged to return them to the original owners, if requested.

Post-genocide Rwanda

The civil war in Rwanda was strongly characterised by its ethnic nature, culminating in the genocide against the Tutsi. It was the invasion by the RPF in October 1990 that started the four year war. The rebel group was organised in the neighbouring country to the north, Uganda, by the second generation of old-case refugees, who had fled the waves of conflicts and persecutions in their homeland since the 'Social Revolution'. The Rwandan government was led by President J. Habyarimana, a Hutu, who had seized power in 1973 in a coup d'état, toppling G. Kayibanda, the country's first president from the PARMEHUTU. The RPF's invasion was launched against a background in which neither of the two presidents had allowed the old-case refugees to be repatriated. While the Arusha peace agreement – concluded in August 1993 – finally recognised the right of return for old-case refugees, it obliged them to abandon their rights to land in cases where the period of their absence exceeded 10 years,[13] which was the case for the overwhelming majority. However, the Arusha peace agreement was immediately broken because of the assassination of Habyarimana on 6 April 1994, which resulted in the genocide and the recurrence of war. The RPF was victorious in the ensuing conflict and established a new political regime in July 1994.[14] For the newly established RPF-led government, land was a critical matter in a double sense: in addition to the population increase and land shortage that had been acute even before the civil war, enormous numbers of Tutsi refugees now came back to the country.

While Rwanda's population was estimated at less than 2 million in the 1930s,[15] it had soared to 7,155,391 by 1991 (République rwandaise 1991), and to 8,162,715 in 2002 (République rwandaise 2003). According to the provisional results of the last census in 2012, the total population was 10,537,222 (Government of Rwanda 2012), giving a population density of 427 persons per square kilometre. The urbanisation rate, which had been very low (5.4 per cent in 1990), increased rapidly in the post-conflict period, reaching 18.3 per cent in 2008 (*World Development Indicators*). While average land holding per agricultural household[16] is less than 0.8 hectares, more than half of the householders have less than 0.5 hectares. In addition, as a result of a lack of agricultural technologies such as animal traction, manure production and irrigation (Republic of Rwanda 2010: 36, 40), productivity remains low and the danger of environmental degradation is great. Due to the population increase and land shortage, customary land tenure, in which extended families play major roles in land management, has been rapidly disappearing in Rwanda.[17]

The second challenge was the return in large numbers of old-case refugees. The population loss caused by the civil war and the genocide was immediately offset by the massive refugee return, as well as natural population increase. It was estimated that 600,000 to 900,000[18] old-case refugees returned to the homeland in a short period following the RPF's victory in July 1994. Coming back to Rwanda after decades of absence, the old-case returnees were virtually landless people: their original family lands had been, in many cases, occupied by and/or redistributed to others. The new government had to deal with the problem as soon as possible – not only because the number of refugees was huge, but also because the old-case returnees constituted the core supporters of the RPF.

Post-conflict interventions in land

Dealing with the massive refugee return

The various land-related policy measures that have been taken in post-civil war Rwanda can be roughly distinguished into three categories. The first includes policy measures that were implemented in the early stage of the post-conflict period in order to deal with the massive return of old-case refugees. The second type was aimed at strengthening land rights, while the third type promoted rational and effective land use. The second and the third categories correspond to the objectives of the NLP. As we will see, the three types are not mutually exclusive, and their basic ideas are related to each other.

Dealing with the enormous numbers of old-case returnees was imperative for the newly established government. As representative policies for this purpose, we examine here 'land sharing' and villagisation. In order to provide land for the old-case returnees, the government first relied on vacant areas that could be found in a game reserve, the national park, communal land and land left after the departure of Hutu refugees (Republic of Rwanda 2004: 14).

While the victory of the RPF brought about the massive return of old-case refugees, it also prompted a tremendous outflow of Hutu refugees: under the threat of RPF retaliation and at the urge of leaders, more than 1.5 million people, together with the leaders of the defeated Habyarimana regime, fled and took refuge in neighbouring countries (Prunier 1995; Adelman 2003). These refugees established themselves mainly in refugee camps in eastern Zaire (now the Democratic Republic of the Congo, hereafter DRC) and Tanzania. Those who took refuge in neighbouring countries in 1994 and the years thereafter are referred to as 'new-case' refugees. The outbreak of an armed conflict in DRC in 1996 triggered their return. In only a few months following November 1996, some 1.5 million returnees moved back into Rwanda.

The return of old-case refugees was concentrated mainly in the eastern part of the country. For many old-case refugees who had lived in Uganda and Tanzania, eastern Rwanda was the nearest and easiest place to access. Furthermore, the approach of Rwandan authorities was to guide the returnees not to their original family lands but to areas where land was relatively abundant. This policy was undertaken on the grounds that most of the land belonging to old-case refugees had, in the course of their long absence, already been distributed to Hutu peasants. It was in this way that large numbers of old-case returnees came to be housed in the surroundings of the national park in eastern Rwanda. When the new-case refugees returned en masse after 1996, they found old-case refugees who had been occupying their land and houses since 1994. To deal with this situation, the Rwandan authorities ordered that houses occupied by old-case returnees be returned to their former owners (namely, new-case returnees) – but with the caveat that the land should be divided equally between the two parties. Through this radical policy, old-case returnees were officially provided with land. The practice was called 'land sharing'. This might be seen as a practical response on the ground rather than a coherent policy, as the occupation of old-case returnees was deemed temporary at the beginning (Van Hoyweghen 1999: 363); later, the practice was endorsed by law without any compensation[19] and formalised through land registration.

This land sharing has greatly impacted post-conflict Rwandan society. It radically changed its land holdings, since in reality it involved a complete division of properties (Musahara and Huggins 2005; Takeuchi and Marara 2005; Bruce 2009; Huggins 2009; Leegwater 2011). The old-case returnees acquired their lands to the detriment of the new-case returnees. In addition, the land transfer has ethnic implications: the old-case returnees were exclusively Tutsi, while the original inhabitants were Hutu – in practice, the properties of the Tutsi survivors from the genocide have been exempted from land sharing (Leegwater 2011: 109).

The villagisation policy was officially established in December 1996, just after the beginning of huge returns of new-case refugees. While Rwandan settlements were traditionally scattered over the 'thousand hills', the new policy aimed to gather settlements in designated areas called *umudugudu* (pl. *imidugudu*), often near to main roads. Although the policy was launched as an emergency action to provide settlements for old-case returnees – who had to hand over houses to new-case returnees – its implementation was not necessarily confined to that objective. There was no doubt that the return of the new-case refugees produced a serious housing crisis, as estimates of the number of families in immediate need of housing ranged from 250,000 to 300,000 (Hilhorst and Van Leeuwen 2000: 266). However, the policy had a long-term perspective, since the government emphasised, as a central rationale of the policy, that it enabled more efficient land use.[20] In addition, it was pointed out that security concerns lay in the background of the policy. Facing the insurgency that rose up in north-west Rwanda during 1997 and 1998, villagisation was considered as 'one way to reduce the likelihood of any recurrence of the insurgency' (HRW 2001: 17).

The results of the villagisation policy varied from region to region. While villagisation was highly developed in the eastern part of the country (Kibungo and Umutara areas), followed by the north-west part (Ruhengeri and Guisenyi areas), development was limited in other regions (Takeuchi and Marara 2000: 30) because the programme did not provide enough incentive for the population. People had to cover all the expense of moving by themselves, and moving increased their vulnerability to thieves in making the distance to their fields much greater (Newbury 2012). As the construction of settlements depended heavily on donors' support, it soon stagnated when, in light of criticism about the ambiguous objectives from human rights groups as well as researchers, donors became hesitant to assist (HRW 2001). Recently, however, the situation has begun to change. The pressure on local inhabitants to move to the designated areas has increased – mainly because of the introduction of the *imihigo* (performance contracts) system. In concluding a contract with authorities higher up, executive secretaries[21] in cells have to show they are competent in the execution of a given set of tasks (Ansoms 2009: 306; Ingelaere 2010: 288). As a result of rising pressure, movement to the *imidugudu* areas has been accelerated. Popular concentration has continuously boosted land prices in the designated areas, thus making moving more difficult for the poor.[22]

Strengthening land rights

The second type of post-conflict land policies focused on strengthening land rights, particularly on an individual basis. While systematic land registration, which started following the adoption of the NLP and the Organic Land Law (OLL) in 2005,[23] might be considered the most typical policy in this regard, the importance of the inheritance law should be emphasised, as it fundamentally challenged traditional custom in recognising women's right to inheritance.[24] Traditionally, Rwanda has been a patrilineal society, in which only sons had the right to inherit land from their father.[25] The inheritance law was adopted in 1999 against the backdrop of a rapid increase in female-headed households as a consequence of the civil war and the genocide. Pottier stated that 'the demographic changes forced women to take on new domestic roles and underscored the need for new legislation' (2006: 519). Once women's land rights had been legally confirmed,[26] a significant change was triggered in Rwandan society as women began to demand them. A considerable number of disputes brought to the local mediation mechanism were related to women's land rights (Lankhorst and Veldman 2009; Takeuchi and Marara 2011). From our observations in the field, women's land rights tend to be well recognised in the justice system, which generally follows government policies, and inheritance of land by daughters is by no means an exceptional case.

The OLL provides the state, on the one hand, with the 'supreme powers to manage all the national land' and 'rights to expropriation due to public interest, settlement and general land management' (Article 3), and stipulates, on the other hand, that registration of land is obligatory (Article 30). Systematic land registration can be a powerful reform for securing property rights. Following the two-year pilot studies, as well as the promulgation of a related law, implementation proceeded rapidly with the assistance of donors including DFID and the World Bank.[27] With the exception of state land, including lakes and rivers, state-owned forests and swamps,[28] demarcation of land plots was completed all over the country in June 2012, and 8.4 million land certificates – relating to the 10.3 million land parcels recorded – had been distributed as of August 2013 (*New Times* 2013). The completion of land demarcation in such a short period of time was without precedent in Africa. Two factors particularly contributed to the swiftness. First, the method of land registration was well designed, as it was village-based and low-cost.[29] Second, the effectiveness of Rwanda's administrative capacity should be highly credited, even if the assistance of donors played an important role.

Although land registration is a powerful tool for establishing private property rights, its effects are arguable in the case of Rwanda. The OLL gives the state particularly strong powers of land control. Land certificates are issued to the general public in the form of 'emphyteutic leases' (*contrats d'emphithéose*) – namely, long-term leases (on this point, see also USAID 2011: 5–7). In general, the leases are available for up to 99 years on land in rural areas and 20–49 years on land in urban areas. While the leases are renewable, people tend to feel that they are only tenants on the state land.

In addition to this supreme power of the state over land, the following two conditions might undermine the establishment of private property rights. First, registered landowners are flexibly defined. The owner can be an individual, or two or more persons. In addition, a land plot can also be registered under the name of the late family head.[30] Such registration tends to be chosen when inheritance among family members has not yet been completed or there are disputes over division. This method of land registration is understandable, considering the fact that disagreement over inheritance between family members is one of the most common types of Rwandan land dispute (Lankhorst and Veldman 2009), and that the inheritance process often takes a long time because of negotiations not only between parents and children but also among children and other family members. It could be impossible to resolve such disputes and to obtain consent for inheritance during the short time-frame of the land registration process. Consent became particularly difficult to finalise during the post-war period because of the absence of significant numbers of Hutus, who were now refugees in neighbouring countries.[31] Registering a plot under a late family head was, therefore, a wise device to postpone dealing with the problem of inheritance, thereby contributing to a reduction in the number of disputes during the registration process.[32]

Another factor that might affect the establishment of private property rights is the regulation prohibiting the division of a land parcel that is equivalent to or less than one hectare. The OLL does not allow people 'to reduce the parcel of land reserved for agriculture of one or less than a hectare' (Article 20). In the process of systematic land registration, all land plots were demarcated and registered, regardless of their size. However, once registered, plots cannot be divided for re-registration if one of the divided parts is less than a hectare. This strict regulation is easy to promulgate, but will be almost impossible to impose on the ground, as demarcation and division of properties are indispensable for inheritance. Considering the importance of land as an asset for rural livelihoods, it is very likely that the regulation will promote the informal division of lands. As a result, dis-crepancies between the land registration records and the reality of land tenure may become widespread in the future. As time passes, these infor-mally divided plots, owned and managed by plural right holders, may turn out to be governed according to something more similar to the previous customary land tenure than to private property rights. Due to the increase in the number of rights holders, disputes will be likely to arise, as was the case before land registration.

Rational and effective land use

The imperative of rational and effective land use is another factor restricting property rights. Against the backdrop of rapid population increase and the general land shortage, this imperative has been repeatedly stressed in Rwan-dan policy documents. This is the second pillar of the overall objectives of the NLP – along with land tenure security. The OLL defined landowners' obli-gations to use the land 'in a productive way' – namely, protecting it from erosion, safeguarding its fertility, and ensuring its production in a sustainable way (Article 62). It may 'impose sanctions ... against the landlord or any other person allowed to lease the land who fails to respect the obligation to efficiently conserve the land and productively exploit it' (Article 73). The sanction includes 'forceful confiscation' if the owner lets the land become degraded and unexploited.

The imperative of rational and productive land use constitutes a basic principle of Rwanda's post-conflict land policy, and the idea can be found in many related arrangements, such as villagisation and registration. One of the clearest examples of this is the policy of land consolidation, which is defined as 'a procedure of putting together small lots of land in order to manage the land and use it in an efficient uniform manner so that the land may be more productive' (OLL, Article 2). While this measure was stipulated in the OLL (Articles 20, 22), its implementation began only in the late 2000s and was limited in the beginning to swamps (marshland), which were defined as state land in the OLL. Under this policy, farmers are requested to plant the same crops in defined areas. Typically, farmers are invited to cultivate designated crops such as maize and rice. The local administration distributes seeds of improved varieties, as well as fertilisers, to farmers, who retain the property rights for the land and crops.[33] Although the government explains that farmers determine what is to be cultivated in the consolidation area through discussion, agricultural officers in the local administration tend to have the power to determine the crops to be planted, and give virtually no other choice to farmers.

From our observation, farmers' opinions on land consolidation are divided. Some were able to take advantage of this opportunity to increase production. However, for others who had only a tiny area of land, which was too small to make sufficient profit through mono-cropped and market-oriented production, it was preferable to cultivate a variety of products for subsistence. Some of them complained about the high-handed attitude of agricultural officers who imposed the designated crops.

These examples demonstrate the tension between private property rights and the demand for rational and effective land use. Clearly, the basic principle in post-conflict Rwanda is that the former should be subjugated to the latter. This means that land tenure security in Rwanda's context does not mean a guarantee of exclusive property rights for individuals. It is the public interest, as defined by the government, that should be first of all secured and prioritised.

The nature of land disputes after the civil war

Land disputes constitute clear symptoms of insecurity over land tenure. While a couple of research projects touched on this subject before the civil war in the 1990s, their judgements varied considerably. Blarel (1994) stated, on the basis of a survey conducted in 1988, that the incidence of land disputes was low and was concentrated on a specific household group: those headed by separated and single women. He concluded that 'land tenure security is fairly high in Rwanda' (1994: 87). On the contrary, André and Platteau (1996) emphasised the insecurity of land tenure. Comparing the data collected in 1988 and those in 1993 in north-western Rwanda, they argued that social tension heightened swiftly as a result of the rapid population increase. Mentioning the exclusion of socially vulnerable groups from land holding and frequent outbreaks of intra-family land disputes,[34] their paper stressed the insecurity of land tenure (1996: 33). The perception that land tenure security was seriously jeopardised seemed to be widely shared by the post-conflict government (Musahara and Huggins 2005: 275) – not only because the pace of population increase did not slow down, but also because new complicating factors such as the massive refugee return had been added.

Two patterns of recent land conflict

The recent situation of land conflict can be traced through some research on Rwanda's local conflict resolution mechanism, *abunzi*[35] (Lankhorst and Veldman 2009; Takeuchi and Marara 2011). The *abunzi* is a village-level judicial system that has been in effect since 2007. *Abunzi* literally means 'reconciliation committee'. These have been established in each cell and are composed of nine elected cell members. Minor offences and conflicts within a cell are mediated by the *abunzi*. Previous studies demonstrated that land-related conflicts were the most numerous among the cases brought to the *abunzi*. There are primarily two patterns in the nature of land conflicts in rural Rwanda.

The most frequently observable land conflicts are those among family members. As the most important livelihood asset, land is a sensitive issue for an overwhelming number of rural inhabitants, thereby readily leading to disputes among them. Inheritance is the most common cause of land disputes between various family members (Lankhorst and Veldman 2009: 29). In the context of a general land shortage, disputes tend to be triggered by intricate family relations, caused mainly by complex conjugality such as polygamy, unofficial marriage, and changes of spouses due to divorce or death. Further exacerbating the land disputes are the new claims to land being made by women according to the 1999 inheritance law upholding women's land rights.

The massive return of old-case refugees has been another important cause of land conflicts. Two different patterns have been found in this kind of land conflict. The first derived directly from land sharing. It is easy to imagine how this radical policy, ordering a transfer of half of the land property to the old-case returnees, has provoked discontent among the new-case returnees. The second pattern occurs between inhabitants and old-case returnees who went back to their family land. Although the majority of the old-case returnees acquired land through land sharing, and therefore stayed in areas where land was relatively abundant, some of them went back to their family land, where they had lived before the 'Social Revolution'. Their claims to land rights in their birthplaces have been recognised because the provision of the Arusha peace agreement that limited the period of claims to ten years became invalid following the victory of the RPF in the civil war. As a result, many landowners were obliged to give their land back to the old-case returnees, even if the former had received certificates from the local authorities at the time of acquisition.

The guidance on restitution, which was given through local authorities, was as follows: 1) if the actual owner does not live on the site claimed by an old-case returnee, and if he/she possesses land elsewhere, the entirety of the claimed land should be given to the returnee; 2) if the actual owner lives on the claimed land, and if he possesses land elsewhere, the claimed land should be given to the returnee – except the house and its surroundings; 3) if the actual owner lives on the claimed land, and if he has no land elsewhere, the land should be equally divided between both parties. This guidance is well known throughout the country.[36] Only a fraction of the old-case returnees have so far decided to go back to their original villages, because of concerns about the high population density in rural Rwanda and possible conflicts with the new inhabitants. Nonetheless, this has also caused a lot of disputes against the backdrop of general land scarcity.

Land disputes that do not come to the surface

In spite of the radical measures such as land sharing and restitution, the number of land conflicts relating to old-case returnees has recently been reduced in the justice mechanism. It is becoming more unusual for people to bring these disputes to the *abunzi* or the courts. As land sharing has been legally authorised, those who have given up half of their property have no chance of winning their case against old-case returnees. Rwanda's conflict resolution mechanisms are well organised in a hierarchical way. A person who wishes to resolve a conflict is first required to consult with a chief of *umudugudu* (the lowest administrative unit). A number of conflicts, particularly minor problems such as quarrels about boundaries, tend to be mediated at this level. The next step is the executive secretary in the cell, who deals with conflicts that cannot be mediated by the *umudugudu* chief. A case will be sent to the *abunzi* only when mediation by the administrative line does not work. In a similar vein, a case will be sent to the local court only when the *abunzi* cannot succeed through mediation. While this hierarchical system of conflict resolution has the merit of alleviating the burden at the higher level by filtering the cases, it can prevent a number of dissenting voices from entering the official judicial mechanism.

People usually accept land sharing, and only bring matters to the *abunzi* when they feel additional injustice.[37] The situation is the same with claims raised by the old-case returnees who go back to their family lands. Once the disputed land has been recognised by the authority as the claimant's family land, it should be returned to them in line with the official guidelines. Consequently, land conflicts regarding old-case returnees have not been numerous at the level of the conflict resolution mechanisms, including the *abunzi*, and recently the number has considerably reduced.[38]

However, this does not necessarily mean that people have completely given up their claims and accepted the division. Rather, they think it is unlikely that the claim will be upheld under the current regime. In post-war Rwanda, where a number of social groups had to renounce adequate compensation for the damage done,[39] requests for reparation for shared land have been prevented from being expressed. In any case, under the current RPF rule, making protests against government policies involves political risks. In addition, improvements in living conditions resulting from donors' active assistance, particularly in the education and health sectors, as well as from the recent economic boom, may have contributed to soothing the discontent. When we asked new-case returnees for their opinions about land sharing and land registration, the interviewees often told us 'we have no choice'. Obviously, they harbour bitter resentment against the loss of their properties and its formalisation through registration,[40] but there is nowhere for them to express these feelings. Through not being brought before justice mechanisms or expressed overtly, this discontent has tended to turn into resignation and remains unresolved among new-case returnees.

Conclusion

Land policies in post-conflict Rwanda have had various effects on land tenure security. With regard to land sharing, their consequences have been contrasting for the old-case returnees and the original inhabitants (or the new-case returnees), as the policies provided land for the former while depriving the latter of a part of their own property. As to the land consolidation introduced after the NLP and OLL, the effects of the policy have been different between large and small (subsistence-level) landholders. The former benefit from the opportunity to increase production for market by using ameliorated seeds and fertilisers, while the latter may feel that their land tenure security is threatened and that their freedom of choice over land use is restricted.

It is not surprising that the policies have different effects on different social groups. However, where a policy is concerned with land tenure security in conflict-affected situations, measures for protecting those who suffer its disadvantageous effects should be carefully considered, because the consequences might be politically dangerous. The case of land sharing is a typical example. Ordering the original inhabitants to give up half of their properties to returnees was certainly a radical measure. However, considering that the old-case refugees had been repeatedly refused the right of return by the previous regimes, some policy intervention was inevitable for securing their land rights. In a situation where their original family lands had been occupied and redistributed during their absence, a Bosnian-type total restitution would be much more complicated and would be likely to provoke social unrest. In this regard, land sharing in the relatively land-abundant areas might be seen as a realistic compromise. While the necessity for intervention should be fully recognised, the fact that its effects were entirely disadvantageous for the original inhabitants should be remembered. The political discontent that land sharing may have created should be borne in mind, not only because it has done serious damage to the livelihood of those who lost their properties, but also because its implementation has strong ethnic implications: Tutsi returnees were provided with lands from Hutu inhabitants. The overlap between economic and ethnic issues may create serious political danger in the Rwandan context.[41]

Rwanda has a long history, in which land tenure security has been continuously threatened by political power. Since pre-colonial times, the state has intervened in the distribution of land for the purpose of providing resources for its own interests, namely for families, friends, favourites, entourage and clients. Such arbitrary distribution provoked discontent among those whose rights were infringed, and invited a backlash each time there was a significant shift in political power. In other words, arbitrary state intervention in land ended up reproducing land tenure insecurity through political instability.

It is important that the vicious cycle of the past be broken. The land sharing in the late 1990s was a major intervention by the state. The government might legitimise this as a necessary redress for landless people who had experienced 'the wrongful and unjust dispossession of land by the pre-1994 regimes' (Republic of Rwanda 2004: 27). In post-war Rwanda, old-case returnees and women, who had previously been deprived of land rights, were officially provided with them. Extending the scope of land rights should be appreciated from the viewpoint of equity. Addressing the abovementioned discontent, however, is critical in order to sustain these positive changes.

The danger of social unrest might not seem imminent, as the discontent has not been loudly expressed. However, the reduction of cases in the *abunzi* or the courts does not mean that the resentment has abated. To avert possible danger, offering help to those who have lost their property through land sharing and other land appropriations would be effective. Although compensation for land sharing was legally denied, other measures for addressing their plight should be envisaged. The land distribution programme carried out in 2008 in the Eastern Province was an attempt that deserved credit in this sense. Huge ranches occupied by military officers in the chaotic period in the immediate aftermath of the civil war were divided into small plots and distributed to small farmers and stockbreeders. This redistribution programme was warmly welcomed by inhabitants. While redistribution for small-scale farmers should have been emphasised, the basic idea of the programme should be appreciated.[42]

There is also ample room for reconsidering the policy of land consolidation. Promoting rational land use for the increase of market production is an important policy, but forceful methods of bringing this about should be avoided. As the provision of ameliorated seeds and fertilisers gives a strong incentive to farmers, coercive land consolidation could be deemed not only unnecessary but also counterproductive, as it might provoke anger among the population. In particular, the possible negative effects for subsistence-level farmers should be addressed. Measures to help this vulnerable social group will also be necessary, as land registration will promote the concentration of land holdings through purchase and land rental markets. In contrast with the strict limit on land division, there is no restriction on land accumulation. While the Gini coefficient in land holdings in Rwanda has significantly increased,[43] registration is likely to accelerate the concentration of land holdings. Preparing safety nets for those who lose their land and move to the towns is vitally important. The increasing numbers of the population whose land tenure rights have been undermined could provoke political unrest through the mobilisation of widespread discontent.

It is undeniable that Rwanda has made remarkable progress since the end of the civil war, with its high economic growth and social stability. At the same time, it is also undeniable that the majority of people have not forgotten the war. In short, the country is still in the process of peacebuilding. With regard to the process of post-conflict statebuilding, it has been argued that not only state capacity, but also state legitimacy in the eyes of ordinary people, will be needed for the prevention of conflict and political instability (Manning and Trzeciak-Duval 2010). In having significant influence over the population, land policy is deeply concerned with the legitimacy of the state (OECD 2010). Measures to assist those who have suffered from the disadvantageous effects of policies will contribute to the enhancement of state legitimacy and therefore sustainable peace.

Notes

1 There is a voluminous literature on ethnicity in Rwanda, as the topic has been one of the most researched areas (Vidal 1969; Newbury 1988). Because of constraints of space, we confine ourselves to providing the minimum information necessary for understanding the current situation. The Rwandan population is composed of three ethnic groups: Hutu, Tutsi and Twa. The Hutu are the majority – having more than 80 per cent of the total population – and the Tutsi are the minority, while the Twa are an extremely small group, with only one per cent of the population. The three groups share the same language (Kinyarwanda) and religion, and they live mixed across the country. The ethnic divide was particularly widened in the colonial period, and political mobilisation on ethnicity has repeatedly resulted in serious violence, including the 1994 genocide.
2 The 'cell' refers to the smallest administrative unit, containing at least one salaried official (an executive secretary). There are more than 2,000 cells all over the country. Several cells compose a sector, of which there are more than 400 in the country, and these are further aggregated into districts. There is a total of 30 districts. A province, composed of several districts, is the largest local unit. Officials in local administration are basically nominated by the government. Mayors (the heads of districts) are elected from among the members of district councils, which are composed of representatives from administrative as well as societal groups.
3 Our research has consistently focused on local dynamics, with special attention to land. Continual visits to two cells and conversations every year with the same interviewees have contributed to improve the reliability of responses. We believe that this method of 'fixed point observation' is useful and appropriate for reflecting the relationship between politics and land – something which is profoundly linked to the everyday lives of the Rwandan people. The two research sites were selected by taking their differences – regarding their historical experiences in terms of refugees and returnees, as well as their geographic characteristics – into consideration. Eastern Rwanda saw a massive return of Tutsi refugees following the RPF's victory in the civil war, while the southern part of the country did not have such a massive inflow of returnees. In addition, due to the difference of geographical conditions, the population density is much higher in the southern part than in eastern Rwanda. While land issues have been the

focus of concern, our interviews with inhabitants have generally been quite free and non-structured. With regard to our methodology, see also Takeuchi and Marara (2005; 2011).

4 For the understanding of land conflicts, the authors collected data on *abunzi* (the local mechanism for dispute resolution) in the two canvassed cells. On the basis of documents written by *abunzi*, we collected additional information on each case through interviews with the president of the *abunzi* committees. The numbers of collected cases are as follows: in Cell B, 127 cases that were brought to *abunzi* between January 2007 and November 2008; in Cell R, 39 cases between September 2008 and January 2009 and 77 cases between December 2010 and September 2012.

5 For information about the traditional Rwandan land tenure system, see Reisdorff (1952), Adriaenssens (1962), André and Lavigne Delville (1998) and Vansina (2001).

6 Notice that Vansina avoids the term '*igikingi*' (2001: 168, n. 22).

7 For a detailed description of Rwanda's land tenure systems and their transformation during the colonial period, see Reisdorff (1952) and Adriaenssens (1962).

8 For a detailed analysis of the 'Social Revolution', see Lemarchand (1970) and Reyntjens (1985). This term has been used mainly by Hutu elites because it imparts 'progressive' connotations to the event: a transition away from feudalism – that is, rule by a minority, towards democratic rule by the majority. Tutsi elites, by contrast, have tended to construe the event as the 'first massacre of Tutsi' (see, for example, the official website of the government of Rwanda). In this chapter, therefore, the term is used in quotation marks.

9 Refugee statistics are referenced from Lemarchand (1970: 172), Reyntjens (1985: 455) and Prunier (1995: 62).

10 An outflow of Tutsi refugees took place once again in 1973, when, following the previous year's mass slaughter of Hutu in Burundi, the politically weakened Kayibanda regime carried out a campaign against the Tutsis.

11 Under the one-party system, local officials were acting as leaders of the ruling parties, namely PARMEHUTU and MRND (*Mouvement révolutionnaire national pour le développement*), under the presidency of Kaybanda and Habyarimana, respectively.

12 The decree dated 11 July 1960 categorised Rwandan territory as areas for customary land laws (mainly rural areas) and those for statutory laws (mainly urban areas). Normally, lands in the customary areas were to be distributed in accordance with the intentions of families and lineages, but the Burgomasters had the ultimate right and responsibility for the areas. A 'commune' was a unit of local administration established at the time of independence after the lowest unit of administration in the colonial period, the 'sub-chiefdom', had been abolished. In 2001 they were reorganised through administrative reform into districts.

13 The Arusha peace agreement stipulated that 'refugees who left the country more than 10 years ago should not reclaim their properties, which might have been occupied by other people' (Protocol of Agreement on the repatriation of Rwandese refugees and the resettlement of displaced persons, Article 4). Following the victory of the RPF in the civil war, however, this accord was abandoned.

14 For details of the Rwandan civil war and genocide, see, for example, Prunier (1995), Jones (2001) and Melvern (2004).

15 The Rwandan population in 1938 was estimated to be 1,888,890 (Everaerts 1939: 375).

16 An 'agricultural household' refers to a household 'where at least one member was engaged in any of the following: agricultural activities, livestock, fisheries, forestry or bee-keeping' (Republic of Rwanda 2010: 9).

17 While extended-family members have basically lost control over land distribution, they have often interfered in the issue. In fact, an objection from one of the family members against the selling of family land is still one of the commonest causes of land disputes (Takeuchi and Marara 2011).

18 Returnees statistics are referenced from Huggins (2009: 69), Bruce (2009: 112) and Office of United Nations Resident Coordinator for Rwanda (2000: 2).

19 The Organic Land Law adopted in 2005 legalised land sharing and exempted it from compensation (Article 87). Ministerial Order No. 001/16.01 of 26/04/2010 (Ministerial Order determining the modalities of land sharing) also determined the detail of the procedure and again denied compensation.

20 Villagisation has been a favourite policy of the RPF since the war. During the peace negotiation in Arusha, the 'RPF delegates were adamant that the new homes must be built in "villages"' (HRW 2001: 7).

21 In a cell, the executive secretary is almost the sole official, receiving a regular salary from the government. He or she is therefore considered to be a delegate of the state in local communities.

22 Our observation in Cell B in September 2012.

23 Organic Law No. 08/2005 of 14/07/2005 determining the use and management of land in Rwanda.

24 Law No. 22/99 of 12/11/1999 to supplement book I of the Civil Code and to institute part five regarding matrimonial regimes, liberalities and successions. O.G. no. 22 of 15/11/1999. Its article 50 stipulates that 'all legitimate children of the *de cujus*, in accordance with civil laws, inherit in equal parts without any discrimination; between male and female children'.

25 In principle, all sons have equal inheritance rights.

26 In addition to the inheritance law in 1999, equal rights for women were confirmed in the OLL (Article 4).

27 The pilot studies of land registration were carried out in 2007 and 2008. See Ali *et al.* (2011) for detail. Ministerial Order No. 002/2008 of 01/4/2008 stipulated the modalities of land registration.

28 'Swamps that may be productive in terms of agriculture' are included in the 'Private state owned land' (OLL, Article 14), though the existent agricultural land use was basically admitted. On this basis, cultivation of designated crops (namely, land consolidation) has been imposed.

29 For the land registration and the system of land administration, see Sagashya and English (2010) and Sagashya (2012).

30 During field research in the Southern Province in September and October 2012, we verified the certificates possessed by canvassed households and found a number of plots registered under the name of the late family head. In many cases, it was the name of the father of the current household head.

31 While two decades have passed since the end of the civil war, around 100,000 Rwandans continue to live outside the country. In spite of the UNHCR's recommendation that their refugee status be discontinued, many African countries still consider that protection is necessary. See IRIN (2013).

32 In the registration procedure, disputed lands are registered separately and their certificates would not be issued until the problem had been resolved. According to the deputy Director-General of the Rwanda National Resource Authority, the number of disputed plots was 5,145 as of June 2011 – less than one per cent of the total number of registered plots (about 6.3 million) at that time (interview 16 August 2011). While a number of factors might have contributed to this, without doubt the registration of family land in the name of a late family head was an important factor.

33 In the case of swamps, the property rights belong to the state; people only have rights for land use. Land consolidation does not expropriate land, but restricts the rights for land use.

34 The examples showed that, in the context of the general land shortage, socially vulnerable people such as orphans and children of illegally married parents were gradually excluded from land tenure, and that disputes over inheritance opposing a father and sons were severely exacerbated (André and Platteau 1996: 28–33).

35 See Organic Law no. 31/2006 of 14/08/2006.

36 Interview conducted with a sector chief in Cell B area on 16 August 2002. (At that time, the area, which was equivalent to current Cell B, constituted a sector.)

37 The following examples from our *abunzi* case file concern land conflicts caused by land sharing: objection against double acquisition through land sharing (a young, unmarried, old-case returnee benefited from land sharing, while his parent had already acquired some plots in another place); objection against the sale of shared land (plots acquired through land sharing were once not permitted to be sold). In these cases, both judgements were favourable to old-case returnees: double acquisition and the sale of shared land were authorised.

38 According to our data, disputes with old-case returnees were as follows: five among 127 cases in Cell B between January 2007 and November 2008; five among 39 cases in Cell R between September 2008 and January 2009; one among 77 cases in Cell R between December 2010 and September 2012.

39 Even the reparation for the genocide survivors, the most seriously affected people from the civil war, has been insufficient. On this point, see Gahima (2013: 174–75).

40 Among our interviewees in Cell R, we have often encountered this kind of feeling. The following are three examples. 1) An old-case returnee expressed his anxiety about his neighbour, who held considerable resentment against him because of land sharing. 2) A new-case returnee, who had provided half of his lands for an old-case returnee, suddenly wanted to revise the border of the divided lands when registration started. 3) A dissenting voice was raised at an explanatory meeting for land registration. A man, whose land had been appropriated by the local authority for the construction of houses for old-case returnees (*imidugudu*), requested that his land be restored on the occasion of land registration. This was not discontent against land registration per se, but against past land appropriation.

41 On this point, see debates regarding horizontal inequalities (Stewart 2008; Takeuchi, 2013).

42 See, for example, *New Times* (2008), as well as Economist Intelligence Unit (2008). According to the Director of the Land Office in the District of Kayonza (Eastern Province), an area of more than 11,000 hectares in the former Akagera National Park was redistributed for 14,616 families (authors' interview on 12 February 2010). Redistribution in favour of cattle keepers seemed to take precedence over that for farmers. In the case of the District of Kayonza, 2,768 cattle keepers benefited from the programme, while the number of farmers who benefited was only 540. From the viewpoint of poverty reduction, the main target of the programme should be farmers rather than cattle keepers, as those who own cattle in Rwanda are relatively rich. For the land distribution programme, see also Huggins (2012).

43 Rwanda's Gini coefficient in 2000 was 0.468, a considerable increase from 0.289 in the mid-1980s (UNDP 2006; 2007); it further increased to 0.510 in 2006 (Government of Rwanda 2007: 13).

References

Adelman, H., 2003, 'The use and abuse of refugees in Zaire', in *Refugee Manipulation: War, Politics, and the Abuse of Human Suffering*, ed. S.J. Stedman and F. Tanner, Washington, DC: Brookings Institution Press, 95–134.

Adriaenssens, J., 1962, *Le Droit foncier au Rwanda*, mimeo.

Ali, D.A., Deininger, K. and Goldstein, M., 2011, 'Environmental and Gender Impacts of Land Tenure Regularization in Africa: Pilot Evidence from Rwanda', Policy Research Working Paper 5765, The World Bank, Washington, DC.

André, C. and Platteau, J.-P., 1996, 'Land tenure under unendurable stress: Rwanda caught in the Malthusian trap', *Cahiers de la Faculté des Sciences Economiques et Sociales*, 164: 1–49.

André, C. and Lavigne Delville, P., 1998, 'Changements fonciers et dynamiques agraires: le Rwanda, 1900–1990', in *Quelles politiques foncières pour l'Afrique rurale? Réconcilier pratiques, légitimité et légalité*, ed. P. Lavigne Delville, Paris: Karthala, 157–82.

Ansoms, A., 2009, 'Re-engineering rural society: the visions and ambitions of the Rwandan elite', *African Affairs*, 108(431): 289–309.

Berry, S., 1989, 'Social institutions and access to resources', *Africa*, 59(1): 41–55.

Bigagaza, J., Abong, C. and Mukarubuga, C., 2002, 'Land scarcity, distribution and conflict in Rwanda', in *Scarcity and Surfeit: The Ecology of Africa's Conflict*, ed. J. Lind and K. Sturman, Pretoria: African Centre for Technology Studies & Institute for Security Studies, 51–82.

Blarel, B., 1994, 'Tenure security and agricultural production under land scarcity: the case of Rwanda', in *Searching for Land Tenure Security in Africa*, ed. J.W. Bruce and S.E. Migot-Adholla, Dubuque, IA: Kendall/Hunt Publishing Company, 71–95.

Bruce, J.W., 2009, 'International standards, improvisation and the role of international humanitarian organizations in the return of land in post-conflict Rwanda', in *Uncharted Territory: Land, Conflict and Humanitarian Action*, ed. S. Pantuliano, Rugby: Practical Action Publishing, 109–31.

Economist Intelligence Unit, 2008, 'The political scene: the president oversees land redistribution under a new law', *The Economist*, 1 May: 13–14.

Everaerts, E., 1939, 'Monographie agricole du Ruanda – Urundi', *Bulletin Agricole du Congo Belge*, 30(3): 343–96; (4): 581–618.

Gahima, G., 2013, *Transitional Justice in Rwanda: Accountability for Atrocity*, Abingdon: Routledge.

Government of Rwanda, 2007, *Economic Development and Poverty Reduction Strategy, 2008–2012*, Kigali.

——2012, 'The provisional results of the 4th population and housing census of Rwanda as of "census night", August 15th 2012, give a total resident population of 10,537,222 people', media release, Government of the Republic of Rwanda, available online at www.gov.rw/The-provisional-results-of-the-4th-Population-and-Housing-Census-of-Rwanda-as-of-census-night-August-15th-2012-give-a-total-resident-population-of-10-537-222-people?lang=en (accessed 24 January 2013).

Hilhorst, D. and Van Leeuwen, M., 2000, 'Emergency and development: the case of *imidugudu*, villagization in Rwanda', *Journal of Refugee Studies*, 13(3): 264–80.

HRW (Human Rights Watch), 1999, *'Leave None to Tell the Story': Genocide in Rwanda*, New York.

——2001, *Uprooting the Rural Poor in Rwanda*, New York.

Huggins, C., 2009, 'Land in return, reintegration and recovery processes: some lessons from the Great Lakes Region of Africa', in *Uncharted Territory: Land, Conflict and Humanitarian Action*, ed. S. Pantuliano, Rugby: Practical Action Publishing, 67–93.

——2012, 'The presidential land commission: undermining land law reform', in *Remaking Rwanda: State Building and Human Rights after Mass Violence*, ed. S. Straus and L. Waldorf, Madison, WI: University of Wisconsin Press, 252–65.

Ingelaere, B., 2010, 'Peasants, power and ethnicity: a bottom-up perspective on Rwanda's political transition', *African Affairs*, 109(435): 273–393.

IRIN, 2013, 'No consensus on implementation of cessation clause for Rwandan refugees', 12 July 2013, available online at www.irinnews.org/report/98409/no-consensus-on-implementation-of-cessation-clause-for-rwandan-refugees (accessed 13 July 2013).

Jones, B.D., 2001, *Peacemaking in Rwanda: The Dynamics of Failure*, Boulder, CO: Lynne Rienner.

Lankhorst, M. and Veldman, M., 2009, 'La proximité de la justice au Rwanda: rapport socio-juridique sur les modes de gestion des conflits fonciers', RCN Justice & Démocratie, Bruxelles.

Lavigne Delville, P., 1998, 'La sécurisation de l'accès aux ressources: par le titre ou l'inscription dans la communauté?', in *Quelles politiques foncières pour l'Afrique rurale? Réconcilier pratiques, légitimité et légalité*, ed. P. Lavigne Delville, Paris: Karthala, 76–86.

Leegwater, M., 2011, 'Sharing scarcity: issues of land tenure in south-east Rwanda', in *Natural Resources and Local Livelihoods in the Great Lakes Region of Africa: A Political Economy Perspective*, ed. A. Ansoms and S. Marysse, Basingstoke: Palgrave Macmillan, 104–22.

Lemarchand, R., 1970, *Rwanda and Burundi*, London: Pall Mall Press.

Mamdani, M., 2001, *When Victims become Killers: Colonialism, Nativism, and the Genocide in Rwanda*, Princeton, NJ: Princeton University Press.

Manning, R. and Trzeciak-Duval, A., 2010, 'Situation of fragility and conflict: aid policies and beyond', *Conflict, Security, and Development*, 10(1): 103–31.

Melvern, L., 2004, *Conspiracy to Murder: The Rwandan Genocide*, London: Verso.

Musahara, H. and Huggins, C., 2005, 'Land reform, land scarcity and post-conflict reconstruction: a case study of Rwanda', in *From the Ground Up: Land Rights, Conflict and Peace in Sub-Saharan Africa*, ed. C. Huggins and J. Clover, Pretoria: Institute for Security Studies, 269–346.

New Times, 2008, 'Kagame winds up land re-distribution launch', 31 January, available online at www.newtimes.co.rw/news/views/article_print.php?13426&a=3857&icon=Print (accessed 1 February 2008).

——2013, 'Land office issues 8.4 million titles', 19 August, available online at www.newtimes.co.rw/news/index.php?i=15454&a=69652 (accessed 19 August 2013).

Newbury, C., 1988, *The Cohesion of Oppression: Clientship and Ethnicity in Rwanda, 1860–1960*, New York: Columbia University Press.

——2012, 'High modernism at the ground level: the *imidugudu* policy in Rwanda', in *Remaking Rwanda: State Building and Human Rights after Mass Violence*, ed. S. Straus and L. Waldorf, Madison, WI: University of Wisconsin Press, 223–39.

Nkurikiyimfura, J.-N., 1994, *Le gros bétail et la société rwandaise, évolution historique: dès XIIe–XIVe siècles à 1958*, Paris: L'Harmattan.

North, D.C., 1981, *Structure and Change in Economic History*, New York: W.W. Norton.

OECD, 2010, *The State's Legitimacy in Fragile Situations: Unpacking Complexity*, Paris: OECD.

Office of United Nations Resident Coordinator for Rwanda, 2000, 'Common country assessment papers', no. 3 (Resettlement & Reintegration), Office of United Nations Resident Coordinator for Rwanda, Kigali.

Payne, G., 2011, 'Land issues in the Rwanda's post-conflict law reform', in *Local Case Studies in African Land Law*, ed. R. Home, Pretoria: Pretoria University Law Press, 21–38.

Place, F., Roth, M. and Hazel, P., 1994, 'Land tenure security and agricultural performance in Africa: overview of research methodology', in *Searching for Land Tenure Security in Africa*, ed. J.W. Bruce and S.E. Migot-Adholla, Dubuque, IA: Kendall/Hunt Publishing Company, 15–39.

Pottier, J., 2006, 'Land reform for peace? Rwanda's 2005 land law in context', *Journal of Agrarian Change*, 6(4): 509–37.

Prunier, G., 1995, *The Rwanda Crisis: History of a Genocide, 1959–1994*, London: Hurst.

Reisdorff, I., 1952, *Enquêtes foncières au Ruanda*, mimeo.

Republic of Rwanda, 2004, *National Land Policy*, Kigali.

——2010, *National Agricultural Survey 2008*, Kigali.

Republique rwandaise, 1991, *Recensement général de la population et de l'habitat au 15 août 1991*, Kigali.

——2003, *Recensement général de la population et de l'habitat Rwanda: 16–30 août 2002, Rapport sur les résultats préliminaires*, Kigali.

Reyntjens, F., 1985, *Pouvoir et droit au Rwanda: droit public et évolution politique, 1916–1973*, Tervuren: Musée Royal de l'Afrique Centrale.

Rose, L.L., 2007, 'Land and genocide: exploring the connections with Rwanda's prisoners and prison officials', *Journal of Genocide Research*, 9(1): 49–69.

Sagashya, D., 2012, 'Rwanda: reforming land administration to enhance the investment environment', in *Untying the Land Knot: Making Equitable, Efficient, and Sustainable Use of Industrial and Commercial Land*, ed. X. Shen and X. Sun, Washington, DC: World Bank, 57–69.

Sagashya, D. and English, C., 2010, 'Designing and establishing a land administration system for Rwanda: technical and economic analysis', in *Innovations in Land Rights Recognition, Administration, and Governance*, ed. K. Deininger, C. Augustinus, S. Enemark and P. Munro-Faure, Washington, DC: World Bank, 44–67.

Stewart, F., 2008, 'Horizontal inequalities and conflict: an introduction and some hypotheses', in *Horizontal Inequalities and Conflict: Understanding Group Violence in Multiethnic Societies*, ed. F. Stewart, New York: Palgrave, 3–24.

Takeuchi, S., 2013, '"Twin countries" with contrasting institutions: post-conflict state-building in Rwanda and Burundi', in *Preventing Violent Conflict in Africa: Inequalities, Perceptions and Institutions*, ed. Y. Mine, F. Stewart, S. Fukuda-Parr and T. Mkandawire, London: Palgrave, 40–65.

Takeuchi, S. and Marara, J., 2000, *Agriculture and Peasants in Rwanda: A Preliminary Report*, Tokyo: Institute of Developing Economies.

——2005, 'Returnees in their homelands: land problems in Rwanda after the civil war', in *Displacement Risks in Africa: Refugees, Resettlers and their Host Population*, ed. I. Ohta and Y.D. Gebre, Kyoto: Kyoto University Press, 162–91.

——2011, 'Features of land conflicts in post-civil war Rwanda', *African Studies Monographs*, Supplementary Issue, 42: 119–35.

UNDP, 2006, *Human Development Report 2006*, New York.

——2007, *Turning Vision 2020 into Reality: From Recovery to Sustainable Human Development, National Human Development Report, Rwanda 2007*, Kigali: UNDP Rwanda.

USAID, 2011, 'USAID country profile, property rights and resource governance, Rwanda', available online at http://usaidlandtenure.net/sites/default/files/country-profiles/full-reports/USAID_Land_Tenure_Rwanda_Profile.pdf (accessed 23 August 2013).

Van Hoyweghen, S., 1999, 'The urgency of land and agrarian reform in Rwanda', *African Affairs*, 98(392): 353–72.

Vansina, J., 2001, *Le Rwanda ancien: le royaume nyiginya*, Paris: Karthala.

Vidal, C., 1969, 'Le Rwanda des anthropologues ou le fétichisme de la vache', *Cahiers d'études africaines*, 9(3): 384–401.

Wyss, K., 2006, 'A thousand hills for 9 million people: land reform in Rwanda: restoration of feudal order or genuine transformation?', working paper, 1/2006, Bern: Swisspeace.

5 Dealing with land problems in post-conflict Burundi

Sylvestre Ndayirukiye and Shinichi Takeuchi

Since long before the end of the protracted civil war, it was widely recognised that land would be one of the most crucial issues for the peace process in Burundi. A surge in land conflicts after the end of the civil war was foreseeable, as huge numbers of refugees had stayed in neighbouring countries for so long and their original properties had been occupied by others during their absence. Confrontations between returnees and present (secondary) occupants were anticipated once peace had been established and the refugees had returned (ICG 2003). The refugee influx and its impact on land was therefore one of the central concerns of the peace negotiations. In addition, many agreed that land problems in Burundi were by no means confined to those related to returnees. Insecurity over land rights, fundamentally caused by land shortages, was widely observed in the country, which is densely populated and heavily dependent on agriculture. There was a general consensus that discussion over a new land policy and a new land law had to start as soon as the war was over.

Against this backdrop, a number of policy measures on land have been taken in the post-civil war period. Concrete arrangements for securing the land and property rights of returnees and internally displaced persons (IDPs) were put in the peace agreement in 2000 (the Arusha peace agreement).[1] The international community, including the United Nations and donors, has helped the Burundian government tackle the problem. Thus, from the outset, land issues constituted one of the important pillars among the activities of the Peacebuilding Commission (UN 2007). In addition, the government adopted a new land policy in 2009[2] and, on this basis, enacted the revised land law in 2011.[3] Land has been one of the top priorities in the Burundian peacebuilding process – at least officially.

Despite the measures taken and efforts made, Burundian society still suffers from land conflicts. More than a decade after the conclusion of the peace agreement, disputes and conflicts about land have been far from alleviated. To tackle these problems, it is indispensable to understand the nature of land conflicts, their background, measures taken to prevent them, and their consequences. For the purpose of examining the conditions for the alleviation of land and property problems in Burundi, this chapter aims at deepening these understandings. Analyses of land problems will also illuminate the background to the recent violent clash that took place over the restitution of houses,[4] as that clash constitutes a part of today's complex land and property problems in the country.

The next section provides information about the main reasons behind Burundian land conflicts, focusing particularly on the history of repeated violence and social transformation since colonial times. Following this, the pattern of current land disputes will be presented on the basis of our field surveys. Finally, policy measures taken to alleviate land disputes will be analysed to evaluate their effects and challenges.

This chapter is based on previous literature and on field research that was mainly conducted from 2010 to 2013. During the field survey, interviews with political authorities were conducted for background information, and various examples of land disputes were collected from the three provinces of Makamba, Bururi and Gitega (see Figure 5.1).[5] Although the amount of data is limited, they provide important information about concrete examples of local land disputes, some of which will be referred to in the following discussion.

The main background to Burundian land problems

Like other conflict-affected countries, Burundi has various types of land disputes, whose causes are manifold but are often closely related to each other. Previous literature has pointed to a wide range of factors as reasons for Burundian land conflicts, including massive displacement caused by armed conflicts, arbitrary distribution of state land, weakened traditional authority and lack of capacity in local courts.[6] This section provides concise information about the background of Burundian land problems, particularly focusing on past armed conflicts and the historical transformation of social settings.

Repeated armed conflicts and the peace process

In Burundian history, massive displacements have repeatedly taken place as a result of large-scale violence and armed conflicts. Two incidents were particularly important as precursors to the present land conflicts. The first was the bloody repression of Hutu in 1972; the second was the indiscriminate persecution and killing of Tutsi in 1993.[7] Ethnicity has been manipulated and mobilised by political elites for the sake of their power struggle. Although the Tutsi–Hutu divide in Burundi was not as pronounced at the end of the colonial period as it was in neighbouring Rwanda, it quickly widened following the assassination of the charismatic leader L. Rwagasore, and, in particular, following political developments in Rwanda.[8] Political confusion following the aborted coup in 1965 resulted in the rise of new Tutsi elites centred upon the army, which arrested and executed a number of Hutu leaders accused of plotting the coup, and took over political power through the dethronement of the *mwami* (king).[9]

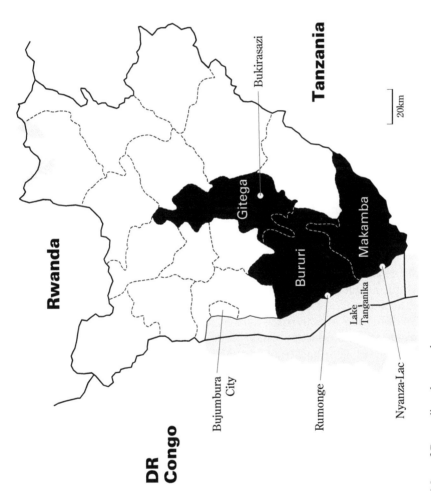

Figure 5.1 Map of Burundi and research areas

In 1972, in response to a Hutu invasion of the southern part of the country and the capital, as well as to the killing of Tutsi civilians, the army carried out brutal reprisals through the wholesale slaughter of Hutu civilians throughout the territory. The number of victims was enormous, though the total is difficult to determine accurately. According to Lemarchand, 'some conservative estimates put the total number of lives lost at one hundred thousand, others at two hundred thousand' (1994: 100). In the chaos, a large number of displaced people fled to neighbouring countries, in particular Tanzania. The refugee flows were most notable in the southern regions, which were heavily affected by the violence. It was estimated that 150,000–200,000 Burundians escaped the country in fear of mass slaughter.[10] The majority of them stayed in refugee camps for the following three decades, and began to repatriate only after the conclusion of the Arusha peace agreement in 2000. According to the UNHCR, the total number of returnees between 2000 and 2011 amounted to 548,720.[11] This number accounts for around 7 per cent of the total population (8,053,574) in 2008 (République du Burundi 2011: 4).

Another massive population displacement occurred in 1993 as the result of a further eruption of violence. In June 1993, in the wave of multi-party democracy that swept through post-Cold War Africa, Burundi saw its first ever free and fair presidential election. As a result, a Hutu, M. Ndadaye, was elected as president. However, only four months later he was assassinated by the military, which feared his possible radical reforms. Because of the indignation among the Hutu provoked by the assassination, and at the instigation of Hutu politicians, Tutsis were killed and persecuted by their neighbours, causing their exodus to camps for IDPs. Circumstances have improved little since then. While 281,628 IDPs resided in 229 camps in 2002, the number in 2009 was 157,167 in 137 camps (Rwabahungu and Nintunze 2009: 9).[12] It should also be remembered that, during the civil war in the 1990s, a lot of Hutu inhabitants were obliged to leave their villages because of attacks by the military.

Following the Arusha peace agreement, a power-sharing system based on ethnicity was introduced (Vandeginste 2009; Takeuchi 2013). The ethnic proportions of Tutsi and Hutu in public institutions was strictly defined, thus making the composition of institutions such as the cabinet, state and local administration, parliament, senate, military, police and political parties mixed in terms of ethnicity and gender. However, in spite of this apparent mingling, the basic power structures of the political parties have not changed. The core of the former Hutu rebels and the current ruling party, *Conseil national pour la défense de la démocratie–Forces pour la défense de la démocratie* (CNDD-FDD), remains a small group of Hutu men. The situation is the same for the former sole political party, *Parti de l'Union et du progrès national* (UPRONA) – now one of the opposition parties – whose real power is in the hands of a few Tutsi men. In the post-civil war political process, the CNDD-FDD has reinforced, on the basis of electoral victories, its political control over public institutions including national and local administrations,[13] which have a critical influence on land governance. As we will see later, the extension of political influence over public institutions has undermined people's confidence in them, particularly in the case of conflict resolution mechanisms.

Limit of the traditional land tenure system

As Van Leeuwen (2010) emphasises, displacement is by no means the only factor behind the land problems in Burundi. Most of the land disputes brought to the courts are not directly related to displacement. Rather, they tend to derive from disagreements with regard to rights to customary land among family members and neighbours (Kohlhagen 2011a). The rapid population increase is one of the most fundamental factors behind such land disputes. While the total population of Burundi was 4,031,420 in 1979 and 5,292,793 in 1990 (République du Burundi 2009b: 17), it exceeded 8 million in 2008, and reached 9.85 million in 2012 (*World Development Indicators*). The urbanisation rate has been gradually increasing, though the level still remains low: it was only 11 per cent in 2011.[14] In 2011 the population density per square kilometre of 16 rural provinces varied from 116.5 in Cankuzo to 474.7 in Kayanza. It tended to be high in the central highlands in the northern and central parts of the country, where the centre of the traditional kingdom was located, and relatively low in areas bordering the Democratic Republic of the Congo and Tanzania (République du Burundi 2011: 21). In spite of the variation, the general feeling of there being a land shortage is today quite real all over the country.[15]

As the traditional order of land governance wanes, population growth is likely to increase land disputes. In the pre-colonial kingdom of Burundi, the *mwami* was at the centre of the land tenure system, which denied exclusive land rights for individuals. Ideologically, all land in Burundi belonged to the *mwami*, and land plots (*itongo*) for each family's subsistence farming were recognised and distributed through the kingdom's hierarchical lines, including chiefs and sub-chiefs. Although this meant that a family's *itongo* could be taken by superiors at any time, it would be an exaggeration to say that they believed that their land rights were persistently unstable. It is safe to say that, in pre-colonial times, Burundians regarded the land tenure system, which was closely connected with the kingdom's political order, as reasonably legitimate.

This legitimacy, however, began to be undermined under European rule, particularly that of the Belgian mandate, granted by the League of Nations after the First World War. The Belgian administration actively intervened in the kingdom's political order, including its land tenure system. By dividing Burundian land into three categories, the colonial authority deprived the *mwami* of the 'state lands' (*terres domaniales*), which were directly managed by the Belgian administration, and of the registered privately owned lands, which were exclusively for Europeans. As a result, the *mwami*'s authority was confined to the 'indigenous lands' (*terres indigènes*). Policies undertaken by the Belgian administration triggered drastic social changes, including population growth,[16] the development of a market economy and a power shift among the political elites,[17] thus bringing about a surge of land disputes that were difficult to manage under the traditional system of land governance. Obviously, these changes destabilised the legitimacy of the traditional land tenure system. In fact, the individualisation of the *itongo* was widely observed in the late colonial period (Kohlhagen 2007: 116–18). At this stage, however, it was evident that land governance still depended fundamentally on the *mwami*-centred political order. After independence, the traditional land tenure system suffered further blows, with chiefdom being abolished in 1960 and finally the *mwami* being dethroned in 1966.[18] Although the new military-based authority did not make fundamental revisions to land governance, the ending of the monarchy resulted in an enlargement of the role of the administrative authorities, particularly that of the chief of the commune.

The decline of the traditional political order also undermined the existing conflict resolution system. Since pre-colonial times, Burundian society has had an ethical system called *bushingantahe*, which constitutes the ideological foundation of the indigenous legal/moral institution. Along with the hierarchical political order in the kingdom – namely the *mwami*, chiefs and sub-chiefs – the *bushingantahe* (that is, individual *bushingantahe* figures) played an important role in conflict resolution.[19] However, manipulation of their status for political purposes began under the Belgian administration, which intervened in judicial affairs and even supplanted their roles after the Second World War: all newly appointed officials were invested as *bushingantahe* (Laely 1997: 707). After independence and the dethronement of the king, the social position of the *bushingantahe* was integrated into the one-party system, which subordinated them to the authority of the party (Laely 1992). As is clearly shown by the recent repeated changes regarding their legal status,[20] this social position has been continually utilised and manipulated for political purposes. Although the idea of *bushingantahe* is widely recognised and respected in Burundian rural communities (Kohlhagen 2009; 2010a), the political manipulation has seriously damaged confidence in the *bushingantahe* individuals. Although they still play an important role in mediating small, everyday disputes, the capacity of the institution is too limited to shoulder the burden of dealing with current land disputes.

Patterns of land disputes

While a variety of factors contributed to the outbreak of land disputes in Burundi, several patterns can be identified. Two criteria are useful to distinguish various disputes. First, disputes are distinguishable according to whether they derive directly from the previous armed conflicts. Another distinction is whether the dispute is concerned more with competition over land rights per se than with their execution and/or enforcement. On the one hand, in a case where various parties are in dispute over a plot, each of them claiming their own rights to it, the dispute is concerned primarily with competition over rights. On the other hand, in a case where obstacles prevent the owner of a plot from exerting land rights, even if the ownership is legally clear, the dispute is concerned primarily with the execution of rights. Following these two criteria of distinction, four types of land disputes are distinguishable. As the purpose of this categorisation is to elucidate the nature of disputes over land in post-conflict Burundi, the four patterns should not be deemed to be distinctly separate from each other; rather, their boundaries are often so blurred that a land dispute may straddle multiple types.

Land disputes directly related to past armed conflicts

In the context of current peacebuilding in Burundi, the land-related disputes that have attracted the closest attention are those caused by the massive numbers of returning refugees. In particular, the return of refugees who had fled Burundi as a result of the events of 1972 has created a huge number of land disputes. Following the conclusion of the Arusha peace agreement in 2000, the 1972 refugees began to return to their homeland and found the secondary occupants (stayees)[21] on their properties. Among the stayees, some had remained in their home village in spite of the turmoil in the 1970s and 1990s; others came to the area in response to government calls or were just seeking opportunities to acquire land. In fact, after the exodus in 1972 the government encouraged immigration into the affected areas in the southern part of Burundi. As a consequence, a lot of people settled in the *imbo* (the lowland area on the shore of Lake Tanganyika) and in the regions bordering Tanzania, which, until recently, had been sparsely populated (Ndayirukiye 1986). A considerable number of immigrants were attracted from the neighbouring highlands, particularly from the interior regions of the provinces of Bururi and Gitega, which were near to the vacant areas and had suffered from land-scarcity because of the mountainous landscape and high population density. While no statistical data are available, it is likely that many Tutsis who had lived in the highlands poured into the vacant areas, as they often had close connections during that period with the local administration, which urgently called for migration. This population movement later resulted in the eruption of a vast number of land disputes in these regions.

Land disputes became markedly complicated in the southern *imbo*, namely in the Rumonge and Nyanza-Lac areas, where immigration was accelerated by state interventions, and in particular as a result of the palm oil development programme, which had the most serious impact of the state interventions.[22] In the mid-1980s the government launched a development project implemented by a local company, *Société régionale de développement du Rumonge* (SRD),[23] which appropriated huge amounts of land to convert into oil palm plantations and distributed them to the settlers. This appropriation of land during the absence of the original owners, and the redistribution of it to the settlers, has made land disputes between returnees and stayees extremely complicated (RCN Justice et Démocratie 2004; Kohlhagen 2011b).

Our interviews, which were carried out in the collines near the town of Rumonge, demonstrated a deep divide between returnees and stayees. On the one hand, returnees generally accused stayees of stealing their lands, and were grieved at their loss of property. On the other hand, stayees refused the division of their plots in favour of returnees, and claimed fair compensation in cases of land division. In this area, although the stayees were a sizeable minority among the population, they were more organised than the returnees and created an association to protect their rights. They expressed deep dissatisfaction with the interventions of the CNTB (*Commission nationale des terres et autres biens*), the national commission in charge of mediating land and property disputes resulting from past armed conflicts, claiming that its intervention policy prioritised returnees without taking stayees' rights into consideration. Germain[24] was one of the stayees who created the association. He expressed considerable anger against the CNTB, which had ruled that he provide half of his land for returnees, without compensation. According to him, the decision was totally unacceptable, as the settlers (that is, the stayees) had paid a lot of money for the purchase, as well as for the improvement of their lands. For this reason, they had sent an open letter to the president of the republic, P. Nkurunziza, condemning the CNTB and asking for compensation.[25] In this case, claims to property rights clearly involve competition among different actors.

Land problems arise even if the legitimate rights holders are obvious. In Burundi, there are cases in which legitimate rights holders cannot safely use their own lands because of the continuing effects of the civil war. A typical example is the difficulties that people living in the IDP camps are facing. As a result of the violence in 1993, a huge number of people have to live in IDP camps. In many cases, IDPs reside in camps located near to their home villages, which they visit to cultivate their own fields. Because of security concerns, they prefer to live in the camps rather than returning to their villages. Their land rights in their villages are not contested, mainly because they undertake regular visits, but they are clearly restricted by the danger of harassment and persecution. This is a particularly serious problem for displaced women, many of whom lost family members in 1993.

The case of Annie, a Tutsi woman with whom we conducted an interview in a colline of Bukirasazi Commune (Province of Gitega), is a typical example.[26] She was born in 1972 and lost most of her family members, including both her parents and six siblings, in the massacre in 1993. After staying in a military camp in the Commune of Makebuko, she has resided in an IDP camp in Bukirasazi since 1999. For the purpose of cultivating her land, she regularly visits her home village, which is located two-and-a-half hours' walk from the camp. This is not only a laborious but also a dangerous task. She has often been harassed when visiting her fields in her home village, where a number of the inhabitants do not hide their hostility towards Tutsi. People have cast aspersions on her, and she once only narrowly escaped rape. Moreover, agricultural produce has often been stolen from her fields, as she is unable to keep watch on them. In short, although nobody has legally contested her land rights, she has enormous difficulty in protecting them.

Land disputes independent from past armed conflicts

Huge numbers of current land disputes in Burundi have no direct connection with past armed conflicts. These disputes are most likely to emerge between family members and neighbours, and regard such issues as inheritance, purchase, property boundaries and the distribution of community properties. Behind the disputes lie politico-legal as well as social factors. While the rapid population growth and complex family relations (exacerbated by the practice of polygamy) have been significant contributing factors in the outbreak of these kinds of disputes, the fact that land rights have never been appropriately secured by the state should be emphasised. Despite the degradation of the traditional land tenure system, Burundi's statutory laws have provided only vague definitions and protection for lands under customary tenure, as we will see in the following section. According to a systematic analysis of the documents in local courts (*tribunaux de résidence*) in Burundi, more than 70 per cent of the cases were related to land; more than 40 per cent had arisen between family members; and one-quarter were concerned with inheritance (Kohlhagen 2011a). Although the importance of the land problems caused by returnees should not be underestimated,[27] it is beyond doubt that land disputes between family and community members are ubiquitous in Burundi.

A typical case involves Florence, a woman living in a colline in the Commune of Gitega (Province of Gitega).[28] According to her explanation, an unknown woman visited her one day and claimed a part of her family land, insisting that she was a grand-daughter of Florence's mother-in-law, who had already died. As neither she nor her husband had any knowledge of the woman, the couple brought the matter to *bashingantahe*. Their recommendation was to divide the family land in half and give half to the woman, but Florence's husband rejected the proposal. Several years later, after her husband had died, the unknown woman again came to Florence and claimed her land. Florence brought the matter to the local court, which also adjudicated that the family land should be divided in half. Although Florence appealed the case, the decision of the High Court (*Tribunal de grande instance*) was the same. She finally brought the case to the Supreme Court, and the case was still under examination as of September 2012. As this example shows, many land disputes arise against the backdrop of a lack of clearly defined ownership, as well as complex kin relationships.

Another example of this kind was the case of Jean, who claimed his rights over former state land.[29] Jean lived in the Commune of Bururi (Province of

Bururi), and in 1984, with the permission of the commune administrator, acquired an area of state land for planting trees. In 1991 the local authority gave an adjoining plot to a neighbour for afforestation. However, the neighbour later encroached into Jean's plot, claiming that the commune allowed him to use all of the state land in the area. Although Jean brought the matter to court, he lost successive cases. He believed that he lost the cases because the neighbour had an informal connection with the court judges through his wife, who was a judge. At the time of our interview, the case was being examined by the Supreme Court. As this case indicates, arbitrary distributions of state land, carried out on the basis of decisions by the commune administrators, have often created disputes between inhabitants, and people generally distrust the courts because of widespread corruption.

The execution of land rights can be problematic not only for residents of the IDP camps, like Annie, but also for ordinary citizens who have encountered these kinds of difficulties regarding court judgements. Even if the ownership of a plot is legally established in the courts, enforcement of the decision can face considerable obstacles. Part of the problem derives from material shortages. For example, lack of transport has constituted a significant obstacle to the execution of judgements on land disputes.[30] Difficulties also stem from people's strong disagreement with court decisions. A number of illegal acts, including the removal of boundary markers, and verbal (and even physical) attacks against judges, have been reported (Kohlhagen 2007: 51–56).

The fundamental reason for all this is a profound distrust of the judicial sector in general. It has been pointed out that the Burundian justice sector has suffered from a number of problems. The backlog of cases is very serious: as a huge number of disputes have been brought to the courts, the process takes a long time and accrues considerable costs.[31] Corruption is another headache in this sector. Although part of the problem stems from necessary expenditures such as transportation costs,[32] the perception that mediators and judges are corrupt is widespread, leading to people contesting the decision when they lose a case on the grounds of alleged corruption. Such an attitude will further damage the legitimacy of the judicial system. In short, the Burundian judicial sector faces enormous difficulties in building up public confidence regarding its decisions. We will see that the CNTB is no exception.

Although land disputes directly related to past armed conflicts have so far attracted the closest attention at national as well as international levels, they are only a part of the problem. The displacements have exacerbated disputes in the social arena, in which a huge number of land disputes have erupted independently of factors related to the previous civil wars. Reasons for the latter include population increase, land shortage, ambiguous land rights in customary tenure and a general distrust of judicial mechanisms. In order to alleviate land disputes caused by armed conflicts, therefore, addressing factors that are independent of armed conflicts will be indispensable.

Policy responses and challenges

A number of policy measures have so far been implemented in post-conflict Burundi for the purpose of alleviating land-related problems. This section examines two types of policy measures directly focusing on land problems. First, policies strengthening land rights for those who are most vulnerable will be analysed. The focus of the analysis is particularly on attempts to secure land rights for returned refugees and land users under customary tenure. Second, the activities of the CNTB, a specialised conflict resolution mechanism for land and property problems deriving from previous civil wars, will be examined.

Securing land rights

The Arusha peace agreement included progressive provisions with respect to the rights of refugees and IDPs. Related settlements can be found in Protocol IV of the agreement. Article 2 recognised the basic principles of this matter, and guaranteed the right of all refugees and IDPs to return to their homes (a, f)[33] as well as the rights to their property (e, g). Issues relating to land and other property were dealt with in Article 8, which guaranteed not only the property rights of refugees and IDPs (a), but also their rights to recover the property (b), rights to compensation if recovery was impossible (c), and rights to compensation as well as indemnification in cases of expropriation (a, d). Although the conclusion of the Arusha peace agreement came about 5 years earlier than the adoption of the Pinheiro Principles (UN 2005), the former had ensured land and property rights for refugees and IDPs, in line with the latter. While this represented laudable progress, one caveat was that it would be technically and politically very difficult to carry out a Bosnian-type total restitution in Burundi. This issue would come to the surface when the CNTB changed its policy with regard to restitution.

The provisions of the peace agreement were not sufficient to guarantee the security of returnees' land and property rights, particularly when the concrete facts about what was to be protected or recovered were not clear. In fact, for the overwhelming majority of Burundians, land rights have never been established with definite demarcation. In general, displaced people, who fled the country in 1972 or 1993, did not have clearly demarcated land rights, thus making restitution very difficult.[34] In fact, Article 8 of the Arusha peace agreement ensured that 'a series of measures shall be taken in order to avoid subsequent disputes over land, including the establishment of a register of rural land ... and ... the conduct of a cadastral survey of rural land' (g), and that 'Burundi's Land Act [sic] must be revised in order to adjust it to the current problems' (i). In short, the agreement recognised that protection and restitution of the rights of refugees and IDPs could not be ensured without establishing well-demarcated land rights in rural areas, and that reform of the land law had to be carried out for this purpose.

The legal framework for land governance in Burundi was based on the system introduced under the Belgian administration in the first half of the twentieth century. After independence, state dominance over land considerably increased as a result of the integration of the 'indigenous lands' into the 'state lands' by the decree of 11 July 1960, and the dethronement of *mwami* in 1966. Consequently, officials in the local administration, particularly the commune administrators,[35] gained significant power regarding land distribution. Although the land law adopted in 1986 – the first land law in Burundi – recognised and protected the rights of customary tenure,[36] the provisions produced no discernible effects.

This ineffectiveness may be attributable to at least two problems inherent in the 1986 land law. First, there was ambiguity about which areas were to be protected under the name of customary rights. Although the law considered 'effectively exploited rural lands' to be the subject of 'exclusive customary rights' (*droits privatifs coutumiers*) in Article 330, what constituted the 'effectively exploited rural lands' was not clear. While a fallow field was acknowledged as usage of customary land (Article 332), the difference between this and wasteland (*les biens fonciers vacants et sans maître*), which the law stipulated as belonging to the state (Article 231), has never been evident. Consequently, how land was dealt with depended mainly on the discretion of local officials. Being endowed with the central role in the process of land registration,[37] it was mainly the commune administrators who made decisions about which areas were to be classified as customary lands. A lot of land disputes have derived from dubious land distributions carried out by heads of communes, as in the case of Jean in the previous section.

Second, for the protection of customary land rights, the law proposed no effective method other than registration, which was conducted by the national registrar of land titles (*Conservateur des titres fonciers*). As no detailed definition of customary lands was provided in the law, virtually any land could be expropriated by the state if it was considered wasteland, the only exception being land that was registered and provided with title. Nevertheless, since the official process of land registration is so complicated and costly for ordinary people, registered lands have remained the exception to date.[38]

Although revision of the 1986 land law began to be discussed soon after its enactment (Kohlhagen 2010b: 68), it was only in June 2009 that the new land policy was adopted (République du Burundi 2009a), and in August 2011 that the revised land law was promulgated. While it is too early to evaluate its full effects, we can examine what was reformed in relation to the above-mentioned drawbacks of the 1986 land law.

On the one hand, aiming to improve access to land registration for rural inhabitants, the revised law decentralised the system of land governance. In addition to the land titles issued by the registrar, the revised law created a new type of land title delivered by the commune-level land department, the *Service foncier communal*. While the former was called *titre foncier* (land title), the latter was labelled *certificat foncier* (land certificate), which would be delivered by a simplified process based on local adjudication.[39] The decentralisation of the land title authority, introduced following the example of Madagascar,[40] is supposed to improve the land tenure security of rural inhabitants. In spite of the simplified delivery process, the revised land law ensures a land certificate that exercises 'all the judicial acts', including onerous and free transfer, inheritance, short-term and long-term lease, and mortgage (Article 408).[41] In addition, a land certificate can be converted into a land title in accordance with due process (Article 410).

On the other hand, the distinction between customary land and wasteland remains unclear in the revised law. In fact, the definition of land that could be the subject of 'exclusive customary rights' has not changed substantially.[42] This means that the commune administrators still play a crucial role in land governance under the new system. In fact, they are in charge of the core functions regarding the issuing of land certificates, including the organisation of local adjudication and judgement regarding eligibility. Customary land rights therefore still remain open to abuses by state officials. Although one of the outstanding reforms in the 2011 law was to prohibit commune administrators from issuing land certificates for themselves, their spouses, their parents and their children (Article 407),[43] the effect of this regulation is as yet uncertain.

Whether this attempt will bring success or not is difficult to predict at this stage, but it is undoubtedly a positive step for enforcing land tenure security. With donors' assistance,[44] some significant developments, including the active participation of inhabitants, have been reported in areas under the pilot project (Munezero and Gihugu 2012). Two additional remarks can be made with regard to the new land law. First, it is not clear whether due consideration has been given to particularly vulnerable groups such as families headed by women and Twa, who have been virtually alienated from land holding in Burundi.[45] Second, providing land certificates for a substantial part of the population will take a long time. Unlike systematic land registration, the provision of title deeds takes much longer, as people have to apply by themselves.[46] What is evident is that the enactment of the revised law will not automatically alleviate complex land disputes in Burundi.

Addressing land disputes

Another important policy measure to address the surge of land disputes was the establishment of the CNTB, which originated from a provision in the Arusha peace agreement.[47] While it originally stipulated the establishment of an organisation with the mandate of assisting the return of refugees and IDPs – the National Commission for the Rehabilitation of *Sinistrés* (CNRS) – the CNRS changed its name in 2006 to the CNTB. The main mission of the organisation is to settle disputes related to land and other properties with relation exclusively to *sinistrés* – those who had been deprived of their properties as a result of the 'tragic events that the country has experienced after independence'.[48] The CNTB was provided with the power of mediation in local land disputes.[49] If one of the parties contests the decision, he or she has the right to lodge an appeal to the CNTB's national-level *ad hoc* sub-commission for appeals. If the decision of the sub-commission is still unacceptable to one of the parties, the case can be brought to court.

However, this option has become increasingly unavailable. As a result of the amendment made in 2009, the CNTB was provided with the legal capacity to execute its own orders without waiting for the court's decisions.[50] This means that the CNTB's decisions are binding for the concerned parties. The CNTB's authority was further strengthened by the revision of the law made in 2011, as authority for supervising the CNTB was transferred from the Office of the First Vice-President to the Office of the President.[51]

During the period between August 2006 (when the CNTB was established) and December 2011, 26,899 cases were registered throughout the country (République du Burundi n.d. (a): 39). Out of 17 provinces, a particularly high number of conflicts were registered in Makamba and Bururi. With 7,883 and 6,467 cases, respectively, the number of registered land conflicts in these two provinces accounted for more than half of the total. Obviously, the registered land conflicts have been concentrated on the areas most affected by the political turmoil of 1972, meaning that the return of the 1972 refugees has caused a huge number of land conflicts. Of 26,899 cases, 15,004 (56 per cent) were resolved – either by mutual understanding (43 per cent) or following the decision of the CNTB (13 per cent); 2,264 cases were closed by the process of the CNTB and were moved on to the court; and 9,631 cases remained unresolved. A comparison between these figures and those of the previous year's annual report shows a sharp increase in land conflicts during 2011: the number of registered land conflict cases rose 31 per cent for the year.[52]

One of the reasons for the recent rise in land conflicts was the acceleration of refugee return. The 1972 refugees started their return just after the conclusion of the Arusha peace agreement, but the numbers rocketed in the late 2000s following a change in Tanzania's refugee policy. Under the *ujamaa* policy, the government of Tanzania settled the Burundian 1972 refugees in planned villages (often called the 'Old Settlements') in Ulyankulu in Tabora Region and in Katumba and Mishamo in Rukwa Region, and provided each settled family with about five to ten hectares of land.[53] However, against the backdrop of recent political developments in Burundi, the Tanzanian government decided to close the Old Settlements. Under the provisions of the Tanzania Comprehensive Solutions Strategy, drawn up with the assistance of the UNHCR in 2007, Burundian refugees in the Old Settlements were asked to choose either repatriation to their homeland or naturalisation as Tanzanians.[54] Following this process, 53,600 refugees returned to Burundi in 2008 and 2009. Many of these returnees have been engaged in land disputes, thus sharply increasing the number of registered cases in the CNTB. The surge of registered land conflicts may result in a serious backlog.[55]

A more fundamental challenge for the CNTB is to preserve political neutrality. Since the installation of the current president of the CNTB, Mgr. S. Bambonanire, in April 2011,[56] the agency has increasingly been considered to be under the influence of the current ruling party, the CNDD-FDD. Opposition parties, such as UPRONA, and civil societies have repeatedly blamed the new president, who has had personal experience as a refugee following the political turmoil in 1972,[57] for his biased stance in favour of returnees.[58] It is widely recognised that the CNTB has changed its policies since the inauguration of the new president, causing serious issues of bias on the ground. The clash on 28 May 2013 in the Ngagara area of the capital was one of the consequences. This was a clash between the police, carrying out a decision of the CNTB, and those who opposed the decision. The decision was to entirely remove occupants from housing belonging to the 1972 refugees. Some of the occupants claimed compensation, arguing that they had bought the houses without any information about the original owners. However, compensation was refused.[59]

The CNTB's policy change has had an enormous impact in rural areas. While dividing land in half between two disputing parties had been the basic mediation principle under the previous president,[60] this has been revised since the installation of the new president, who has clearly stated that the principle of equal division has been 'abolished'.[61] At the local level, the CNTB has recently tended to recommend a division of one-third for the stayee and two-thirds for the returnee.[62] The impact of this policy change has been tremendous, since it has fuelled speculation. People have begun to believe the CNTB is pro-returnee, and this has markedly influenced their behaviour. On the one hand, some returnees are taking a firm stand against stayees, and even asking for a revision of previous decisions to divide the land in half. On the other hand, many stayees, expressing their dissatisfaction and fear about the policy change, have had their confidence in the CNTB undermined.

Following consecutive amendments to the law, the CNTB has been provided with the power of adjudication and execution, and therefore is capable of delivering decisions rapidly and executing them effectively. Through exercising this power, it would be possible to reduce the backlog in a short timeframe. However, in this case, the friction caused by the policy would be considerable, and might provoke serious social unrest. As clearly shown in the fierce reaction of UPRONA, debates about the CNTB have evidently assumed a political character. In post-conflict Burundi, it has often been pointed out that the ruling CNDD-FDD has established control over public institutions in general through legal as well as illegal means (ICG 2011; HRW 2010). Burundians understand the CNTB's recent change under President Bambonanire in this context.

Conclusion

In alleviating Burundian land and property problems, the government, as well as the international community, has a daunting task. From a middle- to long-term perspective, it is critical to ensure land rights under customary tenure. While policy measures for this purpose have already been adopted, they still remain in their infancy. In particular, the provision of land certificates should be accelerated, as this contributes to securing land rights for the majority of the population. Moreover, policies to ensure land rights for the most vulnerable groups, such as families headed by women and Twa, should be promoted, as no effective measures have been taken. The most fundamental question concerns how problems caused by the rapid population increase and land shortages should be tackled. The answers to these difficult questions need to be sought in a wide range of policy fields including industrial development, urban policy and job creation.

While thinking about long-term policies is of course important, the actual situation is so critical that Burundi is obliged to deal immediately with the eruption of land and property disputes. Clearly, the country has not sufficiently succeeded in alleviating these. Although policy interventions to strengthen conflict resolution mechanisms cannot address the root causes of land disputes, the ineffectiveness of the judicial sector aggravates the fragile, post-conflict peace. It creates widespread distrust among the population – not only of the justice sector, but also of the government in general. As Kohlhagen (2009: 65) has stated, Burundi has seen a 'general crisis of conflict management'.

The establishment of the CNTB has not been sufficient to curb this tendency. Rather, it may add the further risk of the politicisation of judicial institutions. In changing its stance in favour of returnees, the role of the CNTB has become increasingly problematic. In a post-conflict situation, where it is difficult to find satisfactory solutions for all, concerned parties are obliged to give up the chase for total victory, and find acceptable compromises. One of the most important functions of conflict resolution mechanisms is to help in finding such compromises, which are often not easy to locate. If the CNTB is considered to be under the influence of a particular political party, confidence in its decision-making abilities will be seriously damaged.

In fact, because of the lack of effective policy interventions to alleviate land and property disputes, hostility between conflicting parties has been exacerbated. Violence has already erupted. The above-mentioned case in Ngagara was not an isolated one. For example, hostility between displaced people living in the IDP camp in Ruhororo (Province of Ngozi), and those who live in the surrounding areas, has resulted in several attacks on both groups. In November 2012 five people were seriously injured.[63] Similar clashes may break out in other areas. We should remember that the violence increasingly tends to be of an ethnic nature. In Ngagara, it was Tutsi youngsters who resisted the police. In Ruhororo, Tutsi IDPs were the target of violence. In many areas, the conflicts between returnees and stayees have the same character, as the 1972 refugees are almost all Hutu and a significant proportion of the stayees are Tutsi.

In politically as well as ethnically complicated situations such as post-conflict Burundi, policies have to strike a balance. As shown in the Pinheiro

Principles, the rights of returnees have been focused on in current discussions on post-conflict land problems. This was an important step forward, but at the same time the basic human rights of all concerned parties, both returnees and stayees, should be ensured in cases of political intervention. Although the CNTB has ardently advocated the securing of returnees' rights, the Burundian government has so far taken no substantial measure to resolve the problems that IDPs are confronting. Pursuing one-sided justice under the name of conflict resolution may bring political benefit to particular parties, but it will never succeed in establishing a durable peace.

Notes

1 Arusha peace and reconciliation agreement for Burundi, Protocol IV, chapter I.
2 République du Burundi (2009a). Regarding the process for adopting the land policy, see Kohlhagen (2010b: 91–97).
3 *Loi no.1/13 du 9 août 2011 portant révision du code foncier du Burundi.*
4 On 28 May 2013, a violent clash broke out between police carrying out eviction orders and the inhabitants of the Ngagara area in Bujumbura. See, for example, *Ibujumbura* 2013, 'Affrontements à Ngagara, alors que la CNTB entend récupérer une maison "vendue" en 1972', 28 May, available online at www.ibujumbura.net/ 2013/05/28/affrontements-ngagara-alors-que-la-cntb-entend-rcuprer-une-maison-vendue-en-1972/ (accessed 26 July 2013).
5 A province is the largest local administrative unit in Burundi. It contains several communes, each of which is composed of several collines: the smallest administrative unit. Of the three provinces, Makamba and Bururi were chosen because the areas have seen a huge number of land disputes caused by refugee returns. Gitega was selected for comparison with the two other provinces. In January 2012, rough data on the land disputes of 270 household heads were collected through structured interviews. In September 2012, the authors visited eight of the 27 collines to conduct semi-structured interviews with around 90 inhabitants. 270 interviewees were selected through the following three stages: 1) three communes were chosen among each of the three above-mentioned provinces (Makamba, Bururi and Gitega); 2) three collines were randomly chosen among each of the nine selected communes; 3) ten household heads were chosen out of each of the 27 selected collines. For the selection of interviewees, we used the snowball sampling method (Cohen and Arieli 2011). With the assistance of chiefs of collines, we made contact with household heads that had any land-related disputes.
6 For an overview of land problems in Burundi, see, for example, RCN Justice et Démocratie (2004; 2006) and Kohlhagen (2007).
7 Space is not available to explain in detail the Burundian ethnic groups. The minimum information necessary for understanding the current situation is that the Burundian population is composed of three ethnic groups: Hutu, Tutsi and Twa. The Hutu are the majority, accounting for more than 80 per cent of the total population, and the Tutsi are the minority; the Twa are an extremely small group, accounting for only one per cent of the population. The three groups share the same language (Kirundi) and the same religion, and have lived in multi-ethnic groups throughout the country. As is the case in Rwanda, the ethnic divide significantly widened during the colonial period. See, for example, Chrétien (1985) and Newbury (2001) for details.
8 The collapse of the Tutsi-centred political regime in Rwanda, which took place in the relatively short period between 1959 and 1961 – often called the 'Social

Revolution' – had a decisive impact on Burundi. For this process, see Lemarchand (1970) and the chapter on Rwanda (Chapter 4).

9 The Burundian Tutsi are not a monolithic group. Traditionally, political power was concentrated within members of the royal family, called *baganwa*. After independence, the turmoil caused by the aborted coup brought about the rise of a Tutsi group based in the army, which resulted in the overthrowing of the monarchy in 1966. The new Tutsi elites came from the Bururi region, from which three consecutive presidents (Micombero, Bagaza and Buyoya) originated. This group, however, had been excluded from power in the pre-colonial kingdom, in which the *baganwa* held most of the power. See Lemarchand (1970).

10 Lemarchand (1994: 104) estimated the number of Burundian refugees who fled after the events of 1972 to be 'approximately 150,000', while another organisation stated the number to be 200,000 (Clark 1987, cited in Sommers 2001: 37).

11 Authors' calculation from *UNHCR Global Reports*.

12 The number accounted for around 2 per cent of the total population in 2008.

13 Among major posts in local administration (province–commune–colline), governors of provinces are politically designated; members of communal councils and chiefs of collines are elected through universal suffrage; and chiefs of communes are nominated from among members of communal councils by the national electoral commission (*Commission électorale nationale indépendante*) in accordance with the constitutional arrangement, in which 'neither of the principal ethnic groups must be represented beyond 67 per cent of the Commune administrators in total at the national level' (Republic of Burundi, The Constitution of the Republic of Burundi, 2005, Article 266).

14 The rate was 6 per cent in 1990. Statistics from the *World Development Indicators*, available online at http://data.worldbank.org/data-catalog/world-development-indicators (accessed 4 August 2013).

15 Burundian population per sq km of arable land reached 828 persons in 2008 (calculated in World Bank 2011). This would be another important factor in stressing the awareness of shortages.

16 Colonial policies on hygiene as well as food security resulted in rapid population growth.

17 As a result of the policy reforms, the power of the chiefs and sub-chiefs was considerably reinforced, thereby intensifying their intervention in land affairs. See Gahama (2001: 313–15) for details.

18 Today, there is no outstanding voice advocating the revival of the Burundian kingdom.

19 For the *bashingantahe* and their historical transformation, see Laely (1992; 1997), Kohlhagen (2010a) and Naniwe-Kaburahe (2008).

20 In the course of the long civil war in the 1990s, the role of *bashingantahe* attracted attention for its potential capacity to reconcile groups in the conflict-affected society. In this context, the Arusha peace agreement called for the installation of the *Conseil des ubushingantahe* [*sic*] in the legal system (Protocol II, Article 9, Section 8). However, the idea of institutionalising the indigenous conflict resolution mechanism was abandoned in the constitution adopted in 2005. See Kohlhagen (2010a: 27–28) for details.

21 The term 'stayees' is hereinafter used, following Fransen and Kuschminder (2012). The term is close to the kirundi term *abasangwa*, which literally means 'those who were found by returnees living on their property'.

22 Although space constraints preclude detailed explanations, other state interventions including the *paysannat* (a policy distributing land plots for fostering small-scale farmers) have also contributed to the complication of land disputes. For the policy of *paysannat* and its effects on land, see, for example, RCN Justice et Démocratie (2004; 2006) and Kohlhagen (2010b).

23 The SRD was later replaced by the Office de l'Huile de Palme (OHP).

24 In this chapter, pseudonyms are used for the interviewees.

25 Interviewed on 12 September 2012. However, Mr S. Ngendakuriyo, the vice-president of the CNTB, rejected the possibility of compensation due to financial constraints (interview, 24 September 2012).

26 The interview was held on 16 September 2012.

27 The same research demonstrated that the proportion of cases related to returnees was less than four per cent. As the author himself explained (Kohlhagen 2011a: 72), however, the statistics did not reflect the seriousness of the returnee-related land disputes, which have been primarily dealt with by the CNTB.

28 Interviewed on 21 September 2012.

29 Interviewed on 13 September 2012.

30 Recently, material conditions have gradually improved, as some local courts have been provided with motorcycles. There is, however, ample room to further improve conditions.

31 According to Kohlhagen (2009: 28–30), the main reason for the delay is that proceedings in the high courts and the Supreme Court tend to take a long time, and this is because of the enormous number of appeals. Too many cases have been appealed to the higher courts, as our cases of Florence and Jean indicate.

32 Judges often require transportation costs for on-the-scene investigations. See Kohlhagen (2009: 25–28) for more detail.

33 The indication '(a, f)' refers to the Sections of the Article, including the related contents.

34 In addition, the provisions of the 30-year rule have complicated restitution for the 1972 refugees, as both the 1986 Land Law (Article 29) and the 2011 Land Law (Article 22) have a positive prescription, which provides a property right for a bona fide owner who has occupied land for more than 30 years. However, the current president of the CNTB, Mgr. Bambonanire, stated his intention to not recognise the provision of the 30-year prescription for land disputes with regard to returnees. See *Burundimega-info*, 'Burundi: "Le partage équitable est une solution hypocrite"-Mgr Sérapion', 21 February 2012, available online at http://burundi-megainfo.blogspot.jp/2012/02/burundile-partage-equitable-est-une.html (accessed 3 August 2013).

35 Chiefdom and sub-chiefdom, the units of local administration under Belgian rule, were abolished just before independence and replaced by the province and commune, respectively.

36 The land law (*Loi portant code foncier du Burundi. 1 Septembre 1986 – No.1/008*) recognised the legal status of the land rights exercised in accordance with custom (Article 329).

37 For the powers granted to local administrators, see related articles of the 1986 land law regarding land registration for more detail – particularly section 2, chapter II, title IV.

38 Even in 2008, registered plots constituted only about one per cent of the total territory of Burundi. For the complexities and difficulties of land registration for ordinary people, see Kohlhagen (2011c: 85–88).

39 For the issue of a land certificate, checks on the situation and boundaries are required on the ground. A 'commission of recognition', which is installed at the colline level, is in charge of this. The commission, which is composed of local officials and notables, investigates and makes judgements about proposed land rights (Articles 393–96). Other processes for certificate application are generally more simple in comparison with those for the land title. The cost for delivery of the land certificate varies in accordance with the size of the land parcel, but on average it is around 5,000 Burundi francs (around US$3.3, as of August 2013). Interview with the director-general of the Ministry of Water, Environment, Land and City Planning on 12 August 2013.

40 In Madagascar, following the failure of the Torrens-model land registration, a new attempt has been made, since the enactment of the law in 2005, to deliver land certificates for customary tenure through land desks (*guichers fonciers*) installed in commune-level local administrations. Speedy and low-cost delivery of land certificates has so far been greatly appreciated. On this point, see Kohlhagen (2011c: 92–97).

41 In spite of this provision, the land certificate is not regarded as guaranteeing exactly the same rights as the land title. According to the director-general of the Ministry of Water, Environment, Land and City Planning, the land certificate may not be acceptable for mortgages, except where the amounts of money borrowed are small – through micro-finance, for example. Interviewed on 12 August 2013.

42 Comparing Article 381 of the 2011 land law with Article 331 of the 1986 land law indicates there was no substantial change.

43 In these cases, the head of the neighbouring commune takes responsibility.

44 European countries and organisations such as the European Union, Switzerland and Belgium have provided technical assistance for this project.

45 On this point, I would like to express my gratitude for the comments of Dr Gregory Myers. See also Kohlhagen (2010b: 72–74). Women's personal rights for land have never been clearly assured, either in statutory or customary laws in Burundi. Being engaged in non-agricultural activities including hunting and pottery in their traditional life, Twa people have been substantially excluded from land holdings.

46 Through systematic land registration, Rwanda has almost finished the entire process in about five years (2009–13). The swiftness of the process has been ensured by active international cooperation, particularly from the UK, as well as by the fact that the land law made registration obligatory (see Chapter 4). In the absence of these factors, it is uncertain how far the land certificate will spread to rural inhabitants in Burundi.

47 Arusha peace agreement, Protocol IV, chapter I, article 3.

48 *Loi No. 1/18 du 4 mai 2006 portant mission, composition, organisation et fonction-nement de la Commission nationale des terres et autre biens*, Article 2.

49 The CNTB has a branch office in each province. In the case of investigations on the ground, the branch office organises a team of several (four to seven) members, including members of the CNTB central office, and they work with representatives of the relevant commune and colline. Following several investigations, they make a decision regarding the mediation process.

50 Article 19 of the *Loi no.1/17 du 04 Septembre 2009 portant revision de la loi no.1/18 du 04 mai 2006 portant missions, composition, organisation et fonctionnement de la Commission nationale des terres et autres biens.*

51 Article 3 of the *Loi no.1/01 du 04 janvier 2011 portant revision de la loi no.1/17 du 04 septembre 2009 portant missions, composition, organisation et fonctionnement de la Commission nationale des terres et autres biens.*

52 The CNTB's annual report 2010 indicated the figures registered between 2006 and 2010. According to the report, the registered number of land conflicts was 20,494: 11,670 of those were settled, 1,379 cases were closed and 7,445 cases remained unsolved (République du Burundi n.d. (b): 42). Comparing this with the total number of registered conflicts in 2011 (26,899) shows that 6,405 cases were registered during the year 2011.

53 According to Milner (2009: 113), the cordial reception granted to the Burundian refugees was part of the *ujamaa* policy, which sought to intensify the productivity of peripheral areas through villagisation.

54 Of 218,234 Burundian refugees living in the Old Settlements, 75 per cent preferred naturalisation; 162,256 refugees were thus granted Tanzanian citizenship by April 2010 (Nordic Consulting Group 2010: 76). However, those who chose the naturalisation option were later informed that only 'permanent residence certificates', not full citizenship, would be provided, and they were required to leave the areas of the

Old Settlements. An official explanation for this relocation was that it followed the Tanzanian citizenship policy in place since the Nyerere era, which requested citizens to move from their home regions. Nevertheless, subsequently revealed information suggested that the decision might have been made under pressure from multinational corporations. AgriSol Energy LLC, an Iowa-based investment company specialising in agribusiness, had acquired land from three 'abandoned refugee camps' before the announcement of the relocation policy. See the Oakland Institute (2012) for details.

55 While the CNTB's backlog problem has not yet come to the fore, some of the interviewees complained that the commission undertook too few visits on the ground and that their progress was too slow. (An interview on 17 September 2012 with a man in a village near to Nyanza-Lac.)

56 Mgr. Bambonanire was nominated to the CNTB presidency following the death of the former president, Abbé A. Kana.

57 Interviewed on 25 July 2013.

58 For example, see @rib news, 'Burundi: Mgr Sérapion Bambonanire dans l'oeil du cyclone', 15 April 2012, available online at www.arib.info/index.php?option= com_content& task = view& id = 5065 (accessed 16 April 2012). On the other hand, Mgr Bambonanire condemned the activities of the CNTB during the incumbency of the former president for having been controlled by UPRONA (Niyonkuru 2012).

59 President Bambonanire justified the decision on the grounds that it would have been impossible for any Burundians to buy the houses without information about their original owners. In short, 'Burundians should know the history' (interviewed on 25 July 2013).

60 According to the previous president, Kana, the principle of division was as follows: if occupants of the land had legitimate certificates issued by the public authorities, the land would be divided equally; if occupants did not have such certificates, two-thirds of the land would be given to the returnees and one-third would be retained for the occupants – this in consideration of the fact that the occupants had taken care of the land for more than three decades (interviewed on 27 October 2010).

61 Interviewed on 25 July 2013.

62 Several interviewees in the provinces of Makamba and Bururi explained to us the policy change regarding land division. The vice-president of the CNTB also admitted the change (interview on 24 September 2012).

63 See, for example, COSOME (*Coalition de la société civile pour le monitoring électoral*), 2012, 'Regain de tension à Ruhororo entre les déplacés et les habitants des collines environnantes', available online at www.cosome.bi/spip.php?article1499 (accessed 11 February 2013).

References

Chrétien, J.-P., 1985, 'Hutu et Tutsi au Rwanda et au Burundi', in *Au coeur de l'ethnie: ethnie, tribalisme et état en Afrique*, ed. J.-L. Amselle and E. M'bokolo, Paris: La Découverte, 129–66.

Clark, L., 1987, *Country Reports on Five Key Asylum Countries in Eastern and Southern Africa*, Washington, DC: Refugee Policy Group.

Cohen, N. and Arieli, T., 2011, 'Field research in conflict management: methodological challenges and snowball sampling', *Journal of Peace Research*, 48(4): 423–35.

Fransen, S. and Kuschminder, K., 2012, 'Back to the land: the long-term challenges of refugee return and reintegration in Burundi', New Issues in Refugee Research, Research Paper, 242, UNHCR, Geneva.

Gahama, J., 2001, *Le Burundi sous administration belge*, 2nd edn, Paris: Karthala.

HRW (Human Rights Watch), 2010, *Burundi: Closing Doors? The Narrowing of Democratic Space in Burundi*, New York: Human Rights Watch.

ICG (International Crisis Group), 2003, 'Réfugiés et déplacés au Burundi: désamorcer la bombe foncière', Rapport afrique, 70, Nairobi/Brussels.

——2011, 'Burundi: du boycott électoral à l'impasse politique', Rapport afrique, 169, Nairobi/Brussels.

Kohlhagen, D., 2007, *Le Tribunal face au terrain: les problèmes d'execution des jugements au Mugamba dans une perspective juridique et anthropologique*, Bujumbura: RCN Justice et Démocratie.

——2009, *Burundi: La justice en milieu rural*, Bujumbura: RCN Justice et Démocratie.

——2010a, 'Les bashingantahe écartés de la loi: La place de la justice traditionnelle burundaise après la loi communale de 2010', in *L'Afrique des grands lacs: annuaire 2009–2010*, ed. S. Marysse, F. Reyntjens and S. Vandeginste, Paris: L'Harmattan, 19–32.

——2010b, 'Vers un nouveau code foncier au Burundi?', in *L'Afrique des grands lacs: annuaire 2009–2010*, ed. S. Marysse, F. Reyntjens and S. Vandeginste, Paris: L'Harmattan, 67–98.

——2011a, 'L'activité judiciaire au Burundi: données quantitatives', in *L'Afrique des grands lacs: annuaire 2010–2011*, ed. S. Marysse, F. Reyntjens and S. Vandeginste, Paris: L'Harmattan, 65–84.

——2011b, 'Conflits fonciers sur ordonnance: l'imbroglio juridique et social dans les "village de paix" de Rumonge', in *L'Afrique des grands lacs: annuaire 2010–2011*, ed. S. Marysse, F. Reyntjens and S. Vandeginste, Paris: L'Harmattan, 41–64.

——2011c, 'In quest of legitimacy: changes in land law and legal reform in Burundi', in *Natural Resources and Local Livelihoods in the Great Lakes Region in Africa: A Political Economy Perspective*, ed. A. Ansoms and S. Marysse, Basingstoke: Palgrave, 83–103.

Laely, T., 1992, 'Le Destin du bushingantahe: transformation d'une structure locale d'autorité au Burundi', *Genève-Afrique*, 30(2): 75–98.

——1997, 'Peasants, local communities and central power in Burundi', *The Journal of Modern African Studies*, 35(4): 695–716.

Lemarchand, R., 1970, *Rwanda and Burundi*, London: Pall Mall Press.

——1994, *Burundi: Ethnocide as Discourse and Practice*, Cambridge: Cambridge University Press.

Milner, J., 2009, *Refugees, the State and the Politics of Asylum in Africa*, Basingstoke: Palgrave.

Munezero, C. and Gihugu, D., 2012, 'Expériences de gestion foncière décentralisée dans la Province de Ngozi au Burundi', in *Rencontres foncières, Bujumbura 28–30 mars 2011*, ed. P. Thinon, A. Rochegude and T. Hilhorst, Bujumbura: Coopération suisse, 57–76.

Naniwe-Kaburahe, A., 2008, 'The institution of bashingantahe in Burundi', in *Transitional Justice and Reconciliation after Violent Conflict: Learning from African Experience*, ed. L. Hayse and M. Salter, Stockholm: IDEA, 149–79.

Ndayirukiye, S., 1986, 'La Plaine occidentale du Burundi, Etude régionale', Phd thesis (planning geography), Université de Nice.

Newbury, D., 2001, 'Precolonial Burundi and Rwanda: local loyalties, regional royalties', *The International Journal of African Historical Studies*, 34(2): 255–314.

Niyonkuru, M., 2012, 'Une guerre de mots entre Sérapion et Pontien', Radio Isanganiro, 21 December, available online at www.isanganiro.org/spip.php?article3307 (accessed 25 January 2013).

Nordic Consulting Group, 2010, *Evaluation of the Protracted Refugee Situation (PRS) for Burundians in Tanzania*, Copenhagen: Ministry of Foreign Affairs of Denmark.

RCN Justice et Démocratie, 2004, *Etude sur les pratiques foncières au Burundi: essai d'harmonisation; enquêtes menées dans 10 Provinces du Burundi en février–mars 2004*, Bujumbura.

——2006, *La Justice de proximité au Burundi: réalités et perspectives*, Bujumbura.

République du Burundi, 2009a, *Lettre de politique foncière*, Bujumbura.

——2009b, *Annuaire statistique du Burundi 2007*, Bujumbura: Ministère du Plan et de la Reconstruction, Institut de Statistiques et d'Etudes Economique (ISTEEBU).

——2011, *Recensement général de la population et de l'habitat du Burundi 2008, synthèse des résultats définitifs*, Bujumbura: Ministère de l'Intérieur, Bureau Central du Recensement.

——n.d. (a), *Commission nationale des terres et autres biens: bilan d'activités période 2006–2011*, Lake House, Bujumbura.

——n.d. (b), *Commission nationale des terres et autres biens: son organisation et ses activités: 2006–2010*, Lake House, Bujumbura.

Rwabahungu, M. and Nintunze, A., 2009, *Rapport sur l'étude d'actualisation de la base de données sur la situation de déplacés et des rapatriés encore dans les sites*, Bujumbura: Ministère de la solidarité nationale du rapatriement des réfugiés et de la réintégration sociale.

Sommers, M., 2001, *Fear in Bongoland: Burundi Refugees in Urban Tanzania*, New York: Berghahn Books.

Takeuchi, S., 2013, '"Twin countries" with contrasting institutions: post-conflict state-building in Rwanda and Burundi', in *Preventing Violent Conflict in Africa: Inequalities, Perceptions and Institutions*, ed. Y. Mine, F. Stewart, S. Fukuda-Parr and T. Mkandawire, London: Palgrave, 40–65.

The Oakland Institute, 2012, 'Lives on hold: the impact of Agrisol's land deal in Tanzania', *Land Deal Brief*, July 2011, available online at www.oaklandinstitute. org/sites/oaklandinstitute.org/files/OI_land_deal_brief_lives_on_hold.pdf (accessed 3 August 2013).

UN, 2005, 'Principles on housing and property restitution for refugees and displaced persons', UN Doc. E/CN.4/Sub.2/2005/17.

——2007, 'Identical letters dated 21 June 2007 from the Chairman of the Burundi configuration of the Peacebuilding Commission to the President of the Security Council, the President of the General Assembly and the President of the Economic and Social Council', UN Doc. PBC/1/BDI/4.

Van Leeuwen, M., 2010, 'Crisis or continuity? Farming land disputes and local conflict resolution in Burundi', *Land Use Policy*, 27: 753–62.

Vandeginste, S., 2009, 'Power-sharing, conflict and transition in Burundi: twenty years of trial and error', *Africa Spectrum*, 44(3): 63–86.

World Bank, 2011, *Africa Development Indicators 2011*, Washington, DC.

6 Property rights in the statebuilding of Bosnia and Herzegovina

Mari Katayanagi

The collapse of the Socialist Federal Republic of Yugoslavia caused multiple armed conflicts, which varied in length and gravity. Bosnia and Herzegovina (BiH) was hit particularly hard because of its ethnic structure, in which none of its three major ethnic groups constituted a significant majority. The General Framework Agreement for Peace (GFAP), the peace agreement signed by representatives of BiH, the Republic of Serbia and the Republic of Croatia in December 1995, marked the end of the three-and-a-half-year armed conflict. Its Annex 4, the Constitution of Bosnia and Herzegovina, provided for a state structure consisting of two entities: the Federation of Bosnia and Herzegovina and Republika Srpska. The Bosniacs, the Croats and the Serbs are recognised as the constituent peoples. BiH, in the immediate post-war period, was, however, divided into territories with three different systems.

The post-conflict transition in BiH has been regarded as a dual process: from war to peace and from socialist economy to free-market economy. Timothy Donais, however, describes it as a triple transition: a transition to democracy and to capitalism, as well as a transition 'from contested to consolidated "stateness"' (Donais 2005: 4). Another scholar suggests that contemporary Bosnia can be described as 'a "virtual", or "neo-feudal" state in which power is concentrated locally, in mini-states, based on patronage, influence peddling, and mafia-like elites' (Stubbs 2001: 101). How far has BiH moved towards statehood since the end of the armed conflict?

This chapter examines statebuilding in BiH from the perspective of real property rights. Property is determined by relationships within a society. It therefore bears historical features and represents social relationships. The issue is so broad and profound that we must limit the scope of the examination. In terms of timeframe, after a brief historical review the bulk of this chapter focuses on the property situation during the latest armed conflict in BiH and subsequent to the GFAP. Regarding the nature of property, our focus is on housing property and agricultural land at the individual level; the state property issue will be analysed separately. The armed conflict deprived a large number of refugees and internally displaced persons (IDPs) of their property. Exerting ethnically exclusive control over a territory became the

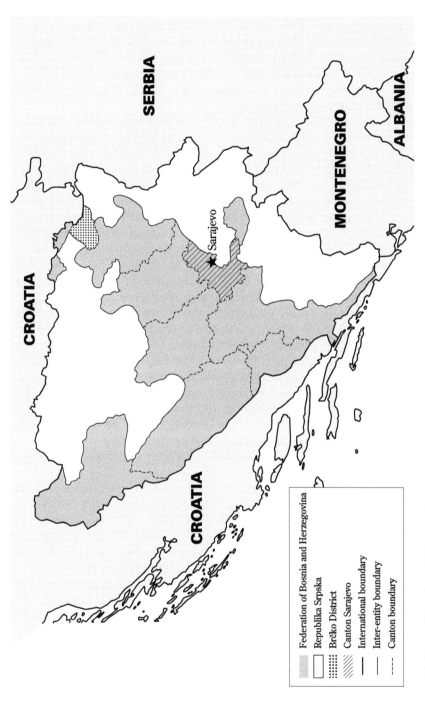

Figure 6.1 Map of Bosnia and Herzegovina

objective of the conflict. The aim of the laborious intervention of the international community for the restitution of those properties was to reverse this manoeuvre and consolidate the country's statehood. Although the restitution has been deemed an unprecedented success in the post-conflict environment, the country is far from enjoying consolidated statehood, as is indicated by the dispute over state property. The politics leave people behind, and ordinary citizens strive for their livelihood.

Peacebuilding in BiH is known for the extensive involvement of the international community, and it cannot be discussed without mentioning a peculiar international presence in the country: the High Representative (HR). According to Annex 10 of the GFAP, the parties to the agreement requested the designation of an HR as a facilitator of the parties' own efforts, and also as a mobiliser and coordinator of international activities concerning civilian aspects of the peace settlement. In December 1997 the Peace Implementation Council (PIC) welcomed the HR's 'final authority in theatre' regarding the interpretation of the GFAP on the civilian implementation of the peace settlement, 'in order to facilitate the resolution of difficulties by *making binding decisions*' [emphasis added], as the HR judges necessary, on certain issues. Such issues include 'interim measures to take effect when parties are unable to reach agreement' and other measures to ensure implementation of the GFAP (OHR 1997: XI). The PIC was established by the Peace Implementation Conference held in London on 8–9 December 1995, and its steering board provides the HR with political guidance.[1] The PIC conclusions of December 1997 effectively reinforced the HR's powers, which are called 'Bonn powers'. The HR is still present in BiH in 2013 and, although the use of the Bonn powers has significantly diminished, the practice so far has included the amendment and suspension of existing laws, the imposition of new legislation and the removal of elected or public officials from office.[2] The power has relevance to the intervention in relation to property restitution, which will be discussed in this chapter.

There is ample literature on peacebuilding in BiH in general (Sokolović and Bieber 2001; Bose 2002; Donais 2005), and also specifically on property restitution (Waters 1999; Philpott 2005; Williams 2005; Buyse 2008). This chapter is unique in shedding light on multiple aspects of the property issue, each of which present hurdles to statebuilding in their own way. The aim here is to deepen the understanding of the peacebuilding process in BiH.

This study is based on a literature review and field research conducted twice in 2011 and 2012, as well as on a survey in Canton Sarajevo. What the present author learned during her eight years of work in the country – communicating with BiH citizens – also provides input to the study.

Property issues in the historical context

Armed conflicts, as well as subsequent regime changes, often have significant effects over tenure security, and those in the history of Yugoslavia are no exception. This section reviews changes in land tenure in the history of BiH.

Under Ottoman rule, *spahis*, the salaried cavalry, could receive *zaim*, a relatively large estate, or *timar*, a smaller estate. The *timar* system was strictly military-feudal and tenure was based on military service. The land was the property of the Sultan, and the heirs of the *timariot* were not legally entitled to inherit the land (Malcolm 1996: 45–48). In the seventeenth century, military-feudal tenure declined along with the emergence of a new kind of local aristocracy holding large estates. Malcolm, a renowned historian, explains that a long process of social and religious polarisation took place, and by the nineteenth century the big landowners were Muslims while the great majority of the non-landowning peasants were Christians (Malcolm 1996: 94).

Austro-Hungarian authorities occupied BiH in 1878 and preserved the feudal relations inherited from the Ottoman period (Ljubojević 2011: 353). Land registration in BiH today goes back to the Austro-Hungarian period, at which time a dual registration system was introduced: a land register (land book) was maintained in the local court, while the cadastre was kept in municipalities (Rose *et al.* 2000: 12–13). During the First World War, the property of the Muslim feudal lords was destroyed, grain, houses and towers were burned, and land was appropriated by ordinary people (Ljubojević 2011: 349). The first major land reform was carried out under the Kingdom of Serbs, Croats and Slovenes, which was established in 1918. Dovring characterises land reforms from 1919 to 1930 as measures to address distinctly different problems of different areas, depending on the governing authorities. In the western and southern parts (BiH, Kosovo and Macedonia), land ownership was transferred from the Turkish *aga*[3] to peasants, which meant the dissolution of the share tenancy systems. In the northern areas (Slovenia, Croatia and Vojvodina), Austrian and Hungarian landowners retained relatively significant holdings (Dovring 1970: 1, 16). As a result of this slow reform, 1,286,000 hectares were subject to transfer of ownership in BiH. The beneficiaries were 250,000 peasants, including 217,000 locals – the rest being war volunteers and other colonists (Dovring 1970: 22).[4] This meant land was transferred from wealthy Muslim landowners to poorer Orthodox Serb peasants (Greble 2011: 9). The government under King Aleksandar also shut down mosques and turned some Islamic religious institutions into military warehouses (Greble 2011: 31).

In April 1941 the Independent State of Croatia (Nezavisna Država Hrvatska, NDH) was founded, and Hitler and Mussolini awarded the new satellite to an ultra-radical pro-Nazi group, the Ustasha Party. Sarajevo fell under this regime and suffered severely from its ethnicity-based policies. Properties were confiscated from Jews, while the Slovenes were brought in as 'colonists' and given priority for prime agricultural real estate in the Sarajevo vicinity. Dozens of Muslims who owned property in Belgrade, wrote in Cyrillic or were 'Serb-oriented' were arrested (Greble 2011: 98–101).

In May 1941 the regime appointed local Aryan trustees – namely Catholics, Muslims and Volksdeutsche – to oversee approximately 200 Jewish and Serb businesses, factories and organisations in Sarajevo. The assigned Catholic and Muslim organisations justified this confiscation in humanitarian terms, claiming that their use of the property would serve the citizens of Sarajevo best (Greble 2011: 105–6).

The second major land reform took place after the Second World War in the Federal People's Republic of Yugoslavia, led by Josip Broz Tito. It was to be renamed the Socialist Federal Republic of Yugoslavia (SFRY) in 1963. The Law on Nationalisation adopted in 1944 covered all property owned by enemy nationals, collaborators and war criminals, which accounted for 80 per cent of Yugoslav industry (Simmie 1991: 172). The land reform of 1945 expropriated all land beyond the prescribed area – in the range of 25 to 45 hectares, depending on the region – regardless of whether it was a part of a large estate or peasant farm. Of some 1.2 million hectares of confiscated farmland, about half was distributed to poor or landless households, and the rest became state property. The Law on Agrarian Reform and Resettlement laid down the principle that land belonged to those who cultivated it, and it was to be registered as private property (Dovring 1970: 1–2, 17–18). In the same year, every building containing more than two apartments was transferred to public ownership (Simmie 1991: 173). In 1953 the maximum size of farms was reduced to ten hectares (in some areas, 15 hectares), and the expropriated farms became a 'land fund', which was managed by district committees and utilised by local agricultural organisations (Dovring 1970: 2, 18).

The Yugoslav economy is known for its workers' management system, whose essential element was socially owned property. According to Mirković, 'social ownership means that resources, productive capacities, and capital goods were owned by the society at large and not by any agency or individual' (1987: 321). Interpretation of social ownership varies and even includes negation of ownership. When it is accepted as ownership, depending on the theorist the owner is claimed to be either the state, society or an economic enterprise. Another view asserts divided ownership between state and enterprises. There is also the view that rights or powers are shared between society and enterprises, but these do not amount to ownership (Van Doren 1972: 83–91; Coronna 1985; Mirković 1987: 323–24).[5]

Social ownership was also relevant to housing. Socially owned enterprises and non-economic institutions were authorised to establish housing enterprises, taking responsibility for the construction and maintenance of socially owned apartments. In 1959 the Law on Housing Relations introduced the 'occupancy right'. It had a family character in the sense that spouses living in the same apartment were considered to be occupancy right holders. If other members of the household were users of the apartment, they were entitled to use it permanently. If the original occupancy right holder(s) ceased to use it, the other household members had to determine, by common agreement, who would be the occupancy right holder. The allocation itself took into account the needs of the household members, including their income and health conditions (UN-HABITAT 2005: 22 note 31; Williams 2005: 479–80).

In 1991, 71 per cent of housing units were privately owned, and 29 per cent socially owned, in BiH (Bosnia and Herzegovina Ministry for Human Rights and Refugees 2005: 63). The private housing units were mostly in rural areas or on the periphery of urban areas, while most of the socially owned housing units were apartments in the urban areas (Williams 2005: 478). Tsenkova states that the hallmark difference between housing systems in socialist and market economies is the role which the public sector plays in ownership and control of housing assets (Tsenkova 2009: 16). In comparison with other socialist countries, the SFRY had a high percentage of privately owned housing, which signifies the limited control over housing on the part of the public authorities. This limited control was also visible in the phenomenon of 'black housing' – self-build production without planning permission (Simmie 1991: 175). There is criticism that housing allocation under the socialist system was not egalitarian, but rather favoured elites. Politicians, bureaucrats, intellectuals and the better-qualified working class acquired a dispropor-tionate share of social housing (Simmie 1991: 179; Petrović 2001: 213). Petrović calls this 'a system of income in kind' (Petrović 2001: 213). Yet the scale of corruption and the consequent gap between the rich and the poor is much larger today than it had been during the period of the SFRY.[6]

The Yugoslav system of social property was designed to limit the state's role. As mentioned earlier, in the mid-1960s responsibility for housing provi-sion was decentralised and borne by socially owned enterprises. However, in the housing reform of the mid-1970s, municipalities came to play the role of coordinating housing supply and demand. The policy was meant to increase state control over market actors (Petrović 2001: 218). In this sense, the exist-ing system was susceptible to the subsequent changes which enabled control of property by local ethno-political elites.

Armed conflict, partitioned territory and legal pluralism

More than half of the pre-war housing units were damaged during the latest armed conflict in BiH. Arson or looting was one of the means of ethnic cleansing, which displaced approximately 1.2 million refugees and one million IDPs (Bosnia and Herzegovina Ministry for Human Rights and Refugees 2005: 21–22). The intention to grab property was evident during this process because people were forced to leave after signing a document declaring that they had abandoned their property (UN 1992: 11). Tuathail and O'Loughlin sharply summarise the ethnic cleansing which took place in BiH as 'ethno-territorial geopolitics, an attack on the existing spatial order, and the imposi-tion of one organized around ethnic division and segregation' (2009: 1046).

During the armed conflict and the following few years, the territory of BiH was partitioned de facto by three ethnic groups, although each territory was not necessarily geographically unified. There were two ways to consolidate ethnically pure territory: one was to prevent the return of other ethnic groups and the other was to maintain the current population – in other words, to make IDPs who took refuge in the municipality stay. These were the two sides of the same coin. The means used to carry out the policy are reviewed below.

First, local authorities reallocated properties that had been 'abandoned' by other ethnic groups 'for humanitarian reasons', giving them to newcomers that had been evacuated from other municipalities (Williams 2005: 476). This had a double effect: preventing the return of the original occupants, and encouraging IDPs to stay. It was particularly easy to justify expropriation of socially owned apartments because the occupancy right was subject to certain conditions, including the actual use of the property (Williams 2005: 476, 480). In the territory under the control of the Republic of Bosnia and Herzegovina, which actually meant Bosniac control, the Law on Abandoned Apartments and the Law on Temporarily Abandoned Real Property Owned by Citizens were applied.[7] In Croat-controlled Hrvatska Zajednica Herzeg Bosna, a sub-legislative Decree on the Use of Abandoned Apartments was issued.[8] In Republika Srpska, which was under Serb control, the local administrative procedure of reallocation was widespread, which was legislated after the signing of GFAP as the Law on the Use of Abandoned Property.[9] This introduced the condition of reciprocity into property repossession, which meant that temporary occupants of property in Republika Srpska were entitled to remain until they had repossessed their own property or had been compensated for their pre-war property (Williams 2005: 483–85). Despite the alleged humanitarian rationale behind reallocation, attractive properties were allocated to 'highly placed political, military, judicial, and police officials as an incentive for their loyalty' (Williams 2005: 484). Such utilisation of property was not novel, as was mentioned in the preceding section.

Second, forced displacement and ethnic consolidation continued beyond the signing of the GFAP. In spring 1996, Bosniacs and Croats were expelled from territories awarded to Republika Srpska (Toal and Dahlman 2011: 176). Also, the Serbs and Croats in Sarajevo fled upon inter-entity territory transfer, either forced by the Bosniacs or because of an order issued by their own political leaders to leave and move to an area controlled by their own ethnic group.

Third, ethnic-based partition was further encouraged by the allocation of public land to IDPs (Dahlman and Tuathail 2005: 652–53). The allocation based on humanitarian justification turned out to benefit only one particular ethnic group. For instance, Croat IDPs from Central Bosnia and Bosniac-controlled parts of the Neretva valley were settled in the southern part of BiH, where there is a high concentration of war veterans. Most of the land was allocated in 1998 and 1999 (ESI 2002: 9). In Republika Srpska, the National Assembly amended its law to allow the allocation of building land free of charge to IDPs in June 1998.[10] Recognising the spread of such practices, in May 1999 the HR suspended the power of local authorities to real-locate socially owned land which was used for residential, religious, cultural, private agricultural or private business activities, as of 6 April 1992 (OHR 1999a).[11] The OHR explained the reasoning behind this decision as being that the land reallocation practice amounted to taking away the livelihood and cultural and religious heritage from refugees and IDPs, and threatened to undermine the processes of restitution and privatisation (OHR 1999b). In April 2000 the HR issued a new decision banning the disposal, allotment, transfer, selling or giving for use or rent of state-owned property, including former socially owned property, but excluding socially owned apartments. Through this decision, the HR introduced a so-called 'waiver' system, which opened the possibility of an exclusion from the ban through a written exemption by the OHR, if the competent entity authorities could prove that the proposed transfer of property was non-discriminatory and in the best interests of the public (OHR 2000a).[12]

Fourth, other benefits were provided to keep particular ethnic groups in the municipality. In particular, Croat IDPs were given financial support from the fund offered by Croatia proper, so that they could stay in the place of displacement where the Croat population was concentrated (Ito 2001: 109; Englbrecht 2004: 123; Phuong 2004: 199; Dahlman and Tuathail 2005: 652–53).

Since controlling territory was the aim of the war, population movement had a strong strategic relevance and property was embedded in this strategy. The creation of three distinctly controlled areas meant a reign of legal pluralism when we look at the entire territory of BiH. In each area, the ethnic authorities were content with their own way of ruling. In order to preserve this situation, the ethno-political elites encouraged IDPs belonging to their own ethnic group to stay permanently, and obstructed the return of other ethnic groups.

Consolidating statehood through restitution and return

International intervention

The GFAP was the first international agreement to provide not only for the right to return to one's own country but for the 'right to return home' (Phuong 2004: 183). The provisions of Article II(5) of Annex 4, Constitution of Bosnia and Herzegovina, and Article I(1) of Annex 7, Agreement on Refugees and Displaced Persons, begin with the exact same sentence: 'All refugees and displaced persons have the right freely to return to their homes of origin.' Both articles set forth that refugees and IDPs 'have the right to have restored to them property of which they were deprived in the course of hostilities since 1991 and to be compensated for any property that cannot be restored to them'. The rationale behind these provisions was that return was necessary in order to reverse ethnic cleansing and regenerate a multi-ethnic society. However, the GFAP also recognised a political structure consisting of two entities: Republika Srpska, dominated by the Serbs, and the Federation of Bosnia and Herzegovina, mainly inhabited by the Bosniacs and the Croats.

The regeneration of a multi-ethnic society in a structure based on ethnic division is contradictory in itself.

As discussed in the previous section, the three ethnic groups largely consolidated their control over specific territories during the armed conflict. The international community could not expect that the above-mentioned provisions would be sincerely and proactively implemented by the domestic authorities. Therefore, in order to realise the return and restitution, as well as the ultimate regeneration of multi-ethnic society, the international community intervened in various ways. The complete picture of this intervention was not in view at the beginning of the process. Rather, it was a step-by-step process that was designed and carried out by the international community, and that encountered different obstacles including strong policies against return, discrimination incorporated in laws and regulations, and the simple shortage of capacity at the municipality level. In this section, we will revisit various measures taken by the international community, including amendments to, suspension of, or imposition of legislation, establishment of and support for a dispute resolution body, removal of obstructive officials, monitoring of property law implementation, and information campaigns.

Before starting the review of intervention measures by the international community, it is important to note the legal ground for property restitution. Two legal sources of the right to property restitution have been discussed by legal experts. The first is the right to return of refugees and IDPs. As mentioned earlier, the GFAP provided for the right to return home. The right to repatriation is set forth in the Universal Declaration of Human Rights, and has been reaffirmed by many UN resolutions. The second potential legal source is reparation for human rights violations (Williams 2005: 457–61; Buyse 2008: 113–60). The linkage between the right to return and the right to restitution is now recognised by the 'Principles on Housing and Property Restitution for Refugees and Displaced Persons', known as the Pinheiro Principles, adopted by the UN Sub-Commission on the Promotion and Protection of Human Rights in 2005.[13] The call for recognition of an independent right to property restitution for refugees and IDPs – in other words, housing, land and property rights – is on the rise among a number of scholars and practitioners (Leckie ed. 2009). While the experience of BiH significantly influenced the drafting of the Pinheiro Principles, the emphasis given in the GFAP to the right to return meant that at the beginning of the restitution process in BiH the right to return was at the forefront.

For property restitution, a legal framework was imperative. As discussed in the preceding section, laws and regulations effectively discriminated against ethnic groups other than the one in control of the particular territory. Under strong political pressure from the international community, the Federation of Bosnia and Herzegovina abolished the law on abandoned properties in April 1998, and Republika Srpska followed in December 1998. The laws adopted by both entities for this purpose are collectively known as 'laws on cessation', which cancelled discriminatory provisions (Williams 2005: 489–90).[14]

Furthermore, when the BiH authorities failed to adopt the required property legislation, the HR introduced a package of property laws.

Although we cannot go into detail due to the limitations of space, there was a legal question on whether the occupancy right to socially owned apartments was a property right. In November 1997 the BiH Human Rights Chamber examined the status of occupancy rights under Article 1 of Protocol 1 to the European Convention for the Protection of Human Rights and Fundamental Freedoms (ECHR), which was directly applicable in BiH in accordance with the Constitution.[15] The Article provides for the peaceful enjoyment of one's possessions. The chamber found that the occupancy right was 'a valuable asset giving the holder the right, subject to the conditions prescribed by law, to occupy the property in question indefinitely'. For the chamber, it was an asset which constituted a 'possession' within the meaning of the said Article.[16]

Following some legislative interventions, the HR further intervened by issuing 13 decisions related to property restitution on 27 October 1999. The decisions had the purpose of harmonising the legislation in the two entities and thus creating equal rights and remedies for all refugees and IDPs across BiH, and also providing the entity authorities with detailed instructions on the application of the property and housing legislation (OHR 1999c: 1).

As a dispute resolution body, the GFAP had provided for the establishment of the Commission for Displaced Persons and Refugees, which was later named the Commission for Real Property Claims of Displaced Persons and Refugees (CRPC). The CRPC consisted of three international members, four members from the Federation of Bosnia and Herzegovina and two from Republika Srpska. The CRPC received property claims from people who wished to repossess their property, and once ownership had been verified it issued a certificate of ownership. However, the CRPC had no means of enforcement and its early decisions were rarely implemented. The aforementioned 13 decisions included laws that incorporated CRPC decisions into domestic claim procedures (OHR 1999d; 1999e). The decisions of the CRPC were made final and binding. On the one hand, there were criticisms that this was a redundant and costly body because parallel domestic procedures existed (Philpott 2005: 16–17; Williams 2005: 508). On the other hand, its role as a neutral body, whose adjudication could not be challenged, has been highly praised (Garlick 2000: 83–84).[17] The CRPC processed over 310,000 claims during its mandate from 1996 to 2003 (Von Carlowitz 2004: 603).

Since the enforcement of CRPC decisions rested on the shoulders of municipal authorities, their obstructive behaviour could easily block the restitution process. In manifest cases, the HR used his special power to remove public officials. In particular, there were two waves of removals concerning restitution and return: the first in November 1999, which removed 22 officials, and the second in September 2000, which removed 15 officials. The first group mainly consisted of politicians, and the second group was mostly made up of officials of housing offices (Moratti 2008: 194–96).[18] These removals were publicly announced and demonstrated the firm commitment of the international community not to tolerate obstruction of the return and restitution process.

Implementation monitoring was another aspect of this commitment. On 22 September 1999, the OHR, the Office of the UNHCR, the Organisation for Security and Cooperation in Europe (OSCE) and the UN Mission in Bosnia and Herzegovina set up the Property Law Implementation Plan (PLIP), which created a well-coordinated monitoring scheme. The CRPC had observer status. One organisation/field officer was designated as a point of contact in each municipality and the information was shared among the organisations in a systematic way. This enabled close monitoring of the progress of property restitution. The PLIP agencies also issued monthly statistics of PLIP implementation by municipality, which enabled comparison of municipalities and identification of municipalities in which restitution was overdue (Philpott 2005: 9; Williams 2005: 509–13).

In order to encourage the return movement, it was necessary to provide accurate information for those who wanted to return to their place of origin and recover their property, as well as for those who would have to leave the occupied property. This ran against the manipulation of IDPs by local authorities, who persuaded IDPs that they could stay in the allocated property permanently. Nationalist elites often used radio and television broadcasts to discourage return, 'exacerbating fears of revenge or re-victimization among the displaced' (Tuathail and Dahlman 2006: 251). Some spontaneous returnees were in fact met with harassment and assault, and some lost their lives through explosions, arson and so on (Englbrecht 2004: 104; Harvey 2006: 92; Stefansson 2006: 116; Toal and Dahlman 2011: 190). The international community therefore conducted an information campaign involving billboards, leaflets and radio and television broadcasts. The '*Poštovanje*/Respect' campaign in 2000, which was conducted by the OHR and the OSCE with assistance from UNHCR, had a message that respect was essential in the property implementation process:

> respect for the right to property and respect for the right to return were the basis for amendments to the property legislation in Bosnia and Herzegovina; that the authorities in Bosnia and Herzegovina, as well as those who seek to repossess their property and those who have to vacate other people's property must respect the law; and finally that respect for human rights and the rule of law are fundamental principles in any democracy.[19]

This was followed by the '*Dosta je*/It's enough' campaign, which expressed 'the frustration felt by claimants waiting to repossess their homes, temporary occupants concerned about their future, and all those involved in the repossession process, who encounter the same obstacles day after day'.[20]

The last extensive amendments to the property laws were carried out by a package of 13 legislative decisions of the HR in December 2001. The HR introduced the principle of chronological processing, by which the first claimant was the first to be processed. The provision aimed at clearing the significant backlog of property applications, but also served to depoliticise the process. In Philpott's words:

> [a] clear non-negotiable order for resolving cases gave the housing officials the political cover *vis-à-vis* nationalist politicians and the public to tackle politically difficult cases; that is, where VIPs or protected persons were occupying property, or where the occupants required alternative accommodation.
>
> (2005: 12)

Furthermore, it was effective in preventing corruption among housing officials (Philpott 2005: 12). Facing massive property claims, the absence of a transparent process could mean the indefinite postponement of pending cases, particularly when these had political implications.

There were, nevertheless, two exceptions to the chronological rule. First, in April 2002 the HR decided to prioritise property repossession claims by returning police officers and members of their 1991 family households (OHR 2002b). This decision was related to police restructuring, which envisaged that the composition of the police in each municipality should reflect the composition of the population in the 1991 census. Therefore, the return of policemen who belonged to an ethnic minority was to be supported. It was also expected that the presence of ethnic minority policemen would accelerate the return process. The second exception concerned residents in collective/transit centres where IDPs were accommodated (OHR 2002c). This was an indirect prioritisation, as it required the transfer of the accommodation of current residents of IDP facilities to those who were occupying their claimed property. This was meant to enable the current residents of collective/transit centres to return home, while the occupants of their former property would move to the collective/transit centres.

While property restitution was pushed forward in order to reverse ethnic cleansing, local politicians began to allocate public land to those who were subject to eviction, as described in the previous section. This was problematic in the sense that the measure appeared to be a part of a population engineering policy. For this reason, the HR intervened and banned the allocation of public land without prior approval by the OHR. Nevertheless, the practice continued in a number of places, and, ironically, it consequently helped to accelerate the return/restitution process, since the temporary occupants of properties moved out once they had succeeded in building their own houses (ESI 2002: 27).

The return issue was a continuation of the war for the ethno-political elites. Against the attempt to consolidate ethno-political territory, the international community tried to reinforce statehood, applying the same principles and harmonised legislation to the entirety of BiH. As far as property restitution was concerned, the international community won the battle, except in a small number of cases. The last published monthly statistics, in January 2004, show 216,904 claims submitted to the CRPC in total, and 201,417 closed cases: an implementation ratio of 92.86 per cent.[21] There were some factors peculiar to the case of BiH which enabled this high rate of restitution. First, there were sufficiently reliable property ownership records in place prior to the conflict. Second, the international community could intervene with forcible measures, if necessary, because of the Bonn powers of the HR. Third, the international community was united in its approach, at least for the important period of the process. Fourth, as Williams rightly points out, despite the separate property administration developed by the conflicting parties, the systems in the three areas were 'largely compatible because they were all based on shared legal and institutional premises' (Williams 2013: 168).

A number of scholars attribute this success to the rights-based and rule of law approach, which replaced the return-based and political approach undertaken at the beginning of the process (Williams 2005: 450, 552–53; Buyse 2008: 339–42). As a matter of fact, not all of those who recovered their property returned, and this fact made it easier for the ethno-political elites to follow the rule of law approach, since their fear was of losing control of the territory through the massive return of other ethnic groups.

Quandaries of the restitution issue

Despite the general success of post-conflict restitution in BiH, there are two quandaries that remain. First, the restitution excluded the occupancy rights of JNA (*Jugoslavenska Narodna Armija*, Yugoslav National Army) officers. Second, it did not take into account the potential restitution of property that had been nationalised under the previous regime.

Prior to the dissolution of the SFRY, property privatisation was ongoing and the transition to the liberal market had begun. It was the socially owned apartments of the JNA officers that were subject to pilot privatisation. The disruption of the process as a result of the conflict significantly affected them. With regard to the JNA apartments, the Federation of Bosnia and Herzegovina Apartments Law held that the occupancy right holder would not be considered a refugee if he or she was in active service for the JNA as of 30 April 1991, and was not a citizen of the Socialist Republic of Bosnia and Herzegovina, unless he or she had approved residence as a refugee or another equivalent protective status in a country outside the former SFRY. If the individual did not fulfil these criteria, they were deemed to have lost occupancy rights. In short, this was the 'collective punishment of the aggressors through expropriation of their apartments' (Williams 2005: 502), since JNA soldiers who were not citizens of the Socialist Republic of Bosnia and Herzegovina were mostly Serbs. Although the provisions were amended in June 2003, in accordance with the Human Rights Chamber decision to set a later date for determining active service and delete the citizenship requirement, the punishment was not entirely withdrawn (Williams 2005: 496–503, 544–48).[22] Cases relating to occupancy rights of JNA apartments were also brought before the European Court of Human Rights (ECtHR). In May 2010 the ECtHR ruled in the *Case of Đokić v. Bosnia and Herzegovina* that there was a violation of Article 1 of Protocol 1 to the ECHR, and ordered BiH to pay pecuniary damages of €60,000, together with other payments (ECtHR 2010b). The applicant, who was a lecturer at a military school in Sarajevo, paid the full amount to privatise a military flat in February 1992, but was denied ownership of the flat. The ECtHR issued similar judgements in May 2010 on three cases, whose pecuniary damages were between €53,000 and €85,000 (ECtHR 2012). The ECtHR explicitly stated in the judgement that despite the alleged rationale for the allocation of 'abandoned' properties as provision of humanitarian shelter to IDPs, 'particularly attractive properties – typically urban flats – were commonly awarded to the military and political elites' (ECtHR 2010b: para. 7). Similar future judgements will severely burden the finances of the Federation of Bosnia and Herzegovina. The issue is not a matter of ethnic interest, but purely in the individual interests of the elites who benefited from the manipulation of legislation, which was enabled by the armed conflict. Ordinary citizens will suffer most from the negative consequences.

Another issue that BiH may face is the demand for restitution of properties nationalised by the earlier regime. Such restitution is common in Central and Eastern Europe today (Pogany 1997; Karadjova 2004; Mungiu-Pippidi and Stefan 2012). There is already a known claim in Kotorsko, in Doboj municipality. The municipal authorities once allocated some 175 residential plots of land to Serb IDPs – this with the approval of the OHR, which considered that the land had been socially owned. Around 400 Bosniac families returned in 2000 to the village across the road from that particular area of land. The returnees vigorously protested to the OHR, claiming that the land in question had been confiscated from them in the 1960s in order to establish an agricultural cooperative, and that it should be returned to them in the future restitution process concerning land confiscated under the socialist regime (ESI 2002: 11).[23] In this light, the certification of property rights, carried out with significant intervention by the international community, might have complicated the matter because the certified rights may be reviewed in future. A widespread problem is likely to be the privatised socially owned apartments. The ownership of land on which socially owned apartments have been built is often uncertain. One of the reasons is that the Yugoslav government failed to register thousands of nationalised properties as state-owned property, although no claims had been submitted (Directorate-General for Internal Policies 2010: 48). In other words, state-owned property may still be registered as private property. Obviously there is an option to compensate the former owners, and not to opt for *restitutio in integrum*.[24] What is required by the BiH government is to find a satisfactory solution for interested parties, without harming the peacebuilding efforts to date.

Securing tenure in the post-conflict context is a highly sensitive issue when the pre-war tenure is not sufficiently clear, or when there are historically pending issues to be resolved. BiH thus needs to take a cautious approach in dealing with the residual property issues.

State property: unseen consolidation of statehood

More than 15 years after the signing of the GFAP, the BiH authorities are yet to determine what state property is, and the issue has direct relevance to statehood. Following the settlement of the challenging question of how to administer the property succession from the SFRY in 2001 (Stanic 2001; Stahn 2002),[25] the BiH government had to deal with the question of how to allocate state property among different levels of government. The Council of Ministers established a commission at the state level in December 2004 to develop criteria for the identification and distribution of state property, for the adoption of regulations on the management of the property, and for proposing relevant draft legislation (OHR 2009: 3). In order to avoid any premature selling of relevant properties, the HR decided on a temporary prohibition on the disposal of such properties.[26] The work of the above-mentioned commission, however, did not produce the expected results for several years.

In February 2008 the PIC set five objectives and two conditions that would need to be fulfilled by the BiH authorities prior to the closure of the OHR. Of the five objectives, two were related to property – namely, acceptable and sustainable resolution of the issue of apportionment of property between state and other levels of government, and acceptable and sustainable resolution of defence property. This highlights the fact that the PIC regarded the property issue as particularly important in statebuilding.[27]

Observing little progress in the state property discussion, in September 2009 the HR decided to prepare an inventory of state properties and then let the BiH authorities resolve their allocation (OHR 2009: 5–6). The OHR delivered an inventory detailing 1,000 state property units to the BiH authorities in December 2009. The major composition of the inventory was as follows: 30 per cent represented defence property registered as property of the former Yugoslav Ministry of Defence; 20 per cent represented property of former 'socio-political organisations' such as the Communist Alliance, Alliance of Trade Unions and Socialist Alliance of Working People;[28] and 12 per cent represented property of the Ministry of Internal Affairs of the Socialist Republic of Bosnia and Herzegovina (OHR 2009: 12). Even upon delivery of the inventory, no expedient action was observed on the part of the BiH authorities.

The long-lasting question surfaced in the political arena in December 2010, when the Republika Srpska National Assembly adopted the Law on the Status of State Property Located in the Territory of Republika Srpska and under the Disposal Ban. The law reflected the authorities' view that BiH 'does not exist without or beyond entities, it is composed of the entities', and that, under the GFAP, Republika Srpska exercises in full capacity its legislative, executive and judicial powers in accordance with the distribution of responsibilities between BiH and the entities (European Commission for Democracy through Law 2011: para. 16). Hence, all property located in the territory of Republika Srpska as of the moment of entry into force of the Bosnia and Herzegovina Constitution is owned by the entity, and, by authorisation of entities, the BiH institutions may use property needed for the exercise of their constitutional and legal responsibilities (para. 28).

In January 2011, Sulejman Tihić, then deputy chairman of the House of Peoples of the BiH Parliamentary Assembly, lodged a lawsuit before the Constitutional Court of Bosnia and Herzegovina requesting a review of the constitutionality of the newly adopted law. In contrast to Republika Srpska's view, the applicant claimed that BiH had continued the international legal personality of the Republic of Bosnia and Herzegovina and was the titleholder to all state property. On this basis, the BiH Parliamentary Assembly could adopt legislation and authorise entities and other levels of government to use or own assets necessary for exercising their respective competences (para. 28).

Regarding this case, the BiH Constitutional Court asked for *amicus curiae* opinion of the European Commission for Democracy through Law (the Venice Commission). The Venice Commission's view was that neither claim was well founded: while the state of Bosnia and Herzegovina was not reducible to the existence of the entities, an international agreement could not directly resolve the constitutional issue of the division of ownership within Bosnia and Herzegovina (paras. 29–30). For the commission, the division of state property was 'substantively a constitutional issue' (para. 31).

The Constitutional Court judgement in this case, upholding the claimant's view that the Republika Srpska law in question was unconstitutional, was issued in July 2012 (Constitutional Court of Bosnia and Herzegovina 2012). The court established that Republika Srpska lacked competence to regulate the legal subject matter of the law under the review. The court is of the view that the term 'Bosnia and Herzegovina' under the Constitution includes several meanings: the highest level of government, a subject of international law, that is, a sovereign state, and the legal successor of the Republic of Bosnia and Herzegovina (para. 72). The court clarified that, pursuant to Article I (1) of the Constitution, 'BiH is entitled to continue to regulate "the state property", both in terms of civil law and public law' (para. 79). The court further expressed its opinion that there were positive obligations on the state of Bosnia and Herzegovina to take into consideration the whole constitutional order of Bosnia and Herzegovina in exercising its responsibilities in taking over the international obligations of the Socialist Republic of Bosnia and Herzegovina and in regulating the issues related to the property of the former Socialist Republic. Such obligations were for the realisation of the normative hierarchy established by the Constitution; incorporating the principle of cooperation, coordination and mutual comprehension amounting to 'justice and tolerance', 'peaceful relations', promotion of general welfare and economic growth; and preservation of the sovereignty, territorial integrity and political independence envisaged in the Preamble (para. 83).

Despite the court's view, which envisages the orderly resolution of the state property dispute in such a way as to conform with the peaceful state-building set forth in the Constitution, the political reality runs against optimistic expectations. Prior to the judgement, six political parties represented at the state level legislature signed an agreement on principles to allocate state property and defence property.[29] However, the inter-party relationship was damaged following the agreement, and it is no longer certain whether the agreement remains effective. The state property turmoil in BiH underscores the fact that property is embedded in power relationships. Despite the international community's endeavours to consolidate statehood, and the state vision of the BiH Constitutional Court, political reality manifests the ethnic divide.

Land and livelihood

Post-liberal peacebuilding scholars criticise the fact that liberal peacebuilding has neglected people's everyday life and welfare (Bojicic-Dzelilovic 2009; Richmond 2009; 2010). Among conflict-affected countries, BiH should have been in a relatively advantageous position because of the high level of attention the country has received from the world, thanks to its location in Europe. Despite this, household economies have not been high on the recovery agenda.

During the armed conflict in BiH, many people in urban areas turned to farming for the first time in order to survive, often using small spaces on their balconies. Subsistence farming is common in post-conflict situations in many parts of the world, as people have no other income source. In the immediate post-conflict period, support for small-scale agricultural activities may sustain people's livelihood. As of 2011, the number of people working in the agricultural sector in BiH was 160,000 (19.6 per cent of the working population) (Čustović and Taletović 2012: 106).

Based on field research in the eastern part of BiH, a researcher has produced the following analysis. The desire to return home is in part due to the returnees' close connection with the agricultural cycle:

> for many elderly people who have yet to return they seem to experience a tangible sense of exasperation at certain times of the year, most notably at planting times, as if they can not fulfil [*sic*] their purpose whilst they are away from their land. This sense of being unfulfilled was exacerbated by the economic necessity of planting crops for self-consumption, particularly as many DPs did not have access to alternative land during displacement.
>
> (D'Onfrio 2004: 16)[30]

The respect for the agricultural cycle transcends ethnic differences. Also in the eastern part of BiH, a returnee told the present author that before recovering his property he had waited for the occupant of his property – which included his farm – to harvest. For him, it was normal that someone who had worked on the land should benefit from the fruits of his labour – even though it was his own land, he did not mind waiting for the harvest.[31]

In the case of BiH, there were some historical factors which worked as a disadvantage for post-conflict subsistence farmers. First, professional farmers were not the majority in the SFRY,[32] because the government promoted industrialisation. This did not help people who had to depend on farming in the post-conflict situation, because of their lack of skills and experience. Another historical weakness was that there was no system to support individual farmers. The SFRY's investment in the agricultural sector focused on state farms, and resources were provided disproportionately to them (Dovring 1970: 42–46). The third limitation was the fragmentation of land, which was on the one hand caused by the limit on the size of private farms, imposed under the SFRY, and, on the other, by the inheritance system (Lockwood 1975: 93). Fragmentation of land causes a number of problems for agricultural development. First, such land is not suitable for mechanisation. Second, farmers have to move from one plot to another, often carrying tools. Third, the border of each plot tends to be wasted in order to avoid conflict with the owner of neighbouring land.[33]

The pre-war industrial sector mainly consisted of socially owned heavy industry. Since the international community believed that decisions regarding the rehabilitation of large-scale enterprises should be led by market forces, the industry sector has been virtually ignored in the rehabilitation process (Donais 2005: 94). Under such conditions, where few signs of industrial development have been observed, agriculture should have been given more attention by the government in order to guarantee sustainability of livelihoods. Unlike some other countries affected by severe armed conflict, BiH is not short of land. Approximately 30 per cent of arable land is uncultivated (Čustović and Taletović 2012: 106).

The only large-scale farms in BiH are those that used to be cultivated by state companies. In the agricultural sector, private property was largely maintained, unlike that in the industrial and service sectors (Medjad 2004: 291). Municipalities, which have the right to permit the use of former state farms, usually rent them to farmers in small portions, and thus inhibit economies of scale.

According to a survey by the JICA Research Institute, property ownership in Canton Sarajevo is structured as 63.8 per cent public property, 34.7 per cent private property and 0.1 per cent the religious community's property;[34] 1.4 per cent does not have ownership data. Figure 6.2 presents the land in Canton Sarajevo according to ownership. The majority of public land is covered by forest. This survey also confirmed the land's fragmentation into parcels, as shown in Figure 6.3. Of the 275,274 parcels of land in the canton, 167,186 are smaller than 0.1 hectare.

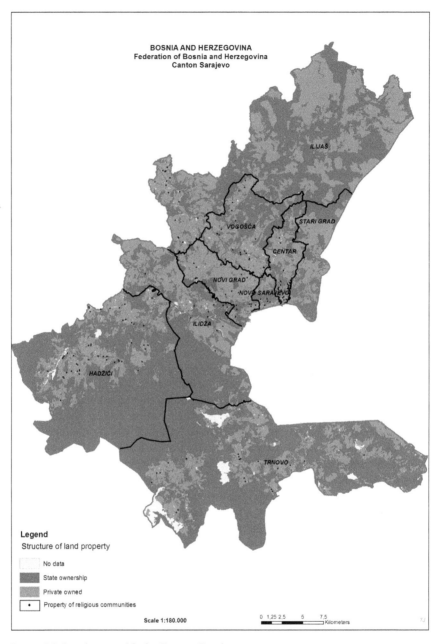

Figure 6.2 Land ownership in Canton Sarajevo

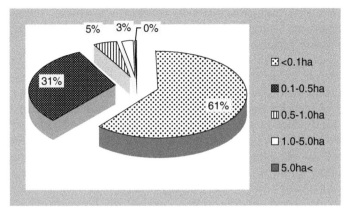

Figure 6.3 Size of land parcels in Canton Sarajevo

According to the BiH Constitution, agriculture falls under the competencies of the entity governments. So far, however, the entity governments have done little to develop agriculture in the post-conflict period, except to provide certain subsidies. It was the Food and Agriculture Organization which started the project 'Inventory of the Post-War Situation of Land Resources in Bosnia', and collected information necessary for land management in the agricultural sector. As a second step, the FAO started a pilot project with three municipalities, introducing Participatory Land Use Development (PLUD); another three projects were added in the following year (Biancalani *et al.* 2004: 8). Based on the PLUD, the municipalities of Ravno (Federation of Bosnia and Herzegovina) and Trebinje (Republika Srpska) were selected for a pilot project for land consolidation. In Ravno municipality, a survey was conducted on landowners' interest in land consolidation. The project is at the phase of preparing a proper design for the process, which is likely to be a voluntary one through buying/selling, leasing or exchanging. In this municipality, a part of the former state-owned farm, which amounts to 300 hectares in total, is leased to approximately 15 users under 25-year contracts. Each user leases only between two and three hectares. This is neither an effective way of using the rare large-scale agricultural land, nor is it helpful in terms of agricultural development. The trial of land consolidation may lead to a different course of development.[35]

Due to uncertainty about the future treatment of the former state farms, some municipalities take a cautious approach in not approving leases of such land. In order to enhance the economic development of the country and improve ordinary citizens' lives, the issue of restitution of property that was nationalised under the previous regime needs to be addressed without delay.

Conclusion

Settling inherited property problems, and drawing up a development policy which properly addresses land use, is rightly a question of transition for the

BiH. Unless BiH politicians start to develop a state-level vision, leaving ethnic and private interest behind, the country will never take steps forward towards positive peace and consolidated statehood.

In the history of BiH, property was subject to power relationships in society, often linked to ethnic politics. The armed conflict in BiH in the 1990s was caused by the desire of ethno-political elites to control territory, and the treatment of property had a striking resemblance to that in earlier historical events. The conflict caused physical destruction of properties and massive displacement. Humanitarian excuses were used to justify the removal of properties from one ethnic group and their allocation among the members of another ethnic group that controlled a particular area. Ethnic politics was also used to enhance the private interests of those who held power.

Against the virtual division of the country, the international community created dynamism in property restitution. To some extent it succeeded in blocking legal pluralism and undermining the ethno-political control of divided territories and people. The rule of law approach was perceived as legitimate because the same rule applied to everyone who had been deprived of his or her property during the armed conflict, and also to those who occupied someone else's property. In other words, it was an approach in which individual property rights were equally respected. However, it was not the state that guaranteed these rights, and therefore the legitimacy of the state was not reinforced.

The consolidation of statehood is a long way off, as symbolically depicted in the issue of state property. For the development of the country, the registration and allocation of state property should be completed without delay.[36] However, one of the entities refuses to recognise the authority of the state to regulate this issue. The state–entity relationship highlighted by this problem is a constant block to statebuilding, and ethnicisation is at its roots. Such politics leaves no space for attention to citizens' needs. In the shadow of the ethno-political debate, people's everyday lives continue. Farmers cultivate fragmented plots of land with limited public support. There are also historical elements that affect current land use, including limits in farm size, the inheritance system and allocation of land in the post-conflict period. On top of this lies the legacy of past nationalisation.

While post-conflict property restitution has been assessed as being successful, the consequent return of displaced populations was lower than expected. In terms of peacebuilding, therefore, the restitution effects appear limited to the establishment of the rule of law in the area of property rights, though this has nevertheless contributed to the stabilisation of the country. The limited scale of return realised by the restitution, however, may have immeasurable implications for the future of BiH. Multi-ethnic society does survive in a number of localities. Sarajevo, before the latest armed conflict, was a lively, multi-ethnic city, of which Sarajevans were proud, although its multi-ethnic character had once been obliterated by the Ustasha regime during the Second World War. Given such historical experience, BiH may have preserved the potential for future social changes that can lead to solid peacebuilding.

Notes

1 The PIC steering board consists of Canada, France, Germany, Italy, Japan, Russia, the United Kingdom, the United States, the Presidency of the European Union, the European Commission and the Organisation of the Islamic Conference represented by Turkey.

2 There has been strong scholarly criticism of the international community's involvement in BiH peacebuilding, particularly regarding the HR's power, although I rather recognise the positive effects of the Bonn powers in BiH peacebuilding and statebuilding. See Knaus and Martin (2003) and Chandler (2006).

3 An owner of an estate in the Ottoman period.

4 There is another account by Ljubojević, who writes that, of 2,804,189 hectares of arable land in BiH, only 1,076,685 hectares were distributed to agrarian interested parties. While seven hectares of land were distributed to former serfs and workers on *beys'* lands, invalids, volunteers and landless peasants received only two hectares (Ljubojević 2011: 368).

5 Since the enactment of the 1976 Constitution, the non-ownership concept has been predominant among Yugoslav legal theorists (Coronna 1985: 234).

6 This was pointed out at a few interviews in Belgrade and Sarajevo in June 2012. One interviewee mentioned that in the SFRY a politician and an ordinary worker would have lived in similar apartments, even if their size or location might have been somewhat different. There would have been no equivalent for the palace-like residences of politicians today.

7 Law on Abandoned Apartments (Official Gazette of the Republic of Bosnia and Herzegovina nos. 6/92, 8/92, 16/92, 13/94, 9/95, 33/95); Law on Temporarily Abandoned Real Property Owned by Citizens (Official Gazette of the Socialist Republic of Bosnia and Herzegovina no. 11/93).

8 Decree on the Use of Abandoned Apartments (Official Gazette of the Croatian Community of Herzeg-Bosna no. 13/93).

9 Law on the Use of Abandoned Property (Official Gazette of Republika Srpska, no. 3/96).

10 Law on Amendments to the Law on City Construction Land (Official Gazette of Republika Srpska no. 23/98). In Republika Srpska, the allocation of land or provision of newly constructed houses is also carried out on behalf of refugees from Croatia. When the present author conducted interviews in a settlement in Prijedor Municipality, which was notorious for the Serb torture of Bosniacs during the armed conflict, the interviewees showed understanding that the refugees needed help, 'as they had nowhere to return to', but also expressed bitterness regarding the fact that the municipal authorities had harassed the Bosniac community – by frequently cutting off electricity, for instance – and that they had had to finance everything by themselves. Interview on 18 October 2011.

11 All High Representative decisions are available online at www.ohr.int (accessed 25 October 2013).

12 The European Stability Initiative reports that the waiver system was largely ignored and the reallocation of public land and construction on such land continued (ESI 2002).

13 Commission on Human Rights, Sub-commission on the Promotion and Protection of Human Rights, Housing and Property Restitution in the context of return of refugees and internally displaced persons. UN doc. E/CN.4/Sub.2/2005/17 (2005).

14 Law on Cessation of the Application of the Law on Abandoned Apartments (Official Gazette of the Federation of Bosnia and Herzegovina no. 11/98); Law on Cessation of the Application of the Law on Temporarily Abandoned Real Property Owned by Citizens (Official Gazette of the Federation of Bosnia and Herzegovina

no. 11/98); Law on the Cessation of the Application of the Law on Use of Abandoned Property (Official Gazette of Republika Srpska no. 38/98).

15 The Human Rights Chamber was a judicial body established in accordance with Annex 6 to the GFAP. Its mandate was to consider apparent or alleged violations of human rights, as provided for in the ECHR and the Protocols thereto – as well as in some other human rights conventions – which were directly applicable to BiH in accordance with the Constitution.

16 Human Rights Chamber for Bosnia and Herzegovina, Decision on the Admissibility and Merits: Case No. CH/96/28: *M.J. v. Republika Srpska* (7 November 1997). On this matter, see Williams (2005: 496–97 and accompanying notes).

17 In an interview conducted in Belgrade, a representative of an NGO working for the restitution of properties located in BiH to Serb owners commented positively about the CRPC, highlighting the fact that it worked together with the local bodies. It is noteworthy that even in Serbia the restitution process in BiH is deemed fair, although there are pending cases to be rectified. Interview on 7 June 2012. According to Garlick, 'CRPC had helped to empower right holders in their dealings with the authorities and related organs exerting influence over access to land and housing' (2000: 83–84).

18 While those removed in 1999 were mainly officials suspected of directly obstructing the return process, the 2000 removals involved housing officials whose work was monitored by the international community. Moratti highlights how those who were giving orders escaped the removals due to lack of evidence, since the orders were given secretly (Moratti 2008: 202).

19 OHR website, www.ohr.int/ohr-dept/rrtf/pics/prop-leg-claim-proc/respect/ (accessed 15 October 2013).

20 OHR website, www.ohr.int/ohr-dept/rrtf/pics/prop-leg-claim-proc/dostaje/ (accessed 15 October 2013).

21 www.ohr.int/plip/pdf/plip_1.04.PDF (accessed 19 September 2013).

22 Human Rights Chamber for Bosnia and Herzegovina, Decision on Merits: Case nos. CH/97/60, CH/98/276, CH/98/287, CH/98/362, CH/99/1766: *Miholić et al. against the Federation of Bosnia and Herzegovina* (7 December 2001); and Decision on Admissibility and Merits: Case nos. CH/02/8202, CH/02/9980, CH/02/11011: *M.P., Dušan Brdar and Zorka Štrbac against the Federation of Bosnia and Herzegovina* (4 April 2003).

23 There is further background to this story, relating to a privatised furniture factory whose current employees are predominantly Serbs (ESI 2002: 11–12).

24 The judgement of the European Court of Human Rights on the *Demopoulos* case presented an interesting view on the relationship between property rights and the passage of time since their deprivation (2010a). The court held:

> [A]t the present point, many decades after the loss of possession by the then owners, property has in many cases changed hands, by gift, succession or otherwise; those claiming title may have never seen, or ever used the property in question. ... The losses thus claimed become increasingly speculative and hypothetical.
>
> (para. 111)

The court was of the view that 'from a Convention perspective, property is a material commodity which can be valued and compensated for in monetary terms' (para. 115). However, this view is strongly criticised by a former judge of the same court (Loucaides 2011). He is absolutely right in arguing that human rights violations should be condemned as long as they persist (Loucaides 2011: 445). The question would be how reparation should be designed to take into account the rights of others and the consequences of the reparation.

25 Agreement on Succession Issues and Annexes A to G, 29 June 2001, Bosn.& Herz.-Croat.-Maced.-Slovn.-Fed.R.Yugo, 41 (ILM 2002).
26 Due to the structure of BiH, three decisions – one at the state level and two at the entity levels – were issued: *Decision Enacting the Law on the Temporary Prohibition of Disposal of State Property of Bosnia and Herzegovina*, 343/05 | 21/3/2005; *Decision Enacting the Law on the Temporary Prohibition of Disposal of State Property of Republika Srpska*, 342/05 | 21/3/2005; and *Decision Enacting the Law on the Temporary Prohibition of Disposal of State Property of the Federation of Bosnia and Herzegovina*, 344/05 | 21/3/2005.
27 The other three objectives were the completion of the Brcko Final Award, fiscal sustainability, and entrenchment of the rule of law. Two conditions were the signing of the Stability and Association Agreement, and a positive assessment of the situation in BiH by the PIC steering board, based on full compliance with the Dayton Peace Agreement (OHR 2008).
28 Socio-political organisations were free political organisations of working people, based on socialist principles and financed from public funds (OHR 2009: 8, note 26).
29 *Dogovoreni principi o raspodjeli imovine* [agreed principles for allocation of property], 9 March 2012 (on file with author).
30 The abbreviation DPs stands for displaced persons. This term was usually used in BiH instead of IDPs because IDPs was used to mean individuals displaced within the same municipality. In this chapter, the term IDPs is used for the easier understanding of readers who are not familiar with the way the term was used in BiH.
31 Interview in Srebrenica municipality, 26 June 2012. In fact, the Cessation Law set out that the deadline for returning arable land might be extended until harvest is completed (Article 12a). I owe this point to Massimo Moratti.
32 Prior to the conflict, agriculture made up approximately 10 per cent of GDP, and accounted for 20 per cent of full-time employment and 20 per cent of part-time employment (Mitchell 2004: 2110, citing European Commission and World Bank 1999: 1).
33 This was pointed out by one of the interviewees in Srebrenica municipality. Such minor conflicts are common, according to him – even among family members. Interview on 25 June 2012.
34 Canton Sarajevo was chosen because digitalised cadastral information was available in some parts of the canton. Since the canton is also the location of the capital, it should be considered as the most urbanised canton.
35 Author's interview of Andrija Simunović, mayor of Ravno, and Jelena Bukvić, the person in charge of the PLUD project, 18 June 2012.
36 The state budget is wasted through renting private premises to accommodate state institutions. *Centar za istraživačko novinarstvo* (The centre for investigative reporting) reports in detail a similar situation in the Federation of Bosnia and Herzegovina. The Federation budget flows to property owners who are close to the political decision-makers. 'The FBiH as a tenant despite its own property', *Izvor*, 15 November 2010.

References

Biancalani, R., Brown, D., DeWit, P., Clementi, S. and Ljuša, M., 2004, 'Participatory land use development in the municipalities of Bosnia and Herzegovina: Guidelines', Food and Agricultural Organization of the United Nations, available online at www.fao.org/fileadmin/user_upload/Europe/documents/Publications/BAguidelines_en.pdf (accessed 25 October 2013).

Bojicic-Dzelilovic, V., 2009, 'Peacebuilding in Bosnia-Herzegovina: reflections on the development-democracy link', in *New Perspectives on Liberal Peacebuilding*, ed. E. Newman, R. Paris and O.P. Richmond, Tokyo, New York and Paris: United Nations University Press, 201–17.

Bose, S., 2002, *Bosnia after Dayton: Nationalist Partition and International Intervention*, London: Hurst.

Bosnia and Herzegovina Ministry for Human Rights and Refugees, 2005, 'Comparative Analysis on Access to Rights of Refugees and Displaced Persons', available online at www.mhrr.gov.ba/PDF/?id=283 (accessed 25 October 2013).

Buyse, A., 2008, *Post-conflict Housing Restitution: The European Human Rights Perspective, with a Case Study on Bosnia and Herzegovina*, Antwerp and Oxford: Intersentia.

Chandler, D., 2006, 'Back to the future? The limits of neo-Wilsonian ideals of exporting democracy', *Review of International Studies*, 32: 475–94.

Constitutional Court of Bosnia and Herzegovina, 2012, 'Decision on Admissibility and Merits', U-1/11, 13 July.

Coronna, M.E., 1985, 'The concept of social property and the rights of the foreign investor in Yugoslavia', *Review of Socialist Law*, 11: 227–47.

Čustović, H. and Taletović, J., 2012, 'Report on the survey on land issues in Canton Sarajevo for the research project on land and property problems in post-conflict state-building and economic development' (unpublished).

Dahlman, C. and Tuathail, G., 2005, 'Broken Bosnia: the localized geopolitics of displacement and return in two Bosnian places', *Annals of the Association of American Geographers*, 95(3): 644–62.

Directorate-General for Internal Policies, Policy Department C: Citizens' Rights and Constitutional Affairs, 2010, *Private Properties Issues Following the Change of Political Regime in Former Socialist or Communist Countries*, Brussels: European Parliament.

D'Onfrio, L., 2004, 'Welcome home? Minority return in south-eastern Republika Srpska', Sussex Migration Working Paper no. 19, University of Sussex.

Donais, T., 2005, *The Political Economy of Peacebuilding in Post-Dayton Bosnia*, Abingdon and New York: Routledge.

Dovring, F., 1970, 'Yugoslavia: socialism by consent?', *AID Spring Review 1970 – Land Reform*, Agency for International Development Spring Review, Country Paper, Yugoslavia, 1–63.

ECtHR (European Court of Human Rights), 2010a, *Demopoulos and Others v. Turkey*, 1 March (Application nos. 46113/99, 3843/02, 13751/02, 13466/03, 10200/04, 14163/04, 19993/04, 21819/04).

—— 2010b, *Đokić v. Bosnia and Herzegovina*, 27 May (application no. 6518/04).

——2012, 'Occupancy rights on pre-war flats in Bosnia and Herzegovina', press release issued by the Registrar of the Court, ECtHR 192 (2012), 3 May.

Englbrecht, W., 2004, 'Bosnia and Herzegovina, Croatia and Kosovo: voluntary return in safety and dignity', *Refugee Survey Quarterly*, 23(3): 100–148.

ESI (European Stability Initiative), 2002, *From Dayton to Europe: Land, Development and the Future of Democratic Planning*, Berlin and Sarajevo: ESI.

European Commission and World Bank, 1999, 'Bosnia and Herzegovina: 1996–1998 Lessons and Accomplishments: Review of the Priority Reconstruction and Recovery Program and Looking Ahead towards Sustainable Economic Development', European Commission, Sarajevo, Annex 13: Agriculture.

European Commission for Democracy through Law (Venice Commission), 2011, 'Amicus Curiae Brief for the Constitutional Court of Bosnia and Herzegovina on the Law of the Republika Srpska on the Status of State Property Located on the Territory of the Republika Srpska and Under the Disposal Ban', Adopted by the Venice Commission at its 88th Plenary Session, CDL-AD (2011) 030.

Garlick, M., 2000, 'Protection for property rights: a partial solution? The Commission for real property claims of displaced persons and refugees (CRPC) in Bosnia and Herzegovina', *Refugee Survey Quarterly*, 19(3): 64–85.

Greble, M., 2011, *Sarajevo, 1941–1945: Muslims, Christians, and Jews in Hitler's Europe*, Ithaca, NY: Cornell University Press.

Harvey, J., 2006, 'Return dynamics in Bosnia and Croatia: a comparative analysis', *International Migration*, 44(3): 89–114.

Ito, A., 2001, 'Politicisation of minority return in Bosnia and Herzegovina: the first five years examined', *International Journal of Refugee Law*, 13(1/2): 98–122.

Karadjova, M., 2004, 'Property restitution in Eastern Europe: domestic and international human rights law responses', *Review of Central and East European Law*, 29(3): 325–63.

Knaus, G. and Martin, F., 2003, 'Lessons from Bosnia and Herzegovina: travails of the European Raj', *Journal of Democracy*, 14(3): 60–74.

Leckie, S. (ed.), 2009, *Housing, Land, and Property Rights in Post-conflict United Nations and Other Peace Operations: A Comparative Survey and Proposal for Reform*, New York: Cambridge University Press.

Ljubojević, R., 2011, 'Land property relations in Yugoslavia during the dictatorship of King Aleksandar', *Megatrend Review*, 8(2): 347–70.

Lockwood, W.G., 1975, *European Moslems: Economy and Ethnicity in Western Bosnia*, New York and London: Academic Press.

Loucaides, L.G., 2011, 'Is the European Court of Human Rights still a principled court of human rights after the *Demopoulos* Case?', *Leiden Journal of International Law*, 24: 435–65.

Malcolm, N., 1996, *Bosnia: A Short History*, 2nd edn, Basingstoke: Macmillan.

Medjad, K., 2004, 'The fate of the Yugoslav model: a case against legal conformity', *The American Journal of Comparative Law*, 52: 287–319.

Mirković, D., 1987, 'Sociological reflections on Yugoslav participatory democracy and social ownership', *East European Quarterly*, XXI(3): 319–32.

Mitchell, S.K., 2004, 'Death, disability, displaced persons and development: the case of landmines in Bosnia and Herzegovina', *World Development*, 32(12): 2105–20.

Moratti, M., 2008, 'Tackling obstruction to property rights and return: a critical assessment of the practice of removing housing officials in Bosnia and Herzegovina', in *Deconstructing the Reconstruction: Human Rights and Rule of Law in Postwar Bosnia and Herzegovina*, ed. D.F. Haynes, Aldershot and Burlington, VT: Ashgate, 177–204.

Mungiu-Pippidi, A. and Stefan, L., 2012, 'Perpetual transitions: contentious property and Europeanization in South-Eastern Europe', *East European Politics and Societies*, 26: 340–61.

OHR (Office of the High Representative), 1997, 'PIC Bonn Conclusions', PIC main meeting, 10/12/1997.

——1999a, 'Decision suspending the power of local authorities in the Federation and the RS to re-allocate socially-owned land in cases where the land was used on 6 April 1992 for residential, religious, cultural, private agricultural or private business activities', 26/5/1999.

——1999b, 'Decision on socially-owned land', press release, OHR Sarajevo, 27/5/1999.

——1999c, 'A comprehensive strategy for a just and efficient returns process in Bosnia and Herzegovina', press release, OHR Sarajevo, 27/10/1999.

——1999d, 'Decision on Recognition and Implementation of CRPC Decisions in the RS', 27/10/1999.

——1999e, 'Decision on Recognition and Implementation of CRPC Decisions in the Federation', 27/10/1999.

——2000a, 'Decision on re-allocation of socially-owned land, superseding the 26 May 1999 and 30 December 1999 Decisions', 27/4/2000.

——2002b, 'Decision prioritising, as an exception to the chronological order rule, the repossession of property by returning police officers', 30/4/2002.

——2002c, 'Decision on the use of collective/transit centre space in Bosnia and Herzegovina to promote the phased and orderly return of refugees and displaced persons', 1/8/2002.

——2008, 'Declaration by the Steering Board of the Peace Implementation Council', PIC SB Political Directors, 27/2/2008, available online at www.ohr.int/pic/default. asp?content_id=41352 (accessed 15 October 2013).

——2009, 'Inventory of state property in Bosnia and Herzegovina compiled under the auspices of the Office of the High Representative', final report.

Petrović, M., 2001, 'Post-socialist housing policy transformation in Yugoslavia and Belgrade', *European Journal of Housing Policy*, 1(2): 211–31.

Philpott, C., 2005, 'Though the dog is dead, the pig must be killed: finishing with property restitution to Bosnia-Herzegovina's IDPs and refugees', *Journal of Refugee Studies*, 18(1): 1–24.

Phuong, C., 2004, *The International Protection of Internally Displaced Persons*, Cambridge: Cambridge University Press.

Pogany, I., 1997, *Europe in Change: Righting Wrongs in Eastern Europe*, Manchester: Manchester University Press.

Richmond, O.P., 2009, 'Becoming liberal, unbecoming liberalism: liberal-local hybridity via the everyday as a response to the paradoxes of liberal peacebuilding', *Journal of Intervention and Statebuilding*, 3(3): 324–44.

——2010, 'A genealogy of peace and conflict theory', in *Palgrave Advances in Peace-building: Critical Developments and Approaches*, ed. O.P. Richmond, London: Palgrave Macmillan, 14–38.

Rose, L., Thomas, J. and Tumler, J., 2000, 'Land tenure issues in post-conflict countries: the case of Bosnia and Herzegovina', available online at www2.gtz.de/dokumente/bib/ 05–0164.pdf (accessed 25 October 2013).

Simmie, J., 1991, 'Housing and inequality under state socialism: an analysis of Yugoslavia', *Housing Studies*, 6(3): 172–81.

Sokolović, D. and Bieber, F., 2001, *Reconstructing Multiethnic Societies: The Case of Bosnia-Herzegovina*, Aldershot: Ashgate.

Stahn, C., 2002, 'The agreement on succession issues of the former Socialist Federal Republic of Yugoslavia', *The American Journal of International Law*, 96(2): 379–97.

Stanic, A., 2001, 'Financial aspects of state succession: the case of Yugoslavia', *European Journal of International Law*, 12(4): 751–79.

Stefansson, A.H., 2006, 'Homes in the making: property restitution, refugee return, and senses of belonging in a post-war Bosnian town', *International Migration*, 44(3): 116–39.

Stubbs, P., 2001, '"Social sector" or the diminution of social policy? Regulating welfare regimes in contemporary Bosnia-Herzegovina', in *International Support Policies to SEE Countries – Lessons (not) Learned in Bosnia-Herzegovina*, ed. Z. Papic, Sarajevo: Muller.

Toal, G. and Dahlman, T., 2011, *Bosnia Remade: Ethnic Cleansing and its Reversal*, New York: Oxford University Press.

Tsenkova, S., 2009, *Housing Policy Reforms in Post-socialist Europe: Lost in Transition*, Heidelberg: Physica-Verlag.

Tuathail, G.Ó. and Dahlman, C., 2006, 'Post-domicide Bosnia and Herzegovina: homes, homelands and one million returns', *International Peacekeeping*, 13(2): 242–60.

Tuathail, G.Ó. and O'Loughlin, J., 2009, 'After ethnic cleansing: return outcomes in Bosnia-Herzegovina a decade beyond war', *Annals of the Association of American Geographers*, 99(5): 1045–53.

UN 1992, 'Report on the situation of human rights in the territory of the former Yugoslavia', UN Doc. E/CN.4/1992/S-1/9 (1992).

UN-HABITAT, 2005, *Housing and Property Rights: Bosnia and Herzegovina, Croatia and Serbia and Montenegro: Security of Tenure in Post-conflict Societies*, Nairobi: UN-HABITAT.

Van Doren, J.W., 1972, 'Ownership of Yugoslav social property and United States industrial property: a comparison', *Rutgers Law Review*, 26: 73–108.

Von Carlowitz, L., 2004, 'Settling property issues in complex peace operations: The CRPC in Bosnia Herzegovina and the HPD/CC in Kosovo', *Leiden Journal of International Law*, 17: 599–614.

Waters, T.W., 1999, 'The naked land: the Dayton Accords, property disputes, and Bosnia's real constitution', *Harvard International Law Journal*, 40(2): 1–81.

Williams, R.C., 2005, 'Post-conflict property restitution and refugee return in Bosnia and Herzegovina: implications for international standard-setting and practice', *International Law and Politics*, 37: 441–553.

——2013, 'Post-conflict land tenure issues in Bosnia: privatization and the politics of reintegrating the displaced', in *Land and Post-conflict Peacebuilding*, ed. J. Unruh and R.C. Williams, Abingdon: Earthscan, 145–75.

7 Colombian land problems, armed conflict and the state

Noriko Hataya, Sergio Coronado Delgado, Flor Edilma Osorio Pérez and Nicolás Vargas Ramírez

What is the relationship between the concentrated land-ownership structure and the six-decade-long internal armed conflict in Colombia? This is the central question of this chapter. In November 2012 a new dialogue began between the Revolutionary Armed Forces of Colombia (*Fuerzas Armadas Revolucionarias de Colombia*, FARC) and the Colombian government, with a view to signing a peace agreement. Even though, in contrast to the other countries studied in this volume, Colombia is the only case which has yet to reach the post-conflict stage.

Previous studies have adopted two general approaches to land problems in Colombia: one analyses the process of agrarian reforms as a political response to the peasant movements and their struggle for land (Zamosc 1986); the other treats the issue through a historical analysis of agricultural colonisation and rural development in the country, with a special focus on the land concentration and structure of land use in Colombia (Machado 2002; Fajardo 2002; Palacios 2006). Since the last decade of the twentieth century, however, there has been a focus on the emerging potential for economic development in Latin America, including Colombia, accompanying the global agro-industry boom (World Bank 2008; PNUD 2011). In this new context, there has been a polemical debate on issues such as rural development without the involvement of peasants (*campesinos*)[1] v. rural development involving peasant modes of production for subsistence (Akram-Lodhi 2007). A more relevant analysis today focuses on a new wave of social movements with diversified actors who have been rendered 'invisible' in the political arena during the past century (Vergara-Camus 2012).

The current land conflict between parties representing international capital and local communities with no guarantee of land entitlement has mostly been analysed by activist advocacy-orientated NGOs, but there has yet to be a detailed comprehensive academic analysis.[2] Today's land conflict, caused by large-scale land purchases by officially approved investors, needs to be analysed in relation to the domestic land tenure structure and local and long-standing regional conflicts between local government, civil society and external actors who have had their own interests in territorial dominance.

There are numerous case studies and monographs on armed conflicts related to land issues in Colombia. They have shown the specific characteristics of the armed conflict in the respective regional contexts, and have treated the armed conflicts and violence from a historical perspective (Vargas 1992; Escobar 2008; Velasco 2009; Moncada ed. 2011; Colombia Land Rights Monitor 2013; Molano 2013). However, there is limited analysis addressing land conflicts following population displacement. In this sense, the regional monograph series on displaced people backed by CNRR[3] are good examples that focus on abandoned land from the point of view and using the voices of displaced persons (CNRR – Grupo de Memoria Histórica 2010a; 2010b). However, there has been no systematic study analysing land conflicts where local people have been deprived of their land due to armed conflict and violence.

Given the above review of the literature on land problems and conflict in Colombia, our methodology and the anticipated results of this study offer the following advantages: first, our approach integrates national and regional perspectives, offering a better understanding of the current nature of land conflicts in Colombia. Second, it examines the performance of regional governments in order to demonstrate that one of the principal causes of today's land conflicts is the vulnerability of local administrations. Most previous studies have thoroughly analysed the weaknesses and limits of national government land policies, but the role and nature of local and regional governments has been ambiguous and needs to be investigated properly. Third, our holistic approach helps to clarify the changing nature of land conflicts in terms of the actors and institutions involved. Most previous studies have dealt with the causal relationships between land issues and armed conflict, but such relationships have become multilateral due to the emergence of new actors – such as officially recognised enterprises – which has not been sufficiently studied.

The chapter is based on a bibliographical and document survey and fieldwork conducted between 2010 and 2013 in two regions of the country: Montes de María and Magdalena Medio. During the field research, semi-structured and non-structured interviews, dialogues, workshops and participatory observations were carried out with inhabitants, NGO activists and public functionaries, focusing on relevant social processes in both regions. As the Colombian state has diverse relationships and societal problems on different administrative levels (local, regional and national), our local and regional approach is indispensable to understanding these themes.

The two regions were selected for their common particularities relevant for the purpose of our comparison: the denominations of these regions are derived from the characterisation based on the social recognition given by local communities, and not from the local administrative division (in fact, this situation is explained by their marginal positions and the lack of state oversight); both regions have been involved in traditional land struggles and have been the scenes of representative rural movements; they rely on NGOs that support local peasant communities; and each relies on an important sector of the rural population that has participated in demanding state recognition of their land rights.

Magdalena Medio is rather homogeneous, with a major part of its population categorised as peasants, whereas Montes de María is more heterogeneous, showing a greater proportion of Afro-Colombians and indigenous people.

Our analysis starts from the following four interrelated hypotheses. 1) The Colombian state is still in the process of formation and has not managed to sufficiently integrate different parts of society and different geographical areas. The degree of consolidation depends on the linkage with central government organisations and the power structures of the regions, and this situation has facilitated the persistence of armed conflict. 2) The war has facilitated a process of rapid and forced dispossession of land by different interests, with the frequent involvement of state functionaries and institutions. The terror caused by the war has led to a new series of forced dispossessions, this time – in the context of the current national policy to prioritise the primary sector of the economy – legalised and legitimised by large international investors. What was done in the past by armies and through violence is done today through bureaucratic processes which facilitate subsoil concessions, to which the formalisation of property rights is no impediment. 3) The armed conflict is a complex and persistent process, which has unfolded over half a century and affected all the relevant actors, including the rural population. This population has developed ways of surviving and strengthening its resistance. 4) The war generates important economic and political benefits for many sectors, which are therefore interested in prolonging it and exercise a certain degree of control. Under such a monopolistic alliance of elite interests with state protection, the concentration of property has accelerated.

This chapter is composed of four sections. The first part provides the national context, describing the nature of the problems related to land and armed conflict, the institutional responses and the struggles led by rural inhabitants. The second and third parts analyse the studied regions, Montes de María and Magdalena Medio, showing the tensions through which the region–centre power relationships are perceived. In the final section, we will consider a series of cross-sectional ideas derived from regional realities and national dynamics.

Problems of land and armed conflict in Colombia

The national context of land concentration and armed conflict

Colombia has maintained a historically concentrated structure of land ownership, which has become more extreme as a result of the war. The war provokes forced displacement from the land, with few opportunities for return. In highly vulnerable conditions, displaced people are forced to take on precarious employment in which they are exposed to new types of exploitation. The impact of the war on the agrarian structure should be seen in the context of a development model exclusively focused on certain social classes and which tends to concentrate wealth through increased efficiency and access to international markets. As a consequence, rural populations have become increasingly impoverished (Osorio and Herrera 2012).

The rural sector has been besieged by legal and illegal investments of four types: those from agro-industrial companies (especially companies dealing with palm oil and timber), those for illicit crops, those for extensive cattle ranching and those from companies in the mining and energy sector. This siege of the rural sector is also based in vertical relationships among those controlling the ownership over the resources and those providing their labour force, usually at a very low cost. In this complex situation it is more likely that large scale companies – rather than other sectors, such as peasants – will benefit (Fajardo 2006). From this general perspective, we identify three relevant tendencies in Colombia, which are as follows.

Land concentration

Inequity in access to land constitutes one of the most important objective outcomes of the armed conflict, as it generates social exclusion and inequality (Comisión de Estudios sobre la Violencia 1987). The economic power of land generates political and social benefits, which in turn provide economic returns for broadening economic power. The bipolarised agrarian structure, as well as limited economic growth in the rural sector, has impeded the Colombian government from responding satisfactorily to demands for access to land.

This situation has intensified social conflicts over demands for access to land from the rural population, impeded the development of a cooperative system for production in the agriculture and cattle-raising sectors, and generated conflicts around land use as a result of excessive or insufficient land use intensity, thus causing economic and social exclusion. In the same way, it has generated a monopoly of a few landowners and favoured their interests in state agrarian policy, which is defined within an institutional framework designed to strengthen their hegemony (Machado 2004).

The historically persistent concentration of rural property has now reached a Gini coefficient of 0.86 (Ibáñez and Muñoz 2012: 301), to which the war has contributed significantly. The tactics of intimidation and complicity on the part of local and regional authorities have facilitated land dispossession via illegal businesses. In the midst of generalised terror, the regions with the greatest concentration of land ownership have been ignored by the state (Ibáñez and Muñoz 2012).

Between 1985 and 2011, around 5.5 million Colombians were victims of forced displacement (Codhes 2012). Eight of every ten displaced families have had to abandon their land, but only two of them have registered title deeds – the rest either have no officially authorised documents to prove their ownership, or only those of private transactions. The high level of ambiguity in the legal status of the land of victims of forced displacement has frequently favoured dispossession. According to Garay and Barbieri (2012), at least 5.5 million hectares, equivalent to 10.8 per cent of all agricultural land in Colombia, are not in the hands of their legitimate owners.

According to the last available data from the end of 2012, forced displacement reflects the intensification of the political conflict – not only because of its magnitude, but also because of the lack of a unified and appropriate approach by the state towards the victims. All 33 of Colombia's departments and 85 per cent of its municipalities are affected by forced internal displacement, which includes both the expulsion of inhabitants and the admission of internally displaced persons. However, the places most affected are the principal cities such as Bogotá, Medellín, Cali, Cartagena and Barranquilla, as well as the intermediate regional cities. This has caused a profound demographic transformation, with serious socio-economic, political and socio-cultural repercussions for the whole of Colombian society. Garay and Bariberi (2012) estimate the value lost by the total of displaced population at US$4.27 billion in 2008 (which is equivalent to 1.96 per cent of GDP in 2007).

The decision to resume the peace dialogue between the government and FARC in 2012 placed the issues of land concentration and deprivation back in the public arena. However, this did not imply any political will to correct problems of land ownership, despite FARC insisting on the 'carrying out of an integral agrarian reform, in terms of socio-environmental, democratic and participative meanings, with a territorial focus' (cited in Agencia Prensa Rural 2013).[4]

Intensification of conflicts over land use

In Colombia, arable land (land of 'potential use for agriculture') stands at 14,362,867 hectares – 12.6 per cent of the national land area (114,174,800 hectares). In 2002 land used for agriculture (5,317,862 hectares) was only 37 per cent of arable land, while that used for cattle ranching was twice as extensive as the area categorised as suitable for it. This has caused the deforestation of around 22 million hectares (IGAC-CORPOICA 2002).[5] The 'forestry' category includes legally protected natural areas (for example, the *Zona de Reserva Forestal*: Forest Reserve Zone) in which the uses of land are limited according to the soil's ecological potentiality, namely for the purposes of forest conservation (Vásquez and Serrano 2009). The overlap of these areas with those occupied by rural inhabitants has been the principal cause of conflicts with the state as a result of restrictions on land use and the acquisition of property rights. This situation especially affects rural communities that are neither indigenous nor Afro-descendant; the latter, because they are protected by a statutory requirement, should be consulted prior to the state's declaration of a conservation area.

Subsoil concessions for resource extraction are another source of land conflict. The state has still not managed to prevent designated institutions from awarding concessions in protected areas. The awarding of concessions can lead to the expropriation of land, or impede the recognition of rights to land already inhabited and used by the rural population. In this way, between 1990 and 2010 around 10 million hectares of concessions were granted for mining activities, and applications were received for concessions on another 26 million hectares (CGR 2011).

On the other hand, statistics for 2010 show significant food dependency in Colombia: rice imports have increased by 64.4 per cent, corn by 67.3 per cent, barley by 35.6 per cent and wheat by 21.1 per cent. Meanwhile, crops such as palm oil, cocoa and fruit have had their production boosted by policies oriented towards competitiveness in exportable tropical products (López 2012). The government shift in priority from food production for the domestic market towards export-oriented agro-industry has had negative effects on income generation and therefore morale in productive activities. This has led to land sales, changes in land use and the migration of peasants – who were hitherto engaged in small- and medium-scale farming – to cities, diminishing their traditional contribution to the internal food market.

Forced displacement and aggravation of impoverishment

A persistently high proportion of the rural population lives in poverty, and this proportion is increasing as a result of forced displacement. Of every 100 rural dwellers, 62 are categorised as poor and 25 as indigent (Bonilla and González eds 2006).[6] In municipalities categorised as 'highly rural' in terms of economic activities and population density, 75 per cent are categorised as populations with unsatisfied basic needs (UBN) (PNUD 2011). There are also significant inequities between regions and even more between rural and urban areas. However, city averages of UBN indicators conceal a profound heterogeneity as well, with many internal contrasts. For example, peripheral urban sectors have higher indicators of indigence, exacerbated by forced displacement caused by the war and migration from the countryside.

The effects of the war in aggravating the impoverishment endured by forcibly displaced families are clear, since the majority of displaced households have been deprived not only of their assets but also of their livelihoods (Garay and Barbieri 2012). The living conditions of families displaced to cities are usually categorised as poverty or indigence, and for them the process of re-establishing themselves is very slow and uncertain. Women are particularly affected: since the majority of survivors of the war are women, they have to assume the role of sole breadwinner for their households.

Measures employed by the state and their scope

As is the case today, the bipartisan violence of the mid-twentieth century generated a large population exodus all over the country, which led to the concentration of land among former landowning elites (Sánchez 1991). Following a four-year dictatorship, which had a pacifying effect, the two opposing parties signed a pact known as the National Front, which established that power would be alternated between them every four years, while excluding and declaring illegal any other political parties (Kline 1995; Palacios 2006).

This elite-led democracy was a factor that promoted the emergence of leftist guerrillas in 1964 – a time at which armed struggle was considered an option for social transformation on the continent. The two most relevant and active groups today are FARC and the National Liberation Army (*Ejército de Liberación Nacional*, ELN) (INDEPAZ 2012); the areas of influence of both are predominantly rural. The former have always flown the agrarian flag, while the latter insist on nationalisation of energy resources. Having mentioned these antecedents, we will now underline some tendencies in state land policy during the last 60 years.

State efforts at agrarian reform with a limited scope

In Colombia, policies and normative frameworks related to land ownership have proved to be insufficient in addressing the concentration of land ownership and changing the inequitable agrarian structure (see Table 7.1). Agrarian reform in Colombia can be understood in relation to the evolution of the legal framework. Instead of land redistribution, the agricultural frontier has been extended to the south and east of the country: sometimes with very little official support, sometimes autonomously, and at other times during the so-called armed colonisation, in other words, led by FARC – this occurred at a time when this armed group did not aim to demolish the state, but rather to achieve 'an agrarian reform promoting small and medium property ownership' (Ramírez 1981: 203).

In the 1980s, the government adopted a productive strategy designed to modernise zones in which the peasant economy predominated. Government actions regarding land were limited to the incorporation of new zones at the agrarian frontier. Productive efficiency, in the context of a process of opening up the Colombian economy, was intensified at the beginning of the 1990s. The current legal framework (Law 160 of 1994) is intended to consolidate a land-rights market approach, which was derived from the emergence of new land disputes and conflicts, and will be analysed in the following sections.

Lack of formalisation of land rights in rural areas

The basic procedure for registering land, including the clarification of whether property is public or private and the delimitation of land boundaries, has been delayed all over the country. There is an evident lack of formalisation of land rights in rural areas: 47.7 per cent of landowners do not have formal property titles, and the situation is even more critical for small landholders (Gáfaro *et al.* 2012). Some of these problems relate to the lack of clarity around property titles in much of the country, a backlog at the land registry office, the high costs of registry transactions and rural property legalisation, uncertainty over property and the lack of clear and definitive delimitation of which lands are public and which private, especially in places such as

Table 7.1 Colombian agrarian reform laws

Name and year	Characteristics
Law 200 in 1936	This law created the concept of the social function of land, meaning that land should be distributed to landless peasants, specifically those occupying wilderness land. One of the main ideas of this law was to recognise the ownership of the land by the peasants working and living on it.
Law 100 in 1944	The purpose of this law was to avoid the land distribution effect caused by the previous land law. This law created barriers against peasants claiming their property rights, by enforcing land rights such as possession and tenure instead of property rights in favour of landless peasants.
Law 161 in 1961	This law was the result of the commitment of the national elite to the distribution of land to landless peasants. The policy created by this law laid the foundation for the National Institute of Colombia for the Agrarian Reform (Incora) and several institutions and norms, with the main purpose of giving land to peasants and recognising and formalising property rights.
Law 4 in 1974	Also known as the 'Chicoral Pact' (named after a province ruled by the landlords at that time). This law was the result of a negotiation between the state and regional elites, and its purpose was to restrain the progress of the agrarian reform law of the 1960s, since agrarian reform was assumed to be a threat to their political and economic power.
Law 160 in 1994	The 1990s amendment of the agrarian reform law implied a shift from the state-oriented land policy to the establishment of a land market supported by the state. Despite this, the law also created Peasant Reserve Zones to protect access to land by peasants in wilderness areas, established limits to private titles to wilderness lands and recognised the territorial rights of indigenous and afro-descendant communities.

Sources: Fajardo 2002; Machado 2002

marshlands, riverbanks and communally used plains. All of this makes the process of identifying and reclaiming property difficult.

The insufficiency and inefficiency of the technical and administrative institutions in charge of land

It is important to add another persistent problem: corruption. In some regions, the links between armed actors and the authorities, including public functionaries in charge of administering systems of registering land rights, have facilitated processes that have led to increasingly concentrated land ownership. This practice has facilitated the co-option of institutional structures at local and regional levels, especially by paramilitary groups. Therefore, although there are comprehensive norms and legal procedures, very few coherent practices are in operation.

New perspective: the land restitution policy and Law 1448/2011

The Land Restitution Law (1448/2011) is an important step towards the reparation and recognition of the rights of victims of the Colombian armed conflict, and is also an expression of the national consensus in favour of reparations for the victims (Bautista 2012; Uprimny and Sánchez 2010). The legal enacting of victims' rights and land restitution was impossible during the Uribe administration, given the government's lack of commitment to the victims. The situation changed under the mandate of President Santos, who showed an interest in this issue from his very first days in power. This law must not be assumed to be an agrarian reform law, because its purpose is not to redistribute land but to repair and restore the rights of the victims of recent violence in the country. It is possible to see that the law has an important background in several international human rights instruments, such as the Deng Principles and the Pinheiro Principles. For example, the law establishes, in Article 71, land restitution as a measure to compensate victims – financial compensation included – and this measure is prioritised over others. Nevertheless, several aspects of the law have been criticised by victims' organisations and human rights NGOs, on the grounds that they do not meet the demands of the international human rights legal framework. Some of these criticisms are as follows:

1 The restriction on the category of victims. Only those who suffered displacement and dispossession after 1991 are recognised. This creates an obstacle for those who were victimised in previous periods, and it clearly forms a limit to the human rights approach of the policy.
2 Limitations on the property within the scope of restitution. The law established that only land can be restored – not property, houses, crops, farm animals or other possessions lost by victims. Overcoming this problem will depend on the enforcement of complementary policies, such as the provision of housing, rural development and technical support to the victims.
3 The inclusion of measures that limit the possibility of restitution. Article 99 stipulates that a restitution judge can establish a legal contract between the victim, as the owner of the restored plot, and the current users of the land only if the current users prove their innocence with regard to the original circumstances in which the land was seized – in which case they can continue to use the land. This can be understood as a limit on the material restitution of the victim's land, because there is no change in the land use – for example, with regard to crops planted during the forced displacement.

Despite these problems, this law is the current legal framework for reparation and the restitution of the rights of more than 4.5 million victims in the country. By the end of February 2013, the Land Restitution Unit had received 32,688 requests from victims to be included in the National Register of Abandoned and Dispossessed Land, and these requests covered an area of

2,368,908 hectares (UAEGRT 2013). The successful enforcement of this law is greatly dependent on the capacity of the state to conciliate the interests of the national elite, who are interested in land restitution and the consolidation of a land market, and the many regional elites who see this policy as a threat. For the national elite, creating a dynamic land market through formalisation of the land tenure system is one of the indispensable conditions for providing security and encouraging foreign investment. The regional elites, however, see land restitution as a land distribution policy which would affect their power, which is founded on land concentration.

Rural inhabitants and their land struggles

In order for any social change to be sustainable, the participation of society is indispensable. Colombian democracy depends upon the active participation of the population. Therefore, despite the unequal power relationships between rural civilians and armed groups, the political elite and powerful business interests, rural civilians' capacity and initiative for resistance has been significant, and they are integral to a successful peace process. We will focus on some of these aspects here.

The peasant struggle for land and lack of a state response

As with any other social demand, redistribution of land and demands for dignified living conditions in rural areas requires that society press for this in the public agenda. The agrarian reform of 1960 was promoted by the National Association of Peasant Land-Users (ANUC) in a process of 'organisation from above', which created a structure 'constructed from below' with four characteristics: a national scope, heterogeneous class content,[7] representation and institutional legitimisation (Zamosc 1987). In this way, as Múnera comments:

> the formation of the ANUC enabled the peasant community to construct a political and social identity in a practical way, as users of state services. The peasants identified themselves as collective consumers of rural public functions, which had been drawn up by the government.
>
> (1998: 284)

Between 1970 and 1978 Colombia experienced a series of invasions of large estates (*haciendas*), which eventually led to 1,031 land occupations by peasants, over almost all the country (Zamosc 1987). Following the Chicoral Pact (see Table 7.1), the peasant movement was slowed down by internal disunity and state repression. This included 'the mobilisation of battalions of the Army, the militarisation of whole regions, massive arrests, long stretches in prison with mistreatment, and the repression of self-defense armed groups of the owners of large estates' (Zamosc 1987: 177). External harassment and internal disputes diminished the energy available for new land occupations, which led to a rapid weakening of the peasants' organisation. The advance of the war, selective persecution of the community leaders and the treatment of social protest as a public order problem diminished the movement's force.

New rural actors and proposals that emerged from the war

Since the intensification of the war, not only the landless peasants but a variety of social groups in rural areas have become involved in the struggle for land and their way of life. Organisations of displaced persons, resistance communities, peasant associations in *Zonas de Reserva Campesina* (Peasant Reserve Zones), women's and victims' groups and Afro-Colombian and indigenous organisations are some of the many socio-political actors in the rural sector, some of which have emerged from the war itself. They are gradually receiving increased national and international recognition. Their efforts have been oriented towards different ends: self-defence, autonomy in the governance of land, and productive agricultural activities and training, as well as proposals to deal with the armed conflict. Many have seen that not only the war, but also the apparent 'peace', has driven people off their land through development projects such as mining exploitation. This generates new activities and networks which allow these groups to face up to powerful adversaries and expand their repertoires of collective action. Hence, the strategy of land occupation that was useful in the 1970s is no longer effective in pressuring the state to redistribute land.

Stigmatisation and persecution against the social movements

In the context of the war in Colombia, social protest has been stigmatised and de-legitimised, as those involved have been considered to be allied with subversive (illegal) groups; this has led to the persecution of leaders and participants. Towards the end of the 1990s and during the first years of the twenty-first century, this situation became more intense as a result of multiple massacres of rural inhabitants, some of whom belonged to agrarian trade unions and protest organisations. This direct persecution by the state, or through paramilitary groups, constitutes political intolerance.[8] The perverse effect of the presence of guerrilla groups, interpreted as the worst and sole enemy of the state, has impeded the formation of a significant democratic left-wing political party. At least 71 leaders have been assassinated in connection with land restitution processes between 2006 and 2011. Many more have been threatened and have had to go into exile (Semana 2012).

Montes de María: land ownership, peacebuilding and state presence[9]

Montes de María is a sub-region located in the Caribbean region, and incorporates 15 municipalities of the departments of Sucre and Bolívar (see Figure 7.1). The process of populating Montes de María goes back to the advance of hacienda-owning elites in the sixteenth century, as well as to the establishment of Afro-Colombian communities which had fled from slavery (Navarrete 2008). The haciendas were consolidated and continued the exploitation of enclave economies, especially through tobacco cropping and cattle ranching, around the beginning of the twentieth century (CNRR – Memoria Histórica 2010b). The peasant population lived in marginal conditions as a result of the domination of food and land markets by the haciendas. The domination over the land market led to the control of the haciendas on the best arable land.

Figure 7.1 Map of political and administrative division of Montes de María

Table 7.2 General information on Montes de María

Land area:	697,312 hectares
Projected 2012 population:	676,428 inhabitants
Urban dwellers – percentage of population:	74%
Rural dwellers – percentage of population:	26%
Percentage of population with UBN:	65%
Percentage of rural population with UBN:	68%
Population displaced by violence (1997–2011):	215,923 persons

Source: Created by authors based on data from DANE, SIPOD

During the second half of the twentieth century, the peasantry's organi-sational processes transformed the region's political landscape. In some municipalities, organised landless peasants initiated activities to pressure the state to hand over land, and created a scenario of negotiation for land redistribution during the 1960s and 1970s. The National Institute of Colombia for Agrarian Reform (Incora) negotiated with some large landowners and awarded property rights to peasants organised within ANUC, through a mechanism of title and tenancy in common (*proindiviso*). From the peasants' point of view, Incora partially fulfilled the task of awarding land access to those members of the population who lacked it. Although many peasants lacked basic social and economic rights, some had partial access to land.[10]

Nevertheless, the institutional action which facilitated this partial access of peasants to land in the region was diminished by two phenomena that occurred during the second half of the 1990s and the early years of the 2000s. First, neoliberal reforms weakened those institutions in charge of promoting peasant access to land, and facilitated the importation of the types of food products that were produced in the region – which led to the financial ruin of many peasant producers.[11] Second, the escalation of paramilitary violence, which led to forced displacement and theft of land, undermined the position of the peasant population in making demands of state institutions.

Three phases can be identified in the armed conflict in Montes de María. The first was marked by the arrival of FARC in the region in 1985, occupying territories where there was no state presence. The second began in 1997, when large-scale landowners, politicians and business people encouraged the arrival of paramilitary groups, intensifying the armed conflict against the civil population and dispossessing peasants of close to 40,000 hectares of land in the region (Ministerio de Agricultura 2011). The population did not have the capacity to act against the state, nor did the state have the institutional capacity to respond to the demands of the peasants. The country is currently witnessing a third phase, marked by the demobilisation of certain para-military structures and the emergence of new ones, as well as the limited presence of guerrillas in some zones. Although security conditions have improved, the presence of armed actors is still felt, as it is in many other places around the country, and they are linked with processes of concentration of rural land ownership and dispossession of land.

Land ownership disputes

Rural inhabitants of the Montes de María region are currently faced with different conflicts related to land ownership rights. These conflicts can be explained in relation to the agrarian structures resulting from the period of intensification of the armed conflict against the civil population (1997–2010), as well as the institutional reforms which transformed the presence of the state in the region. The typology presented in Table 7.3 gathers some of the land ownership disputes identified in fieldwork.

Two tendencies can be observed in the region with regard to property rights and land disputes. First, there is a process of re-concentration of ownership of agrarian land, derived from the usurping of land as a result of the armed conflict, and this process has become linked to the expansion of agro-industrial, timber and cattle-ranching production. This process is categorised in the typology as type 1 (Table 7.3), and notable cases include the rapid growth in land ownership by private companies in Carmen de Bolívar – increasing from 3,889 hectares in 2000 to 8,325 hectares by the year 2010 – and that of Hacienda la Europa (province of Ovejas), where 1,321 hectares awarded in 1969 to 114 peasant families through agrarian reform were later bought through irregular transactions by a private businessman from another region of the country, after the forced displacement of local inhabitants (Verdad Abierta 2012). According to the national authority of notaries and land registration, the large-scale purchase of land belonging to displaced persons could have involved a total of 37,273 hectares (ILSA 2012).

Second, there are demands for access to, and formalisation and protection of, land rights by peasants and ethnic groups.[12] This is the case for the community of Pueblo Nuevo (province of María la Baja), who were victims of two forced displacements and who demanded that the state formally recognise their property rights over the land. This community and other organisations have forged links via the Organisation of Displaced Population, which represents their interests to the government. Discussions in recent years between peasants and the state have centred on access to land and guaranteeing property rights, identifying the possibility of establishing a Peasant Reserve Zone, and moving forwards with the recognition of the territorial rights of ethnic groups.

In disputes of type 1 and 2, the strong presence of government administration favours the consolidation, by investors and third parties, of property rights to land usurped from peasants.[13] Disputes of type 2 allow the identification of the requirements in terms of prioritising land for the peasants who were displaced and returned, and for those who have resisted displacement. Many peasants do not rely on formal property rights to their land, and some even consider that this situation protects them in the face of the growth of

Table 7.3 Main types of land disputes in Montes de María

Land dispute	Actors involved	Description and causes	Relationship with the state
1 Displaced peasants demand the restitution of their land, which was subject to concentration of ownership and mass buying after the violence.	Displaced peasants v. investors (companies, individual owners) and/or illegal armed groups (mainly paramilitaries)	Private agents purchased the land abandoned by or dispossessed from peasants. Some of these cases were legal purchases when prices were very low because of the violence, with the complicity of public authorities.	Currently, the state is trying to remedy its intervention against the land rights of the displaced peasants by the enforcement of the Land Restitution Law. This law aims to recognise and formalise property rights over land stolen from or abandoned by peasants due to the violence.
2 Peasants demand the protection of their land because of the threat of growing agribusiness and monoculture.	Peasants (returned communities, or persons who did not abandon their land) v. local and national authorities and/or investors (companies, individual owners)	Investors arrived in the region for the purpose of buying land. In some cases there are links between the buyers and illegal armed groups, led by corrupt state functionaries.	The state authorities are studying the possibility of constituting a Peasant Reserve Zone for the region with an area of 441,673 hectares.
3 Lack of land access programmes or agrarian reform to benefit the economically active rural population	Landless peasants (mainly rural women and young people) claim against local and national authorities.	Agrarian reform via the land market is insufficient to address the demand for access to rural land by the poor peasants.	The state response has been limited. In some cases, access to land is achieved via the intervention of NGOs with international financial support.
4 Land grabbing of areas designated for common use (agricultural suitability, forests, plains and river banks)	Peasant communities v. local and national authorities, and/or investors (companies, individual owners)	Land for common use was appropriated for the development of large-scale productive or extractive projects, which was approved by public authorities in charge of land policies at the regional level.	The state is trying to revise the demarcation of communal land. 1,822 hectares are currently being collectively titled to the Afro-descendant groups.

Source: Author, based on fieldwork

large-scale estates, in that it makes buying their land more difficult because of the lack of documentation.[14] The state could resolve this situation through protective measures, such as Peasant Reserve Zones or the recognition of territorial rights for ethnic groups.

Dispute types 3 and 4 demonstrate situations of a limited state presence, which reflects an institutional transition resulting from the implementation of neoliberal policies. While the land market expands, peasants are excluded from the land, which leads to a high level of concentration of land ownership in municipalities such as Palmito or Toluviejo (Gini coefficient 0.83).

In many situations, the absence of the state is compensated for by the actions of NGOs that provide land for peasants. This is the case for the Feminine Agricultural Association of San Cayetano, in the province of San Juan Nepomuceno. Dispute type 4 shows the absence of the state in terms of its obligations to protect the rural population's access to land. The lack of state action and the problems of bringing the land registry up to date for land that is public but designated as being for communal use, or for ancestral territories of ethnic peoples, facilitates the process of monopolising land and concentration of ownership. Some black communities have asked the state to protect their territories through collective land titles – for example the community councils of Eladio Ariza and Santo Madero (in the province of San Jacinto). Other organisations carry out processes of defending their collective land, such as the Council for the Defence of the Communal Riverbanks (province of Mahates).

The disputes given in Table 7.3 occur simultaneously. The absence of public institutions to protect the community's rights to access land is related to the presence of another public institution which recognises, through an illegal bureaucratic procedure, property rights over this same land, in favour of private agents. The presence of the state might promote the protection of the peasant population's land rights through existing legal means. However, in recent years the formalisation of property rights has mainly favoured the interests of private actors who use them to gain juridical security for their investments – to the detriment of peasants' rights. This situation has been denounced by the local population and prosecuted by public authorities at the national level, and various notaries have therefore been dismissed for having links with illegal armed actors (Ministerio de Agricultura 2011).

The characteristics of the disputes also allow the identification of general tendencies related to access and control of land in the region. One aspect to take into account is the nature of institutional behaviour. In general, these institutions are far from what would be hoped for in terms of a redistributive agrarian reform, because of the effect of the agrarian structure and pre-existing power structures (Borras 2007). Institutional responses do not take into account local conditions, where private property rights have been demonstrably incapable of regulating all the complex relationships in rural societies. The state needs to put in place diverse institutional measures oriented towards addressing diverse situations in order to protect and guarantee the rights of the rural population in the context of large-scale land grabbing and threats endangering their ways of life.

The Magdalena Medio region: rich resources, peasants' land struggles and stigmas[15]

The Magdalena Medio region is located in the north central region of the country. It has 33 municipalities,[16] situated in marginal zones of four departments, and communication among them is mainly via the Magdalena River (Figure 7.2). Settlement in Magdalena Medio accelerated after the construction of a railway towards the end of the nineteenth century, as well as after the discovery of oil in 1918. This brought a wave of migrants attracted by the increased labour demand from these infrastructure projects. Towards the middle of the twentieth century, the region received a new settlement wave as a result of the forced displacement of people from different regions of the country fleeing bipartisan violence; this expanded the agrarian frontier without taking into account any formalisation of property. This process intensified as a result of the growing number of disputes over territorial domination between legal and illegal armed groups, which were closely related to drug trafficking.

The high economic potential of oil, gold and other mineral exploitation, together with an unequal land ownership structure dominated by large-scale agro-industry and cattle ranching, are the most significant causes of land conflict in Magdalena Medio. The central driver of the Magdalena Medio economy has been oil exploitation, which has shaped Barrancabermeja and the surrounding municipalities. Extensive cattle ranching and subsistence agricultural production have been combined in the Santander region, although the former is advancing more rapidly and is replacing the latter (Archila *et al.* 2006). The south of Cesar department has been principally dedicated to the agro-industrial production of palm oil and cotton, as well as to cattle ranching. The economy in the south of Bolívar department is based on peasant agriculture, artisanal fishing and timber exploitation. In addition, in the San Lucas Range (in the south of the Bolívar department), the economy is dominated by legal and illegal small-scale gold mining. In this area there has been an increase in the cropping of coca in the last two decades, to which the government has responded via aerial fumigation, which has generated new forced displacement.

Following the construction of a refinery in Barrancabermeja, the Unión de Sindical Obrera (USO), the nation's first oil industry trade union, was founded with the aim of protesting against poor working conditions. Some of the USO leaders, together with the peasant leagues and communist leaders, founded the ELN, which has its base in the San Lucas Range (Romero 1994). This historical process of social struggle in Magdalena Medio, driven by social and revolutionary movements, has also met with strong state repression. The process of agrarian reform led by the ANUC, while influential in the peasant struggle, has had limited impact here.

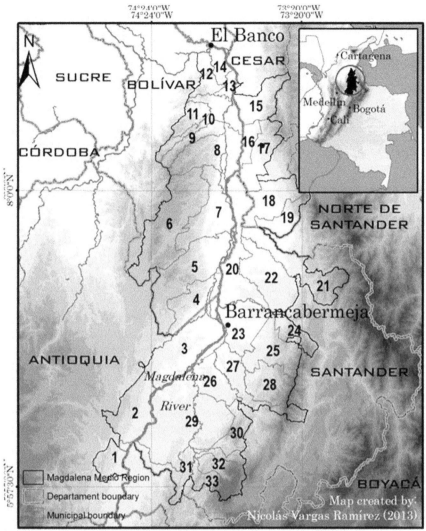

ANTIOQUIA (1 Puerto Nare, 2 Puerto Berrío, 3 Yondó) BOLÍVAR (4 Cantagallo, 5 San Pablo, 6 Santa Rosa del Sur, 7 Simití, 8 Morales, 9 Arenal, 10 Rioviejo, 11 Norosí, 12 San Martin de Loba, 13 Regidor, 14 El Peñón) CESAR (15 La Gloria, 16 Gamarra, 17 Aguachica, 18 San Martín, 19 San Alberto) SANTANDER (20 Puerto Wilches, 21 Rionegro, 22 Sabana de Torres, 23 Barrancabermeja, 24 Betulia, 25 San Vicente de Chucurí, 26 Puerto Parra, 27 Simacota, 28 El Carmen, 29 Cimitarra, 30 Landázuri, 31 Bolívar, 32 El Peñón, 33 Sucre).

Figure 7.2 Map of political and administrative division of Magdalena Medio

Control of the region around the middle of the 1980s by FARC and the ELN was linked to coca crops, and was openly disputed between paramilitary groups that were present in many municipalities during the 1990s. This violent confrontation led peasants and artisanal miners to organise themselves to

Table 7.4 General data for Magdalena Medio

Land area	3,329,528 hectares
Population projected for 2012	862,946 inhabitants
Urban dwellers – percentage of the population	61%
Rural dwellers – percentage of the population	39%
Population with UBN 2010	43%
Rural Population with UBN 2010	59%
Forcibly displaced population (1997–2011)	143,440 persons

Source: Author, based on data from DANE and SIPOD

resist the violence in their territories, demanding the presence of the state via marches and peasant 'exodus' events. Although negotiation between peasant organisations and the state did take place, and included the issue of land protection, there was also strong repression of the peasantry by para-militaries, with the frequent involvement of state organs (Bonilla 2007).

Land ownership disputes

Given the high level of concentration of land ownership and presumed informality in the possession of land, as well as the significant potential for agro-industrial and mining-energy investment, access to land ownership for peasants is increasingly limited. This is due to the insufficiency of state pro-grammes for redistributing rural land and the pro-development tendency of agrarian policies, who are focused on benefiting large-scale agro-industrial enterprises. This selective benefit is also apparent in the mining and energy sector and expresses itself in the new national mining regulations, which favour foreign investors.

The stimulus of large capital investments has enabled the construction of large roads such as the Magdalena Trunk Route and the projected track of Pan-American Highway, which has boosted land-grabbing activities, accom-panied by a strong presence of armed groups. Given these threats, various popular civic organisations made up of peasants, artisanal miners and dis-placed agricultural workers have been energised to resist the usurping of their land, despite their continual stigmatisation by different actors, including state institutions.

The most conventional response of the state to dispute cases of type 1 (Table 7.5) has been the awarding of titles to land occupied by peasant set-tlers. This process usually requires moving the boundary of the Forest Reserve Zone, created by Law 2 of 1959, so that it does not overlap the relevant Peasant Reserve Zone. Peasants turn to already-existing Peasant Reserve Zones as a more collective method of gaining access to land; this requires persistence in demanding better technical assistance from the state to improve production on the land, since, if the land is not cultivated, the Peasant Reserve Zone designation may be invalidated.

Table 7.5 Main types of land disputes in Magdalena Medio

Type of dispute	Actors involved	Description and causes	Relationship with the state
1 Peasants demand protection from displacement and/or from dispossession by buyers or supposed landowners.	Peasants who have settled on wilderness land v. local and national authorities, investors (companies, individual owners) and/or illegal armed groups	Peasants do not rely on due protection of land, as they have expanded the agricultural frontier, including the Forest Reserve Zone. In some cases there are links between the buyers and illegal armed groups, assisted by corrupt state functionaries.	The state has created two Peasant Reserve Zones: one of 29,110 hectares in 1999 in the south of Bolivar, and the other of 184,000 hectares in 2002 in the valley of the Cimitarra River.
2 Displaced peasants claim the restitution of their land, which was subject to concentration of ownership and large-scale purchase.	Returned peasants and peasants who are resisting being displaced v. investors, illegal armed groups and/or drug traffickers	Private agents purchased the land abandoned by or stolen from the peasants. Some of these cases occurred as legal purchases when prices were very low because of the violence, with the complicity of public authorities.	The solution has to do with clarifying the possession of land and its possible forfeiture in cases where there is a proven occupation. The 'Victims' and Land Restitution Law is being applied, both individually and collectively (1,500 hectares by September 2012 in the south of Bolivar).
3 Lack of assistance and land access programmes to displaced and relocated people	Displaced and relocated peasants in the urban area, particularly young women and the young claim against local and national authorities.	When they are relocated in a suburban rural area, assigned land may be abandoned due to the lack of technical assistance.	The state response is limited. Remaining on the land depends on the help from NGOs with international cooperation.
4 Land grabbing of areas designated for common use (agricultural suitability, forests, plains and river banks).	Peasant and artisanal miners v. local and national authorities, investors and/or developers (agro-industry and mining)	Communal-use land is invaded for illegal exploitation. The construction of infrastructure has taken land from peasant agriculture. The drying out of marshes and wetland for artisanal fishing has increased due to the expansion of illegal mining, cattle ranching and palm oil production.	The state has awarded the Special Reserve Area (ARE) to informal mining, but technical and financial assistance has been lacking. Policies to promote biofuel production have favoured the expansion of palm oil cropping. Rigorous environmental control is lacking.

Source: Author, based on press sources, PDPMM and fieldwork

Despite being designed to protect the ability of peasants to stay on their land, concrete cases do not always show favourable results. In the case of El Garzal (Simití), the intervention of supposed landowners linked to para-militarism and drug-trafficking, together with the corruption of regional and local functionaries, has impeded the process of awarding titles to peasants. The peasant organisation asked for the process to be centralised at the Colombian National Institute of Rural Development (Incoder)[17] in Bogotá, demanding greater transparency in the state's actions.

A Peasant Reserve Zone in the valley of the Cimitarra River was suspended between 2002 and 2011 by order of the Uribe government as a result of the stigmatising of the peasants as 'guerrillas'. The resistance of the Peasant Association of the Valley of the Cimitarra River (*Asociación Campesina del Valle del río Cimitarra*), with the help of various NGOs such as the Development and Peace Programme of the Magdalena Medio (*Programa de Desarrollo y Paz del Magdalena Medio*), led to it being awarded the National Peace Prize in 2010 and, later, to the suspension order against the Peasant Reserve Zone being lifted. Currently they are bringing their internal development plans up to date in order to negotiate investment from the local government.

Cases categorised as type 2 deal with the restitution of land rights to the original possessors, who had been dispossessed through violent forced displacement. These complaints are processed based on the Victims and Land Restitution Law, and one of the first cases where it was applied was in Monterrey, where the intervention of paramilitary groups was evident. On the Las Pavas hacienda, peasant farms were occupied first by drug traffickers and later by the palm oil agro-industry. Some palms were apparently planted legally by a business consortium; however, the peasants asked the state to initiate a process of asset recovery on the grounds that the company was not making full economic use of the land. Another reason invoked was the fact of the involvement of illegal armed actors and drug traffickers. The state pronounced in favour of the peasants[18] and is now waiting to resolve a legal action taken by the business consortium in order to restore 1,290 hectares to its legitimate owners.

Cases in type 3 involve displaced peasants who have been relocated to rural and suburban areas. Example are the resettlement of San Marcos, Rancho K5 and La Palmita (Barrancabermeja), and the region of Las Pampas (Sabana de Torres).[19] In these cases, the land was assigned by state institutions with the aim of re-establishing victims of forced displacement. In spite of the formal assignment of land, the lack of appropriate criteria for the selection of families and relocation sites, as well as limited technical, financial and basic sanitation assistance, has generated new conflicts between the re-located people, who, given their difficult circumstances and in spite of the legal restrictions, sell their land to other peasants. The success of these re-establishment processes is subject to various threats, but they persist thanks to the help of NGOs and international cooperation.

Land disputes of type 4 arise from the interest in the natural resources in the subsoil, which, because of exploration and exploitation work backed by the public authorities, affects settlers in the use and control of their land. Given that the majority of subsoil in the region is under concession, peasants and miners who subsist on such land see their rights to it being infringed, especially when they cannot rely on legal processes that would guarantee their ownership. This is the case with the peasants of El Carmen de Chucurí (Santander) who have denounced water supply contamination resulting from coal mining by the company Centromin SA. It has been impossible to stop this exploitation because the company has permission from the relevant state mining and environmental authorities (Vanguardia 2010).

In the mining zone of the San Lucas Range, the organisation of around 3,000 artisanal miners in the Federation of Farmers and Miners of the South of Bolivar (*Federación de Agricultores y Mineros del Sur de Bolívar*, Fedeagromisbol) has allowed them to resist being forcibly displaced for more than 30 years, despite pressure from different armed actors. Fedeagromisbol has led the struggle against paramilitary stigmatisation by the public armed forces and has managed to maintain its economic activities. Under the new mining code, the state has declared Special Reserve Areas (*Áreas de Reserva Especial*, ARE)[20] to protect the inhabitants' preferential rights over the subsoil. However, the mere declaration of an ARE does not guarantee that the artisanal miners will be able to stay on their land, as they also need technical and financial assistance.

Land disputes in Magdalena Medio are very diverse, owing to the economic, environmental and social heterogeneity of the region. In spite of this, various common elements can be found. First, the peasant organisations engaged in resistance on their land have been stigmatised in their struggles and have been the victims of violence from illegal armed groups and the state. Second, the changing local context, the geographical heterogeneity and the varying dispossession strategies generate an ongoing transformation of the conflicts: cases which can be categorised today as being one type of conflict could later be located in another category, and even give rise to new categories.

Conclusions

It is unquestionable that there is a profound relationship between armed conflict, inequity in the distribution of land, the interaction between state and society, and a fragile democracy. This study affirms that these links are structural and go beyond the policies of formalisation and titling of land.

The negative effects of these problems have a fundamental impact on the forever-excluded rural inhabitants, such as peasant, indigenous and Afro-Colombian people, given the persistent and profound subordination of the countryside and its inhabitants in Colombia's national life. The re-evaluation of the countryside's resources stems from the drive to expand the extractive agro-industry and mining and energy industries at the expense of the rural inhabitants – who are consequently dispossessed and displaced.

The formalisation and clarification of property rights could be a useful tool for the resolution of land conflicts and for peacebuilding. However, regional experiences make its limitations clear. 1) Property rights can be used to protect peasants' access to land, but can also fail to take into account social relationships behind communal use of this resource, and can even be used to formalise dispossession. 2) The formalisation of individual land rights over communal or public land restricts the access of settlers to these resources, which generates conflicts. 3) Property rights over land can impede monopolisation if they are accompanied by measures to protect peasant systems of possession and production on their land (such as the Peasant Reserve Zones, ARE and/or the recognition of the collective territorial rights of ethnic groups). However, our analysis of the local experience of such measures suggests that their effectiveness is limited. In fact, in the absence of state protection, peasant organisations backed by local NGOs are now pressing local administrations to address these issues. 4) Property rights do not sufficiently protect rural inhabitants from abuses deriving from the use of the land by large investors, who do not always seek ownership of the land but rather the usufruct of it. Property rights provide even less guarantee to rights over the subsoil. 5) Private property rights can be a mechanism for effecting an institutional response to the provision of rural land, following protests by landless peasants to state institutions. However, this requires state intervention that goes beyond the mere formalisation of the property rights of rural inhabitants, so as to balance the unequal power relationships which the war has deepened, and to counteract the new problems generated by state intervention. Such state intervention is at the moment lacking, and the mere provision of a legal framework is insufficient.

Policies to formalise land ownership and restore land will not favour a peace process if they are not backed by the political will to recognise and strengthen the values of the peasant economy. This would require not only the protection of peasants from both legal and illegal armed actors, but also the guarantee of their rights in the context of government decisions regarding strategic zones for economic growth policies and the entry of global capital, stimulated and favoured by state policies. In short, the issue is the recognition and guarantee of rural inhabitants' central and permanent place in society, which requires that their particular way of life – and their world view and understanding of what constitutes a better way of life – is recognised independently of the system of administering land rights and the currently dominant model of concentrated development in 'hegemonic globalisation'.[21]

It is apparent that historical regional processes, and the role of the state in them, are fundamental in the construction and adjustment of rural organisational dynamics. State intervention has been erratic, varying between recognition and stigmatisation of rural protests, and its absence has frequently been made up for by NGOs supported by international cooperation (donations and other funding). The recognition of the citizenship of peasants, indigenous communities and Afro-Colombians must go beyond the juridical formalities. The attainment of peace in Colombia depends on whether concrete policies to realise genuine rights for such people are achieved.

The lack of credibility of the state's institutions and of their effective power in the regions, resulting from its negligence, co-option and corruption, is a structural obstacle to state action. As a result, simply formalising the possession of land and restoring land to victims is already a monumental challenge, since it requires a state presence that is active, efficient, timely and independent of local power structures – both legal and illegal; in addition, it demands sufficient coherence between the various state entities involved. It is important to add that there is a significant historical debt owed to the rural populations with regard to the provision of basic services and the infrastructure necessary for a decent standard of living, independently of the degree of formalisation of land ownership.

Peace negotiations should deal with the various power structure problems of the Colombian state and the concentration of land ownership as processes linked to the continuance of the armed conflict. Peace, understood as a process that must be built in a permanent and ongoing way, requires models of land use that suit the soil, that respect the environmental conditions and that meet the needs of the population. Another challenge that will enhance the peacebuilding process is the progressive recognition from the state institutions of the autonomous land governance by peasants. This not only guarantees their access but also their control over the territories in question; it also guarantees their economic, political, social and cultural rights.

It is worth remembering that the monopolisation of land and concessions by extractive industries demands a huge quantity of rural land inhabited by peasants – who are at great risk from these processes – regardless of whether the land in question is public, private or community land. The peace dialogues are an excellent opportunity to configure a development model that strengthens the organisation of land and the formalisation of land tenure and land ownership, and to solve conflicts over land usage. This will strengthen not only land rights, but also the capacity of rural inhabitants for decision-making and for the management of their own territories and resources.

Notes

1 For this chapter, we adopt the conceptual definition of a 'peasant' proposed in the 'Declaration on Rights of Peasants and other people working in rural areas' (UN A/HRC/19/75 'Final study of the Human Rights Council Advisory Committee on the advancement of the rights of peasants and other people working in rural areas'). According to the Declaration, 'a peasant is a man or woman of the land, who has a direct and special relationship with the land and nature through the production of food or other agricultural products. Peasants work the land

themselves and rely above all on family labour and other small scale forms of organising labour ... The term "peasant" also applies to landless people.'

2 Borras *et al.* (2012) is an initial effort to analyse the diagnostic situation of land grabbing in 17 Latin American countries, based on the survey conducted by FAO.

3 *La Comisión Nacional de Reparación y Reconciliación* (National Commission of Reparation and Reconciliation).

4 Despite the maintenance of armed confrontations, the strong opposition of right-wing political sectors led by former president Alvaro Uribe, the increasing scepticism among several groups towards political life, and the hope of others within civil society, by December 2013 the Colombian government and the FARC guerrillas were still continuing peace talks in La Habana, Cuba. At this time there is agreement on two of the five points of the agenda: rural development and political participation. The third point, related to the production of drugs and trafficking policies, was being negotiated at the time of writing. Going forward, the negotiation teams must pursue the next topics: mechanisms for disarming the guerrillas, and victims' rights. Although some details of the points already negotiated are now available to the public, according to the public statements of the representatives of both sides the final agreement will embrace the negotiations as a whole, and therefore there will be no partial agreement involving one or two points on the agenda until the negotiations conclude. Some of the issues regarding the lack of certainty of the peace talks can be traced to this condition. Despite this, it is possible to identify the general direction of the agreement over rural development, including the promotion of access to land for landless rural inhabitants, the formalisation of rights to land, the creation of an agrarian jurisdiction to resolve land disputes, and the modernisation of the rural cadastre. The agreement also includes the prioritisation of health, education, housing and infrastructure policies for rural areas, the strengthening of the Peasant Reserve Zones and the closing of the agrarian border in order to preserve forests and other areas through environmental protection.

5 The data for current use is based on satellite images and aerial photography. Potential use is defined according to the environmental and ecological attributes of regions.

6 The population in poverty is that whose income level is under the poverty line, based on the 'basic family basket' – a value equivalent to the minimum expenditure required to provide the food and other basic needs to maintain tolerable life. Indigence indicates an income level which cannot adequately supply the minimum food for the people to survive.

7 This included independent peasants, tenants, sharecroppers, settlers and agricultural day-workers.

8 At the trial of Herbert Veloza, a former paramilitary commander, the Court of Peace and Justice of Bogotá (a special judiciary authority in charge of trials of former paramilitaries) acknowledged that the mass murder of militants of the Unión Patriótica (a leftist political party of the 1980s linked to a previous peace process between the government and FARC) was genocide related to political victimisation, and placed the responsibility on paramilitary groups whose actions were coordinated with the Colombian police and national armed forces. See www.coljuristas.org/documentos/adicionales/control_de_legalidad_HEBERT_VELOZA.pdf (accessed 20 September 2013).

9 The regional case study in Montes de María is based on fieldwork conducted mainly by Sergio Coronado and Nicolás Vargas during the period from August 2012 to February 2013. Where no other sources are given for facts regarding land disputes in Montes de María, these are derived from data collected during our fieldwork.

10 Field diary. Minutes of session of the Citizenship School in Montes de María, 31 August 2012, María La Baja, Bolívar.
11 Contribution of Carlos Salgado, director of Planeta Paz, in *Forum on Rural Development* in Montes de María, María La Baja, Bolívar, 18 August 2012.
12 In Colombia, 'ethnic groups' or 'ethnic communities' are concepts used to define either indigenous or Afro-descendant communities living in rural areas. These concepts are related to the definition of tribal peoples in ILO Convention 169.
13 In Montes de María, a strong institutional presence favoured the dispossession of land rights, and it can be observed that a key role was played by authorities and institutions such as notaries and other officials who permitted the sale of lands belonging to displaced people. In September 2011 the Prosecutor began an investigation against 23 notaries, officials and other members of administrative authorities in the region of Montes de María regarding possible collaboration in the dispossession of land rights of displaced peasants of the region. This modality is called 'dispossession via administrative corruption' (CNRR–Grupo de Memoria Histórica 2010b: 44).
14 Authors' interview with a peasant of the municipality of San Juan Nepomuceno.
15 The regional case study in Magdalena Medio is based on fieldwork conducted mainly by Noriko Hataya and Nicolás Vargas during the period from August 2010 to February 2013. Where no other sources are given for facts regarding land disputes in Magdalena Medio, these are derived from data collected during our fieldwork.
16 We use the figures and delimitations established by the Development and Peace Programme of the Magdalena Medio (*Programa de Desarrollo y Paz del Magdalena Medio*).
17 Incoder (*Instituto Nacional Colombiano de Desarrollo Rural*) was created in 2005 to assume the administrative functions of the Incora.
18 According to Sentence T-267/2011 of the Constitutional Court, Incoder ultimately decided to confiscate these lands from the palm oil company in November 2012. For more detail see Hurtado and Pereira (2011) and http://retornoalaspavas.wordpress.com/ (accessed 20 September 2013).
19 A pilot case was the productive alliance with a palm-cropping company on land assigned in 2007 by Incoder to victims of forced displacement. The alliance was not economically viable, but the displaced people have sown 500 hectares of oil palm, thanks to the technical assistance of the Association of Small-Scale Palm Croppers (Vanguardia 2009).
20 Article 31 of the current Mining Law establishes Special Reserve Areas (AREs). The purpose of this classification is to restrict the number of mine contracts and concessions granted to companies or investors in areas where there is artisanal or informal mining by local inhabitants. The ARE statement implies the beginning of studies and research to identify better options for mining in such areas, with regard to social and economic conditions.
21 The term 'hegemonic', implying a critical view of current globalisation, refers to the 'counter-hegemonic globalization' argued by Santos (Santos and Rodríguez-Garavito 2005).

References

Agencia Prensa Rural, 2013, 'Las Farc proponen una reforma rural y agraria integral, socioambiental, democrática y participativa, con enfoque territorial', *Agencia Prensa Rural*, 14 January 2013, available online at www.prensarural.org/spip/spip.php?article10024 (accessed 19 January 2013).

Akram-Lodhi, A.H., 2007, 'Land, markets and neoliberal enclosure: an agrarian political economy perspective', *Third World Quarterly*, 28(8): 1437–56.

Archila, M., Bolívar, I.J., Delgado, Á., García, M.C., González, F.E., Madariaga, P., Prada, E. and Vásquez, T., 2006, *Conflictos, poderes e identidades en el Magdalena Medio, 1990–2001*, Bogotá: CINEP.

Bautista, A.J., 2012, 'Restitución ¿realidad o ficción? Balance de los derechos de las víctimas del despojo y del abandono forzado de tierras en Colombia', master's thesis, Universidad Andina Simón Bolívar.

Bonilla, L., 2007, 'Magdalena Medio: de las luchas por la tierra a la consolidación de autoritarismos subnacionales', in *Parapolítica: la ruta de la expansión paramilitar y los acuerdos políticos*, ed. M. Romero and L. Valencia, Bogotá: Corporación Nuevo Arco Iris-Intermedio Editores, 341–92.

Bonilla, R. and González, J. (eds), 2006, *Bien-estar y macroeconomía: 2002/2006: crecimiento insuficiente, inequitativo e insostenible*, Bogotá: Universidad Nacional de Colombia-Contraloría General de la República.

Borras, S., 2007, *Pro-Poor Land Reform: A Critique*, Ottawa: University of Ottawa Press.

Borras, S., Kay, C., Gómez, S. and Wilkinson, J., 2012, 'Land grabbing and global capitalist accumulation: key features in Latin America', *Canadian Journal of Development Studies/ Revue canadienne d'études du developpment*, 33(4): 402–16.

CGR, 2011, *Informe del estado de los recursos naturales y del ambiente 2010–2011*, Bogotá: Contraloría General de la República.

CNRR – Grupo de Memoria Histórica, 2010a, *Bojayá: la guerra sin límites*, Bogotá: Ediciones Aguilar.

——2010b, *La tierra en disputa: Memorias del despojo y resistencias campesinas en la costa caribe 1960–2010*, Bogotá: Ediciones Aguilar.

Codhes, 2012, 'Desplazamiento creciente y crisis humanitaria invisibilizada', *Boletín Codhes informa*, 79, available online at www.codhes.org/images/stories/pdf/bolet%C3%ADn%2079%20desplazamiento%20creciente%20y%20crisis%20humanitaria%20visible.txt.pdf (accessed 23 August 2012).

Colombia Land Rights Monitor, 2013, 'Justicia evasiva: la lucha por la tierra y la vida en Curvaradó y Jiguamiandó', available online at http://colombialand.org/wp-content/uploads/2013/06/Justicia_Evasiva.pdf (accessed 30 May 2013).

Comisión de Estudios sobre la Violencia, 1987, *Colombia: violencia y democracia*, Bogotá: Universidad Nacional.

Escobar, A., 2008, *Territories of Difference: Place, Movements, Life, Redes*, Durham, NC: Duke University Press.

Fajardo, D., 2002, *Para sembrar la paz hay que aflojar la tierra*, Bogotá: Universidad Nacional – Idea.

——2006, 'El desplazamiento forzado: una lectura desde la economía política', in *Territorio, patrimonio y desplazamiento (Seminario Internacional)*, vol. 1, Bogotá: Procuraduría General de la Nación – Consejo Noruego para Refugiados, 103–42.

Gáfaro, M., Ibañez, A. and Zarruk, D., 2012, *Equidad y eficiencia rural en Colombia: una discusión de políticas para el acceso a la tierra*, Bogotá: Universidad de los Andes.

Garay, L. and Barbieri, F., 2012, 'Usurpación y abandono de tierras y demás bienes de la población desplazada', in *Justicia distributiva en sociedades en transición*, ed. B. Morten, C.R. Garavito, P. Kalmanovitz and M. Saffon, Oslo: Torkel Opsahl Academic EPublisher, 277–99.

Hurtado, M. and Pereira, C., 2011, 'Legitimidad empresarial, conflicto de tierras y producción palmera en Colombia', *Revista-Bogotá*, 6(2): 91–110.

Ibáñez, A. and Muñoz, J., 2012, 'La persistencia de la concentración de la tierra en Colombia: qué pasó entre 2000 y 2009?', in *Justicia distributiva en sociedades en transición*, ed. B. Morten, C.R. Garavito, P. Kalmanovitz and M. Saffon, Oslo: Torkel Opsahl Academic EPublisher, 301–32.

IGAC-CORPOICA, 2002, *Zonificación de los conflictos de uso de Tierras en Colombia*, Bogotá: Instituto Geográfico Agustín Codazzi.

ILSA, 2012, 'Montes de María; entre la consolidación del territorio y el acaparamiento de tierras: aproximación a la situación de derechos humanos y del derecho internacional humanitario en la región (2006–12)', ILSA, Bogotá, available online at http://ilsa.org.co:81/biblioteca/dwnlds/otras/montes1/informe.pdf (accessed 20 September 2013).

INDEPAZ, 2012, 'Cartografía del Conflicto: narcoparamilitares y guerrilla', *Punto de Encuentro*, 58, available online at http://ediciones.indepaz.org.co/wp-content/uploads/2012/03/No.58-Punto-De-Encuentro.pdf (accessed 23 January 2013).

Kline, H.F., 1995, *Colombia: Democracy under Assault*, Boulder, CO: Westview Press.

López, D., 2012, 'Disponibilidad de alimentos básicos en Colombia 2000–2010: ¿producción nacional o importaciones?', Master's thesis, Faculty of Economics, Universidad Nacional de Colombia.

Machado, A., 2002, *De la estructura agraria al sistema agroindustrial*, Bogotá: Universidad Nacional.

——2004, 'Tenencia de tierras, problema agrario y conflicto', *Desplazamiento Forzado dinámicas de guerra, exclusión y desarraigo*, ACNUR, Universidad Nacional, Bogotá, available online at www.virtual.unal.edu.co/cursos/humanas/2004945/docs_curso/descargas/2da%20sesion/Basica/Absalon%20Machado.pdf (accessed 15 April 2013).

Ministerio de Agricultura, 2011, *Libro blanco de las irregularidades de la tenencia de la tierra en Colombia*, Bogotá: Ministerio de Agricultura.

Molano, A., 2013, *Dignidad campesina*, Bogotá: Icono Editorial Ltda.

Moncada, J.J. (ed.), 2011, *Realidades del despojo de tierra: retos para la paz de Colombia*, Medellín: Instituto Popular de Capacitación.

Múnera, L., 1998, *Rupturas y continuidades: poder y movimiento popular en Colombia, 1968–1988*, Bogotá: IEPRI-CEREC.

Navarrete, M., 2008, *San Basilio de Palenque: memoria y tradición*, Cali: Universidad del Valle.

Osorio, F. and Herrera, M., 2012, 'Prácticas de seducción y violencia hacia la quimera del progreso: la combinación de las formas de lucha del capital', in *Autonomías territoriales: experiencias y desafíos*, Observatorio de Territorios Étnicos, Bogotá: Pontificia Universidad Javeriana, 297–325.

Palacios, M., 2006, *Between Legitimacy and Violence: A History of Colombia, 1875–2002*, trans. R. Stoller, Durham, NC: Duke University Press.

PNUD, 2011, *Colombia rural: razones para la esperanza*, Bogotá: Informe Nacional de Desarrollo Humano.

Ramírez, W., 1981, 'La guerrilla rural en Colombia: ¿una vía hacia la colonización armada?', *Estudios Rurales Latinoameriacanos*, 4(2): 199–209.

Romero, A., 1994, *Magdalena Medio: luchas sociales y violaciones a los derechos humanos 1980–1992*, Bogotá: Corporación AVRE.

Sánchez, G., 1991, *Guerra y política en la sociedad colombiana*, Bogotá: El Ancora Editores.

Santos, B. and Rodríguez-Garavito, C.A. (eds), 2005, *Law and Globalization from Below: Towards a Cosmopolitan Legality*, New York: Cambridge University Press.

Semana, 2012, 'Reina impunidad en asesinatos de líderes de tierra', available online at www.semana.com/nacion/articulo/reina-impunidad-asesinatos-lideres-tierras/256131-3 (accessed 30 May 2013).

UAEGRT, 2013, 'Estadísticas de la unidad administrativa especial para la gestión y restitución de tierras, Bogotá', 3 February, available online at http://restituciondetierras.gov.co/media/descargas/estadisticas/estadisticas-20130204.pdf (accessed 20 September 2013).

Uprimny, R. and Sánchez, C., 2010, 'Los dilemas de la restitución de tierras en Colombia', *Revista Estudios Socio-Jurídicos*, 12(2): 305–42.

Vanguardia, 2009, 'En La Pampa se resistieron al despojo de las tierras', available online at www.vanguardia.com/historico/48187-en-la-pampa-se-resistieron-al-despojo-de-las-tierras (accessed 10 January 2013).

——2010, 'Denuncian contaminación por explotación de carbón', available online at www.vanguardia.com/historico/74864-denuncian-contaminacion-por-explotacion-de-carbon (accessed 21 January 2013).

Vargas, V., 1992, *Magdalena Medio Santanderiano: colonización y conflicto armado*, Bogotá: CINEP.

Vásquez, V. and Serrano, M., 2009, *Las áreas naturales protegidas de Colombia*, Bogotá: Conservación Internacional-Colombia & Fundación Biocolombia.

Velasco, A., 2009, 'The mobilization of Colombian ethnic minorities', in *Rural Social Movements in Latin America: Organizing for Sustainable Livelihoods*, ed. C.D. Deere and F.S. Royce, Gainesville, FL: University Press of Florida, 138–59.

Verdad Abierta, 2012, 'La Europa y su misterioso comprador', available online at www.verdadabierta.com/component/content/article/241-especial-ovejas/4350-la-europa-y-su-misterioso-comprador (accessed 15 June 2013).

Vergara-Camus, L., 2012, 'The legacy of social conflicts over property rights in rural Brazil and Mexico: current land struggles in historical perspective', *The Journal of Peasant Studies*, 39(5): 1133–58.

World Bank, 2008, 'The World Bank annual report 2008', available online at http://siteresources.worldbank.org/EXTANNREP2K8/Resources/YR00_Year_in_Review_English.pdf (accessed 15 May 2013).

Zamosc, L., 1986, *The Agrarian Question and the Peasant Movement in Colombia: Struggles of the National Peasant Association 1967–1981*, New York: Cambridge University Press.

——1987, *La cuestión agraria y el movimiento campesino en Colombia*, Instituto de Investigaciones de las Naciones Unidas para el Desarrollo Social, Bogotá: CINEP.

8 Land problems in Cambodia

The historical influence of conflict

Ryutaro Murotani

Land problems are widespread in Cambodia. Conflicts over land have been widely reported by the media in recent years, while the international community is concerned by the slow response of the government. In urban areas, there are large-scale forced evictions, mostly in poor urban settlements. In rural areas, local people, including indigenous communities, are threatened by investors trying to purchase land for plantation farming or other economic activities. In both cases, people often face difficulties in protecting their land, even though they have lived on the land peacefully for many years. Public institutions in Cambodia cannot effectively protect these people's daily lives.

Since the signature of the Paris Peace Agreements that formally ended the armed conflict in 1991, Cambodia has gone through the transition from a war-torn country to a vibrant developing economy. Although there had been violent clashes up until 1998,[1] the country has been relatively stable during the past 15 years. While the democratisation progress is said to be slow, the Cambodian economic performance in recent years has been very impressive. In fact, improved public safety and stability is one of the drivers of the recent economic development in Cambodia. On the other hand, as economic development stimulates more investment in land, land problems are becoming more acute in the country.

As there are many notable cases of land problems in Cambodia, many analyses have been carried out. Many scholars and practitioners attribute the cause of land problems to the weak legal systems and institutions and to a dysfunctional justice sector (Adler *et al.* 2008; Sekiguchi and Hatsukano 2013). Others indicate more structural problems in Cambodian politics – neo-patrimonialism – as the main reason for ineffective land policies and political elites' unwillingness to address the problems (Un and So 2011; Williams 2013).

However, the land problems today are not independent of events in the history of Cambodia. The history of long years of violent conflict certainly poses challenges to the country in tackling its problems. Williams (2009), for instance, points out the lack of consideration by the United Nations Transitional Authority in Cambodia (UNTAC) towards protecting HLP (housing, land and property) rights as one of the factors that has undermined the protection of these basic human rights in the country.

Recognising the importance of these historical antecedents, this chapter tries to understand the broader structural issues that weaken the land tenure security of ordinary citizens in Cambodia. Though respect for HLP rights was obviously weak in the UNTAC's repatriation operations, there were other underlying problems that needed to be addressed. Even in cases in which returnees received land, their land tenure security was very weak because local authorities had the discretion to control and revoke their land rights. Since many land plots are without legal titles, donors have supported land registration, but this has been slow and not as effective as expected. Moreover, land registration alone cannot be a solution, as there must be mechanisms to secure land titles after registration as well.

This chapter will examine historical developments in the country that have affected land tenure problems, and look at the policy measures to mitigate them. It finds that land tenure security is weak for various reasons, including historical contexts, and that policy response needs to be based on a deeper understanding of these structural problems, as well as the potential interactions of new policies and the underlying societal norms.

Land problems in Cambodia

In recent years in Cambodia, landlessness has increased and inequality in land distribution has grown. The problem is exacerbated by increased population pressure and economic demand for land, often resulting in large-scale land disputes and forced evictions. While the government's conflict resolution mechanisms can solve some of the smaller-scale land disputes, they are not as effective in dealing with large-scale land disputes.

Landlessness and inequality in land distribution

In Cambodia, inequality in land holdings is among the highest in the region. The Gini coefficient of land distribution is 0.65 – much higher than those of neighbouring countries (for example, 0.41 in Thailand, 0.49 in Indonesia, 0.51 in Malaysia and 0.55 in India) (Un and So 2011: 300–301). While refugee repatriation, urbanisation and population growth increase pressure on land, land ownership is being more concentrated in fewer people through investment in land. The distribution of land has become increasingly inequitable. Since the 1980s, 20–30 per cent of the country's land has passed into the hands of less than 1 per cent of the population (USAID 2011: 5). Large-scale land disputes have often resulted in the forced eviction of poor families who have no formal documents to protect their rights. These incidents further exacerbate the inequality of land ownership.

The number of landless people is on the rise. The landless increased from 13 per cent in the late 1990s to 20 per cent in 2004; 20–40 per cent of rural households were landless in 2009. Young families and female-headed households are more likely to be landless or near landless. Many of the families of

Figure 8.1 Map of Cambodia

demobilised soldiers and returnees during the period of 1992–93 have still not received land (USAID 2011: 5).

Large-scale land disputes

Large-scale land disputes in both urban and rural areas are widely reported in the media. In urban areas, urban dwellers without formal title documents are threatened with eviction. In Phnom Penh alone, 133,000 people are said to have been forcibly evicted since 1990. More than 80 per cent of evictions have happened since the early 2000s (Un and So 2011: 297). Around Boeng Kak Lake, 4,252 families were evicted in 2009, although most of them had lived in their houses for many years (Grimsditch and Henderson 2009). In rural areas, increased investment in agricultural plantations and economic land conces-sions (ELCs) threaten local villagers, including indigenous communities. About 50,000 people were reported to have been evicted for development projects in 2006 and 2007 (IRIN 2008). The impact of ELCs is as widespread as 1 million hectares – that is, 5.5 per cent of Cambodia's entire territory is now under ELCs (Ullenberg 2009).

Although it is difficult to get an overall picture of land disputes in the country, the NGO Forum on Cambodia (2011) provides us with an analysis of land disputes of a relatively large scale. Recording land disputes involving more than five households, they report an upward trend of occurrences since the mid-2000s, with a peak in 2008. In 2010, 28 new land disputes were reported to have occurred. According to their analysis, most land disputes have occurred in areas of strong economic growth, such as Battambang and Preah Sihanouk provinces. The average number of households involved is 158 per case, while the largest land dispute involved 1,362 households. The majority of these disputes occur over agricultural land, and they are likely to have negative impacts on income-generating activities and the livelihoods of the local population.

The report points out that these large-scale land disputes tend to involve 'influential, powerful, or rich' individuals and/or local authorities. In 38 per cent of cases, land is acquired for agricultural or plantation/farming reasons. Of 41 disputes resulting in forced evictions, most occurred in Preah Sihanouk province and Phnom Penh municipality, and 26 cases involved 'powerful or rich' people. Of all 282 land disputes recorded, 39 cases have been rooted in ELCs. Although people bring these disputes to local authorities, provincial halls and provincial courts, only 20 per cent of all cases were either fully or partially resolved (NGO Forum on Cambodia 2011: 5–12).

Smaller land-dispute cases

Besides the large-scale land disputes that are often reported in the media, there are a lot of small-scale land-dispute cases at local levels. Having reviewed the record of the Cadastral Commission (CC),[2] established to deal with disputes over unregistered land, we can attest to the fact that small-scale land disputes are very common.

Adler *et al.* (2006: 17–21) found in their survey of the CCs in Kampong Cham province that the majority of cases (53 per cent) were disputes between villagers and neighbours, while another 15 per cent of cases were conflicts between family members and relatives. They also found that the CCs deal mainly with cases over smaller amounts of land: the median size of land in dispute was 963 sq m, and even disputes over as little as 2.4 sq m were being reported. Although cases between local villagers are clearly the majority in the CC, cases involving 'more powerful people'[3] made up 17 per cent, while another 14 per cent of cases involved local authorities. Cases involving 'more powerful people' had the lowest resolution rate (Adler *et al.* 2006: 21).

Among various land disputes, large-scale disputes and disputes involving someone from outside are more difficult to resolve. Concerning intra-village small-scale disputes, local villagers often approach the CCs, who sometimes manage to resolve cases. In defending their land from neighbours, local villagers do not have to validate their land rights with formal land titles. However, when it comes to disputes with someone from outside the village, the CC is not effective in protecting the rights of people without formal land titles. A villager's land tenure security is weak against people who have obtained registered titles.

The weakness of these people's land tenure security has a historical background, and can be explained in relation to Cambodian history, with its decades of conflicts. The following section illustrates how armed conflicts in Cambodia have influenced land problems, particularly weakening land tenure security for ordinary citizens. Because this problem has been generated over decades, policy makers need to understand the structural problems behind it in designing solutions.

The historical influence of conflict on land problems

The history of violent conflicts affects today's land problems in various ways – most notably through multiple changes in political regimes and property orders, movement of people and struggles in post-conflict statebuilding. Repeated changes of political regime have created multiple layers of land rights based on different legal systems. These changes have created confusion and slowed down institutional capacity building. Massive movements of people have also complicated the situation. On many occasions, people have moved to new places without any formal land titles and settled on unoccupied land. Finally, in the post-conflict environment the government has had to handle various challenges, despite its weak capacity and confusing legal structures. While Cambodia has been successful in terms of political stability and economic development, development of the justice sector and the protection of land rights are more complicated tasks.

Multiple regime changes

One important characteristic of land rights in Cambodia is the historical inconstancy caused by the changes in political regime. While traditional and customary land tenure remains strong in some developing countries, property claims dating to before 1979 are officially disallowed in Cambodia under Article 1 of the Law on Land of 1992. Although there are a few cases in which people try to claim back their land based on their rights prior to 1975 (four cases out of the 70 reviewed in the CC in Adler *et al.* 2006), traditional land rights are not valid in the current legal system in Cambodia. There is a clear separation between before and after 1979, and the basis of today's land rights was established in the 1980s.

In 1975–79, the ruling Khmer Rouge introduced collective agriculture, denied private ownership, and destroyed documents and human resources regarding land rights (Amakawa 2001; Williams 2009). In Cambodia, private ownership of land was introduced during the French colonial period, although its application was limited to Phnom Penh City and plantation farms (Williams 2009). Before 1975, only 10 per cent of landowners had received property rights certificates (Un and So 2011). As documents and other resources were completely destroyed during the Khmer Rouge period, it is very difficult to trace ownership records prior to 1975.

When the new socialist government, backed by the Vietnamese government, defeated the Khmer Rouge regime in 1979, it introduced a new collective agriculture mechanism. This formed the basis for land distribution among the Cambodian people. Although the new government of the Kampuchean People's Revolutionary Party (KPRP) introduced an agriculture cooperative system called *Krom Samaki*, in reality it functioned as a collective agricultural cooperative for only a limited period. When *Krom Samaki* was in practice dissolved after several cultivating seasons (in the early- to mid-1980s), land was distributed to each family in each village. The pattern of land distribution prior to 1975 was restored in some areas, but in many villages distribution disregarded the pre-1975 land rights. In most cases, land distribution was proportional to the size of households (Amakawa 2001: 168). In effect, this produced an equal distribution of land among households in rural villages. Amakawa (2001) examined the Gini coefficients of land distribution in two villages and found very low figures (0.15 and 0.13) at the time of the dissolution of *Krom Samaki*. Private ownership of residential land was officially recognised in 1989, when the government introduced a free market economy.

However, this historical instability has caused two problems. First, because land was distributed at a certain point in the early- to mid-1980s, those who were absent from the villages at that particular point were not entitled to their land rights. Regardless of land rights before 1975, families who returned to the villages after the land distribution were disadvantaged, and some became landless (Amakawa 2001: 170–79). In fact, a large proportion of returnees in 1992–93 had difficulties in finding land to live on, as discussed later in this chapter.

The other problem is that distribution during this period was discretionally decided by local village leaders, and not properly registered in official documents. As local leaders who were close to the KPRP had discretion in decision making, there are cases in which people with political backing received favourable treatment in land distribution (Williams 2009). Also, because the land was divided among local village residents, and the lease and transfer of ownership mostly happened within local villages, people did not feel the need to register their claim and protect their land rights. This was probably one of the reasons why the sporadic land registration that started in 1989 made very slow progress (Amakawa 2001).

Movement of people

Another impact of conflict on land problems in Cambodia has been the large-scale movement of people. Frequent movements of a large number of people have complicated people's understanding of land rights. Those who were forced to move during the series of violent conflicts had to find a place to settle without consolidated land tenure security. Returnees in the massive repatriation in 1992–93 typically faced the challenge of finding land to depend on. Repatriation and economic development after the UNTAC period promoted urbanisation, which resulted in many urban settlers without legal land titles.

Displacements from 1975–91

The large-scale movement of people started in the Khmer Rouge era, when some two million people were forced to relocate from cities to rural areas (Williams 2009). Under the Khmer Rouge regime, nearly two million Cambodians – one person in four – died as a result of Khmer Rouge policies and actions: 400,000 people were killed outright as enemies of the revolution, while others died of starvation, disease or overwork (Chandler 2008: 259). While internal displacement was widespread in Cambodia in the Khmer Rouge era, 34,000 Cambodians managed to escape into Thailand between 1975 and 1978; another 20,000 went to Laos and 170,000 went to Vietnam (UNHCR 2000a: 92).

When the KPRP came to power in 1979, the new regime offered the displaced the right to return to their native land and freedom of residence; however, pre-1975 land rights were never restored. As the new regime maintained control of the land and continued a policy of collective farming, not all survivors returned to their original homes. Some fled to the cities and became squatters, while others left the country. Some former urban residents were drafted into the new administration, but more opted to flee to Thailand (Williams 2009).

As a result, in addition to the 164,000 refugees who had already arrived from Cambodia and Laos,[4] Thailand faced a new wave of tens of thousands of incoming Cambodian refugees in 1979. In that year, the UNHCR pledged nearly US$60 million to meet the needs of up to 300,000 Cambodian refugees. By the time of the Paris Peace Agreements in 1991, there were 353,000 refugees in Thailand, while another 180,000 Cambodians were internally displaced. From 1975 to 1992, more than 235,000 Cambodian refugees in Thailand were resettled overseas (UNHCR 2000a: 92–93, 96–97).

As mentioned in the previous section, land rights were distributed at the end of the *Krom Samaki* period of collective agriculture. During this complicated period, there were many who failed to receive land rights because they could not return to their original village in time for the land reallocation.

Repatriation during the UNTAC period[5]

The next large-scale movement of people occurred after the signing of the Paris Peace Agreements in 1991. Between 1981 and 1988, only one Cambodian refugee officially returned from a UNHCR camp. From March 1992 to May 1993, the UNHCR coordinated a repatriation of more than 360,000 (UNHCR 2000a: 96–97).

In April 1989 – before the Paris Peace Agreements – the Cambodian government introduced the private ownership of land. This policy consolidated the land allocation under the KPRP regime that had denied pre-1979 land rights. In the peace negotiations, property restitution to Cambodian refugees and IDPs was carefully avoided. As a result, neither restitution nor the return of refugees to their homes of origin was mentioned in the Paris Peace Agreements (Williams 2009). In fact, many refugees did not return to their original villages, but rather went to villages in the north-western region of Cambodia or to urban areas. They did not have any claims to the land, and only received small cash grants from the UNHCR on their return (Eastmond and Öjendal 1999; Williams 2009). Returnees had to live in rural areas and cities without any land titles. In rural areas, landless returnees had difficulties in making a living. In urban areas, most of them occupied the land without formal land titles. Lacking consolidated tenure security, they faced threats of eviction, as discussed in the following section.

Urbanisation and squatter shantytowns

During the course of the wave of repatriation, followed by reconstruction and development, more people moved into cities and settled without formal land titles. Many returnees sought economic opportunities in urban areas because they had freedom in choosing where to return. Economic development after the UNTAC period also attracted people to urban areas. Because many of those who moved into cities were not able to obtain formal land titles, they chose to remain on unoccupied land.

As both the 1992 Law on Land and the 2001 Law on Land in Cambodia allow for entitling land ownership if the land has been held peacefully and unambiguously for five consecutive years, urban settlers tried to occupy spaces without formal land rights. Because these laws cut off pre-1979 claims but recognised adverse possession, they invited returnees and other Cambodians to obtain new property interests through squatters' rights, rather than by pursuing restitution claims (Williams 2009: 57). For instance, in the 1989 land reform, many poor people living on highly valued land in urban districts were left out of the distribution and subsequently evicted from their homes, forcing them to seek refuge in informal urban settlements on 'state land' (Un and So 2011). As early as the UNTAC period, speculators were already buying up land on the edges of urban centres, and causing land disputes with informal occupants (Ledgerwood 1998: 132).

Recently, as the Cambodian economy has grown, there has been a substantial increase in rural-to-urban migration. Rural migrants to Phnom Penh were often unable to afford formal housing, and generally sought low-cost accommodation through rental or purchase of homes in the shantytowns on 'state land' – with initial acquiescence from local authorities (Un and So 2011). Under the law, they would be entitled to land ownership after five years of peaceful settlement, but most of them were not issued with a formal land title even after the five-year occupation. The land registration system in Cambodia works very slowly, and does not deal effectively with registration requests on ambiguous and/or contested plots of land. The problems of the land registration system will be further discussed later in this chapter.

Post-conflict statebuilding and land governance

With a series of changes of political power and regimes, the legal and administrative structure in Cambodia has been very fluid, making institution building for land governance challenging. In the first years of its post-conflict statebuilding endeavour, Cambodia experienced some unstable periods. Only after the violent incidents of 1998 did the country regain political stability.

On balance, people appreciate the political stability and economic recovery, though problems such as corruption and nepotism still remain. According to an opinion survey by the International Republican Institute (IRI 2013), a large majority of people (79 per cent in January 2013) think that the country is moving in the right direction.[6] People consistently offer improvements in infrastructure – with more roads built (74 per cent in the January/February 2013 survey), more schools built (58 per cent) and more health clinics built (34 per cent) – as the primary reasons for their positive judgement. On the other hand, of those who believe that the country is moving in the wrong direction (21 per cent), 24 per cent think that more corruption is the problem for the country. In fact, Transparency International ranks Cambodia 157th among 176 countries in the 2012 Corruption Perception Index (Transparency International 2012).

However, the mechanism that has maintained political stability also allows the ruling political party to make the most of the flexible legal structure. When the armed conflict ended, the CPP (Cambodian People's Party, successor of the KPRP) had already consolidated its system of controlling the state security apparatus and local village communities, and it became the dominant party – particularly after the violent clashes that destroyed its rivals in 1998. The CPP has even established grassroots network connections to the villages that govern the local communities, based on patron–client relations (Blunt and Turner 2005; Richmond and Franks 2007; Roberts 2009; Murotani *et al.* 2010; Takeuchi *et al.* 2011; Un 2011).

In this political environment, political elites within the patronage networks can impose favourable outcomes on disputes. Under the 2001 Land Law (Articles 4 to 28), land is classified into five categories: private land, state public land, state private land, common property and indigenous land. As state public land cannot be sold or transferred by lease or concession to private parties, the government must convert state public land into state private land if it wishes to use it for ELCs. Without transparent and accountable monitoring mechanisms, these rules can easily be manipulated (Williams 2013).

Post-conflict statebuilding in Cambodia has been successful in realising political stability and economic development, but state institutions that prioritise stability over transparency and accountability are less effective in addressing land and property issues. In various post-conflict societies, Takeuchi *et al.* (2011) have observed the common tendency of states to become authoritarian while they consolidate the capacity to maintain stability. The ability to suppress opposition can also be used to restrict the accountability mechanisms that are essential for resolving land and property problems.

Policies to mitigate land problems and their impacts

Against these complex historical backgrounds, post-conflict Cambodia has failed to address structural problems at the levels of repatriation, reintegration and long-term institution building. Because the international community prioritised safe and rapid repatriation of refugees over land tenure problems, returnees suffered from weak land tenure security. Land problems were also obstacles to the reconciliation between returnees and local villagers. Even if returnees obtained plots of land, these tended to be of low quality and with weak tenure security. In some cases, returnees lost their land to local villagers. The government's policies to expedite land registration and to strengthen dispute resolution mechanisms have not been very successful in protecting the rights of the people. As these policies on land governance are interlinked, policies should be designed in coordination with each other and with due consideration to informal norms and customs.

The examples below illustrate the limitations of partial solutions to the complex problems of land tenure. The consolidation of land tenure security needs to be based on various elements such as respect for land and property rights, land registration and land dispute resolution mechanisms. Solutions need to be comprehensive in order to simultaneously address various elements that can reinforce or obstruct each other. The following cases exhibit unsatisfactory results because of a lack of awareness of local contexts and interactions between various policies.

Repatriation operations by the UNTAC/UNHCR

Repatriation operations by the UNTAC and the UNHCR were successful in bringing the large number of refugees safely back into their home country, but did not pay sufficient attention to the land rights of returnees. Although many of the 360,000 refugees had previously left behind homes and land in Cambodia, neither restitution nor return of refugees to their homes of origin were mentioned in the Paris Peace Agreements. As a result, refugees were expected to return to Cambodia without guarantees that their rights to their assets would be respected. The notion of a right of return to one's home, as well as HLP rights, is a relatively recent assertion, established by the Dayton Peace Accords for Bosnia and Herzegovina in 1995. This view was not commonly held at this period, as the UNTAC was one of the first post-Cold War UN peacekeeping operations. Even the Universal Declaration of Human Rights (UDHR) only recognises the right of every person 'to return to his country' (Williams 2009: 51–54). Land rights of the returnees were not properly secured in the UNTAC/UNHCR repatriation operations for Cambodia.

In fact, restitution might not have been a feasible option, because most of the land in Cambodia had not been clearly registered, having been governed under the customary system before 1975.[7] The destruction of documents and human resources during the Khmer Rouge period exacerbated the ambiguity of land ownership. To successfully organise the general elections in 1993, the international community needed efficient and speedy repatriation operations. Rather than recommending that they return to their original homes, the UNHCR offered refugees several options, including land and other material assistance, upon their return to Cambodia. Initially, the UNHCR presented a land option offering two hectares per individual returnee. However, their assumption that there were 240,000 hectares of available land in Cambodia was an overestimate (Williams 2009: 41–42).[8] When the UNHCR recognised the insufficiency of available land, a range of other alternatives were offered to the returning refugees.[9] In the end, around 85 per cent of all returnees chose the cash option (UNHCR 2000b: 147).

The refugees themselves did not necessarily wish to go back to their original villages.[10] When returnees chose their destinations, rather than going back to their homes of origin, 58 per cent went to the two provinces closest to the Thai border: Banteay Meanchey and Battambang. They were popular because they are close to Thailand and it would be easier for returnees to escape if things went wrong. Fears of a recurrence of violent conflict were still real for returnees. Many refugees also had previous connections to the two provinces. Phnom Penh (including Kandal province) received 8 per cent of returnees (Bernander *et al.* 1995: 103).

On the other hand, refugees wanted to receive land for their livelihood upon their return. In an early UNHCR survey, a majority of the refugees in the border camps indicated that they wanted land – in particular in Battambang, which they believed to have fertile soil. However, the land option forced refugees to wait in camps until land had been identified, and many feared they would be the last to leave and would end up with no land at all. The cash option encouraged them to give up waiting for available land. In the end, only 3 per cent of all returnees chose the land option. After repatriation, the UNHCR assisted returnees – not limited to those who had taken the land option – in obtaining land titles, totalling an estimated 9,500 titles in 1993 and 10,000 in 1994 (Bernander *et al.* 1995: 103–4).

Though land restitution might not have been feasible or even desirable, returnees needed to secure their own land to make their living. Prioritising efficient return, the international repatriation operation had to sacrifice land tenure security for returnees. The issue remained problematic in the next stage of reintegration.

UNDP's support for reintegration after return

After their return, reintegration and reconciliation between returnees and local villagers were major challenges in rural villages. Competition for land further intensified the tensions between returnees and local villagers. As a joint response with the UNHCR to repatriation and reintegration,[11] the UNDP's CARERE (Cambodia Resettlement and Reintegration Project)[12] programme promoted reconciliation and reintegration, but the land problems remained a major obstacle.

The UNDP's review (2001: 15) looked back over the UNHCR's failure to recognise the gravity of the land issue, and described how it created difficulties for reintegration in resettlement areas. When the returnees came back to Cambodia, local villagers were also suffering from land scarcity. With a growing population, new households received increasingly small plots. Historically, Cambodia enjoyed a relative abundance of land compared to other countries in the region. The population density in Cambodia (57 people per sq km in 1995) was much lower than in Thailand (115) and Vietnam (225). Access to free land had always been easy (Grant 1999: 16). But in the mid-1990s, arable land became scarce, and land acquisition became a competitive bargaining process.

There were several reasons for the land scarcity for returnees. First, the widespread presence of landmines limited the areas of arable agricultural land. Second, as returnees were given the right to select where to return to, they were concentrated in the north-western provinces of Banteay Meanchey and Battambang, making the demand for land in those two provinces excessive. Third, since the Khmer Rouge withdrew from the Paris Peace Agreements and extended their territorial control, the areas open to returnees simply decreased (UNDP 2001: 41–42).

Under such circumstances, the UNHCR had to rely on the will of provincial and communal authorities to make land available; however, local authorities frequently refused to give up their lands for the returning refugees and IDPs (UNDP 2001: 42). As the privatisation of land had made it a valuable commodity, they were not likely to give land to returnees willingly. Land allocated to returnees was reportedly taken back the following year, with the 'original owner' showing up and simply selling the land to a third person. Because returnees' land was often not secured by land titles, it was easily confiscated by local elites after the UNHCR closed its offices in the area (Bernander *et al.* 1995: 106; UNDP 2001: 42).

In one of the villages in Battambang province, despite joint efforts based on a contract between the village chiefs and the UNHCR, returnees were expelled from the good land originally allocated – and mostly even titled – to them the previous year, and 'given' bad land in exchange. Although the village chiefs agreed to give state property land and unused land to both returnees and local villagers, local villagers seemed to obtain lands with better access after the UNHCR left. Returnees who had had land close to the village were shifted more or less forcibly to distant fields. There was resentment on the part of the local villagers because the returnees' lands were titled more quickly than their own (Bernander *et al.* 1995: 107). These resentments threatened the land tenure security of returnees, even if they had land titles.

In another case in Battambang, returnees were given land in remote areas without formal titles, but they were not able to cultivate the land because of the security threat from the Khmer Rouge. As they could not live on the given land, they paid to borrow land from their neighbours or asked their relatives to let them use their land. In this case, the quality of land was so poor that the returnees faced more difficulties. While the presence of relatives was assumed to be a key factor for reintegration, relatives' support was limited and unsustainable, and sometimes not offered at all. The relatives were also constrained by the scarcity of land and other means of livelihood. Since village heads often controlled the distribution of day labour, returnees were reported to be at a disadvantage in getting opportunities for work as well. According to the UNHCR survey, 30–35 per cent of returnees lived from hand to mouth, whereas the figure for locals was 17 per cent (Bernander *et al.* 1995: 106, 109, 113–14).[13]

Facing a serious shortage of land, the CARERE programme aimed to increase the land available for both returnees and local villagers in order to promote reintegration. However, this new land was not always secured for returnees. The programme assisted in clearing close to 18,000 hectares of land, affecting some 70,000 people. The programme's focus on infrastructure is partly explained by the need to create access to water, roads and markets for the newly cleared agricultural areas (Bernander *et al.* 1995: 56–57). In Pursat province, the programme tried to facilitate the issuance of land titles, but was not successful due to the lack of capacity in the land titling departments of the government. In another village in Battambang province, people lost their land, despite legal land title documents provided to villagers through the support of the programme (Grant 1999: 21–22).

Though the CARERE programme could not resolve the land conflict, it mitigated tensions by promoting reconciliation and establishing elected village development councils (VDCs). The programme encouraged interventions that benefited entire communities without differentiating between non-returnees and returnees. As the programme required community participation in building local infrastructures, it provided opportunities for people to work together and support each other. In addition, the members of the VDCs were elected by a secret ballot with external observers, which enabled the returning population to have a fair chance of gaining representation on the councils. It also opened the decision-making process to women, for whom three of the seven positions on the VDCs were reserved. Once the VDC structure had been accepted in early 1995, CARERE was able to assist in establishing 111 VDCs in two months. Although the projects selected by the VDCs were not very different in type from those selected through other processes, this at least promoted broader consensus by bringing together divergent sectors of the communities (UNDP 2001: 43–44). Having reviewed various evaluation reports on the CARERE, Hughes (2007) acknowledged its success in building the capacity of the government and promoting the participation of local villagers. Though she also points out the limitations of its impact on transparency, accountability, attitudes among officials and villagers and sustainability, gradual improvements in local governance and reconciliation certainly served to mitigate the land conflicts between villagers and returnees.

Landlessness was a problem not only for returnees but also for other local villagers, and it needed to be tackled in a coordinated way. As the village chiefs had the authority to decide on the allocation of land, as well as other means of livelihood, resentment of local villagers and/or village chiefs regarding returnees needed to be avoided. Reconciliation between returnees and local villagers was important for mitigating the tensions over land tenure.

Long-term institution building

After repatriation and reintegration, the Cambodian government passed a series of legislative and policy measures for long-term institution building for managing land problems. They introduced a new Land Law and related policies on land to protect people's rights by registering more titles, acknowledging indigenous communities' collective rights and introducing social land concessions (SLCs). However, in reality these policies have not been effective in protecting people's land rights.

No one single policy measure is sufficient for strengthening people's tenure security, because many of these policies are dependent on one another. For example, the 2001 Land Law presumed an effective land registration system, as it aimed to strengthen tenure security through land registration. At that time, the land registration process was slow and ineffective, in part at least because dispute resolution mechanisms were not efficient enough to mediate competing claims to land. Long-term institution building can only be effective if it can strengthen land governance as a whole.

The 2001 Land Law and related policies

The first Land Law in 1992[14] was enacted by the government of the State of Cambodia to codify the CPP's land policy by explicitly extinguishing all pre-1979 rights to the land. The HLP policy was left primarily to the domestic authorities because UNTAC did not adopt any systematic policy on HLP issues, except in relation to repatriation. The law stipulated that peaceful occupation of land would give rise to title within five years, but the state administration lacked the capacity to ensure that the law was applied even-handedly. In the post-UNTAC period, political stability, the return of refugees and the opening up of the economy led to increased demand for land and housing, and HLP issues became a major human rights agenda for the international community (Williams 2009: 43–45).

Cambodia introduced the new Land Law in 2001, with the support of the Asian Development Bank. The 2001 Land Law extended private ownership rights to residual and agricultural land, established a system for the systematic titling of land and created a comprehensive dispute resolution system (USAID 2011: 5). Article 30 also allowed people 'the right to request a definitive title of ownership' after five years of 'peaceful, uncontested possession of immovable property', but, unlike the 1992 Land Law, it added the condition that possession should be initiated before the promulgation of the law. While the old Land Law had no such condition regarding the start of the five-year possession (Article 74), the new law introduced the condition, aiming to end the custom of getting land titles through occupation. There was a strong intention under the new law of clarifying land ownership, rather than allowing people to occupy vacant land in various places.

Articles 23 to 28 of the 2001 Land Law recognised the right of indigenous communities to the collective ownership of their land. However, the sub-decree on Procedures for Registration of Land of Indigenous Communities was issued only in 2009, and required communities to register as legal entities before registering their own rights (USAID 2011: 6). Only a few indigenous communities have been able to register their collective rights to date.[15]

To mitigate the inequality of land distribution, Article 49 introduced a mechanism called social land concessions (SLCs), on which the government established a sub-decree in 2003. SLC is supposed to grant state private land to poor, landless families, but its implementation is very limited (USAID 2011: 6).

The Declaration of the Royal Government on Land Policy on 1 July 2009 set forth a vision of land policy in Cambodia. In this policy, the goals of land administration described are: to clearly register ownership and other rights over immovable properties (state and private); to conduct official transfer of those rights; to prevent and resolve land disputes in order to strengthen land tenure security; and to ensure reliability and efficiency of the land market.

The 2001 Land Law was drafted by a team sponsored by a development bank, and introduced an Australian-based system that emphasised clarity and simplicity in land titling by recognising ownership exclusively on the basis of formal registration with a centralised cadastral agency. The emphasis on registration to achieve legal effect is the essence of the Australian-inspired Torrens-style registration system. Experts from multilateral development banks believed strongly that a free market in land required the clear and definitive title system promised by a Torrens-style registration system (Trzcinski and Upham 2012: 130–36). The next sub-section will look at the impact of the registration system on people's land rights.

Land registration

Land registration in Cambodia is slow, and has not strengthened the tenure security of the people. Formal land registration started in April 1989 – even before the first Land Law of 1992 – but its coverage is still limited. Some people estimate that it will take more than 10 years to complete the registration process, while others say it may need 45 years. Since those who try to benefit from land registration can manipulate and register land without formal titles, those who have not registered their land rights are threatened.

When formal land registration – which would be called sporadic land registration in contrast to the systematic land registration introduced under the 2001 Land Law – started with land privatisation in 1989, competition over land was fierce and land distribution became less equitable. Unlike user rights in the communist era, the new rule granted stronger ownership rights, including the right to exclude others, and it led to a property boom and some confusion. The registration process was slow as a result of disputes, confusion, corruption of local cadastral offices and a simple lack of capacity. By 2001, only an estimated 15 per cent of some 4 million applications submitted for land tenure certificates had been processed. The incomplete and corrupt implementation of the registration process undermined legal certainty in Cambodian property relations (Williams 2009: 39–40).

While land disputes already existed at the introduction of private property rights in 1989 (Un and So 2011), many local farmers did not feel the need to prioritise their registration. In a UNHCR survey, the vast majority (over 98 per cent) of interviewees who did not hold land titles reported that they were confident that their neighbours, village and commune chiefs knew where their land began and ended, and for this reason they thought that they did not need a title. As a result, most of the land distributed following the economic liberalisation in 1989 was not properly documented (Grant 1999: 16). However, in legal terms, any land without issued ownership documents remained formally the property of the state.

As the speed of land registration was slow, the government introduced the systematic land registration and cadastral index map[16] (Un and So 2011) – but its coverage was also limited. Systematic land registration started in 1995 as a pilot project, and was expanded with the LMAP (Land Management and Administration Project),[17] supported by the World Bank, Canada, Germany and Finland from 2002. The LMAP was introduced for smooth implementation of the 2001 Land Law. Using modern technology, systematic land registration issued 1.1 million titles. However, because of limited capacity and budget, this process has been conducted in only 14 of the 24 provinces in the country (Sekiguchi and Hatsukano 2013: 444). Trzcinski and Upham (2012) estimate that there are up to 10 million land parcels in the country, and at the current rate it would take another 45 years to register all of them.

While the LMAP helped to register more than one million land parcels, the project aimed to speed up land registration by avoiding contested areas.

Registration by the LMAP covered only undisputed areas, because the project was designed to overlook land where 'disputes are likely until agreements are reached on the status of the land' (World Bank 2002: 24). The project was supposed to promote clarification of the status of these contested lands through dispute resolution, and thereby enable these disputed areas to be titled. However, these processes were not effectively implemented, and disputes over contested land areas remained unresolved. These areas are difficult to register, and there is no concrete plan to clarify their land titles. As a result, forced displacement of people who live in disputed areas without formal land titles continues to be a problem in urban areas, and the World Bank has suspended its support to the LMAP since 2009.

While many people have not formally registered their land rights, some have taken advantage of the system to claim their rights. In large-scale land disputes, people often claim ownership by presenting official supporting documents, including informal letters issued by village or commune authorities, receipts and other documents. However, only 0.7 per cent of complainants are able to produce strong evidence such as official land titles. Others use 'soft titles' such as family books and acknowledgements of ownership issued by the authorities. On the other hand, investors in ELCs can present official documents related to ELCs, such as a concession agreement (NGO Forum on Cambodia 2011: 10–11). Since the introduction of the land registration system, 'soft titles' are often denied and labelled 'illegal' because of the lack of formal 'hard titles' (Grimsditch and Henderson 2009: 39). Those without formal land registration can be disadvantaged in disputes with registered land title holders.

Land registration as promoted by the LMAP is important and necessary, but there are disputed lands that are difficult to register, and not everyone makes use of the services equally. While those who received formal land titles have undoubtedly benefited, those who were left out of this initiative were left relatively much worse off (Trzcinski and Upham 2012: 139).

The 2001 Land Law and the 2007 Civil Code

With the land registration system not managing to properly protect people's land rights, the 2007 Civil Code provided a different approach. Supported by the Japan International Cooperation Agency (JICA), the Civil Code aimed to unify the various statutes dealing with civil law – including the Land Laws of 1992 and 2001 – to be consistent with the Constitution of 1993, and to facilitate Cambodia's entry into the World Trade Organization. It was enacted in December 2007, and became applicable by the enactment of the Law on Application of the Civil Code in 2011 (Trzcinski and Upham 2012: 133–34).

First, the Civil Code acknowledged informal possession and acquisition more widely. It allowed for acquisition of private property after 20 years of peaceful and open possession, without reference to the pre- or post-2001 commencement of the possession (Trzcinski and Upham 2012: 134). Second, the Civil Code rejected the Torrens-style registration system, and introduced a system closer to the American deed registration system (Trzcinski and Upham 2012: 134–35). Article 137 (1) of the Civil Code provided only that 'where a right is registered ... it is presumed that such right belongs to the person to whom it is registered'. This allowed Cambodians who had failed to register their land titles to still claim their rights. It also solved the problem of updating the registered information. According to the Land Law, land transfers should be registered – otherwise, the law does not protect the new landowner's rights. However, as land transfer registration is time-consuming and the institutions may be corrupt, landowners tend to transfer registered land to new owners informally (So 2010: 2–4).

The interpretation of these two different provisions of the Land Law and the Civil Code remained uncertain until they were finally reconciled by the Law on Application of the Civil Code, which took effect in early 2012. The 2001 registration system remains in place, but various forms to prove possession and use rights have been recognised as valid in the determination of ownership. The courts would be responsible for deciding on the validity of various certificates (Trzcinski and Upham 2012: 137).

Trzcinski and Upham (2012: 143), though cautious, saying that 'other effects of the law remain to be seen', lauded the Civil Code for acknowledging the social context. In an environment in which the government is incapable and/or unwilling to register all land titles and protect people's rights, the land registration system was not the best system for strengthening people's tenure security in an equitable manner. The Civil Code secured flexibility in ways that allowed people to protect their land rights. On the other hand, it also left ambiguity because the land title cannot by itself prove ownership. Any disagreements over land ownership require a formal or informal institution in order to be resolved. Therefore, it is crucial to have effective land dispute resolution mechanisms that can resolve, mediate and decide upon the status of land rights in each individual case.

Land dispute resolution mechanisms

To resolve land disputes, the Cambodian government has established multiple mechanisms, but all of them have some limitations in their effectiveness. They do not function independently from formal and informal judicial and decision-making mechanisms. These mechanisms are the courts, the CC and the NALDR (National Authority for Land Dispute Resolution). Cambodian citizens can also consult with local authorities, such as village and commune chiefs. Legally, each of these authorities is supposed to function for a different purpose, though people seem to choose their preferred authority for their own problems. The courts are responsible for any disputes over registered land. Disputes over inheritances and contracts should also be dealt with in courts in line with the Civil Code. However, the judiciary is widely viewed as corrupt, incompetent and biased (Richmond and Franks 2007: 38–40).

Any disputes over unregistered land should be dealt with by the CC. As the CCs are established at the district level and upwards, many local disputes are brought to village and commune authorities before going to the CCs (Adler *et al.* 2006). The NALDR is supposed to deal with cases 'beyond the jurisdiction of the CC', though its authority is sometimes unclear (Grimsditch and Henderson 2009). By the end of 2009, it had received 1,271 cases – many of which were sent from the national CC, as they could not be resolved in the CC or the court (Sekiguchi and Hatsukano 2013: 446). According to the NGO Forum on Cambodia (2011: 8), of the 282 land disputes they recorded,[18] the local authorities received the largest number of cases (202), while 112 complaints were sent to the provincial halls. The third largest number of cases (84) was dealt with in the CC. As various mechanisms exist for dispute resolution, both complainants and defendants seek out intervention by different means. In some cases, complainants and defendants negotiate among themselves outside these authorities (NGO Forum on Cambodia 2011: 9).

However, these land dispute resolution mechanisms are mostly ineffective in cases involving powerful politicians. Land use is subject to multiple conflicting norms, and powerful elites often manipulate various rules and norms against vulnerable groups who do not have formally recognised legal rights but base their claims only on social norms (Adler *et al.* 2008: 2–3). The rule of law and judicial institutions are still weak. Alternative measures for land dispute resolution, such as traditional and customary authorities, are not effective enough to deal with large-scale investments either. In fact, for ordinary citizens there is no mechanism that can assure their land tenure security. As foreign investment increases in Cambodia, there may be more cases in which foreign investors are involved. Land dispute resolution mechanisms will become more and more important as more foreign investors become interested in land in Cambodia.

Conclusion

Land problems in Cambodia have many historical antecedents. In particular, the series of changes of political regime, massive movements of people and weak government capacity – the consequences of conflict – have in turn confused the land and property order in Cambodia. As a result, it is very difficult for ordinary citizens to consolidate their land tenure security. As people have experienced changes in political regimes – and, furthermore, as some have been displaced from their homes – it is difficult for people to claim their land rights based on traditional and customary authority. With weak government capacity, land registration is slow and ineffective, while dispute resolution mechanisms can be manipulated by powerful elites. To strengthen the land tenure security of ordinary citizens, the complex nature of land problems and the historical influence of conflicts need to be carefully examined. The international community's engagements in the past were not necessarily based on sufficient awareness of the local context. Gaining a better understanding of local contexts should be the first step in assessing the potential impacts of any future policy options.

In addition, policy interventions should be designed not as a specific single policy tool, but as a coordinated comprehensive intervention. The repatriation programmes organised by the UNTAC/UNHCR gave priority to a safe return to the country, and did not address land rights problems. The reintegration programme of the UNDP/UNHCR tried to help landless returnees, but it was partially successful only when combined with reconciliation activities as well as the establishment of participatory governance mechanisms. Legislation has not yet been successful in enhancing land tenure security, because the improvement of dispute resolution capacity has not caught up with expectations. Policy interventions such as land registration, dispute resolution and protection of the rights of vulnerable people, including returnees, are mutually dependent. No single policy can improve land tenure security. Rather, land governance as a whole needs to be strengthened.

As economic development continues, Cambodia may experience more foreign direct investment and other threats to land tenure security. Land tenure security can be strengthened only if the policy measures are designed based on a careful understanding of the complex nature of the problem, and as a package of mutually dependent components of land governance.

Notes

1 The largest violent clash after the Paris Peace Agreements happened in July 1997, when the then Second Prime Minister Hun Sen used his personal bodyguard to launch a pre-emptive coup against FUNCINPEC troops and followers in Phnom Penh. Over 100 FUNCINPEC officials and supporters were reported to have been killed. As a result of the incident, several donors suspended aid, and Cambodia's accession to ASEAN was delayed. After the general elections in 1998, the CPP maintained control over the security forces and Hun Sen became the sole Prime Minister (Chandler 2008: 290–91).

2 The Cadastral Commission (CC) was established by Article 47 of the 2001 Land Law, and its organisation and functions were specified by sub-decree No. 47 on Organization and Functioning of the Cadastral Commission in 2002. The CCs have three levels: DKCC (district/*khan*), PMCC (provincial/municipal) and NCC (national). Complaints are first submitted to the DKCC, and are then referred to the PMCC and subsequently the NCC if no resolution is realised. By January 2009 the CC had dealt with 5,059 cases, of which 1,653 were resolved (Grimsditch and Henderson 2009: 49).

3 This is defined as someone who works for or is described as having connections with the government or military at the district level or above (Adler *et al.* 2006: 21).

4 There were even more Laotian refugees than Cambodians in Thailand in the late 1970s. By December 1975, when the Lao People's Democratic Republic was officially established, 54,000 Laotian refugees were in Thailand. Faced with the large number of Cambodian and Laotian refugees, the government of Thailand tried to push back the new wave of Cambodian refugees in 1979 (UNHCR 2000a: 92, 97–98).

5 During the violent clashes in 1997 and 1998, 45,000 Cambodians fled to Thailand. These refugees had returned to Cambodia by the end of March 1999 (Grant 1999: 1).

Although this was another large-scale forced displacement, in this chapter 'returnees' and 'repatriation' refer to the returning population in 1992 and 1993.

6 The figure has always been above 70 per cent since January 2007.

7 Pre-1975 pre-war property records consisted primarily of records of land ownership in urban and some lowland areas. Between 1925 and 1975, only 10 per cent of landowners were issued with ownership titles (Un and So 2011: 291).

8 According to the UNHCR's own review (UNHCR 2000b: 146), its primary calculation was based on the data from a 1989 survey, and it was unaware of subsequent economic changes in the country. It admits that this illustrates the difficulties for peacekeeping missions in engaging in countries without reliable and up-to-date information.

9 According to Whiteside (1996: 17), the three options officially offered to returnees were: 1) up to two hectares of rice land, a housing plot, wood for a house frame, US$25 for thatch and bamboo, a household/agricultural kit and 400 days of food; 2) a housing plot, wood for a house frame, US$25 for thatch and bamboo, a household/agricultural kit and 400 days of food; and 3) cash (US$50 per adult and US$25 per child under 12), a household/agricultural kit and 400 days of food.

10 After recognising the land scarcity, the UNHCR encouraged returnees to go back to their native villages, in the hope that their relatives would help them and reintegration would be less difficult (Bernander *et al.* 1995: 55).

11 The UNHCR and UNDP concluded a Memorandum of Understanding to promote collaboration between the UNHCR's quick impact projects and the UNDP's medium and long-term support for reintegration and development (UNDP 2001: 11). CARERE was an integral part of strengthening the collaboration between the two organisations.

12 This is the project title for phase 1. Phase 2 first used the same abbreviation CARERE for a different project title: Cambodia Area Rehabilitation and Regeneration Project. During Phase 2, the project was renamed *Seila*.

13 Apparently, there was variation in returnees' treatment across regions and political situations in each region. In Banteay Meanchey, most returnees wanting rice land have reportedly been given access to some kind of land, even if it's not necessarily very good or near to their village. In Siem Reap, about 85 per cent of the returnees have received titled land, according to the UNHCR (Bernander *et al.* 1995: 104).

14 Many of the provisions in the 1992 Land Law were simply copied from the 1920 Civil Code. The government was willing to adopt 'only the minimum provisions necessary to establish a sense of order' before the elections (Trzcinski and Upham 2012: 131).

15 McAndrew and Il 2009 and Simbolon 2009 explain challenges for indigenous communities to protect their communal land rights

16 The cadastral index map contains a Unique Parcel Reference Number for each land plot, which serves to provide information about the geographic location of the property that has been registered (Un and So 2011: 293).

17 Later renamed as LASSP (Land Administration Sub-Sector Program).

18 As stakeholders can visit more than one institution, multiple answers were allowed to this question.

References

Adler, D., Porter, D. and Woolcock, M., 2008, 'Legal pluralism and equity: some reflections on land reform in Cambodia', Justice for the Poor Briefing Notes, vol. 2, issue 2 (April), World Bank.

Adler, D., Chhim, K., Path, H. and Sochanny, H., 2006, *Towards Institutional Justice? A Review of the Work of Cambodia's Cadastral Commission in Relation to Land Dispute Resolution*, Phnom Penh: GTZ and World Bank.

Amakawa, N., 2001, 'Nouchi shoyuu no seido to kouzou: Poru Poto seiken houkai-go no saikouchiku katei' (Institutions and structures of farm land ownership: reconstruction process after the fall of the Pol Pot regime), in *Kambojia no fukkou-kaihatsu (Reconstruction and development in Cambodia)*, ed. N. Amakawa, IDE Research Series 518, Chiba: Institute of Developing Economies-JETRO, 151–211 (in Japanese).

Bernander, B., Charny, J., Eastmond, M., Lindahl, C. and Ojendal, J., 1995, *Facing a Complex Emergency: An Evaluation of Swedish Support to Emergency Aid to Cambodia*, SIDA Evaluation Report, Stockholm: Swedish International Development Authority.

Blunt, P. and Turner, M., 2005, 'Decentralization, democracy, and development in a post-conflict society: commune councils in Cambodia', *Public Administration and Development*, 25: 75–87.

Chandler, D., 2008, *A History of Cambodia*, 4th edn, Boulder, CO: Westview Press.

Eastmond, M. and Öjendal, J., 1999, 'Revisiting a "repatriation success": the case of Cambodia', in *The End of the Refugee Cycle? Refugee Repatriation and Reconstruction*, ed. R. Black and K. Koser, New York: Berghahn Books, 38–55.

Grant, K., 1999, 'Access to land and property rights for returnees to Cambodia', UNHCR Cambodia, Field Office Battambang.

Grimsditch, M. and Henderson, N., 2009, 'Untitled: Tenure Insecurity and Inequality in the Cambodian Land Sector', Bridges Across Borders Southeast Asia, Centre on Housing Rights and Eviction, and Jesuit Refugee Service.

Hughes, C., 2007, 'The *Seila* programme in Cambodia', in *Aid that Works: Successful Development in Fragile States*, ed. J. Manor, Washington, DC: World Bank, 85–121.

IRI (International Republican Institute), 2013, 'Survey of Cambodian public opinion' (12 January–2 February 2013), available online at www.iri.org/news-events-press-center/news/iri-cambodia-survey-finds-high-interest-national-elections (accessed 9 March 2014).

IRIN, 2008, 'Cambodia: questions over legality of evictions in name of development', August 18, available online at www.irinnews.org/report/79863/cambodia-questions-over-legality-of-evictions-in-name-of-development (accessed 9 March 2014).

Ledgerwood, J.L., 1998, 'Rural development in Cambodia: the view from the village', in *Cambodia and the International Community: The Quest for Peace, Development, and Democracy*, ed. F.Z. Brown and D.G. Timberman, New York and Singapore: Asia Society and ISEAS, 127–47.

McAndrew, J.P. and Il, O., 2009, 'Access to natural resources: case studies of Cambodian hill tribes', in *Land and Cultural Survival: The Communal Land Rights of Indigenous People in Asia*, ed. J. Perera, Manila: Asian Development Bank, 93–124.

Murotani, R., Wakamatsu, E., Kikuchi, T., Nagaishi, M. and Ochiai, N., 2010, 'Statebuilding in fragile situations: Japanese aid experiences in Cambodia, Afghanistan, and Mindanao', JICA-RI Working Paper 5, Tokyo: JICA-RI.

NGO Forum on Cambodia, 2011, 'Statistical analysis on land disputes in Cambodia, 2010', available online at www.ngoforum.org.kh/administrator/components/com_ngoforum/files/lip_final_land_dispute_report_2010_english.pdf (accessed 9 March 2014).

Richmond, O.P. and Franks, J., 2007, 'Liberal hubris? Virtual peace in Cambodia', *Security Dialogue*, 38(1): 27–48.

Roberts, D., 2009, 'The superficiality of statebuilding in Cambodia: patronage and clientelism as enduring forms of politics', in *The Dilemmas of Statebuilding:*

Confronting the Contradictions of Postwar Peace Operations, ed. R. Paris and T. Sisk, Abingdon: Routledge.

Sekiguchi, M. and Hatsukano, N., 2013, 'Land conflicts and land registration in Cambodia', in *Land and Post-conflict Peacebuilding*, ed. J. Unruh and R.C. Williams, Abingdon: Earthscan, 437–49.

Simbolon, I., 2009, 'Law reforms and recognition of indigenous people's communal rights in Cambodia', in *Land and Cultural Survival: The Communal Land Rights of Indigenous People in Asia*, ed. J. Perera, Manila: Asian Development Bank, 63–91.

So, S., 2010, 'Land rights in Cambodia: an unfinished reform', *Asia Pacific Issues: Analysis from the East–West Center*, no. 97, August, Honolulu: East-West center.

Takeuchi, S., Murotani, R. and Tsunekawa, K., 2011, 'Capacity traps and legitimacy traps: development assistance and state building in fragile situations', in *Catalyzing Development: A New Vision for Aid*, ed. H. Kharas, K. Makino and W. Jung, Washington, DC: Brookings Institution Press, 127–54.

Transparency International, 2012, 'TI corruption perception index 2012', available online at http://cpi.transparency.org/cpi2012/results/ (accessed 9 March 2014).

Trzcinski, L.M. and Upham, F.K., 2012, 'The integration of conflicting donor approaches: land law reform in Cambodia', *Journal of International Cooperation Studies*, 20(1): 129–46.

Ullenberg, A., 2009, 'Foreign direct investment (FDI) in land in Cambodia', Deutsche Gesellschaft für Technische Zusammenarbeit (GTZ) GmbH, December.

Un, K., 2011, 'Cambodia: moving away from democracy?', *International Political Science Review*, 32(546): 546–62.

Un, K. and So, S., 2011, 'Land rights in Cambodia: how neopatrimonial politics restricts land policy reform', *Pacific Affairs*, 84(2): 289–308.

UNDP, 2001, *Peace-building from the Ground Up: A Case Study of the UNDP's CARERE Programme in Cambodia: 1991–2000*, Phnom Penh: UNDP/Cambodia (Emergency Response Division).

UNHCR, 2000a, 'Flight from Indochina', in *The State of the World's Refugees in 2000: Fifty Years of Humanitarian Action*, New York: Oxford University Press, 79–103.

——2000b, 'Repatriation and peacebuilding in the early 1990s', in *The State of the World's Refugees in 2000: Fifty Years of Humanitarian Action*, New York: Oxford University Press, 133–53.

USAID, 2011, 'Cambodia – property rights and resource governance profile', USAID Land Tenure and Property Rights Portal, available online at http://usaidlandtenure. net/cambodia (accessed 9 March 2014).

Whiteside, M., 1996, 'Assistance to vulnerable elderly repatriating from the Thai-Cambodia border', Help Age International Cam/10 Programme Evaluation Report.

Williams, R.C., 2009, 'Stability, justice, and rights in the wake of the Cold War: the housing, land, and property rights legacy of the UN Transitional Authority in Cambodia', in *Housing, Land, and Property Rights in Post-conflict United Nations and Other Peace Operations: A Comparative Survey and Proposal for Reform*, ed. S. Leckie, Cambridge: Cambridge University Press, 16–60.

——2013, 'Title through possession or position? Respect for housing, land, and property rights in Cambodia', in *Land and Post-conflict Peacebuilding*, ed. J. Unruh and R.C. Williams, Abingdon: Earthscan, 437–49.

World Bank, 2002, 'Project Appraisal Documents on Land Management and Administration Project', Washington, DC: World Bank.

9 Land, state and community reconstruction

Timor-Leste in search of a sustainable peace

*Antero Benedito da Silva and
Kiyoko Furusawa*

Timor-Leste became fully independent in 2002. However, during the following decade, disputes over land have continued to cause confrontation between the state, communities and individuals. These disputes have been complicated by the processes of displacement, resettlement and reoccupation that have occurred over the country's long history of foreign domination and violent conflict. As a consequence, land claims are often duplicated.

From the nineteenth century, the Portuguese colonial authorities forcibly relocated people to expand plantations or to exercise control over native rebels. Soon after the Carnation Revolution in Portugal on 25 April 1974, the native people began to respond to the call for decolonisation by organising political parties. Australia, Indonesia and other foreign powers orchestrated a two-week-long civil war in 1975 that forced tens of thousands of people to leave the country. This led to the brutal Indonesian military occupation from late 1975, and by the 1980s the military had forcibly reallocated people into resettlement camps or newly created 'strategic hamlets' to isolate them from guerrilla forces. However, through the mid-1980s the Timorese guerrilla resistance persisted in the mountains. Timorese calls for self-determination continued to be a diplomatic problem for Indonesia. To reinforce its new development-oriented campaign, from the early 1980s the Indonesian government fostered political assimilation by encouraging migration from other Indonesian provinces, with Balinese farmers establishing new transmigration colonies in some relatively more peaceful zones of the country. Suharto's regime also promoted massive development projects and urbanisation, most of which involved taking land from the local population.

The Asian economic crisis and the popular revolt against Suharto's regime in 1997 aborted this Indonesian soft war of development and assimilation. Under the new civilian leadership, Indonesia allowed a referendum as the proper mechanism to address what has been called a pebble in the shoe of the Indonesian Republic. The United Nations successfully organised the popular consultation in 1999. Following the result in favour of secession from Indonesian control, the Indonesian army and pro-Indonesian militia groups burned cities and forced 250,000 people to flee to settlement camps in West Timor. The native Indonesian civilians who had been evacuated earlier from Timor-Leste had to return to their original provinces or were settled elsewhere in Indonesia. During the first two years following the referendum – until 2002 – Timor-Leste was a kind of protectorate under the UN. It was during this period that refugees and the diaspora Timorese community that had abandoned Timor since 1975 began to return home, and subsequently proceeded with their land claims.

In 2006 a major political crisis emerged out of a rivalry within the security organisations and evolved into a quasi-ethnic conflict in which westerners (*kaladi*) attacked easterners (*firaku*), leading to more than 100,000 people, mostly easterners, being displaced from the capital, Dili. This led to new land disputes, further adding to the already complex land situation.

Interestingly, Timor-Leste has emerged as a focus of research and intellectual discussion over the last decade. Several researchers have studied land conflict in Timor-Leste. Fitzpatrick (2002) published a comprehensive study on existing claims based on previous titles and customary rights in Timor-Leste, and made policy recommendations. Da Silva *et al.* (2010) questioned the role of international agencies in shaping neoliberal land policies and proposed an alternative land policy in which the state and local communities become key agents in establishing a new model of land ownership and management. Anderson (2010), in line with da Silva *et al.* (2010), criticised the aid agencies' proposal for land reform as a tactic to induce farmers to give up their land for commercial exploitation. He argued that monoculture and modern agriculture had undermined customary land ownership that served people's subsistence needs, and that the proposed land reform would endanger the country's food security.

Timor-Leste is struggling with not only a post-conflict situation but also a post-colonial one. After all the turmoil, no community in Timor-Leste has been left intact. Bringing together the above-mentioned studies and our own fieldwork,[1] this chapter aims to identify the roots of land conflict in Timor-Leste in the complex situation arising from its post-conflict, post-colonial and economic development experiences, and to review policies – such as the new land law – and people's efforts to achieve a just and sustainable society in Timor-Leste.

Land, people and power

Pre-colonial Timorese society consisted of small and independent communities with territorial boundaries, which the Portuguese called *reinos* (kingdoms). In the eighteenth century there were two alliances of such small communities, or 'provinces', on the island of Timor: Servião and Belu. Servião comprised 11 *reinos,* while Belu had no less than 43 (Hagerdal 2012: 52–53). The chiefs of these *reinos* accepted gifts and military titles such as 'colonel' or 'lieutenant' from the Portuguese as a token of respect, but they were still independent of Portuguese influence.

The Portuguese Governor de Castro characterised *reinos* as 'small republics' built on family alliances and governed by aristocrats (Gunn 1999: 35).

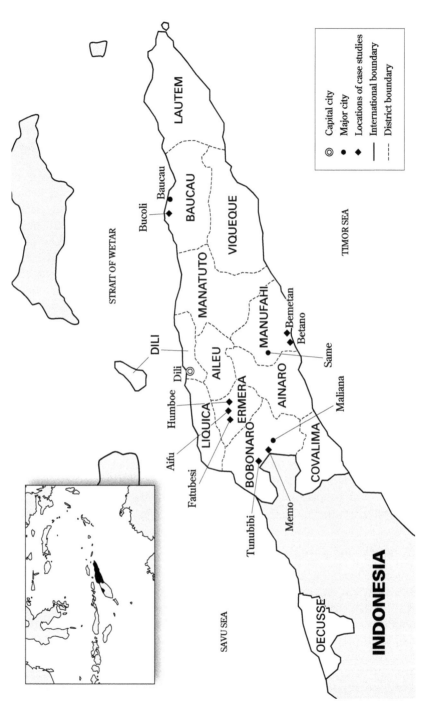

Figure 9.1 Map of Timor-Leste

A family alliance is formed through a *festa-umane* (husband giver–wife giver) relationship and an *uma-lisan* or ancestral house that maintains the original ancestral link through generations. Ancestral houses still wield powerful authority over land. The community leadership, consisting of *dato* (nobles) and *liurai* (a chief elected from among the *datos*), does not own land but plays a role in distributing land to members (Fitzpatrick 2002: 41).

By the nineteenth century, however, the independence of the Timorese *reinos* had begun to change. Oral accounts tell us how the Portuguese inter-vened in local rivalries to gain control over *reinos*. For example, in the early twentieth century the Portuguese supported the *reino* of Luca in its war against the community of Bina-Boraboo, which gave support to a separatist movement in Luca. Luca destroyed Bina-Boraboo completely with the assis-tance of the Portuguese colonial rulers in 1906.

In the nineteenth century colonial economic policy shifted its focus from the declining sandalwood trade to coffee production. In 1815 Governor P.A. de Sousa introduced coffee trees to Timor, and the cultivation of sugar cane and cotton then followed. Governor Celestino da Silva established an agribusiness company – the Sociedade Agricola, Patria e Trabalho (SAPT) – in 1899, and allowed it to forcibly take control of a significant amount of land (Taylor 1999: 30). The policy resulted in the displacement of the native people. As coffee exports decreased towards the end of the century (Gunn 1999: 137), Governor da Silva further allowed Portuguese companies, which ran major cocoa plantations in São Tome in Africa, to invest in Timor, and as a result competition over the coffee business became severe (Gunn 1999: 196). Abilio Araujo, a Timorese politician and historian, stated at a public seminar in Dili in 2013 that in 1905 Portugal introduced a new regulation that limited the jurisdiction of a *reino* to 50 hectares, which invited open resistance from the local rulers. The Manufahi war led by Dom Boaventura in 1912, he said, was a well-known example of such resistance. Gunn also writes:

> The first major attempt to impose a colonial land regime took the form of a special decree of 5 December 1910. Under this act the Governor had exclusive responsibility for all grants of land on a 'quit-rent' or àfor-amento tenure and for transfer of property up to 2,500 hectares. District administrators were also empowered to make grants of 'unoccupied' land up to 100 hectares, under certain conditions, to Portuguese subjects or foreigners taking up residence in the colony.
>
> (Gunn 1999: 197)

The Republican Revolution in 1910 in Portugal brought about a short period of liberal politics with strong anti-clerical and anti-feudal orientations. How-ever, this chaotic republicanism was soon overthrown by a military coup in 1926, which paved the way for one of the longest dictatorships in Europe, the *Estado Novo*, based upon Catholicism and the exploitation of the colonies.

Under colonial policies, land began to acquire a certain level of liquidity. The collection of *finta* or tax drove local leaders to give up land to Portuguese administrators. This became state land and was handed over to Portuguese allies and officials. This land was known as *aforamento*. In the midland Mombae community, native people were employed in quasi-slavery conditions by these new landlords, and the landlords would pay taxes to the colonial administration. The Portuguese administration also recruited through the local kingdoms auxiliaries and *moradores* (local militias) to supply cheap labour. In the process, some of these hard-working *moradores* managed to acquire lands in Dili, and became small landholders. The king of Doeloi, Daraloi of Matebian, sent his people to the SAPT, which occupied land in Dili, as workers, and some of them settled in an area known today as Quintal Boot (da Silva *et al.* 2010: 10). Dili grew into a cosmopolitan city with a population including Timorese (both original inhabitants and migrants), Chinese, Arabs and Portuguese.

The Chinese, whose population prior to 1811 numbered around 300, spread around Kupang, Atapupu and Dili, were involved in the sandalwood trade. Governor da Silva banned commercial activities by Chinese outside specifically designated areas. By 1870 Chinese commercial houses were concentrated in an area called Bidau in Dili (Gunn 1999: 112, 127–29). In the early twentieth century, Portugal encouraged Chinese to settle in Timor, in the hope that their business acumen would increase local economic activity. The number of Chinese settlers grew, and at the time of the Portuguese departure in 1975 there were around 15,000 Chinese in Timor-Leste (Kwartanada 2001: 8).

In a recent article, Johnston claims that Muslim traders were present in Timor by at least the nineteenth century. Of 2,400 Muslims currently in Timor, 600 are Hadhramis. The rest are Indonesian Muslims who remained after 1999. They are concentrated in the suburb of Kampong Alor in Dili (Johnston 2012). The Alkatiri family used to be landlords, benefiting from the employment of native workers, and they still hold a large amount of land around Kampung Alor, Fatuhada and Bebonuk – all in Dili. Some of this land was traded to the Indonesian government. Members of the Alkatiri family have threatened to evict a few families who used to be their family helpers from land which they had acquired through *aforamento*, in the interest of business and economic development.

After the 1926 coup, Lisbon exiled a number of convicted political activists to Timor. Grants of *aforamento* were given to these *deportados,* among whom was the Carrascalão family, which managed a large area of coffee plantations in Liquiça and still occupies a large amount of land in Comoro in Dili. Another such family was the Sebastiao da Costa family, which possessed a large amount of land in Hera, east of the capital. They sold part of the land to the Indonesian government, and made another portion available to local farmers for cultivation. The Albano family possessed substantial lands south of the Comoro river, and sold some plots to the Indonesian government for a public housing project. Today this is a wealthy family.

The Carnation Revolution that toppled the dictatorship in Lisbon in 1974 inspired one of the two major parties advocating independence – FRETILIN (*Frente Revolucionaria do Timor-Leste Independente*, Revolutionary Front for an Independent East Timor) – to adopt a land reform programme. This aimed at economic decolonisation through breaking up plantations or transferring them to joint management by Timorese (FRETILIN 1974: 27–34). However, other political forces such as the UDT (*União Democratica de Timor*, Timorese Democratic Union), which mainly consisted of local feudal landlords and *deportados* including some heads of villages under fascist administration, Timorese colonial elites and the Catholic Church[2] which wanted to maintain their vested interests in land, opposed this progressive political agenda. The conflict formed part of the background to the brief civil war in August 1975, which led to Indonesian military intervention.

The Indonesian occupation of Timor-Leste from 1975 until 1999 was generally harsh and exploitative. In its land policies, Indonesia accepted Portuguese land titles, which benefited the Church and large landowners. Interestingly, Indonesia returned 500 hectares of coffee plantations to the then pro-integration leader Manuel Carrascalão in 1980 (Budiardjo and Liem 1984: 105). Meanwhile, Indonesia requisitioned lands abandoned after 1975 (Fitzpatrick 2002: 93). Coffee farmers took some plots on plantations which they regarded as their own property, but the price given for their coffee by the Indonesian army-backed company, PT Denok, was half the price given for Carrascalão's coffee. This was a penalty for the farmers who had 'reoccupied' land that should have reverted to the state. Government officials said 'the farmers are the laborers picking coffee that doesn't belong to them' (Budiardjo and Liem 1984: 105).

Cases of land conflicts with their roots in Portuguese colonialism

The coffee business and peasants in Ermera

The district of Ermera is a major coffee-producing area and an area of tense land conflict. It is, therefore, highly instructive for us to take a close look at the history of the area and how it became a coffee-producing area under Portuguese colonialism.

Local oral stories say that Ermera means 'red water', since *er* means 'water' and *mera* 'red' in Mombae, and three Mombae-speaking brothers lived there: Bereleki, Lakuleki and Mauleki. Their descendants were identified with the three mountains of Kituria, Lalimlau and Kailitilau, respectively, as their ancestors had lived, died and been buried there. Bereleki, possibly the eldest brother, lived in Lalimlau. There were three *uma-fukun* or local totem communities in Lalimlau at the time when Timorese chiefs received military titles from the Portuguese in 1701–3: Wehali, Tenenti and Maior. While the latter two are obviously military titles of Portuguese origin, the first, Wehali, indicates some link with the kingdom of Wewiku-Wehali. It is known that

Ermera paid *finta,* or tax, in the form of ten slaves and 20 picos to the Portuguese to sustain the *Praca* (military post) of Lifau in 1733. In 1815 the ruler of the *reino de Erimeira alias Ermera* was a queen with the name of Coronela Dona Dam. Artesabe or Atsabe, a subdistrict of Ermera, was a separate community, and Dom Antonio Hornay was mentioned as its ruler. By 1850 Ermera was one of the 48 districts under Portuguese rule. In 1896, when the total population of Timor was approximately 301,900, Ermera had a population of 10,000, out of whom 50 were Christians who spoke Mombae. In 1913 Dom Miguel Hornay of Ermera was killed while siding with Dom Boaventura's Manufahi revolt against the Portuguese (Belo 2011: 27, 36, 37, 38 and 50). Oral stories confirmed that Dom Miguel was killed in Batugade, where the Portuguese had a military post.

Governor da Silva developed coffee plantations in Ermera. Later – in the early twentieth century – the colonial administration handed over SAPT plantations to Portuguese *deportados* or Chinese, marking the beginning of *latifundiarios* (large landownership) and *fazendas* (plantations). Locals who were unable to pay a head tax had to become cheap labourers on *fazendas*. An old man, Mauleto, who was from the sub-village of Lequisi and more than 100 years old, told us in 2000 that the Portuguese paid wages only when they remembered.

Conflict over state concessions

The case of a well-known large coffee plantation located in Fatubesi in western Ermera is illustrative. There were originally two communities in the area, Mau-Ubu and Fatubolu, both of which originated in Lalimlau. In order to develop a seedling project for coffee and other trees, in the late nineteenth century Governor Celestino requested a local *liurai* to expel inhabitants, so as to confiscate their land for coffee production. The land was handed over to the SAPT, and inhabitants who resisted were beaten or imprisoned. The governor brought in labourers from other areas such as Bobonaro, Manufahi, Aileu, Ainaro, Baucau, Lospalos and Viqueque, as he did not trust the locals (Matadalan ba Rai 2013:56). The two communities, Mau-Ubu and Fatubolu, eventually became *sucos* (villages) under the colonial administrative system. Indonesia created a new *suco* with the name of Fatubesi for the original inhabitants of Mau-Ubu and Fatubolu. Through this process, conflict developed between the SAPT workers and the original inhabitants.

After Indonesia withdrew, the original inhabitants began retaking the land of which they had been forcibly deprived. The peasant group coordinated the allocation of abandoned land among the original inhabitants and settlers in 2001. They called this 'popular land reform', and hoped it would be recognised by the FRETILIN government. To the local's surprise, the FRETILIN government developed an agribusiness project to hand over 3,000 hectares of land, including the coffee plantation in Fatubesi, as a concession to a Singaporean–Timorese joint venture, Timor Global. The decision was based on Law No. 1/2003 on Land, which transfers abandoned properties previously controlled by foreigners to the state (Ministério da Justiça 2003).

In an interview,[3] the former Minister of Agriculture of the FRETILIN administration, Estanislau da Silva, denied that the principles of FRETILIN's land policy had changed, as well as the claim that there was any intervention by donors or any other country in making the decision. The purpose was the full utilisation of the land, which needed investment for regeneration which the government could not afford. The contract between the government and Timor Global guaranteed that the farmers would not be evicted without the offer of alternative land, and that the company would bring a profit to the farmers, as it promised to purchase their coffee at a competitive price. As there had been no other coffee buyers at that time, the minister added, the deal should have been acceptable for the farmers.

The lack of political consultation during this policy's development might have contributed to conflict. The decision generated resentment, and in December 2005 thousands of farmers and NGOs protested against the company and the government. The farmers initiated dialogues with the government, calling for a change of policy. The Ministry of Agriculture and the Ministry of Justice represented the government, but it failed to adequately respond to the call of the farmers. The NGOs and the farmers suggested an alternative policy by which the land would remain in the hands of the people and would be leased to the company. The prime minister, Mari Alkatiri, endorsed this alternative policy, and at present the farmers continue to use the land and maintain coffee plantation. Timor Global buys coffee beans only from the farmers and supports them in replacing old trees with new ones, and terracing the land.[4] Tension remains, however, and the farmers fear that they might lose their land rights if a new land regime turns out not to support the original communal land rights.

Conflict between aforamento *holders, NGOs and the community*

Ermera has another area of land conflict: *aldeia* (hamlet) Aifu in *suco* Poetete. During the Portuguese colonial period in the 1920s, Jose Babo, a Portuguese, obtained a portion of land from *liurai* Bersik to develop a seedling project for coffee and other types of tree. When the coffee trees were planted, Jose Babo declared that the land belonged to him as he had obtained a document of *aforamento* (right to use) for 169 hectares of coffee plantation from the Portuguese. The locals initially refused to leave the land, but when threatened with imprisonment in a notorious prison in Weberek, Manufahi, they abandoned the land and became labourers on the plantation to earn money to pay their head tax (KSI 2004: 2).

Just before the civil war in August 1975, the Babo family left for Australia. During the war period between 1976 and 1984, the native people reoccupied their land. A son of Jose Babo passed a letter of attorney to an Indonesian businessman in Kupang, in Indonesian West Timor. In 1984 the Indonesian came to Aifu with the letter and began to manage the coffee plantation. The farmers were again expelled and became labourers on the plantation. By that time, the Indonesian military elites had established a company, PT Denok, and this company monopolised Ermera's coffee.

Immediately after independence, a dispute emerged in Aifu between the Babo family's Timorese descendants and the CCT (*Cooperativa Café Timor*, Timor Coffee Cooperative), the biggest cooperative firm of coffee farmers in east Timor-Leste. From interviews we conducted with leaders of the farmers union, local chiefs and the CCT, the history of the conflict can be summarised as below.[5] As a result of an initiative by the Clinton administration in 1994, there was a breakthrough in the Indonesian monopoly on Ermera's coffee. The plight of the East Timorese had attracted world attention because of the Santa Cruz massacre in 1991, and so the new Clinton administration in the US was under pressure to do something about Timor-Leste. Against this backdrop, the non-profit National Cooperatives Business Association (NCBA), with the help of USAID, succeeded in obtaining a licence to purchase and export coffee from Timor-Leste. The *chefe de suco* mediated an agreement between NCBA and the PUSKUD, a centre of government-manufactured village cooperatives. NCBA concluded a 20-year contract with the PUSKUD. NCBA built its first processing factory in Aifu and began to introduce Ermera's organic Arabica to the global coffee market. One of the main buyers of CCT products was Starbucks, in America. However, the change in buyer did not affect the status of the farmers in relation to the land.

In 1997 or 1998 the Indonesian manager left Timor. The management of the plantation was handed over to the *chefe de suco*, who was a member of the underground resistance organisation. After the Indonesian withdrawal, some of the farmers formed a union called UNAER (*União Agricultores Ermera*, Ermera Peasants Union). In 2001 the *chefe de suco* and the farmers held a dialogue and agreed that management should be returned to the farmers. In 2000, under the Timor Economic Rehabilitation and Development Project, USAID started a capacity-building programme for the CCT, which was reorganised from PUSKUD with the support of NCBA. A clash occurred in December 2002, when Timorese nephews of the Portuguese, who held the *aforamento* document for the plantation, brought in 140 ex-guerrillas and squatted on the land to 'retake their own lands'. They destroyed newly planted vanilla trees and a coffee-processing machine at the CCT's factory. The CCT took the matter to court. The court ruled that the lease contract of NCBA/CCT was valid. Despite the court decision, the squatters stayed in Aifu for six months. In 2004 the CCT's contract ended and its factory moved elsewhere. While CCT continued to purchase organic coffee from certified farmers, a Japanese fair trade company also started supporting the farmers by purchasing their coffee in 2008. So far there has been no violent confrontation between the farmers and the Portuguese family, but people are worried about their land rights because the family holds the *aforamento* document.

Cases of land conflicts with their roots in the Indonesian occupation

Three patterns of land conflict can be discerned as having their basis in the period of Indonesian occupation. The first is conflict caused by the massive relocation to 'strategic hamlets' in the 1980s. The second is conflict caused by Indonesia's transmigration policy in the 1990s. The third is conflict caused by the requisition of land for public use.

'Strategic hamlets' and their aftermath

After the fall of the resistance base at Mount Matebian and the surrender of FRETILIN followers in late 1978, the TNI (*Tentara Nasional Indonesia*, Indonesian National Army) transferred people into what they called 'strategic hamlets'. These were designed to isolate people from the guerrillas. The military built a few such hamlets in every district (Aditjondro 1994: 65).[6] These areas were not unpopulated. However, as Myat Thu (2008) noted, people successfully recreated livelihoods in cooperation with the host community. Today, there is tension over land between the original villagers and the settlers. What follows is a story we heard in Bucoli,[7] Baucau District.

Bucoli is a village near the city of Baucau, where the legendary FRETILIN leader Vicente dos Reis (Sahe) was born. In 1974–75 it was a base for FRETILIN's social economic programme. After the fall of the resistance base at Mount Matebian in 1978, people of all *aldeias* of Bucoli, Makadai de Baixu, Waisemu, Lurihene, Lekirewatu, Aobaka and Makadai Desima were confined in the churchyard, before being moved to nearby hamlets, from which their movement was restricted. In the camps they were given only corn powder, and therefore they had to seek other food themselves, such as tubers or jackfruit. For three years they were not allowed to cultivate or release animals beyond the limited vicinity of the hamlets. Later they were allowed to live and cultivate beyond the hamlet limit. However, if there was an attack by the FALINTIL (*Forças Armadas para Libertação Nacional de Timor-Leste*, Timor-Leste National Liberation Army), they were prohibited to go beyond the hamlet limit. People were ordered to live in settlements facing the road so that the TNI could easily watch their movements.

These people had no choice but to build houses on land owned by somebody else. People from other areas were brought in to these 'strategic hamlets' as well. For survival reasons, people sought a way to live together, and to some extent created internal patron–client relationships. For example, landowners allowed residents to continue to stay in the houses facing the road. As for cultivation, the settlers who were taken in from other areas within Bucoli had to cultivate their original plots. Those from outside Bucoli were allowed to cultivate the fields of the original owners, but they had to share the harvest with the landowners. It was decided that they could plant corn and cassava for food, but they could not plant trees such as jackfruit, cumin, coconut or teak. These arrangements were generally made by negotiation between the owners and the settlers.

After independence almost all of those who had come from outside Bucoli returned to their original homes, except those who were now married to locals. On the other hand, the settlers from other places within Bucoli continued to live in the houses along the main road, as this was advantageous for transport and business. As the settlers began to build new houses on the land of the original owners, tensions increased between the landowners and the settlers. While the former assert that the land should be kept for their children, the latter respond that they are the victims of Indonesian military operations. As tension rises, small-scale confrontations are now happening. Villagers as well as local leaders worry about what the result of the new law will be.

Indonesian transmigration policy and its consequences

Indonesia's transmigration policy had the purpose of transferring farmers from overpopulated Java and Bali to the sparsely populated Outer Islands to reduce population pressure and introduce the more advanced agriculture of the Javanese or Balinese farmers to 'backward' Timor-Leste. From the early 1980s Indonesian migrants were settled at 19 sites, mainly on the south coast (Durand 2002: 103). This policy also aimed to consolidate security in problematic areas such as Timor-Leste, West Papua or Aceh through cultural assimilation. Here we describe the situation of the transmigration site in Tunubibi, Bobonaro District, as an illustrative case of land conflict caused by the policy.

Maliana is the capital of Bobonaro District near the border with Indonesian West Timor. The area was greatly affected by Indonesian military operations. The plain surrounded by the rivers Nunura (north), Bulobo (east) and Malibaka (west) was a destination for both internal and external migrations. Tunubibi is an *aldeia* located in the northern part of Memo village, Bobonaro District. Aditjondro described the land conflict at Tunubibi as a land grab by the Indonesian authorities (Aditjondro 1994: 63), while Fitzpatrick presented it as a dispute between the local people and settlers (Fitzpatrick 2002: 176–78, 180), as we saw in Bucoli and Ermera. We conducted an interview with the *chefe de suco* of Memo, who was the village secretary during the Indonesian occupation, two *lia nain* (traditional elders) in Memo, and *the chefe de aldeia* of Tunubibi. The following is a summary of the stories they told us.[8]

In 1982 the Indonesian administration started a 'model village' programme in Tunubibi. Under the scheme, the government brought into Tunubibi 50 families from Bali (*Trans Bali*) and 50 families from nearby villages in Maliana such as Memo, Holsa and Odomau (*Trans Lokal*). The government provided each family with a house, a plot of farmland and provisions for five years. The leaders of the local administration, including the district administrator, who was also the *liurai* of Memo, used the threat of military force to compel landowners to give up their land without compensation, saying that this would be a temporary arrangement. However, the settlers were provided with certificates of ownership (*hak milik*)[9] by the government. Later the government constructed irrigation facilities, and the rice harvest became stable. In 1999 the Balinese farmers returned to Bali in fear of possible turmoil resulting from the referendum. They left their land and houses in Tunubibi. A dispute arose when inhabitants of other places such as Oeleu, Odamau, Marobo and Sekar[10] returned from refugee camps in West Timor and occupied the abandoned Balinese houses and lands.

In the transitional period when the CNRT (*Conselho Nacional de Resistencia Timoresnse*, National Council of Timorese Resistance) was in charge of village administration, the leader of the CNRT in Tunubibi campaigned to upgrade Tunubibi to a village, which meant that it would separate from Memo. This proposal was opposed by the original landowners of Memo, and it did not materialise. When the original owners began to sow seeds on the land abandoned by the Balinese, there was a fight between the landowners and some of the occupants, including Sekar people. As a result, one person was severely wounded and five people were imprisoned for three months. The dispute was brought to the District Office of Land and Property. However, the Office could not judge on the matter, instead urging the parties to negotiate an agreement for use of the land only.

If the new land law is to recognise customary rights, then since the Memo originally asserted their ownership by stating that they dug the first earth canal in 1973, they have the land rights. On the other hand, the settlers contend that the land abandoned by the Balinese foreigners became state land. In 2013 the government started a new project to regenerate the irrigation system of the Malibaka river. It is probable that the dispute will flare up again when the original owners find that they have lost their rights.

Land requisition for public use

The Indonesian authorities, both military and civilian, often took land from people for public use. The village of Humboe, near Ermera, the old capital of Ermera District, is one such case. In an interview,[11] the *chefe de suco* in Humboe told us that there was a 'demonstration plot' of coffee trees of 33 hectares that the Portuguese colonial government seized in 1973. Villagers had worked as labourers on the plot. After the Indonesians occupied Timor-Leste, the plot was transferred to the Department of Agriculture. In 1995, through negotiations with government officials, army and police commanders and members of the district legislative body, the villagers gained permission to utilise the land themselves, which included re-establishing coffee trees. In return for this arrangement the villagers agreed to pay additional tax, and still cultivate the land today. They are worried that the government will take the land because the proposed land law provides that abandoned public property should be transferred to the state.

A similar case can be found in Maliana, Bobonaro District.[12] A Timorese family owned a piece of land in the village of Holsa, and they built a house and cultivated the land. However, the Indonesian police seized the land to build its district headquarters in 1985. In September 1999 the police head-quarters was the site of a massacre by pro-Indonesian Timorese militia and Indonesian soldiers. After independence, in accordance with the new land law, the Timorese government decided to rehabilitate it as the district head-quarters of the PNTL (*Policia Nacional Timor-Leste*, the Timor-Leste National Police).

The government takeover of the land prompted the original landowners to take the case to the district administration land and property committee.[13] The committee decided that the process of reclamation had been done in an appropriate way, and that if the family wanted to persist with their claim they should take the case to the upper level. Later, the PNTL occupied an addi-tional piece of land next to the police headquarters to build a dormitory for officers. In 2007, with the support of the *chefe de suco* of Holsa and the head of the Land and Property Office, the family agreed to submit to the Minister of Justice a letter stating that they would allow the PNTL to use the premises where the headquarters and a dormitory had already been built. At the same time they requested the minister to order the PNTL not to occupy any more land and to return the remaining land to the family. Up to now the family has neither received a response nor compensation from the government. Now the PNTL has occupied more land on another side of the headquarters to build houses for officers. This has further infuriated the family, who have long suf-fered from the occupation of their land.

Bitter feelings remain in the family, as they feel they have dedicated so much to the liberation struggle. One member of the family fought alongside FALINTIL guerrillas in the mountains and was killed by the TNI. Another member was an activist of the women's organisation of FRETILIN, and other members also actively participated in the underground resistance. In marked contrast with the case of this family, land that had been owned by the Catholic mission in central Maliana, and that was confiscated by the Indo-nesian army's district command, was returned to the mission after indepen-dence.[14] Now the construction of a Catholic school complex is under way.

Cases of land conflict in post-independence Timor-Leste

Dili today, after the referendum exodus and the crisis of 2006

As explained earlier, after the referendum in 1999 about 250,000 people fled or were forcibly taken to Indonesian West Timor when Timor-Leste des-cended into chaos under the Indonesian military's scorched earth policy. When these refugees returned to Timor-Leste, some of them had nowhere to go, as their houses had been destroyed or burnt down. Many were attracted to the capital, Dili, as it was benefiting from an economic boom stimulated by the UN. Others feared reprisals if they went back home, as they might be suspected of links with the pro-Indonesian militia. Against this backdrop, many decided to remain in Dili and occupied 'empty' houses that Indonesians had lived in before the referendum.

In January 2006, eight months after the downsizing of the UN presence, Timor-Leste began to slip into crisis when a split between 'easterner' commanders and 'westerner' soldiers within the armed forces emerged, and a large group of disgruntled soldiers deserted with their weapons. By May 2006 their action had evolved into a major conflict that divided not only the security services but also the political leadership and society as a whole. The death toll reached 37 and more than 100,000 persons were displaced. These were mostly residents of the capital, who originated from the eastern region. Even after the prime minister resigned in June 2006, the disaffected soldiers continued to refuse to surrender; this led to a shooting incident in February 2008, in which the leader of the group was killed and the president of Timor-Leste was shot and seriously wounded (Matsuno 2009: 40–41).

We conducted interviews with the previous *chefe de aldeia* in Kampung Alor[15] (1999–2005) and the present *chefe de suco* in Bekora[16] (2005–) in order to trace what had happened in their communities since 1999. In both areas disputes over houses and lands left by Indonesians still remain unresolved.

Kampung Alor is an area of Dili that has a mosque and is traditionally inhabited by Arabs. In the Indonesian period many Muslim Indonesian migrants also settled there. When the post-referendum refugees from this area returned home, these Indonesians found their houses already occupied by Timorese who had previously returned from West Timor. They asked the squatters to leave, telling them that they loved Timor and wanted to live in Timor-Leste. They paid compensation from US$1,000–3,000 to the squatters to retrieve their houses. However, after obtaining certificates of residence, they sold the houses and went back to Indonesia. Seeing this pattern, Timorese squatters began refusing to leave. Some even rented out the houses to UN staff, and when those staff left they sold the houses to other Timorese. Those who occupied the houses were said to be easterners, mostly from Lautem District, who might previously have had no houses. When the 2006 crisis broke out, easterners in Dili were attacked and became IDPs. The houses squatted in by easterners in 1999–2000 were reoccupied by other people. Neither side had legal rights over the properties.

In Bekora, a south-eastern suburb of Dili, both easterners and westerners – according to the *chefe de suco* – occupied houses that Indonesians had left behind, as they had no places to settle. They did not occupy houses in the possession of Timorese, even if the owners did not return from West Timor. At the time of the 2006 crisis, in which easterners became the target of violence, their houses were burnt, looted or occupied.

In order to put an end to the IDP problem, in December 2007 the government launched a 'cash for return' programme that provided the victims, mostly easterners, with compensation to reconstruct or repair their houses. The amount of compensation was determined according to the level of damage – which was established in assessment by the Ministry of Social Solidarity and the Ministry of Public Works – and ranged from US$500 to US$4,500 (Lopes 2009: 12). However, the government executed this programme without resolving the problem of land titles. One consequence was that there were many cases of irregular use of money. For example, IDPs, when they returned and found their houses occupied, often had to pay money to the squatters so that they would leave. The *chefe de suco* of Bekora sometimes mediated a negotiation between the two parties, neither of whom had any legal right over the property. The two parties would agree, for example, that the 'victim' party would receive compensation of US$4,500 from the government and give US$1,000 to the squatter party. This profit sharing might be a practical solution, but it rewards the perpetrator of a crime. After all, the problem is in how to deal with the properties left by the Indonesians. The *chefe de suco* of Bekora proposes that anyone, easterner or westerner, should pay rent to the government because the proposed law stipulates that abandoned land and properties should be returned to the state.[17]

Harrington (2007) suggested that illegal occupations of houses in 1999 were mainly carried out by easterners. However, up to now no effort has been made by the government to establish the truth. Fitzpatrick and Monson (2009) and Harrington (2007) pointed out that the inability of both the United Nations Transitional Administration in East Timor (UNTAET), which lacked resources and mandate, and the Timorese Consultative Council, which lacked political will, to build a transitional land administration in order to manage arbitrary housing occupations and transactions contributed to the outbreak of violence in Dili in 2006.

Development, farmers and landlords in Betano

Betano is a town located in the southern coastal area of Manufahi District, facing the Timor Sea. Behind it spreads a vast area of flat land, and on the seabed of the Timor Sea there is drilling for oil and gas. In the Portuguese period there were communities in Bemetan, Loro and Otorita.[18] In the late 1960s or early 1970s the Portuguese government gave *aforamento* of 203 hectares to a Portuguese businessman, Mateus Ferreira,[19] to build a palm wine brewery in Loro. At the same time it also gave *aforamento* to a Chinese businessman, San Tai Hoo, to build a fabric factory.

Under the Indonesian occupation, Betano became a centre of the government's resettlement programmes for security and development. The Indonesian authorities resettled people from Same, from other districts such as Ainaro, Ermera, Dili or Baucau, and also from within Betano. For example, the *aldeia* of Pemuda Tani ('young farmers' in Indonesian) was constructed for people from a mountain village in Same, with the aim of discouraging their support for the FALINTIL guerrillas and diverting their energy into 'productive activities'. Pemuda Tani was constructed on land where San Tai Hoo had his *aforamento*.

In 1996 the Indonesian government developed modern irrigation facilities that gave some 600 hectares of rice fields access to water from the Caraulun river. After independence in 2006, the irrigation facilities were rehabilitated under the Agricultural Rehabilitation Project (ARP) III, co-funded by the European Union and the World Bank. A warehouse and an office were constructed by the ARP for Akadiruoan Water Users Association. From the Indonesian period until today, Ferreira's family have been claiming their rights over the land. In 2006 the family put forward their claim against the Ministry of Agriculture and farmers. The case was brought to court, but a decision has been suspended. Since the rehabilitation was not complete, the District Agriculture Office and farmers in Betano submitted a request to the government that the weir across the river should be reconstructed. The renewal of this system started in July 2013. However, the dispute with Ferreira is not yet resolved.

Meanwhile, some different government projects have been in progress in Bemetan, an *aldeia* of Betano. The first one was the construction of a power plant.[20] Some of the farmers have opposed this project, and the first clash took place when the government tried to expropriate land for the purpose.[21] The lack of a clear legal framework for land titles and compensation is a factor here, but there was also miscommunication, and the local authorities adopted an authoritarian approach towards the claimants. Initially the landowners did not object to the project. The community decided to offer the four hectares of land that the government designated, without asking for compensation. However, it turned out that the power plant needed 16 hectares. This time the landowners would not agree to offer such a wide area of land without compensation. However, the village chief thought that the government was not ready to pay compensation. He turned to the subcontracting company, Tinolina, and asked it to give a small amount of money to each claimant as a recompense.

The claimants received money as *kosar been* – literally, 'reward for their sweat'. The company emphasised that it was not official compensation. The claimants gave their signatures to a document because they thought that it was merely a receipt for *kosar been*. However, this was used as a proof of their agreement. The company cleared the land using heavy machinery, destroying all the crops and plants, without first informing the claimants that this would take place. The claimants felt that they had been cheated. On 30 August 2011 the claimants and their supporters demonstrated at the site of the power plant. Despite the fact that the organisers abided by regulations and informed the relevant authorities, including the police, about the action, the police made a violent intervention, shouting obscenities at female landowners and arresting people (Front Mahasiswa and RBR 2011; *Diario* 2011).

After this incident, government officials and members of parliament made a series of visits to the area. In an attempt to persuade the locals of the necessity for a large amount of land for power plant construction, and to quell concerns about the environmental impact, the government invited some claimants to visit a power plant in Hera, near the capital, Dili. In July 2012 the government also invited community leaders to a meeting in Dili to explain the planned expansion of the project with an oil refinery and other infrastructures. On neither occasion did the government mention compensation. The DNTPSC (*Direcção Naçional de Terras e Propriedades, Serviços Cadastrais*, National Directorate for Land, Property and Cadastral Services) claimed that the land for the power plant had been abandoned. The community firmly opposed this view, stating that the land had been used for farming, planting trees and grazing.

Bemetan has another dispute over land that the government expropriated under the MDG Suco Program.[22] According to the government's Strategic Development Plan 2010–30, the programme aims to build houses for vulnerable people in every *aldeia*. Each prefabricated house is to be equipped with solar power facilities, piped water and a bathroom. For the first phase, the plan was to build five houses in each hamlet by 2015. The total number of houses to be built in the phase would be 2,228 (Government of Timor-Leste 2011: 110–11). However, the land acquisition did not go smoothly. The National Development Agency (ADN) then changed its plan and decided to build a new settlement in one place to cover several villages. But the new plan has brought another problem to Betano.

By 2012 the site in Bemetan had already been expropriated and the construction of about 100 houses had started. These houses are intended for 'vulnerable people', but no one knew who would get them. The landowners had offered their land for this project, but the document in which they agreed to offer the land mentions neither the right of the landowners of access to the house nor compensation. The landowners' understanding is that they can obtain all the houses built on their land; but this was denied by the ADN. Landowners are also opposed to accepting vulnerable people from other villages, because nobody will take care of them. This lack of accountability and transparency has caused a degree of anxiety and distrust.

Land administration and conflict resolution

From the historical background and the cases of land conflict described here, we can see that there are two sources of land claims in Timor-Leste: titles authorised by two previous administrations[23] and customary rights. However, the situation is much more complex. First, titles from the Portuguese and Indonesian periods are not always seen as legitimate in the eyes of many people. Some are clearly cases of dispossession, and in such cases automatic recognition of previous titles or nationalisation may be felt to be unjust. Second, customary or traditional rights have never been clearly defined and are not yet legally authorised. Third, expelling 'illegal' occupants unconditionally may be regarded as unjust when often the occupants themselves have been the victims of forcible relocation or displacement. How to settle disputes between original people and new settlers is linked with the issue of who should benefit from 'customary rights'.

The government's capacity to deal with this complex situation is far from sufficient. Almost all public documents were destroyed by the post-referendum scorched earth policy of the Indonesian army and militia. Institution building is urgently needed, especially in the three areas of law, land registration and conflict resolution mechanisms. The most fundamental is law, because without a clear law it is impossible to sort out claims. Registration must be systematic and universally implemented. The Portuguese and Indonesian authorities did register land, but they issued only a limited number of titles.[24] As for a land administration mechanism, the government established the DNTP (*Direcção Naçional de Terras e Propriedades*, National Directorate for Land and Property)[25] by Law No. 1/2003, which not only administers immovable property but also develops policies and draft legislation, and settles disputes through a non-judicial mechanism.[26]

In 2007 the government accelerated institution building for land and property, with the assistance of USAID. The project is called Strengthening Property Rights in Timor-Leste, and was given a Tetun name, 'Ita Nia Rai' (Our Land) or INR. The Ministry of Justice was responsible for the project, and it was implemented through subcontracting consultancies between 2007 and 2011.

Land registration[27]

The INR project included a pilot land registration programme carried out in the capitals of 13 districts. The procedure was systematic. GPS photo data was collected, interviews with claimants were conducted, a cadastral map was made public with all the claimants' names and photographs, and – if there was no dispute, or after any dispute had been resolved – measurement was done. If the ministry received duplicate claims, the plot would be shaded in red and the application number encircled. There was a 30-day period for objections before the process was closed. With the Decree Law of July 2011, the Ministry of Justice started issuing certificates for non-disputed land. From this process it emerged that there was a huge number of disputes. This was positive, since with this information illegal transactions could be prevented. However, our concern is the capacity of the DNTPSC to deal with these disputes and to proceed to the second phase on farmland in rural areas. In rural areas outside the capital, land claims relate to customary land held by families or clans, and hence without in-depth anthropological studies this registration system will only foster new disputes within and among communities.

The new land law

In March 2011 the cabinet finalised a legal package comprising the Law on Special Regime for Determination of Ownership of Immovable Property, the Law on Expropriation[28] and the Law on Real Estate Financial Fund.[29]

The laws were passed by parliament in February 2012, but the then president, José Ramos Horta, rejected their promulgation, arguing that people's rights were not fully accommodated. As of August 2013 the parliament is yet to hold a final debate on the laws. What we discuss here, therefore, is the cabinet version of the Law on Special Regime for Determination of Ownership of Immovable Property (Government of Timor-Leste 2012). We will focus on this law because it determines ownership rights, and so is the foundation for the application of the other two laws. We examine four major issues – previous titles, foreigners, public property and special adverse possession – and present their implications for the disputes we have presented in this chapter.

Previous titles

The Special Regime recognises uncontested previous titles (Article 27). In cases of dispute between indigenous claimants holding previous primary rights (ownership), when one of the claimants owns the immovable property or part thereof, the claimant will be granted property rights over the part of the property he owns (Article 31). In cases of dispute between previous primary rights (ownership) holders and previous secondary rights (right to use) holders, the former are given priority (Article 32). In disputed cases between holders of the previous secondary rights, those who have present possession will be given priority (Article 33). If neither party has present possession, the most recent holder of rights is given priority (Article 36).

Foreigners

Under the Special Regime, the immovable property of foreign claimants who hold previous rights shall revert to the state, except in cases of special adverse possession by nationals (Article 8–1). If foreign claimants wish to use the property, they can do so by making a lease contract with the state (Article 8–3). All immovable property of foreigners that is identified as abandoned by the DNTPSC under Law No. 1/2003 shall be considered to be under current state possession (Article 6–3).

Public property

Property previously used by the government of Portugal and/or Indonesia shall be considered as the state's domain (Article 6–5). State ownership of properties in its possession shall prevail over any previous rights, but there is a right to compensation under the provisions of this law (Article 6–2).

Special adverse possession

Special adverse possession means the acquisition of property through its peaceful maintenance over a certain period of time. The concept is intended to cover most of the customarily and individually possessed lands in rural areas. Importantly, the definition is designed to exclude both the occupation of land and property left by the Indonesians in 1999 and the reoccupation of houses in 2006. Special adverse possession does not apply to the public domain (Article 18), and it must meet the following requirements. First, the claimant must be a Timorese citizen and possess the property with the intention of ownership continuously, publicly and notarially. Second, possession must have begun in a peaceful fashion before or on 31 December 1998, without the use of physical violence or psychological coercion (Article 19). Further, even if the claimant fulfils the above two requirements, this does not supersede previous primary rights of a national claimant (Article 34). However, in a dispute with a national claimant with previous secondary rights, the present possessor is granted ownership (Article 35). In this case the loser could receive reparation from the Real Estate Fund (Article 39), and the person assigned ownership rights shall reimburse the state (Article 43).

Community protection zones

A community protection zone is defined as an area protected by the state for the purpose of safeguarding the common interests of local communities. The areas concerned include residential areas, agricultural areas (either cultivated or fallow ground), forests, culturally relevant sites, pastures, water springs and areas with natural resources that are shared by the population and are necessary for its subsistence (Article 21). Community property is immovable property acknowledged as being for the common and shared use of a group of individuals or families, organised in accordance with local practices and customs (Article 26). The DNTPSC will issue ownership titles in the name of the local community.

Implications of the new law

What are the implications of these provisions for the cases of land conflict presented above? The Special Regime upholds two major principles. One is the absolute priority of effective previous titles, the Regime taking no account of how a previous title was obtained. The other is the wide authority of the state. The state has claims on land abandoned by foreigners, land possessed by the Portuguese or Indonesian authorities, and land deemed not in use. The only condition that allows people to use the property they occupy now is special adverse possession with the deadline of 31 December 1998. In view of these principles, the implications for our cases are as follows.

The 'popular land reform' farmers in Ermera are not likely to be granted ownership. Their land can be identified as abandoned, since the Portuguese owner is dead, and hence the government's action in taking it over and leasing it as a concession may be justified. The farmers started to use the land only after the withdrawal of the Indonesians, thus not fulfilling one of the two requirements of special adverse possession. Article 95 of the new land law confirms the government's position, as it stipulates that all *lease* contracts entered under Law No.1/2003 of 10 March, and related to abandoned immovable property, shall continue to be effective until their termination dates, and the private holder who was granted the ownership right shall become the landlord.

The UNAER farmers in Aifu are also unlikely to regain ownership of the land they were dispossessed of in the Portuguese period. Even though the farmers started using the land peacefully before 31 December 1998, they would have to compensate the holder of Portuguese *aforamento* through the Real Estate Fund. It would be the same for the villagers of Betano who have 'occupied' the land of *aforamento* holders.[30]

The land abandoned by Balinese migrants in Tunubibi may revert to the state, and hence the people of both Sekar and Memo may have to refrain from using the land for free. The use of the abandoned land in Tunubibi is not in any way illegal, but since Memo's original villagers argue that the Indonesian authorities took their land by coercion, they will feel it unjust that this land reverts to the state.

The land that the farmers in Humboe are using may also be taken by the government. Although this may be a case of dispossession, the land was public property in the Portuguese and Indonesian periods. For that reason alone, the villagers will lose the right to land that they have used since 1995 as a result of their struggle against unjust colonialism and foreign occupation.[31] There seems to be no chance that the land on which the Maliana police headquarters was built will be returned to the family that possessed it. It was clearly public property in the Indonesian period. The cases of Humboe and the Maliana police headquarters may fall under the provisions for compensation of Article 6, but this provision is so vague that nothing can be said with certainty about this.

Occupants of houses abandoned by Indonesians in 1999 have no chance of being granted ownership. The vast majority of cases of occupation occurred after 31 December 1998, and hence do not constitute a case of special adverse possession. Here, the principle that property abandoned by foreigners reverts to the state will be strictly applied.

With regard to the disputes in the former 'strategic hamlet' in Bucoli and the problem in Tunubibi, the law is not useful, because it does not touch on disputed claims based on customary rights. In this situation it is a matter of how the original villagers accommodate the settlers' rights. In the case of Bucoli, special adverse possession does not apply to the occupants, because the land was not possessed peacefully.

The procedure by which the government took 16 hectares of land in Bemetan for a power plant now appears to be problematic. It has been made clear that the strict procedures on valuation and payment of compensation ensured by the Law on Expropriation were not executed in Betano. However, the issue still revolves around determination of ownership. In Betano, after the incident of August 2011, the Ministry of Justice prepared an application form for compensation, on which only the crops destroyed by the land clearance could be listed. This proposal was rejected by the owners.

It is clear that the Special Regime is unfavourable to people struggling for their rights in the cases we have described. The fundamental problem is that the Special Regime does not take account of how a previous title was obtained. With its unconditional recognition of previous titles, the Special Regime is likely to end up only strengthening the injustices that colonialism and foreign occupation inflicted upon these people. The only possible remedy is compensation, but the Special Regime is not clear about this.

How could the Special Regime be of help for claimants in both old and new types of land conflicts, such as the case of Ermera and the construction of the power plant and vulnerable people's houses in Betano? First, it should accommodate a provision for redressing past injustice. To do this it would be necessary to set up a technical procedure, such as the rights inquiry recommended by the CAVR (*Comissão dé Acolhimento, Verdade e Reconciliação de Timor Leste*, the Commission for Reception, Truth and Reconciliation),[32] to certify the fact of dispossession or abuse of customary rights. This decision should be made by a court. Once the victim has been designated, the state should be responsible for restitution or provision of compensation to settle the case. As for disputes with the state, it is crucial that the present state of possession should be proved in order to prevent arbitrary decisions by the state concerning whether land is abandoned or not. The cases in question may be more appropriately discussed as cases of expropriation. Under current conditions in Timor-Leste, customary landowners need to be protected from all kinds of manipulative transactions.

The issue of gender equality should also be mentioned here. The land law upholds the principle of gender equality in Article 4. However, in reality women's claims on land are not respected in the patrilineal and patriarchal Timorese society (Huang 2009). In the case of the Betano power plant, a female landowner who participated in the demonstration against the land clearance told us that she was invited neither to a briefing by the village chief to landowners nor to a meeting where they received money from the subcontracting company. On both occasions a male member of her family was invited. To promote gender equality on land rights, the Secretary of State for Promotion of Equality has been carrying out a campaign with the INR.[33] We can see some progress in the level of women's participation in the registration process. According to the statistics on land claims (30 June 2011), claims by individual females constituted 20.54 per cent,[34] joint claims by married couples made up 11.71 per cent, while claims by individual males accounted for 39.72 per cent(USAID 2011: 43).

Community dispute resolution and mediation

Mediation of land disputes was introduced in 2001, after the Timorese leaders of the National Council, the consultative body to the UN, opposed the establishment of a land claim commission at the time of the UNTAET.[35] The UNTAET established the Land and Property Unit, and authorised it to file and record claims, to supervise systems of mediation and to allocate public and abandoned properties through temporary lease contracts. The Unit (after 2003, the DNTP) gave intensive training to mediators in 2001 and 2005. In 2003 the Draft Mediation Law was publicised (Fitzpatrick 2008: 180–81). Community or traditional leaders, such as *liurai*, *lia-nain*, *chefe de suco* or *chefe de aldeia*, worked together with the DNTP's mediation staff.[36] In some cases NGOs were also involved.

The *chefe de suco* of Ritabau in Maliana, for example, said that mediation should not rush to the issue of compensation or how to share the land, but that the first thing to do was to invite the parties in conflict to listen to the history of both communities in order to appreciate their respective claims.[37] This approach is important because, while the Timorese experienced numerous displacements and migrations under foreign domination, their histories are not recorded. Furthermore, land possessions are often found in different locations because of food security or as fallow land for cyclic cultivation. Disputants can go on to a formal judicial track only when they cannot reach agreement. The government also used mediation to resolve land disputes related to the 2006 crisis. The Ministry of Social Solidarity formed dialogue teams and dispatched them to IDP camps to encourage IDPs to return, and to the recipient communities to facilitate their acceptance (Lopes 2009: 14). The INR project also has a component of mediation.

However, according to the statistics of the INR in June 2011, of 4,011 disputes 2,579 had gone to court, 79 had been dealt with within families, 66 cases were in mediation and 270 were in process with the INR. The extremely low success rate for mediation can be explained by two factors: one is the lack of capacity of hastily trained mediators, and the other is the fact that the mediators had no mandate to deal with disputes where the state was involved. The number of disputes involving the state was 2,381, all of which were referred to the courts. By June 2013 only 28 of the cases involving the state had been settled in the courts (USAID 2011: 41).

In a recent development, the Ministry of Defence and Security has created the DNPCC (*Direcção Nacional de Prevenção de Conflitos Comunitários*, National Directorate for Prevention of Community Conflict) and appointed its mediators in all districts.[38] At the presidential office there are two advisors on land issues. This might offer an alternative, in the sense that the government could be more participatory in developing its plan and implementing projects in communities. A well-made progressive law and mechanisms can be effective in facilitating this progress.

People's initiative for social justice: agrarian reform

Regarding the vitality of agrarian reform, coffee farmers have been resisting alongside FRETILIN since 1975, with the objective of achieving a better life after independence. Agrarian reform, according to UNAER, means both equal distribution and sustainable management of land directly by the farmers. This will allow people to reclaim their identity and their original land titles from the colonial government and former associated landlords, which had enslaved their ancestors.

Following the withdrawal of Indonesian forces, the farmers occupied and distributed land – first in Lequisi in 1999, and then in other areas in Ermera. A local NGO, Kdadalak Sulimutuk Institute (KSI), had started working with the coffee farmers to assist them in advocating non-violent agrarian reform, hoping that a FRETILIN government would implement its 1975 agrarian reform policy. The case has been discussed in a previous section.

In 2012 the union persuaded FRETILIN, now an opposition party, to include agrarian reform in its political agenda. FRETILIN's commitment is to be tested soon, as the new land law will be back in parliament. On the ground, the farmers have attempted to organise cooperatives and direct coffee trade links with the green cooperative movement in Japan and South Korea, and they are on their way to succeeding.

Fitzpatrick has pointed out that the SAPT had plantations totalling 10,000 hectares, and other Portuguese planters owned at least 6,000 hectares (Fitzpatrick 2002: 148). KSI and UNAER have recently identified 14,069 hectares of coffee plantations in 21 locations, and 5,467 families have occupied most of these plantations. There are four other locations of coffee plantations – such as Damata Metan and Hurbohei of Mirtitu village, Hatuhu of Legimea village, and Naimorema of Riheu village – that have been occupied by farmers, but the total hectarage and number of households are still not identified.[39]

In support of the farmers' struggle, UNAER and KSI have built international links with La Via Campecina – a farmers' international movement – and its partners in the Asian region. Locally, the farmers have also supported the establishment of a network on land in an alliance with other NGOs, forming a sound social movement campaigning for agrarian reform. Among its members is *Assosiasaun Hak*, which conducted major research on land issues in the 1990s (Fitzpatrick 2002: 117–34). The *Haburas* Foundation, an environmental NGO, recently coordinated a survey entitled 'Community's Voice on Land', which covered 35 villages in seven districts. The *Lao Hamutuk* has been monitoring land policies and has built up a rich database. In 2012, UNAER and the *Rede ba Rai* (NGOs Land Rights Network) successfully lobbied the president of the republic, Jose Ramos Horta, to veto the land law, because it did not incorporate their demands for the recognition of indigenous land tenure (KSI 2012).

In the latest development, KSI and UNAER, in cooperation with local authorities and progressive Catholic priests in Ermera, have successfully revived the practice of *Tara Bandu*, which literally means 'to place a prohibition' – a communal traditional resource management and conflict prevention mechanism. All 52 villages in Ermera District have implemented *Tara Bandu*, with the participation of President Horta during its initial ceremony in 2012. KSI has attempted to develop *Tara Bandu* beyond ecological protection and resource management to include limiting dowry practice or reducing the number of animals slaughtered in traditional feasts and rituals. The impact of this has been encouraging. Families have paid more attention to sending their children to school than to organising traditional rituals or wedding parties, each of which consume dozens of water buffalos, goats and pigs. The *Haburas* Foundation has long advocated *Tara Bandu* to protect the environment in other districts, and this practice is beginning to reclaim a space in the modern law system. The current prime minister, Xanana Gusmao, has himself on a number of occasions appealed to local authorities to consider reviving the positive aspects of *Tara Bandu*, in addition to the formal legal system. In Ermera, land distribution, sustainable land management and *Tara Bandu* could be complementary programmes aimed at a more just and sustainable community.

Conclusion

This chapter has attempted to describe the history and current situation of land conflicts in Timor-Leste. Colonialism and foreign occupation have caused massive dislocation and displacement, have disconnected people from the customary land system, and have created an unjust society of the privileged and the dispossessed. The legacy of foreign domination has continued to shadow people's lives since the liberation of the country. However, the authorities, from UNTAET to the FRETILIN government and the current coalition government, have failed to respond sincerely and effectively to the post-colonial situation in independent Timor-Leste and to people's efforts to overcome its problems. It was a fatal mistake when the land issue was detached from the transitional justice mechanism in Timor-Leste. As a result the CAVR had no mandate to settle land and property issues. Where, then, lies hope in this situation?

First, and most essentially, the Law on Special Regime should include a provision to redress past injustices regarding land. Parliament has for years been discussing not only land laws but also implementation of the recommendations of the CAVR. It is high time that property issues were integrated into the arguments about redressing what happened in the past. Without this provision, no policy on land reform is assured. International donors and NGOs should pay more attention to this issue in order to prevent future conflicts and human rights abuses on their project sites.

Second, this chapter has described grassroots efforts to resolve land disputes. People have been struggling to find what they think is a just solution to their complex problems. As we saw in Ermera, people are even prepared to accommodate the rights of those who were relocated by foreign rulers, as these people are victims of the conflict too. In a way, this is a grassroots effort to achieve communal reconciliation and sustainable peace. These efforts and the spirit in which they are carried out should become a foundation for reconstructing communities and for making best use of the section on 'communal rights and community protection zones' of the land law.

Finally, the land law perceives customary landowners as legitimate stakeholders. However, some of the land problems have apparently derived from a lack of attention on the part of officials to the views and opinions of stakeholders with customary titles. Holders of customary titles are more vulnerable and prone to all kinds of manipulation. In this respect, additional measures to protect customary rights will be needed.

Notes

1 This included semi-structured interviews with those involved in disputes, NGOs, national and local government officials, chiefs and members of Commission A (legal affairs) of the national parliament, donor agencies, as well as a survey of major newspapers from 2011 to 2013.
2 In January 1975 the bishop issued a Pastoral Letter on 'the New Situation in East Timor'. In this letter he emphasised the Church's role in East Timor and people's right to property (Hill 2002: 134).
3 Interview by Furusawa in Dili (28 March 2013).
4 Interview by Furusawa with two executives of Timor Global (13 September 2012).
5 Interviews by Furusawa with farmers in Lequesi, staff of KSI and members of UNAER (13 September 2012, 2 January 2013), the president of CCT/former *chefe de suco* of Poetete (27 December 2012) and the director of Strengthening Cooperative/CCT (31 December 2012). We were provided with a copy of some legal documents by UNAER relating to the family's claim, as well as the form on land claims submitted by the farmers to the Ministry of Justice in 2004.
6 Da Silva's students at Timor-Leste National University also identified such disputes in former strategic hamlets in Uato-Lari, Lalerek Mutin, both in Viqueque District, and Seixal in Baucau District for this study.
7 Interview by Furusawa with the *chefe de suco* of Bucoli and the *chefe de aldeia* of Waisemu (6 September 2013). They talked about the situation in Bucoli as of present administrative area not including Triloka. Triloka was separated from Bucoli in Indonesian time and a dispute has been seen between settlers from a different district and original people.
8 Interviews by Furusawa with the *chefe de suco* of Memo (22 March 2013, 3 September 2013), two *lia nain* of Memo (3 September 2013) and the *chefe de aldeia* of Tunbibi (2–3 September 2013). Maliana is known to be the most successful irrigation rehabilitation project in Timor-Leste. However, many disputes have occurred over the irrigated fields within families or between communities.
9 The certificate shown by the *chefe de aldeia* includes the ownership of a house, farmland, and land on/surrounding the house.
10 The people of Sekar have been residents in Memo since the Portuguese period. They were originally from neighbouring Atsabe, in the mountains. In the 1950s they escaped from Atsabe as they could not pay a head tax to the Portuguese. They were captured and handed over to the *liurai* in Memo. Conflicts over land between the Sekar people and Memo residents had already started in the Portuguese period. Under Indonesian rule, Holsa and Memo became two different villages, and villagers of Sekar chose to be registered for Holsa village (interview with the *chefe de suco* of Memo, 22 March 2013).

11 Interview by Furusawa in Humboe (3 January 2013).
12 Interview by Furusawa with staff of Asosiasaun HAK (Association of Law, Human Rights and Justice) (1–3 September 2012). HAK was involved in the case of the police station in 2007. A case of land grabbing for the construction of Secondary School No. 1 is also known from Maliana.
13 The committee was a temporary system during the UNTAET period. The membership included representatives of the Timorese administration, political groups and local religious and civil society organisations (Fitzpatrick 2002: 185).
14 Aditjondro noted that the largest landowning institution in Timor-Leste was probably the Catholic Church (1994: 55). Many disputes have occurred over Church lands – either with traditional landowners or the state.
15 Interview by Furusawa in Dili (15 September 2011).
16 Interview by Furusawa at the Office of Suco Bekora (19 March 2013).
17 According to Law No.1/2003, users of state land must pay a rent to the state. However, this law has so far been executed only sporadically and not consistently.
18 The historical background of the communities was derived from an interview by Furusawa with the former *chefe de aldeia* of Loro (8 September 2012). An interview was carried out with a son of Mr Ferreira in Same (9 September 2012).
19 He was a member of the UDT and was killed by FRETILIN during the civil war in 1975.
20 The government has also drawn up a blueprint for the so-called 'Tasi Mane [Men's Sea] Project' in Betano, according to which the area will become the centre of the oil industry, with a power plant, an oil refinery and a highway that passes through the middle of the area of the Caraulun irrigation scheme (Government of Timor-Leste 2011: 140–42).
21 A group interview with 35 villagers by Furusawa in Bemetan (28 December 2011). Interviews with the district administrator, the director of DNP Manufahi and the *chefe de aldeia* of Bemetan were also conducted (27–30 December 2011).
22 Interview by Furusawa with the landowners, the *chefe de aldeia* of Bemetan and the Office of the MDG Suco Program at the National Development Agency in Dili (10 September 2012).
23 Two of the main titles recognised by Portuguese administration were *propriedade perfeita* (ownership rights) and *aforamento* (right to use). The main titles recognised by the Indonesian administration were *hak milik* (ownership rights), *hak guna-bangunan* (right to use) and *hak guna-usaha* (right to use the state land) (Draft Land Law, p. 2).
24 The applicant must pay a registration fee and those who hold the title have to pay a property tax to the state. A property tax will be introduced by the Special Regime.
25 Later the DNTPSC.
26 Furusawa had a discussion about major land issues with the State Secretary and National Director in charge of DNTPSC, and found that the problems in Ermera, Maliana and Betano were well known (7 September 2012).
27 The information was obtained through an interview with the chief of the consultants team for the INR by Furusawa at its headquarter in Dili (16 September 2011).
28 The law enables the state to expropriate private property in the public interest, and prescribes the procedure to be followed. However, it emphasises the duty of the state first to try to acquire the property through other means, such as settlement by fair compensation. If the amount of compensation cannot be agreed, it will be determined by arbitration on appeal to the courts. An appeal against the arbitration ruling can be lodged.

29 The fund is a single public instrument for financing compensation payable by the state under the Special Regime, and for providing payment for damages due and resettlement operations by the application of the Expropriation Law. The Law prescribes its purposes, revenue, operations, executive body and inspection.

30 The Special Regime does not refer to the matter of the expiration of titles, which can be a matter for argument.

31 The land in Hunboe is no longer used by the state. The villagers could be allowed to use the land under the contract with the state.

32 The CAVR shed light on the problem of forced displacement as a violation of the right to livelihood, and recommended 'the Parliament and the Government to institute an inquiry into land disputes that have arisen as a result of the wide-scale resettlement programs undertaken during the political conflicts' (CAVR 2005: 164).

33 Interview by Furusawa with the policy advisor of SEPI (13 September 2011).

34 Many of these cases come from matrilineal areas such as Manatuto District. However, in light of the experiences in other nations where women have lost their vested interest when land registration was executed, these statistics can still be seen as positive.

35 Fitzpatrick noted that the cabinet of the National Council reportedly wanted to postpone enacting this type of legislation until there was a democratically elected government. The cabinet also reportedly wanted to keep a free hand over the status of Indonesian property titles in negotiations with Indonesian government. A final factor many have been fear of political conflict over land issues (Fitzpatrick 2002: 197).

36 In Timor-Leste there is a traditional conflict resolution mechanism called *Nahe Biti-Boot,* meaning 'spreading a big mat'. It is a gathering of community elders to collectively solve a dispute (Babo-Soares 2004). Now discussion is ongoing as to how to incorporate protection against discrimination and abuse of power into this system.

37 The interview was conducted by Furusawa with the *chefe de suco* at Ritabau (1 April 2013, 23 March 2013).

38 Interview by Furusawa with the chief of the Directorate (7 January 2013). Most of the appointed mediators are local or traditional leaders who have experience of mediation in the community. The nomination of women – for example the *chefe de suco* of Ritabau – is being promoted.

39 Field research was conducted in March and September 2013.

References

Aditjondro, G.J., 1994, *In the Shadow of Mount Ramelau: The Impact of the Occupation of East Timor,* Leiden: Indonesian Documentation and Information Centre.

Anderson, T., 2010, 'Land reform in Timor-Leste? Why the Constitution is worth defending', in *Understanding Timor-Leste,* ed. M. Leach, N.C. Mendes, A.B. da Silva, A.C. Ximenes and B. Boughton, Hawthorn, Victoria: Swinburne Press, 213–18.

Babo-Soares, D., 2004, '*Nahe Biti*: the philosophy and process of grassroots reconciliation (and Justice) in East Timor', *The Asian Pacific Journal of Anthropology,* 5(1): 15–33.

Belo, D.C.F.X., 2011, *Os antigos reinos de Timor Leste,* Timor Leste: Edicao Tipografia Diocesana Baucau.

Budiardjo, C. and Liem, S.L., 1984, *War against East Timor,* London: Zed Books.

CAVR (Comissão dé Acolhimento, Verdade e Reconciliação de Timor Leste), 2005, 'Chega!: the report of the commission for reception, truth and reconciliation Timor-Leste' (CAVR), Executive Summary.

Da Silva, A.B., Perreira, A., De Oliveira, D., Savio, L.J. and Nunes, A.C.N., 2010, 'Reforma agraria no modelu dezenvolvimentu: agenda IFIs ho Donor sira iha Pos-Okupasaun Timor-Leste', in *Understanding Timor Leste*, ed. M. Leach, N.C. Mendes, A.B. da Silva, A.C. Ximenes and B. Boughton, Hawthorn, Victoria: Swinburne Press, 9–12.

Diario, 2011, 'Manifestasaun hasoru projeitu sentral elektrikal Betano: Polisia Kaer Ema Nain 9', 2 September.

Durand, F., 2002, *Timor Lorosa'e – pays au carrefour de l'Asie et du Pacifique: un atlas geo-historique*, Paris: Presses Universitaires de Marne-La-Vallee, and Bangkok – IRESEC.

Fitzpatrick, D., 2002, *Land Claims in East Timor*, Canberra: Asia Pacific Press, the Australian National University.

——2008, 'Mediating land conflict in East Timor', in *Making Land Work, Volume 2: Case Studies on Customary Land and Development in the Pacific*, Canberra: Australian Agency for International Development (AusAid), 175–97.

Fitzpatrick, D. and Monson, R., 2009, 'Balancing rights and norms – property programming in East Timor, the Solomon Islands, and Bouganville', in *Housing, Land, and Property Rights in Post-conflict United Nations and Other Peace Operations – A Comparative Survey and Proposal for Reform*, ed. S. Leckie, New York: Cambridge University Press, 103–35.

FRETILIN (Frente Revolucionaria do Timor-Leste Independente), 1974, *Manual e Programa Politicos*, FRETILIN, Dili, Timor-Leste.

Front Mahasiswa and Rede ba Rai (Land Rights Network), 2011, *Resolution*, Dili.

Government of Timor-Leste, 2011, *Timor-Leste Strategic Development Plan 2010–2030*, Dili: Government of Timor-Leste.

——2012, 'Law on Special Regime for Determination of Ownership of Immovable Property, Law on Real Estate Financial Fund and Law on Expropriation' (unofficial translation by the Council of Ministers).

Gunn, G.C., 1999, *Timor Lorosa'e 500 Years*, Macau: Livros de Oriente.

Hagerdal, H., 2012, *Lords of the Land, Lords of the Sea: Conflict and Adaptation in Early Colonial Timor, 1600–1800*, Leiden: KITLV.

Harrington, A., 2007, 'Ethnicity, violence, and land and property disputes in Timor-Leste', *East Timor Law Journal*, available online at http://easttimorlawjournal.blogspot.com.au/2012/05/ethnicity-violence-land-and-property.html (accessed 25 September 2013).

Hill, H., 2002, *Stirrings of Nationalism in East Timor: FRETILIN 1974–1978: The Origins, Ideologies and Strategies of a Nationalist Movement*, Otford (Sydney), Kuala Lumpur and Dili: Otford Press.

Huang, M., 2009, 'Strengthening property rights in Timor-Leste "Ita Nia Rai": gender and land rights', presentation to the Sector Consultation Workshop on Customary Law/Local Justice, Dili, Timor-Leste, 27 February 2009.

Johnston, M., 2012, 'A "Muslim" leader of a "catholic" nation? Mari Alkatiri's Arab-Islamic identity and its (inter-) national contestations', *Austrian Studies in Social Anthropology*, 1, available online at www.univie.ac.at/alumni.ksa/images/text-documents/ASSA/ASSA-SN-2012-01-Art4-Johnston.pdf (accessed 25 September 2013).

KSI (Kdadalak Sulimutuk Institute), 2004, 'Historia Lekesi', unpublished record of an interview on the history of Lekesi, p. 2.

——2012, 'Submisaun UNAER ba regime Espesial konaba definisaun nain ba bens imoveis: Lei de Terras', *Lian Toos Nain*, 3: 10–11.

Kwartanada, D., 2001, 'Middlemen minority in an isolated outpost: a preliminary study of the Chinese in East Timor to 1945', in 'Research Report: Formation of 'Nation State' in East Timor and its International Environment', ed. K. Goto, available online at www.waseda.jp/gsaps/faculty/goto/pdf/didi.pdf (accessed 25 September 2013).

Lopes, I., 2009, 'Land and displacement in Timor-Leste', *Humanitarian Exchange*, 43: 12–14 (Timor-Leste).

Matadalan ba Rai, 2013, 'Komunidade Nia Lian Konaba Rai: Resultadu Husi Konsultasaun Matadaln ba Rai', Fundasaun Haburas research project, Haburas Foundation, Dili, Timor-Leste.

Matsuno, A., 2009, 'Security and democracy in post-conflict East Timor: the political system and the crisis in 2006', in *Still Under Construction: Regional Organisations' Capacities for Conflict Prevention*, ed. H. Wulf, Essen: Institute for Development and Peace, Universitat Duisburg.

Ministério da Justiça, 2003, *República Democrática de Timor-Leste 10/3/2003*, Legislaçao de Terras: Lei No.1/2003.

Myat Thu, P., 2008, 'Land forgotten: effects of Indonesian re-settlement on rural live-lihoods in East Timor', in *Democratic Governance in Timor-Leste: Reconciling the Local and the National*, ed. E. Mearns, Darwin: Charles Darwin University Press, 143–59.

Taylor, J., 1999, *East Timor: The Price of Freedom*, London and New York: Zed Books and Annandale: Pluto Press.

USAID, 2011, 'Strengthening property rights in Timor-Leste project', available online at www.acdivoca.org/site/Lookup/East-Timor-Fact-Sheet/$file/East-Timor-Fact-Sheet.pdf (accessed 25 September 2013).

10 Conclusion

Confronting land and property problems for peace

Shinichi Takeuchi, Mari Katayanagi and Ryutaro Murotani

This book has examined a range of land and property problems that people have endured in conflict-affected settings. In this concluding chapter, we will compare our eight case studies to classify those problems and identify the measures taken to combat them in the respective countries, and further evaluate the effectiveness of those measures. The evaluation will help us draw lessons from the experiences of the different cases. Our aim is to find an approach to addressing land and property problems in conflict-affected settings with a long-term vision for development. In the following section we will first present the analysis framework, and then, comparing our eight case studies, we will look at the observable phenomena regarding land and property rights during and following armed conflicts. Key measures taken to combat land and property problems will be examined in order to explore the policy implications. The last part discusses general policy implications.

Analysis framework

The primary purpose of this book is to re-examine the policy measures that can be used to confront land and property problems in conflict-affected settings. The contributors have illustrated in each case study the nature of the land and property problems, as well as policy measures that have been taken in the respective countries. The case studies support our basic standpoint that the nature of property rights (effectiveness, scope, durability, etc.) is dependent on the relationship between the state and society. Conflicts in most cases transform the power relationship in the given society, and thus change the order that regulates property rights. An armed conflict usually damages property rights through physical destruction of property and forced displacement, which is often massive in scale. When the society loses stability through such calamities, it is likely that an increasing number of actors will try to grab land and property, taking advantage of the lack of rules and regulations, or the lapse in their enforcement. This is why land and property problems are generally aggravated in conflict-affected situations.

Most of the large-scale armed conflicts today have arisen in developing countries in the form of internal conflict. Scholars in international politics have argued that one of the critical reasons behind the concentration of violent conflicts in particular regions is the peculiar nature of certain states and their state–society relationships that have been deeply affected by state formation processes such as colonisation (Buzan 1983; Holsti 1996). This peculiar state–society relationship can also be considered one of the most fundamental causes of the land and property problems that have arisen in the areas in question. Fitzpatrick aptly summarised the property rights failure in the Third World:

> The enforcement of property rights depends on the nature and strength of the social order. Property enforcement is more than a question of law, or institutional choices between agreements, court decisions and state regulation. Well before the creation of modern nation-states, social norms developed to maintain order in multiple-user environments. The degradation of these norms, often in circumstances of state antagonism and illegitimacy, is at the heart of modern property rights failures in the Third World.
>
> (2006: 1046–47)

Land and property problems in conflict-affected settings tend to emerge as a consequence not only of armed conflict but also of the inherent predicaments shared by many developing countries. The two factors are inextricably connected to each other.

Furthermore, the state–society relationship is fundamentally connected with international factors. In the globalised world, state governments in developing countries are often deeply and structurally connected with the international community. This external influence also directly affects societies in the Third World through, for example, the activities of international donors and NGOs, as well as multinational companies. International influence tends to increase in a conflict-affected context as a result of special activities such as mediation of warring parties, transitional administration and various efforts towards recovery. In short, the nature of property rights depends on the state–society relationship, which is in turn deeply connected to international factors.

Land and property problems in conflict-affected settings are connected to peacebuilding and statebuilding in a double sense. On the one hand, both land and property problems and armed conflicts are attributable to the fragile state–society relationship. On the other hand, these problems are aggravated by factors caused by armed conflict. It is therefore evident that attempts to tackle land and property problems in conflict-affected situations cannot be isolated from peacebuilding and statebuilding efforts.

Statebuilding is an integral part of peacebuilding, and is considered to be the central objective for overcoming fragility (OECD 2007). For this purpose, it is important to enhance both the state's capacity to provide basic services and the state's legitimacy in the eyes of citizens (Manning and Trzeciak-Duval 2010). Not all of our case study countries seem to run the risk of a recurrence of armed conflict on the grounds of land and property problems. Yet dealing appropriately with these issues will enhance state legitimacy in the eyes of ordinary people, thereby contributing to the establishment of a sustainable state–society relationship. In cases that involve violent conflicts at local levels or have a higher risk of large-scale fighting, rapid and effective measures are additionally required to reduce tension and build capacity for delivering adequate services for affected people.

Property rights affected by armed conflicts

Deprivation of property rights by displacement

In all of the eight case studies in this book, large-scale displacement was one of the serious consequences of armed conflict. People have to leave their property behind and may not be able to return to regain it. In 1994 almost all Rwandans were forced to flee from their homes because of the recurrent civil war and genocide. Internally displaced persons (IDPs) in Colombia between 1985 and 2011 numbered 5.5 million. Large-scale migrations transform social order and structure – both in the origin and host societies.

The length of displacement varies. Some cases persist for decades, as was the case in Burundi, Cambodia, Colombia, Rwanda, South Sudan and Timor-Leste.[1] In these cases, returnees are second-generation refugees who remember little about their homeland. On the other hand, displacement in Bosnia and Herzegovina and northern Uganda was relatively short term; many refugees and IDPs returned within 10 years.[2] Also, there are people who decide not to return or are unable to return.

In the case of repatriation, various factors influence people's decisions about whether to return to the place of origin or to settle in another place in the country. These decisions are made by individuals or families, but the policies of the government and the international community have a significant influence. Without international engagement, the process of repatriation to Bosnia and Herzegovina, as well as to Burundi, would have been totally different. These decisions also depend on a range of domestic factors, including government policies, power relationships in the post-conflict society, the property situation, socio-economic conditions and psychological elements. One phenomenon that may be common in many post-conflict settings is the choice of settling in urban areas and not returning to rural areas. The population pouring into urban areas swells the number of poor and vulnerable inhabitants there. In Timor-Leste, many returnees, coming back from the refugee camps in Western Timor (Indonesian territory) in 1999 and 2000, occupied intact houses in the capital city, Dili, instead of returning to their original place in the eastern part of the country. In the Colombian case, official measures to assist those who settled in urban areas tend to be insufficient, and some refuse such assistance against the backdrop of general distrust of the government.

Large-scale land acquisitions

Several cases demonstrate significant problems caused by land grabs. Land acquisitions tend to be regarded as land grabs if they fall under one or more of the following five conditions: (1) they violate human rights (2) they lack the free, prior and informed consent of the affected land-users (3) they lack fair assessment (4) they lack transparent contracts (5) they lack effective democratic planning (International Land Coalition 2011).

While large-scale land acquisitions can be observed in many developing countries, conflict-affected situations intensify the problem because of conflicting property right claims, changing power relations, exceptionally weak governance and increased land and property value after the end of conflicts. In conflict-affected settings, those in power may take advantage of ambiguities in land tenure in order to grab vast and valuable areas of land. As our case studies show, large-scale land grabs have taken place with the involvement of actors such as military officers, state officials and private companies, and these actors are often closely connected to each other. For these reasons, South Sudan, northern Uganda and Cambodia have witnessed significant land grabs in the post-conflict period. Large-scale land grabs have been generally supported by national elites, who have acquired political power through the armed conflict. The necessity to increase state revenue urges governments to utilise land concessions, but this has often been used as an excuse for manipulation by the elites.

As land values tend to rise after the end of armed conflicts, the private sector becomes more interested in investment in land. In addition, governments have widely adopted economic liberalisation policies, which often enable foreign and national investors to have an advantage in purchasing land on a large scale. Generally, land grabs have not yet caused a massive expulsion of residents in Africa, but in Colombia, large-scale and persistent land grabs and evictions have constituted a major cause of the protracted internal armed conflict.

Unstable and vulnerable property order

All of our case studies are characterised by instability as well as vulnerability in the property order, caused by the transformation of state–society relations in conflict-affected settings. Land claims become complex particularly in places that have experienced multiple regime changes. New regimes often establish new property orders and deny any previous basis for claims, or in some cases restore an older basis for claims as a legitimate order. There can be cases where each claimant has a title issued under a different regime. In Timor-Leste, those who are entitled to claim restitution can be classified into various groups: (1) holders of pre-1975 Portuguese titles (2) customary landholders dispossessed during the Portuguese colonial period (3) holders of titles from the Indonesian era (4) those who were dispossessed of land under the Indonesian administration (5) those who were displaced or dispossessed in 1999 (Fitzpatrick and Monson 2009: 112).

The parliament of Timor-Leste is now in the final stage of discussions to regulate ownership under the Land Law. Competing claims caused by regime change are also evident in Cambodia, Rwanda and Burundi.

Traditional authorities tend to decline during armed conflicts, as illustrated in the case studies of Uganda and South Sudan, and consequently the given society's capacity to resolve land disputes over customary land weakens. Even when the customary mechanism still functions, it may not be sufficient to deal with problems emanating from large-scale population movement and new population structures. Also, there can be conflict between different customary orders. In South Sudan, the Madi used to live in Nimule in Eastern Equatoria. Dinka IDPs who settled in Nimule refused to follow the customs of returned Madi, and reconstituted their own customary institution. Although the Dinka are not original inhabitants in Nimule, they have a close relationship with the Dinka Sudan People's Liberation Army (SPLA) soldiers stationed there. The dispute is hence certainly affected by the local power structure. The customary conflict resolution mechanism does not function as it used to, because the population movement has transformed local society.

While factors peculiar to post-conflict settings add new complexity to land and property problems, land problems are usually commonplace even in the absence of armed conflicts. For various reasons – including significant population increase, the decline of customary governance and arbitrary actions of the state – land rights are not well secured in many developing countries. Once an armed conflict takes place, ordinary land disputes over inheritance or demarcation between land plots can be exacerbated by conflict-related factors such as displacement. Armed conflicts may add another layer to legal pluralism by introducing an additional order, or destroy the existing property orders and thus intensify the competition between claims over land.

Examining measures to address land and property problems

On the basis of the case study analyses, we consider that three areas of policy intervention have had particular importance in confronting land and property problems: securing housing and land for the displaced, establishing and strengthening conflict resolution mechanisms and protecting the land rights of vulnerable people. This section looks into the measures taken in different countries in each of the three areas and assesses their consequences.

Securing housing and land for the displaced

As mentioned above, armed conflicts typically deprive people of houses and land through destruction, landmines or displacement. The measures taken to address this situation are not consistent, even among our eight case studies. These measures vary in the degree to which they attempt to restore the status quo ante. While restitution in Bosnia and Herzegovina aimed to respect and restore all pre-conflict property rights, the repatriation operation in Cambodia did not attempt this at all. Financial compensation for deprivation of pre-conflict property rights is another measure taken, although this method was not actually implemented in any of our case studies. Although in both Burundi and Rwanda the policy of land sharing was introduced as a principle, these had differing natures: the former could be seen as partial restitution, while the latter had an element of redistribution. Neither land allocation in Cambodia nor villagisation in Rwanda had any relevance to pre-war property rights: people started their lives in a new place where the land and/or housing was offered. One-time payment is an option that leaves the entire responsibility for securing housing and land to those who receive the money. In many of these contexts, it is not easy to identify the most desirable option, because what is just for a particular society is inevitably contextual. Policy choices for dealing with pre-conflict rights should therefore be made in a way that secures the widespread support of the population. We further discuss the effectiveness of these measures and the required conditions for their application below.

Restitution

When people are forced to leave their homes as a result of armed conflict, it is likely that their property will be occupied by secondary occupants, if not destroyed. Such forced displacement constitutes a human rights violation that will lead to the question of reparation. Reparation may take the form of either *restitutio in integrum* (restoration to the original condition) or financial compensation.

The principle adopted in Bosnia and Herzogovina after the General Framework Agreement for Peace (GFAP) was *restitutio in integrum*, which was successful in protecting the pre-conflict property rights of both property owners and occupancy right holders. Consequently, the restitution rate reached over 90 per cent. This success significantly influenced the adoption of the Pinheiro Principles by the international community. Since the principle of protecting pre-conflict property rights under the GFAP was effectively implemented, restitution and property rights became a standard issue for peace agreements, as was the case in Burundi.

Although restitution in Bosnia and Herzogovina did not lead directly to the return of refugees and IDPs, the extremely high restitution rate should be recognised as having contributed to the promotion of social justice. Nevertheless, since there are several factors that make the case of Bosnia and Herzogovina unique, it may not serve as a model for other cases under completely different conditions. First, property rights were relatively clear in Bosnia and Herzogovina prior to the conflict, although there were some deficiencies, as described in the case study. Second, the period of displacement was comparatively short, ranging from a few months to several years – but mostly less than ten years. Third, the international presence in Bosnia and Herzogovina was extraordinarily strong because of the Bonn powers of the High Representative, and this was therefore able to overcome obstacles set up by nationalistic political leaders. In this case, because the solution was perceived as fair and equitable by ordinary people across different ethnic groups, it had a significantly positive impact on peacebuilding.

In contrast, South Sudan is a case in which the conditions of Bosnia and Herzogovina were not met. Although the Land Act of 2009 entitled returnees who had been displaced as a result of the civil war from 16 May 1983 to restitution of their original land or compensation, restitution, in reality, was not effectively executed. Colombia is an interesting case for further comparison. Following the land restitution law in 2011, more than 30,000 requests for restitution, which cover more than 2.3 million hectares, have been submitted to the organisation in charge. What are the prospects for these requests? On the one hand, in comparison with the Bosnian case, the conditions for restitution are not promising. Informality in land holdings has been frequent, and the length of displacement has been decades. Furthermore, confrontation with local elites would be unavoidable because their power base generally lies in the control of land. On the other hand, in comparison with other developing countries the country has a fairly high capacity in terms of state institutions, and human suffering because of land deprivation has been quite serious. The government could make considerable progress in restitution if it demonstrates strong political will. Obviously, such will was missing during the Uribe administration, but the situation would appear to be different under the leadership of President Santos. The international community should provide the necessary assistance to foster the commitment of the government.

Compensation

Although restitution is a desirable policy measure for the restoration of property rights, it can be applied only in limited circumstances, as described above. If *restitutio in integrum* is not feasible, the other reparation option is compensation.

In Bosnia and Herzogovina, the GFAP had a provision for compensation for lost property that could not be restored. Nevertheless, the compensation fund envisaged in the GFAP has never materialised, primarily because such funding was regarded as support of ethnic cleansing, in the sense that it would consolidate its effects. Some scholars consider that overemphasis on restitution precludes alternative solutions such as compensation (Rosand 2000; Ballard 2010; Smit 2012).[3] Rosand, writing before the minority return gathered pace in Bosnia and Herzogovina, contended that relocation of those displaced was a reality that the international community must recognise (2000: 126). For him, therefore, compensation should assist them in resettlement, and he further maintained that if the funding responsibility fell on local governments, it might induce them to remove the existing obstacles to return (Rosand 2000: 133). While this argument is theoretically interesting, it is not difficult to imagine that such a policy would have drained the compensation fund, because local governments' budgets were short and they might have been content neither to pay nor to remove the obstacles to return. As a consequence, displaced people would have been left without either restoration of property or compensation.

There may be cases where compensation funds become functional, and effectively serve to address loss of land and property caused by armed conflict. It may be particularly useful when the period of displacement is very long and the rights of secondary occupants require comparatively weighty consideration. This seems to be the view that the European Court of Human Rights has taken regarding recent claims by Greek-Cypriots on their properties located in northern Cyprus.[4] However, unless the conditions are created for potential returnees to make voluntary decisions in a real sense, policy makers should be aware of the risk that this option might deprive returnees of the possibility of returning to their place of origin, even in the case of relatively brief displacement.[5]

Land sharing

In sharp contrast to the Bosnia and Herzogovina case, the population displacement in Rwanda and Burundi lasted for decades, and land was scarce even prior to the conflict, due to the rapid population increase. In such conditions, land sharing might be regarded as an unavoidable choice.

Land sharing in Burundi can be considered as partial restitution, because the returnees are rights holders over the land, which is shared with those who have occupied it during their absence (the so-called stayees). The special commission used to adjudicate the division of land between the stayees and returnees in a ratio of one to one; this later shifted to one to two. This proportion is a point of dispute in Burundi, and the sudden change by the commission in favour of the returnees invited stayees to doubt its impartiality.

In Rwanda, the policy of land sharing was carried out more rapidly and more effectively than in the case of Burundi. The new-case returnees (those who had fled temporarily to neighbouring countries in 1994, after the victory of the Rwandan Patriotic Front, RPF) were officially ordered to transfer half of their land to the old-case returnees (those who had fled around independence in 1962 and returned after the RPF's victory). In an overwhelming number of cases, the old-case returnees were not the original owners of the land, and thus this measure has the characteristics of land distribution. Despite the massive scale of return, this policy assured most people a place to live, and a humanitarian crisis was averted. However, it is important to consider how people perceive the policy. The policy may be deemed as ethnic-based revenge, because the new-case and old-case returnees have completely different ethnic compositions: the former are exclusively Hutu, and the latter are Tutsi. If those who had to give up half of the land they used to cultivate perceive that their land was taken away as a result of regime change, this sense of victimisation may grow into a conflict factor in the future. Having been carried out exclusively in favour of the old-case returnees and without compensation, Rwanda's land sharing may have negative effects on long-term peacebuilding.

In Timor-Leste, the practice of land sharing has been voluntarily chosen as a means of compromise. Although it was not a state policy, land disputes between original holders and secondary occupants were solved in some cases through mediation, and actual land sharing took place. Historically, both parties have experienced displacement/migration due to policies under Portuguese colonial rule and Indonesian military operations. In this case, since there was no state policy to deal with the problems, the society found a way to resolve the issue on its own, as far as claims on customary land rights could be legally recognised.

Land allocation

In the case where securing pre-conflict property rights is not feasible and realistic, it is necessary to consider alternative options to provide housing and land. Land allocation may be an effective measure if enough land of sufficient quality is available for allocation and if it is distributed equitably in accordance with needs. However, these conditions are hard to meet, as the cases of Cambodia and Bosnia and Herzogovina illustrate.

In the case of Cambodia, although agricultural land was one of the options presented to the returning refugees during the period of the United Nations Transitional Authority in Cambodia (UNTAC), land scarcity prevented this from being an effective option. The UNHCR had to rely on the cooperation of local village leaders, but they secured less land than expected, and only three per cent of returnees chose the land option. Even in cases where land was allocated and a certificate was provided, some returnees were pushed off the land and forced to move to infertile land after the departure of the international organisation that had been monitoring the situation. In Bosnia and Herzogovina, land allocation was politically manipulated, and distribution was not equitable. Although local authorities carried out land allocation under the pretext of humanitarian concerns, it was in fact an ethnic-based policy. Local authorities provided public land to IDPs, but only to those belonging to the dominant ethnic group in the area. Land allocation can be an effective option, but it requires that difficult conditions are met in terms of land availability and political impartiality.

Land allocation is not a measure that solely concerns return. Recently, there have been attempts at land allocation for the purpose of reintegrating demobilised soldiers.[6] It is quite often one of few available options and can be effective for those who choose farming as their way of life. While demobilisation is an important step for the stabilisation of society, land allocation requires sensitivity regarding the perceptions of ex-combatants and other members of the population in terms of equity and fairness in assistance.

Housing arrangements

If returnees are not able to recover their original properties, housing policies are necessary to respond to humanitarian needs. There may be situations where housing provision is more efficient than restitution of lost property as a short-term measure – for example, when a settlement has been completely destroyed. As an emergency response especially, temporary settlement sites or collective centres may mitigate human suffering. However, providing adequate living conditions for permanent residence is not as easy as it may seem.

In Rwanda, housing policy through villagisation addressed the immediate needs of more than 250,000 households of old-case refugees who had to vacate the houses they had occupied during the absence of the new-case refugees. However, this policy has been criticised for several reasons. Because the houses were located far from their cultivated land, people had to spend a long time commuting to their farms. In addition, those whose land was expropriated for housing construction did not receive adequate compensation. Some critics even suspect the government's intention with villagisation was to reduce the likelihood of insurgency, as the setup made people's movements easy to monitor.

Other examples also show negative results. In Cambodia, settlement sites for returnees were in remote areas and were not adequately equipped with basic infrastructure. In Burundi, newly constructed villages for returnees ('peace villages') have suffered a number of problems similar to those in Rwanda (Falisse and Niyonkuru 2013). In addition, Tutsi IDPs who were persecuted in 1993 still remain in IDP camps after two decades. The protracted existence of the IDP camps in the country has exacerbated the segmentalisation of the IDPs and Hutu in the neighbourhood.

While offering housing is important, creating permanent residential areas is not simple. In the past, government-led collectivisation policies have often failed in developing countries. We need to be cautious about such measures, except as a temporary emergency response.

One-time payments

When people who have lost land and property seek a place to settle after an armed conflict, one-time financial payment is one potential measure to support their livelihood. In Cambodia, as the pre-war property rights of returnees were not fully recognised, and as not many attractive alternatives were suggested, the majority of refugees chose this option instead of land allocation. However, such a measure can sustain livelihoods only for a short period. People may not be able to obtain housing and/or land with the money provided, and landlessness may become a serious problem in the post-war period. Therefore, additional measures to secure people's livelihood should be considered in addition to this measure. In Timor-Leste after the 2006 political crisis, the 'cash for return' programme was implemented before the ownership of properties was established. As a result, those who occupied the houses that were originally taken over by Easterners managed – upon vacating the property – to gain part of the state compensation that was offered to the returning Easterners. This was a private solution agreed by the parties concerned, without the involvement of any state officials. If the new land law is applied, those who occupied someone else's house and land after 31 December 1998 will be required to pay rent to the state in those cases where the original owner does not return.

Establishing and strengthening conflict resolution mechanisms

Strengthening the capacity of conflict resolution mechanisms contributes to people's everyday security. The frequent occurrence of conflicts over land and property may cause social disturbance and increase the risk of conflict recurrence. Therefore, this policy has significant importance. However, we must bear in mind that such a mechanism cannot adjust a social structure that causes land and property problems. Policy interventions in this field vary, because there are a range of mechanisms for conflict resolution. States provide such capacity through formal institutions, while customary authorities or civil society sometimes supplement the lack of state capacity. Measures taken regarding both formal and informal mechanisms are examined below.

Strengthening the formal capacity of conflict resolution

Basically, there are two approaches to enhancing formal conflict resolution mechanisms, though they are not mutually exclusive. One is to establish specialised institutions for property disputes, and the other is to strengthen existing institutions so that they can handle property disputes more efficiently.

Among our case studies, there are more examples of the first approach: the National Commission for Lands and other Properties (CNTB) in Burundi; the Commission for Real Property Claims of Displaced Persons and Refugees (CRPC) in Bosnia and Herzegovina; the Cadastral Commission (CC) and National Authority for Land Dispute Resolution (NALDR) in Cambodia; the National Directorate on Land, Property and Cadastral Services (DNTPSC) in Timor-Leste; and the Land Commission, district land boards and parish land committees in Uganda. The CNTB in Burundi and the CRPC in Bosnia and Herzegovina specifically dealt with conflict-related property disputes, while the Cambodian, Timorese and Ugandan organisations did not have such limits. In order to process a large number of land

and property disputes after armed conflicts, it may be useful to establish a specialised conflict resolution institution. The CRPC in Bosnia and Herzegovina was an example that had positive results. It processed a large number of claims through a standardised procedure, and the enforcement of its decisions by local institutions was secured thanks to various interventions by the international community.

However, creating a specialised institution does not guarantee effective resolution of disputes. To resolve disputes effectively, the institutions need to be independent, equitable and effective. If the conflict resolution mechanisms are influenced by political and/or economic power, institution building does not lead to protection of property rights for all. In reality, such cases are common, as discussed in the case studies. In Burundi, the CNTB is considered to be under the influence of the ruling party, and therefore is in grave danger of facing popular distrust. In other cases, the specialised organisations cannot deal with critical cases involving the state and/or power elites. In Cambodia, while the CC resolves small-scale land disputes between local villagers relatively well, its effectiveness in settling large-scale conflicts with political elites is weak. The DNTPSC and its district offices in Timor-Leste deal with a variety of disputes regarding land and property. However, they cannot handle disputes to which the state is a party, although such disputes are frequent. Since the DNTPSC's mandate is limited to non-judicial mediation, cases involving the state are solely dealt with by the courts, where claimants may wait for adjudication for an indefinite period.

Strengthening the existing justice system is another measure to enhance the resolution of land and property disputes. Rwanda offers one example of this approach. Following the reorganisation of the justice system, Rwanda has a clear chain of conflict resolution mechanisms: from mediation by local administrators and the *abunzi* (local level mediators) to local and national courts. In spite of radical changes to land holding caused by land sharing, the number of land disputes involving returnees brought before the *abunzi* and the courts has been decreasing. Following the military victory in the civil war, the former rebel RPF has made extensive efforts to establish dominance over society. The reconfiguration of the conflict resolution mechanism can be considered as part of these efforts. One of the important reasons for the reduction in land disputes is that the overwhelming majority of claims and grievances have been dealt with at the local administrator level: local administrators tend to dissuade those who are dissatisfied from taking their cases to the higher administrative levels, and people simply give up because their efforts are clearly in vain and may be politically dangerous. The reduction of the number of disputes, therefore, should not be considered as a resolution of the problem. This case shows that a procedurally efficient conflict resolution mechanism does not necessarily contribute to a constructive state–society relationship. Short-term stability through repression would not contribute to peacebuilding in the long run.

Given the nature of disputes over land, mediation and reconciliation should be promoted as a means of strengthening the capacity of formal conflict resolution mechanisms. Generally, the justice system clearly distinguishes the winner and the loser. However, this may not be desirable in the case of land and property disputes, in which multiple parties often have competing but legitimate claims. In many of these cases, land and property rights are vaguely defined, and making a clear judgement is an arduous task. For the loser, the deprivation of land and properties may destroy their livelihood. Protracted trials and increasing costs would threaten the livelihood of the complainant, and would also burden defendants and judges. Naturally, there are cases that ought not to be dealt with by mediation: for instance, the case of a large-scale land grab threatening the livelihood of local communities. However, the possibility of mediation and reconciliation should be actively pursued, particularly in a case where the complainant and the defendant belong to the same local community.

Effective use of mediation for the resolution of land and property problems can be found in the historical experience of developed countries. As part of its modernisation process, Japan established in the 1920s a mediation mechanism to deal with two major sources of social unrest in urban and rural areas. One source of social unrest was conflict over houses. Against the backdrop of rapid urbanisation, conflicts between owners of rented houses and their tenants proliferated. The other source of unrest was conflict over tenanted farmlands. Suffering from unstable land rights and high levels of rent under the tenancy system, the tenants repeatedly took strong actions to voice their discontent. Both problems were in essence concerned with the ambiguity of property rights, as tenancy rights either for houses or farmlands were not clearly defined and were under limited protection. Following the introduction of the Leasehold Mediation Law in 1922 and the Tenancy Mediation Law in 1924, the mediation mechanisms for rented houses as well as tenanted farmlands greatly contributed to conflict resolution and quelling social unrest. Interestingly, the former mechanism had not been utilised much until the Great Kanto Earthquake of 1923. A large number of disputes between landlords and tenants in the aftermath of the earthquake necessitated an efficient conflict resolution mechanism, and such urgent demand helped develop the system (Ishihara 1970). Japan's experience shows the advantage of the mediation system when existing laws and regulations do not provide sufficient protection for legitimate right holders, and also when there is an upsurge in property disputes that require prompt resolution.[7]

Activating societal mechanisms

In a post-conflict setting, the capacity of a formal justice system is often limited, and while in some cases the society utilises its endogenous capacity to resolve disputes, in other cases external assistance enhances conflict resolution.

The Ugandan case study showed how an NGO provided an alternative dispute resolution (ADR) mechanism and commendably resolved a case through its mediation. The Colombian case also showcases the significant role of NGOs. They have the capacity to address problems through the justice system, provide legal information for protecting the rights of vulnerable people, promote the legal acknowledgement of customary land rights of rural communities and lead the social justice movement.

In Timor-Leste, the local mediation system resolved disputes in the post-conflict period with the support of the international community. The United Nations Transitional Administration in East Timor (UNTAET) Land and Property Directorate provided intensive mediation training to both traditional and administrative chiefs from 2001 to 2005. While local communities are likely to be deprived of a part of their capacity in conflict-affected situations, their potential for dealing with local disputes is still considerable. External assistance that enhances the local capacity for dispute resolution should therefore be promoted.

Protecting the property rights of vulnerable people

In order to conduct long-term strategies to deal with land disputes arising in conflict-affected situations, it is indispensable to secure land rights for those who are vulnerable and under the threat of deprivation. Customary land rights require special attention in this regard, since their formal and legal status tends to be ambiguous. A number of countries have recently introduced a range of policy measures for their protection. These new policies mostly aim at enhancing the protection of the property rights of the vulnerable population. In fact, the majority of our case study countries have experienced reform in adopting new land laws. As we have seen, it is a recent global trend in land law reforms to formally recognise customary rights. In defiance of the male-centric tendency of customary systems, women's rights are also highly respected in the new laws. Countries with high land inequality often require redistribution in their land reforms. Some laws create reserve zones to protect the rights of socially vulnerable groups. Numerous countries expedite land registration to formalise and protect people's property rights. However, the impact of these measures varies, depending on how thoroughly they are implemented.

Customary rights

Vast areas of land in developing countries are left out of the formal registration process, instead being governed under customary systems, while new land laws increasingly recognise customary tenure. In four of our eight case studies – Burundi, Cambodia, South Sudan and Uganda – the protection and strengthening of customary land rights is, in one way or another, incorporated in the land laws and/or land policies. Rwanda issued an official certificate for land owned through custom. In Timor-Leste the proposed land law has provisions on 'special adverse possession' that recognise customary land rights over undisputed land. However, recognition of customary rights in the land law does not guarantee enhanced tenure security, because law enforcement in reality is another question. Community chiefs, as traditional authorities, may abuse their power in ways that harm the community's rights. More importantly for our analysis, since armed conflicts transform power structures and increase people's movements, customary authorities are likely to see their legitimacy weakened, as illustrated in the South Sudanese and Ugandan cases. In such conflict-affected settings, formal recognition of customary land rights is a necessary measure, but it is not sufficient on its own to secure these rights. Improvement of public land governance as a whole, and clear positioning of customary land tenure in the system, are indispensable. For this purpose, recently developed guidelines and policy tools, which we will discuss later, will be useful.

Women's rights

We ought to be aware that securing customary rights is not a perfect solution, particularly with regard to women's rights. An increasing number of countries make an effort to strengthen women's rights to land when introducing a new land law or amending the existing one. Rwanda is a good example of this. When the Inheritance Law of 1999 recognised the land rights of women and the Organic Land Law of 2005 provided equal rights for women, the number of disputes before the local mediation mechanism in regard to women's land rights notably increased. This clearly shows women's stronger awareness of their rights over land. Inheritance of land by daughters is no longer exceptional in Rwanda. Serious commitment on the part of the state can realise rapid reform of society, even if managing social friction remains a difficult challenge.

    In some other countries, however, implementation has not caught up with the notion of equal land rights for women set forth in civil codes, as well as land law and policy. In Timor-Leste, for instance, female landowners may not be invited to events for landowners, although some women manage to submit land claims either as an individual or as part of a married couple. Since armed conflicts usually increase the number of widows, women's rights to land need to be strengthened in order to protect both their livelihood and that of their family members who are dependent on them.

Land redistribution

When significant inequalities in land holding exist in a society, land redistribution is a measure to protect farmers' rights. Since the end of the Cold War, land reforms have mainly focused on the enactment or amendment of land-related laws. Nevertheless, significant inequalities in land holding can still be one of the causes of armed conflict. Land distribution to adjust inequalities in land holding has been carried out in many countries since the end of the Second World War, and it remains an important policy option even today, particularly in Latin American and southern African countries.

However, as shown in Chapter 7 on Colombia, the effectiveness of the policy can be significantly undermined for the profit of political elites. This is why the authors of the case study remain cautious about the value of recent agreements on land reform between the government of Colombia and the rebels.[8] Although it is too early to assess the results of the agreement, past experience of land distribution policies deserves appropriate attention so that the latest efforts will bear fruit.

After the Indonesian withdrawal from Timor-Leste, the coffee farmers in the Ermera district united and carried out the 'Popular Land Reform' in order to recover their ancestral land that had been taken by the Portuguese colonial administration. This example shows farmers' strong desire to reclaim their land rights, though the state may not recognise them under the new land law. It is not hard to imagine the difficulties, given the number of decolonised countries, including Kenya and Zimbabwe, that still have the burden of unresolved legacies of colonial-era-related land dispossession decades after independence.

Reserve zones

Some countries designate reserve zones to protect the rights of vulnerable peasants, local communities and indigenous groups. In Colombia, the government established Peasant Reserve Zones, with the purpose of restricting the concentration of land ownership, protecting the peasant economy and collectively organising productive activities and environmental resources. Although this can be a useful method for protecting the land rights of Colombian peasants[9] collectively, formal recognition of the Peasant Reserve Zones is often delayed in the country.

The proposed law of Timor-Leste provides for Community Protection Zones, which are defined as areas – including agricultural areas, cultural sites and areas containing natural resources – protected by the state for safeguarding local communities' common interests. While this could have important effects, we are not able to evaluate the effectiveness of this measure since the law is yet to be discussed anew in the country's parliament. In Cambodia, the 2001 Land Law allows indigenous communities to designate the areas they live in or use for agriculture as their collective land, which will be managed by traditional authorities and mechanisms for decision making. However, the actual implementation of this has been limited. Concrete procedures to register collective rights had not been clear until they were finally defined in 2009. Even after the adoption of a sub-decree to define such procedures, many indigenous communities have not been able to formalise their rights, as the process is too complicated.

Like attempts to secure customary land rights, the designation of reserve zones does not necessarily ensure the rights of vulnerable people. While adequate governance capacity is required to sustain and manage the reserve zones, the solidarity of local communities inhabiting the zones is often weak and rapid social change diminishes their internal coherence. The reserve zones are therefore likely to be susceptible to abuse by those who have political power. We should thus be aware that the policy measures will not bear fruit without improving the quality of land governance.

Land registration

Land registration aims to clarify and protect landowners' rights by formally recording land tenure. Advocates believe that it also increases farmers' access to the credit market by enabling the collateralisation of titled land, and thereby expands their opportunities for income generation and poverty reduction (De Soto 2000). With international support, it has been promoted in a number of countries, including Bosnia and Herzegovina, Burundi, Cambodia, Rwanda and Timor-Leste.

   While land registration certainly clarifies and strengthens tenure security for those who have registered their land, not every entitled person enjoys the benefits, for two main reasons. First, most of the property rights under traditional systems in developing countries, particularly conflict-affected ones, are vague and sometimes overlapping. The ambiguous and complex property rights, often shared collectively by local groups or communities, are extremely complicated and therefore difficult to record fully; the registration system consequently needs to be designed so as to recognise them accurately. Second, if the process is time-consuming and/or costly, poor local villagers tend to find no reason to register their land plots. Particularly if threats to tenure security are not foreseen, many people do not realise the importance and usefulness of having their land registered. On the other hand, people who understand the benefits of land registration work out the advantages from their knowledge of the system. In many countries, large enterprises, including foreign investors, secure the registration of their rights. Consequently, their property claims become much stronger than unregistered claims by local communities and the local population.

   The land registration process needs to be accessible for every individual and community to prevent fraudulent usage by certain groups of people. The introduction of modern technologies such as Geographic Information Systems can make the process less costly and faster, as was the case in Rwanda. The example of Timor-Leste highlights an interesting effort to make the land registration process more inclusive. At first, GPS photos were taken and interviews with claimants were conducted. If there were no disputes over a plot, measurements followed. While all the plots were published with cadastral maps, disputed plots were published together with all the claimants' names and photos. As a consequence, a large number of existing disputes were identified and recorded, and the findings will help prevent those disputed plots being put on the market. This procedure serves as clarification of property rights with the safeguard that the land is not registered by the first claimant. A similar attempt to provide accessible land certificates has recently been made in Burundi. However, we still do not know to what extent these land certificates will be accepted and how far their usage will spread among rural inhabitants.

While the Rwandan land registration has been praised for its swiftness, its sustainability in the future is questionable. In Rwanda, while land can be registered in the name of a family or someone who has died, the registration of a land plot of less than one hectare is not allowed. This could be a cause of great disparities between the land register and actual land holding in the future, because in reality plots will be further fractured through inheritance, regardless of the official record. Furthermore, if post-registration transfer is not reported, the disparity between the register and reality increases even further. In Cambodia, to cope with the disparity the 2007 Civil Code introduced a system closer to the American deed registration system. It limits the protection of the registered land plots and allows Cambodians who failed to register their land titles to claim their rights nonetheless.

Since land registration has its limitations and can potentially create adverse effects, a cautious approach is required in its execution (Bruce 2012). Without a certain level of good governance, land registration will neither enhance economic development nor contribute to the protection of the rights of vulnerable people (Deininger and Feder 2009). It is worth considering whether this measure should be given priority in the post-conflict setting. In conflict-affected situations, both formal accountability mechanisms and customary mechanisms tend to be weak, and transparency is liable to be low. Efforts should be made to control unscrupulous actions of the state (or national and local elites) through improvement of public land governance. In the same context, it is also important to empower local inhabitants through information sharing, as well as through education and training.

General policy implications

In this last section, we will discuss the policy implications of our studies. As we have already examined major policy measures relevant to land and property problems in conflict-affected situations, and assessed their consequences, the discussion in this section will be concerned with overarching issues. We begin by examining policy implications with regard to the relationship between land and property problems, statebuilding and peacebuilding, and, on this basis, the role of external actors will be discussed.

Improving land governance as an important step for sustainable statebuilding

Our case studies illustrate fragile state–society relations in conflict-affected countries. As armed conflicts ruin human relations and people's confidence in the state, reconciliation among national groups and confidence-building between the state and society are major challenges. In fact, our case study countries are still confronted with a number of obstacles that hinder constructive state–society relationships. Characteristics including ethnic and regional rivalry, the patrimonial nature of elites and enormous disparities in power have been widely observable in these countries. In this regard, land and property problems in conflict-affected situations are substantially political, and insecurity regarding land and property is more often than not caused and aggravated by the fragile state–society relationship. In other words, in order to tackle land and property problems, it is necessary to address fragility in these states and state–society relations. Policies for dealing with land and property problems should therefore be coherent with statebuilding efforts.

With regard to international engagement in statebuilding, the Development Assistance Committee of the OECD has highlighted two important areas for building a constructive state–society relationship. One is 'supporting the legitimacy and accountability of states' and the other is 'strengthening the capability of states to fulfil their core functions' (OECD 2007). We would argue that tackling land and property problems has important implications for statebuilding in general, and particularly for legitimacy building. Regulating property order is one of the fundamental functions of the state. Considering the vital importance of land and property rights for ordinary people, not only in terms of livelihood but also from the viewpoint of political and spiritual meanings, governance that effectively ensures people's property rights would enhance the legitimacy of the state.

In affirming the close relationship between statebuilding and land and property problems, what are the concrete policy measures that need to be taken? In this regard, recently developed guidelines and policy tools are very instructive. For instance, the voluntary guidelines, laid out by the Food and Agriculture Organization and endorsed by the Committee on World Food Security, seek to

> improve governance of tenure of land, fisheries and forest … for the benefit of all, with an emphasis on vulnerable and marginalised people, with the goals of food security and progressive realisation of the rights to adequate food, poverty eradication, sustainable livelihoods, social stability, housing security, rural development, environmental protection and sustainable social and economic development.
>
> (FAO 2012: 1)

Having the primary objective of improving land governance, the guidelines lay out the principles of implementation that are critical for the state–society relationship: human dignity, non-discrimination, equity and justice, gender equality, rule of law, transparency and accountability (FAO 2012: 4–5).[10] If the guidelines were properly implemented, it would significantly contribute to tackling land and property problems, simultaneously building a constructive state–society relationship.

In order for these guidelines to be effective, policy tools for assessing land governance should be made use of. A report published by UN-Habitat in 2012, based on the activities of the Global Land Tool Network, has the purpose of developing practical ways to solve problems in land administration and management. With its broad scope, including tenure security in armed conflict, the report provides a range of findings and practical recommendations for policy makers and practitioners. In this regard, the handbook published by Bruce with Holt (2011) also deserves specific mention as a valuable source for practitioners, containing a series of information and policy tools concerning the issue of land and conflict prevention, which is closely related to land governance. Finally, the Land Governance Assessment Framework developed by the World Bank is a detailed assessment tool for land governance (Deininger *et al.* 2012). Through its five thematic areas and 21 land governance indicators,[11] detailed assessment is made possible. These efforts to improve land governance are steps forward for statebuilding, given the close relationship between the two that has been repeatedly emphasised in this book.

As the guidelines and policy tools are not necessarily based on the assumption of conflict-affected settings, adjustment may be required for their proper application in such contexts. The first step is to examine the specific situation on the ground and the country context. Conflict-affected situations are often characterised by an extremely unequal power balance, both at national and local levels, and therefore the distribution of political power should be taken into account. In order for policy intervention in land and property to contribute to peacebuilding, it is critical to understand whose rights are undermined and how, so that those whose rights are infringed can be supported. In such interventions, impartial external actors can play a crucial role.

The role of external actors

Although statebuilding is inherently an endogenous and long-term process, policy interventions can make a significant difference. This is empirically proven for land and property problems in conflict-affected situations. Despite the deep and complicated roots of land and property problems in each society, governmental and/or international interventions can have influence, either positively or negatively. The inaction of UNTAC or UNTAET has certainly affected the subsequent aggravation of land and property problems in Cambodia and Timor-Leste, while the strong support of the international community extensively contributed to Bosnia's property restitution process. Given the potential impact of these policies on land and property problems, all the stakeholders ought to pay attention to and address the problems so that their work can positively contribute to their resolution.

In considering the policy options, the timeframe should be thoroughly examined and options should be appropriately combined, since both swiftness and a long-term perspective are required. On the one hand, it is obvious that land and property problems should be tackled with urgency in a post-conflict context, because it is critical for the restoration of political order. On the other hand, measures taken during an emergency period will have significant influence in the long run. Urgent demands in the immediate aftermath of conflict should be carefully examined from the viewpoint of sustainable peace. For instance, although the land sharing and housing arrangements secured land and houses for Rwandan Tutsi returnees, resentment among Hutu at not receiving any compensation for expropriated land may threaten sustainable peace in the long run, unless this is adequately addressed.

In this regard, coordinating policy interventions in land and property problems is crucial for peace consolidation. As the importance of this issue has been recognised in the context of peacebuilding, UN agencies and humanitarian organisations are now keen to address problems from the early stage of the post-conflict period or even before any ceasefire. In contrast, development agencies have not been as active as they could be, despite the related research emphasising the necessity of a long-term perspective (Pantuliano 2009; Unruh and Williams 2013). While, in the past decade, both humanitarian and development agencies have worked to close the gap in post-conflict assistance, coordination between the two still remains insufficient in regard to land and property problems.

Given that land and property have been central topics in development for a long time, the role of development agencies ought to be reinforced. The humanitarian agencies were ahead of development agencies in recognising the need to tackle land and property problems in conflict-affected situations. As the necessity of introducing a long-term perspective has been stressed, the role of development agencies has been increasingly highlighted. While interest in the nexus of land and conflict has been rising among development agencies, their primary focus was conflict prevention rather than the post-conflict phase (Bruce and Holt 2011; USAID 2013). To supplement previous studies, we would argue that special consideration is required for dealing with these problems in conflict-affected situations. On the basis of recent experience in supporting various statebuilding efforts, development agencies could also make a considerable contribution to tackling these problems, including enhancing land governance, mitigating land inequalities, protecting property rights and helping land law reforms. For this purpose, development agencies need to deepen their knowledge and experience in the field where land and property problems and statebuilding overlap.

We further emphasise that the following three points are particularly important. The first is speed of action. Development agencies should move into the field quickly enough to cooperate with the host government as well as other actors such as humanitarian and UN agencies. The experience and knowledge of development agencies will be indispensable for other actors to make urgent policy interventions, which will eventually have a long-term influence. Filling the gap between humanitarian and development agencies in land and property issues is an urgent concern.

The second is an improvement in understanding the nature of land governance in each country and coordinating policy measures. Since land and property problems are complicated by various factors, particularly in conflict-affected situations, intensive land governance assessment can be an effective tool. Besides assessments at the national level, surveys on local communities can also be informative, enabling a better understanding of the unique nature of land-related problems in each locality. Based on a better understanding of land and property problems, donors need to pay sufficient attention to 'do no harm'. As their policy interventions may have unexpected consequences, donors need to at least be aware of their influence on land and property problems. Coordination among donors is essential, as land and property problems are deeply linked to other political, economic and social problems.

The third issue is political consideration. Since land problems are inherently political, they may require measures beyond technical changes in some conflict-affected situations. Development agencies need to be aware of their potential impact on politics, fully take into account the progress of statebuilding in conducting operations, and look for opportunities to create political consensus to address difficult challenges.

Windows of opportunity

Our case studies showed that there are a number of cases where a part of society has in the history of its country suffered significant deprivation regarding property. As Bernadette Atuahene has strongly argued, such cases may require a transformative conception. Bearing in mind the case of South Africa, she stresses the danger 'when inequality emanating from past property theft has the potential to cause backlash and destabilize the state' (2010: 804). While under the classical conception of exclusive property rights, 'only the property claims of present title-holders are recognized, and thus they are placed in a dominant societal position', the transformative conception 'seeks to mitigate this power asymmetry by protecting the rights of current title-holders and also defending the rights of those unjustly dispossessed' (Atuahene 2010: 804).

Like South Africa, conflict-affected countries face enormous challenges in reconciling various competing land and property claims, which can be based on different but grounded justifications. Obviously, reconciling these claims will not be easy. However, this challenge also provides windows of opportunity to transform state–society relationships and build sustainable peace. Some scholars, as well as practitioners, have noted the potential of the post-conflict period for reforming societies (Unruh 2003: 365–67; UN-Habitat 2012: 101; Unruh and Williams 2013: 568). It may well be an occasion to help mend past injustice. We would echo this view, as our case studies include positive examples such as the development of women's land rights in Rwanda. While we might tend to emphasise critical issues, positive aspects are also observable in every country. The development of a mediation system in the aftermath of a serious earthquake in Japan in the 1920s is an example of a positive social change following a chaotic situation. What we need is cautious optimism. The international community unquestionably needs to make an adequate effort as well as offer assistance to maximise the potential of these windows of opportunity.

Notes

1 In Cambodia and Timor-Leste, there have been various displacement experiences, some lasting more than a decade and some relatively short.

2 This classification is based on the comparison of different forced migration cases, and we note that the notion of length could be subjective. A period of even weeks or months could be long for those who have had to leave their place of living behind.

3 Interestingly, those who have written academic pieces on the subject of Bosnian restitution based on their experience as practitioners have not strongly regretted the lack of compensation funds (Garlick 2000; Williams 2005). Philpott, however, recognises the usefulness of compensation as an obvious solution for unresolved claims as well as specific cases including those who missed claim deadlines (Philpott 2006).

4 See Chapter 6.

5 Although this is not a case of compensation, the Cambodian returnees' choice between the land option and the cash option is an example that shows that people will choose a realistic and immediately viable option, rather than following their genuine wishes. In an early survey, the majority of refugees wished to receive land. However, as they gradually recognised that not enough land was available for everyone, in the end 85 per cent of returnees chose the cash option in contrast to 3 per cent who opted for land allocation.

6 We owe this point to Carl Bruch, Senior Attorney and Co-Director, International Programs, Environmental Law Institute. For examples of countries such as Indonesia (Aceh), Angola and El Salvador, see Unruh and Williams (eds 2013).

7 In its support for community mediation capacity building, JICA introduced the Japanese mediation mechanism to Nepal. The community-based mediation mechanism supplements the capacity of formal judicial institutions. Many of the cases they deal with are related to land problems in local communities.

8 The joint statement of 26 May 2013 reads: 'This agreement will be the start of a radical transformation of rural Colombia'. 'Colombia and FARC rebels reach agreement on land reform', BBC News Latin America & Caribbean, 27 May 2013, available online at www.bbc.co.uk/news/world-latin-america-22676049 (accessed 9 March 2014).

9 The term 'peasant' has a specific meaning in the Colombian context. See Chapter 7 for details.

10 Recognition of the political importance of land governance can also be found in the guidelines proposed by African stakeholders. 'Framework and guidelines on land policy in Africa' states that '(s)tructures governing access, control and management of land are as much about the consolidation of democracy as they are

about asset stewardship' (African Union Commission–Economic Commission for Africa–African Development Bank 2010: 14).
11 The five thematic areas, which include several land governance indicators, are as follows: 1) legal and institutional framework, 2) land use planning, management and taxation, 3) management of public land, 4) public provision of land information, 5) dispute resolution and conflict management.

References

African Union Commission–Economic Commission for Africa–African Development Bank, 2010, 'Framework and guidelines on land policy in Africa', Addis Ababa.

Atuahene, B., 2010, 'Property rights and the demands of transformation', *Michigan Journal of International Law*, 31: 765–819.

Ballard, M., 2010, 'Post-conflict property restitution: flawed legal and theoretical foundations', *Berkeley Journal of International Law*, 28(2): 462–96.

Bruce, J.W., 2012, 'Simple solutions to complex problems: land formalisation as a "silver bullet"', in *Fair Land Governance: How to Legalise Land Rights for Rural Development*, ed. J.M. Otto and A. Hoekema, Leiden: Leiden University Press, 31–55.

Bruce, J.W. and Holt, S., 2011, *Land and Conflict Prevention*, Colchester: University of Essex.

Buzan, B., 1983, *People, States and Fear*, Brighton: Wheatsheaf Books.

De Soto, H., 2000, *The Mystery of Capital: Why Capitalism Triumphs in the West and Fails Everywhere Else*, New York: Basic Books.

Deininger, K. and Feder, G., 2009, 'Land registration, governance, and development: evidence and implications for policy', *The World Bank Research Observer*, 24(2): 233–66.

Deininger, K., Selod, H. and Burns, A., 2012, *The Land Governance Assessment Framework: Identifying and Monitoring Good Practice in the Land Sector*, Washington, DC: World Bank.

Falisse, J.-B. and Niyonkuru, R.C., 2013, 'Peace villages for repatriates to Burundi', *FMR online*, available online at www.fmreview.org/fragilestates/falisse-niyonkuru (accessed 9 March 2014).

FAO (Food and Agriculture Organization of the United Nations), 2012, *Voluntary Guidelines on the Responsible Governance of Tenure of Land, Fisheries and Forests in the Context of National Food Security*, Rome: FAO.

Fitzpatrick, D., 2006, 'Evolution and chaos in property rights systems: the Third World tragedy of contested access', *The Yale Law Journal*, 115: 996–1048.

Fitzpatrick, D. and Monson, R., 2009, 'Balancing rights and norms: property programming in East Timor, the Solomon Islands, and Bougainville', in *Housing, Land, and Property Rights in Post-conflict United Nations and Other Peace Operations: A Comparative Survey and Proposal for Reform*, ed. S. Leckie, New York: Cambridge University Press, 103–35.

Garlick, M., 2000, 'Protection for property rights: a partial solution? The Commission for real property claims of displaced persons and refugees (CRPC) in Bosnia and Herzegovina', *Refugee Survey Quarterly*, 19(3): 64–85.

Holsti, K.J., 1996, *The State, War, and the State of War*, Cambridge: Cambridge University Press.

International Land Coalition, 2011, 'Securing land access for the poor in times of intensified natural resources competition', Tirana declaration, available online at www.landcoalition.org/sites/default/files/aom11/Tirana_Declaration_ILC_2011_ENG. pdf (accessed 9 March 2014).

Ishihara, T., 1970, *Minji-choteihou jitsumu-souran* (General practice in civil conciliation act), Tokyo: Sakai Shoten.

Manning, R. and Trzeciak-Duval, A., 2010, 'Situation of fragility and conflict: aid policies and beyond', *Conflict, Security, and Development*, 10(1): 103–31.

OECD, 2007, 'Principles for good international engagement in fragile states and situations', Paris.

Pantuliano, S., 2009, 'Charting the way: integrating land issues in humanitarian action', in *Uncharted Territory: Land, Conflict and Humanitarian Action*, ed. S. Pantuliano, Rugby: Practical Action Publishing, 193–212.

Philpott, C.B., 2006, 'From the right to return to the return of rights: completing post-war property restitution in Bosnia and Herzegovina', *International Journal of Refugee Law*, 18(1): 30–80.

Rosand, E., 2000, 'The right to compensation in Bosnia: an unfulfilled promise and a challenge to international law', *Cornell International Law Journal*, 33: 113–58.

Smit, A., 2012, *The Property Rights of Refugees and Internally Displaced Persons: Beyond Restitution*, Abingdon and New York: Routledge.

UN-Habitat, 2012, *Handling Land: Tools for Land Governance and Secure Tenure*, Nairobi: UN-Habitat.

Unruh, J., 2003, 'Land tenure and legal pluralism in the peace process', *Peace & Change*, 28(3): 352–77.

Unruh, J. and Williams, R.C., 2013, 'Lessons learned in land tenure and natural resource management in post-conflict societies', in *Land and Post-conflict Peacebuilding*, ed. J. Unruh and R.C. Williams, Abingdon: Earthscan, 535–76.

Unruh, J.D. and Williams, R.C. (eds), 2013, *Land and Post-Conflict Peacebuilding*, Abingdon: Earthscan.

USAID, 2013, 'Land and conflict: land disputes and land conflicts', Property rights and resource governance briefing paper #12, Washington, DC.

Williams, R.C., 2005, 'Post-conflict property restitution and refugee return in Bosnia and Herzegovina: implications for international standard-setting and practice', *International Law and Politics*, 37: 441–553.

Index

Note: Italic numbers indicate figures; boldface type indicates tables

For Product Safety Concerns and Information please contact our EU
representative GPSR@taylorandfrancis.com
Taylor & Francis Verlag GmbH, Kaufingerstraße 24, 80331 München, Germany

www.ingramcontent.com/pod-product-compliance
Ingram Content Group UK Ltd.
Pitfield, Milton Keynes, MK11 3LW, UK
UKHW021833240425
457818UK00006B/179